ALBERT CAMUS

ALBERT CAMUS
FROM THE ABSURD TO REVOLT

John Foley

McGill-Queen's University Press
Montreal & Kingston • Ithaca

ISBN 978-0-7735-3466-7 (hardcover)
ISBN 978-0-7735-3467-4 (paperback)

Legal deposit fourth quarter 2008
Bibliothèque nationale du Québec

Published simultaneously outside North America by
Acumen Publishing Limited

McGill-Queen's University Press acknowledges the financial support of the
Government of Canada through the Book Publishing Development Program
(BPIDP) for its activities.

Library and Archives Canada Cataloguing in Publication

Foley, John, 1974–
    Albert Camus: from the absurd to revolt / John Foley.

Includes bibliographical references and index.
ISBN 978-0-7735-3466-7 (bound).—ISBN 978-0-7735-3467-4 (pbk.)

    Camus, Albert, 1913–1960—Criticism and interpretation. 2. Camus, Albert,
1913–1960—Political and social views. I. Title.

PQ2605.A3734Z6426 2008   848'.91409   C2008-903736-7

Typeset by Graphicraft Limited, Hong Kong.
Printed and bound by Biddles Limited, King's Lynn.

For my mother and for Farah

It may be that the ideal of freedom to choose ends without claiming eternal validity for them, and the pluralism of values connected with this, is only the late fruit of our declining capitalist civilization: an ideal which remote ages and primitive societies have not recognized, and one which posterity will regard with curiosity, even sympathy, but little comprehension. This may be so; but no sceptical conclusions seem to me to follow. Principles are not less sacred because their duration cannot be guaranteed. Indeed, the very desire for guarantees that our values are eternal and secure in some objective heaven is perhaps only a craving for the certainties of childhood or the absolute values of our primitive past. "To realise the relative validity of one's convictions," said an admirable writer of our time, "and yet stand for them unflinchingly, is what distinguishes a civilised man from a barbarian." To demand more than this is perhaps a deep and incurable metaphysical need; but to allow it to determine one's practice is a symptom of an equally deep, and more dangerous, moral and political immaturity.

Isaiah Berlin, "Two Concepts of Liberty" (1958)

CONTENTS

ACKNOWLEDGEMENTS

I wish to thank the following individuals or institutions: the Irish Research Council for the Humanities and Social Sciences for the award of a postdoctoral fellowship 2004–6, during which much of this research was done; Kevin Barry and Nicholas Canny of the Moore Institute for Research in the Humanities and Social Studies, at the National University of Ireland, Galway, where I worked for the duration of my IRCHSS fellowship; Mme Catherine Camus, who granted me extraordinary access to materials at the Centre de Documentation Albert Camus, Bibliothèque Méjanes, Aix-en-Provence, in the spring and summer of 2003, and Marcelle Mahasela, Director of the archive, who greatly assisted me in my research; the Harry Ransom Humanities Research Center, at the University of Texas at Austin, which awarded me a Mellon Fellowship in 2007, permitting the consultation of those papers in the Alfred Knopf Collection pertaining to Camus; the Beinecke Rare Book and Manuscript Library, Yale University, for assistance in finding my way through a small part of the John Gerassi Collection of Jean-Paul Sartre; Joe Mahon, at the Department of Philosophy, NUI Galway, who supervised this research through its initial stages; the editors of *Albert Camus in the 21st Century* (Rodopi, 2008), in which a version of Chapter 5 has appeared; Steven Gerrard of Acumen, for his support for this project and for his patience.

The following individuals kindly responded to various queries, offered advice, or gave support: Hédi Abdel-Jaouad, Ronald Aronson, the late Konrad Bieber, Ian Birchall, the late Jo Campling, Cairns Craig, Conor Cruise O'Brien, Colin Davis, Phil Dine, Peter Dunwoodie, Raymond Gay-Crosier, John Gerassi, Daniel Gri-Gri, Eddie Hughes, John Kenny, Paschal O'Gorman, Eric Sellin, the late Pat Sheeran, Frank Shovlin, Joe Sweeney, Maurice Weyembergh. I am particularly grateful to David

Carroll and David Sprintzen, both of whom read the book in manuscript for the publisher and made several valuable suggestions.

I owe a very great deal to my family, Mary, Charles and Stephen, and to Farah, without whom this work would not have been completed.

John Foley

NOTES ON THE TEXT AND ABBREVIATIONS

In almost all cases the dates given for entries to the *Carnets* or *Notebooks* are approximate, as most entries are not dated. If no reference is given for a translation from the French, it is my own; if a reference to a translated text is followed by an asterisk (*), the translation has been revised. Finally, the following abbreviations have been used throughout:

C1	*Carnets I: mai 1935–février 1942* (Paris: Gallimard, 1962).
C2	*Carnets II: janvier 1942–mars 1951* (Paris: Gallimard, 1964).
C3	*Carnets III: mars 1951–décembre 1959* (Paris: Gallimard, 1989).
CAC 1–8	*Cahiers Albert Camus Vols 1–8* (see bibliography for full references to each volume).
CC	*Camus at* Combat*: Writing 1944–1947*, ed. J. Lévi-Valensi; fwd D. Carroll; trans. A. Goldhammer (Princeton, NJ: Princeton University Press, 2006).
COP	*Caligula and Other Plays: Caligula, Cross Purpose, The Just, The Possessed*, trans. S. Gilbert *et al.* (Harmondsworth: Penguin, 1984).
E	*Essais*, Introduction par R. Quilliot; Edition établie et annotée par R. Quilliot et L. Faucon (Paris: Gallimard/Bibliothèque de la Pléiade, 1965).
LACE	*Lyrical and Critical Essays*, trans. E. C. Kennedy; ed. P. Thody (New York: Knopf, 1968).
MS	*The Myth of Sisyphus*, trans. J. O'Brien (Harmondsworth: Penguin, 1975).
NB1	*Notebooks 1935–1942*, ed. & trans. P. Thody (New York: Knopf, 1963).
NB2	*Notebooks 1942–1951*, ed. & trans. J. O'Brien (New York: Knopf, 1965).

OCI   *Œuvres Complètes: Tome 1, 1931–1944*, ed. J. Lévi-Valensi *et al.* (Paris:
          Gallimard/Bibliothèque de la Pléiade, 2006).
OCII   *Œuvres Complètes: Tome 2, 1944–1948*, ed. J. Lévi-Valensi *et al.* (Paris:
          Gallimard/Bibliothèque de la Pléiade, 2006).
R   *The Rebel: An Essay on Man in Revolt*, revised and complete trans. A.
          Bower; fwd H. Read (New York: Knopf, 1956).
RRD   *Resistance, Rebellion and Death*, trans. J. O'Brien (New York: Knopf,
          1960).
SCHC   *Sartre and Camus: A Historic Confrontation*, eds & trans. D. Sprintzen &
          A. van den Hoven (New York: Humanity, 2004).
SEN   *Selected Essays & Notebooks*, ed. & trans. P. Thody (Harmondsworth:
          Penguin, 1979).
TO   *The Outsider*, trans. J. Laredo (Harmondsworth: Penguin, 1983).
TP   *The Plague*, trans. S. Gilbert (Harmondsworth: Penguin, 1960).
TRN   *Théâtre, Récits, Nouvelles*, Préface par J. Grenier; Textes établis et
          annotés par R. Quilliot (Paris: Gallimard/Bibliothèque de la Pléiade,
          1962).

INTRODUCTION

It is essential for us to know whether man, without the help of the eternal or of rationalistic thought, can unaided create his own values . . . the uneasiness that concerns
us belongs to a whole epoch from which we do not want to dissociate ourselves. . . .
We know that everything is not summed up in negation and absurdity. But we must
first posit negation and absurdity because they are what our generation has encountered and what we must take into account.[1]

(Albert Camus, "Le Pessimisme et le Courage", *Combat* 3 November 1944)

Despite his popular image, strictly speaking Camus was not an existentialist. His
first major philosophical essay, *The Myth of Sisyphus* (1942), was explicitly intended
as a critique of existentialism, especially the Christian existentialist tradition of
Kierkegaard, Jaspers and Chestov. According to Camus, starting from the premise
that nothing in the world has meaning or depth, existentialists proceed, through a
leap of irrational faith, to find meaning and depth in it. He thus criticizes representatives of the philosophical movement with which he is most closely associated for
"deify[ing] what crushes them and find[ing] reason to hope in what impoverishes
them" (*MS*: 35; *E*: 112). Moreover, although in France in the 1940s and 1950s to be
an existentialist was, most probably, to be a follower or admirer of Sartre's atheistic
existentialism, we find in this period both Sartre and Camus repeatedly insisting
that Camus was definitively neither an existentialist nor a Sartrean. Indeed, in 1939,
reviewing Sartre's short story collection *The Wall*, Camus can be seen to object to
Sartre's depiction of human freedom as both total and futile. For Camus, as David
Sprintzen notes, the characters of Sartre's fiction have "absolutised their freedom
to compensate for a transcendent absolute by whose absence they are haunted".
Furthermore, this freedom "bears witness to a deeper isolation from the world
around them and, most particularly, from nature" (Sprintzen 1988: 44). In the world
described by Sartre, the individual is "reduced to self-contemplation", is conscious
of "his profound indifference to everything that is not himself", is "alone, enclosed
in this freedom". This solipsism is symptomatic of the discovery of the absurd but,
says Camus in a review of Sartre's *Nausea* in 1938, "the realisation that life is absurd
cannot be an end, but only a beginning. This is a truth that nearly all great minds
have taken as their starting point. It is not this discovery that is interesting, but the
consequences and rules for action that can be drawn from it."[2]

Although the "absurd", as we shall see, constitutes Camus's "first principle", he nevertheless defines his intellectual programme precisely in contrast with existentialism. In 1943, for example, he declares that the purpose of *The Myth of Sisyphus* is to define "an absurd way of thinking [*une pensée absurde*], that is, one delivered of metaphysical hope, by way of a criticism of several themes of existential philosophy".[3] In 1944 he declares that, although it is a "great philosophical adventure", he believes the conclusions of existentialism to be "false"; a few weeks later, Sartre characterizes Camus as a proponent not of existentialism but of a "coherent and profound . . . philosophy of the absurd".[4] In November 1945, a month after the first issue of Sartre's journal *Les Temps modernes* appeared, Camus declared:

> No I am not an existentialist. Sartre and I are always surprised to see our names associated. We think that one day we may publish a short statement in which the undersigned affirm that they have nothing in common and that they each refuse to answer for the debts that the other may have incurred . . . Sartre and I had published all of our books, without exception, before becoming acquainted. Our eventual meeting only confirmed our differences. Sartre is an existentialist, and the only book of ideas I've written, *The Myth of Sisyphus*, is directed against the so-called existentialist philosophers.[5]

Two days later in another interview Camus reiterates the same points, adding that "if one is an existentialist because one poses the problem of human ends, then all literature, from Montaigne to Pascal", deserves to be called existentialist.[6] In an interview in December 1945, Sartre responds unequivocally to the "almost habitual" association of his work with that of Camus: "It rests", he says, "on a serious confusion. Camus is not an existentialist." His "real masters", says Sartre, are not "Kierkegaard, Jaspers and Heidegger" but "the French moralists of the 17th century".[7] In the same month, Camus reaffirms his differences with existentialism, and suggests that the confusion whereby he is treated as a "disciple" of Sartre in the popular media may derive from the fact that few people seem to understand the meaning of existentialism. He affirms that he is not a philosopher, on the basis that he has not "sufficient faith in reason to believe in a system", and criticizes theistic existentialism for its irrational leap of faith.[8] Critically, in this interview Camus goes on to introduce another criticism of existentialism, one which, I would suggest, is directed primarily if not exclusively at Sartre. In *The Myth of Sisyphus*, as we have noted, Camus accused the existentialists (theistic existentialists in particular) of "deifying what crushes them". In this interview he criticizes atheistic existentialists for what he considers to be a similar resort to divine mystery, this time in what he sees as a divinization of history: "they no longer believe in God, but they believe in history", history considered as an absolute value, an idea rooted in Hegel and Marx, for whom the totalizing "meaning" and direction of history were discernible. Although Camus admits to understanding the attraction of the religious "solution" and, most especially, he appreciates the importance of history, he believes in neither "in their absolute sense". "It makes me very uneasy", he says, "that I am being forced to choose between Saint Augustine and Hegel. I have the impression that there must be a tenable truth between the two extremes."[9]

Although such an appeal to "history" as a transcendent value may seem alien to existentialism, it was entirely relevant to Sartre, who, as is well known, sought to reconcile his existentialism with Marxism, and who had in the interview just quoted identified himself as a Marxist.[10] To this extent, Camus's rejection of existentialism became more a focused rejection of Sartrean existentialism and what he considered the incompatibility of its alleged deification of history with its affirmation of human freedom.[11] A month later, in January 1945, Camus responded to a review of his play *Caligula*, which suggested that the play "is but an illustration of the principles of Sartre's existentialism". Camus replied, pointing out that, first, the play had been written in 1938, before Sartre's existentialist works had been published, secondly, his only book of ideas, *The Myth of Sisyphus*, explicitly criticizes existentialism (and part of this critique may still be applied to Sartre) and, thirdly, that although he recognized the "historical importance" of existentialism he had not sufficient faith in reason to subscribe to a system, to the point that even Sartre's manifesto in the first issue of *Les Temps modernes* seemed to him "unacceptable".[12] As we shall see, this critique of Sartrean existentialism achieves its ultimate expression in *The Rebel* (1951), the essay that provoked a spectacular end to their association in the public eye. Here Camus notes that while "atheistic existentialism" may wish to "create a morality", it has yet to respond to the "real difficulty" involved in creating such a morality "without introducing into historical existence a value foreign to history".[13]

For the present purposes, the merits of Camus's criticism of existentialism are not at issue – the point is simply that he went to considerable effort to distinguish himself from existentialism, particularly Sartrean existentialism, and that any attempt to read Camus as an existentialist should take this into account. Camus, in this account, can be seen to object to what we might call philosophical existentialism on the basis that: (a) although, broadly, he agrees with the initial absurd premise of existentialism, he claims that in its response to the absurd it "deifies what crushes it" (this was especially the case for theistic existentialists); and (b) in its Sartrean form, its "deification of history" is incompatible with the existentialist affirmation of radical human freedom.

There is of course another, less technical way in which the term existentialist can be deployed, and identifying Camus with this group is hardly problematic. How we want to describe this broader group of writers is open to debate, but it seems that we could do far worse than use Camus's reference to a literature concerned with "the problem of human ends". In any event, although classifying Camus as an existentialist constitutes a singularly unhelpful way of assessing the merits of his thought (because he was a critic, not an exponent, of existentialism), reading him as a *moraliste* or, to use his own term, "an existential writer" may provide little assistance in determining the value of his writing.[14]

This book suggests that Camus's *oeuvre* can be read in a relatively systematic way if we concentrate on two pivotal concepts in his writing: the absurd and revolt. It argues that they are both intellectually coherent, meaning that they admit a fair degree of analytic scrutiny, and, furthermore, that they are mutually dependent upon one another, by which I mean that, according to Camus, if the absurd is not to degenerate into moral nihilism it must rehabilitate itself in the light of revolt, and that if revolt is not to deteriorate into a regime of tyranny and oppression, it must remain conscious of its origins in the absurd premise.[15] There have been a number of important critical contributions that share this view of the relation between the two concepts (notably those of David Sprintzen and Thomas W. Busch), but there remains an influential critical perspective according to which Camus eventually rejected the absurd in favour of revolt (most recently in Avi Sagi and Richard Kamber).[16] The problem with such a perspective is that it inevitably leads to a distorted view of both the absurd and revolt and, as we shall see, can result in Camus's concept of the absurd being identified with nihilism, and his concept of revolt with political quietism, bourgeois liberalism and even pacifism.[17] However, if we recognize an intellectual continuum between the absurd and revolt, we are led to an entirely different perspective, since we recognize the details of the absurd in the light of revolt, and the contours of revolt in the light of the absurd. The aim of this book, therefore, is not simply to affirm the coherence of the absurd and revolt, but also to illustrate the centrality of this coherence to an accurate understanding of Camus's political and philosophical commitments, and the writings that were grounded on those commitments.

In 1945, an interviewer suggested that the Camus that France had grown to know through *The Myth of Sisyphus* and *The Outsider* was fundamentally different from the Camus who had emerged in the post-war era. Rejecting this oft-repeated assumption, he declared:

> I consider that there is a coherence. . . . All that I can hope to do, in respect of my creative work, is to show that generous forms of behaviour can be engendered even in a world without God and that man alone in the universe can still create his own values. That is, in my opinion, the sole problem posed by our era. We give everything in order to try to clarify this, in our lives as well as in our writings. I take my place among others in the search for that solution, that is all. . . . But why not admit that a mind which is pessimistic about the human condition can still feel within himself a solidarity with his companions in servitude, and to find there reason to act?   (Arban 1945: 2)

In the context of this coherence between the absurd and revolt, in the course of this study, I examine at length Camus's engagement with a series of contemporary political and moral questions, including capital punishment, Algerian independence and, most especially, the issue of political violence. This perspective also informs my analysis of Camus's relationship with Sartre, something that has received a fair degree of critical scrutiny in recent times.[18]

1 | THE ABSURD

At this point of his effort man stands face to face with the irrational. He feels within him his longing for happiness and for reason. The absurd is born of this confrontation between the human need and the unreasonable silence of the world.

(*MS*: 31–2; *E*: 117–18)

The Myth of Sisyphus

Written in 1940 amidst the French and European disaster, this book declares that even within the limits of nihilism it is possible to proceed beyond nihilism. In all the books I have written since, I have attempted to pursue this direction. Although *Le Mythe de Sisyphe* poses moral problems, it sums itself up for me as a lucid invitation to live and to create, in the very midst of the desert. (*MS*: 7; *E*: 97)

Not without reason, the term "absurd" rarely now makes an appearance in academic discourse, even academic discourse on existentialist philosophy, with which the term is usually associated. However, the importance of the concept to Camus's intellectual trajectory cannot be overstated, and a detailed account of what he means by the absurd would be necessary for any serious discussion of his ideas. A convenient way of introducing this analysis is to contrast Camus's concept of the absurd with those versions articulated by the existentialists Kierkegaard and Sartre. Such a contrast will further serve to highlight the extent to which Camus was not an existentialist. For Sartre, with whom the idea is perhaps most usually associated, the term "absurd" denoted the contingent nature of human existence, the realization of which brings what he called *nausea*. In Hazel Barnes's translation of *Being and Nothingness*, the Sartrean absurd is defined as "That which is meaningless. Thus man's existence is absurd because his contingency finds no external justification" (Sartre 1956: 628). In marked contrast, for Kierkegaard, the absurd refers to that quality of Christian faith that runs counter to all mundane human experience or, in

Kierkegaard's terms, "The absurd, precisely by reason of its objective repulsion, is the dynamometer of the inwardness of faith" (Lowrie 1938: 336; cf. Kierkegaard 1941: 189). In his *Journals*, Kierkegaard asserts that "The absurd, or to act by virtue of the absurd, is to act upon faith, trusting in God" (Kierkegaard 1938: 291). As we shall see, in *The Myth of Sisyphus* Camus explicitly rejects this faith proposed by Kierkegaard, calling it "philosophical suicide". Furthermore, while Camus's conception of the absurd can be said to correspond to a significant extent with that of Sartre, it should also be noted that Camus was inclined to criticize Sartre for the implications he construed from the absurd. Reviewing Sartre's *Nausea* in 1938, as we have seen, Camus criticizes the author for "thinking that life is tragic because it is wretched", and argues that "the realisation that life is absurd cannot be an end in itself but only a beginning". "It is not the discovery which is interesting," argues Camus, "but the consequences and rules for actions which can be drawn from it."[1]

For reasons such as these, it is important to examine Camus's ideas regarding the absurd carefully, and in order to understand his conception of the absurd accurately it is necessary to examine his essay *The Myth of Sisyphus* (1942). Here Camus claims that the absurd arises out of the "confrontation between human need and the un-reasonable silence of the world" (*MS*: 32; *E*: 117–18). Human beings are naturally inclined to want and expect the world to be intelligible "in the full and familiar ways that religious and philosophical systems have portrayed it". This kind of intelligibil-ity purports to be comprehensive, to explain the world as a whole, and crucially, it purports to explain the world "in terms that human beings care about", in ways that make sense "with respect to human values". In Camus's view, neither human exis-tence nor the world are themselves absurd. Instead the absurd arises because the world is resistant to this kind of intelligibility: "we want the world to make sense, but it does not make sense. To see this conflict is to see the absurd" (Kamber 2002: 52). "If there is an absurd," Camus says at one point, "it is in man's universe" (*MS*: 38; *E*: 124). What normally brings the individual into confrontation with his absurd con-dition, suggests Camus, is the awareness not of human mortality per se, but of his own personal mortality.[2] In the case of Camus himself, this awareness came with his first attack of tuberculosis, in 1930 or 1931, at the age of seventeen. For someone whose juvenile writing displayed a profound bond with the natural world, the sud-den visceral awareness of his own mortality, the imperviousness of nature to the pri-vate traumas of humankind, the feeling of dying slowly *from the inside*, the painfully asphyxiating experience of the pneumothorax treatments that denied him even the pantheistic prayer of uninhibited respiration, left clear fissures in the latent panthe-ism of his earliest, mainly lyrical, writing.[3] However, this is not to say that the absurd is born of an irrational response to the realization of human mortality. While feel-ings of the absurd may thus be awoken, awareness of the absurd, Camus insists, is specifically a rational, intellectual discovery, deduced from the recognition of the division between our expectations of the world and the world itself, unresponsive to those expectations (*MS*: 26; *E*: 112). Camus finds the strongest evidence for this concept of the absurd in what seems the unimpeachably empirical domain of the physical sciences. He argues that science ultimately relies on poetry, meta‸ art to explain itself. To illustrate, he mentions atomic theory, and its descripti‸ the building blocks of physical reality:

> At the final stage you teach me that this wondrous and multicoloured [*bariolé*] universe can be reduced to the atom. . . . But you tell me of an invisible planetary system in which electrons gravitate around a nucleus. You explain this world to me with an image. I realise then that you have been reduced to poetry . . . that science that was to teach me everything ends up in hypothesis, that lucidity founders in metaphor, that uncertainty is resolved in a work of art. (*MS*: 25; *E*: 112)

In a review of *The Myth of Sisyphus* in 1946, the logical-positivist A. J. Ayer characterizes Camus's assertions as "what modern Cambridge philosophers would call a 'pointless lament'", and argued that the kind of intelligibility demanded by Camus is impossible. Of course, this is precisely the point being made by Camus.[4] In his estimation, then, even the so-called hard sciences ultimately rely on the language of poetry to explain the physical make-up of the world. Camus is here not simply concerned by the fact that the world remains unintelligible, but more importantly he in concerned by the fact that it remains unintelligible in ways meaningful to humankind. "The mind's deepest desire", he says, "is an insistence upon familiarity, an appetite for clarity. Understanding the world for a man is reducing it to the human, stamping it with his seal" (*MS*: 22–3; *E*: 110). It is Camus's contention that ordinary human existence tends to take this level of perfect coherence for granted, but that occasionally, or perhaps inevitably, "the stage-sets collapse", and one is wrenched from one's ontological complacency and forced to confront the radical incoherence perceived to be at the heart of the relation between the self and the world, that sense of absurdity which a recent critic has characterized as "the *feeling* of radical divorce, of living in a once familiar but now suddenly radically alien homeland, of being adrift between past and future and unable to rely on either to give meaning to the present, of being a stranger to the world and to oneself" (Carroll 2007b: 56–7).

While Camus is convinced of the world's unintelligibility in the sense described, he nevertheless believes that there are certain claims about which one can be reasonably confident: my existence as a conscious being and the existence of the world I can touch. "This heart within me I can feel, and I judge that it exists. This world I can touch and I likewise judge that it exists. There ends all my knowledge and the rest is construction" (*MS*: 25; *E*: 111). Camus insists that no other knowledge is available to him, that beyond these claims regarding his own existence and the existence of an external reality, all is invention and speculation, in logic and science as much as in psychology and philosophy. Despite this view, Camus's absurd is not a prelude to nihilism, to a rejection of all value-claims, and he himself compares it (with a due sense of proportion) to Descartes's systematic doubt, in so far as it is a sceptical deconstruction of ingrained assumptions about our knowledge of the world, designed to identify what grounds, if any, can be found on which to construct a positive ethics. He asserts repeatedly that it is the implications of the absurd that interest him: "I was looking for a method and not a doctrine. I was practicing methodical doubt. I was trying to make a *tabula rasa*, on the basis of which it would be possible to construct something."[5] The absurd, then, as conceived by Camus is fundamentally an epistemological claim addressing an ontological need; that is, a claim regarding the knowledge we can have of the world. From this premise, Camus progressively extends the absurd perspective to a critique of all transcendental truths or values: "No code of ethics and no effort are justifiable *a priori* in the face of the cruel mathematics that command our condition."[6] Within the context of this critique and without in any way "overcoming" its ontological implications, Camus begins to investigate ways in which, he argues, it may be possible to respond positively to the absurd. This creative capacity eventually becomes the core of his theory of revolt, which I will discuss in detail in later chapters.

The Myth of Sisyphus itself is concerned primarily with an examination of other responses to the absurd, and in the essay Camus argues that hitherto philosophers concerned with the absurd have sought ultimately to overcome or transcend it. For example, he accuses Kierkegaard of reducing the problem of the absurd to the hubris of the human desire to reduce the world to clarity and coherence. For Kierkegaard this desire for truth and clarity "is a sin against a creature's finitude".[7] The absurd, the "very thing that led to despair of the meaning and depth of this life", becomes for Kierkegaard "its truth and its clarity". He calls, says Camus, quite plainly for "the third sacrifice required by St Ignatius Loyola, the one in which God most rejoices: 'The sacrifice of the intellect'." In doing this Kierkegaard makes of the absurd "the criterion of the other world", whereas for Camus the absurd "is simply the residue of the experience of this world". Substituting "for his cry of revolt a frantic adherence", Kierkegaard is led at once "to blind himself to the absurd which hitherto enlightened him" and "to deify the only certainty he henceforth possesses, the irrational". Kierkegaard, put simply, advocates a "leap" of faith which expressed the individual's nothingness without God, but for Camus this leap constitutes a suppression of the very tension that is at the heart of the human condition, the absurd, "the metaphysical state of the conscious man" (*MS*: 40, 42; *E*: 125–6, 128).

Similarly, although he considers Husserl's concept of intentionality (the idea that consciousness was always consciousness *of something*) entirely consistent with the absurd, since intentionality made no claims regarding the object beyond the perception of it, Camus is less convinced by the introduction of the concept of eidetic intuition, which allows Husserl to claim that the universal can be *seen* in the individual, and which permits him to speak of "extra-temporal essences". To discover "the point where thought leaves the path of evidence", says Camus, one needs only to consider Husserl's

> reasoning . . . regarding the mind: "If our insight extended to the exact laws of mental process, these too would be eternal and unchangeable, as are the laws of theoretical natural science; they would therefore hold even if there were no mental processes at all." Even if the mind were not, its laws would be! I see

then that of a psychological truth Husserl aims to make a rational rule: after having denied the integrating power of human reason, he leaps by this expedient to eternal Reason.[8]

Husserl's effort to import a quasi-scientific discourse into talk of basic human experience would inevitably fall out of favour with Camus, for we have already seen his caustic attitude to the pretensions of the hard sciences, accusing them of sophistry in their resort to poetic language in order to describe physical reality.[9]

Camus somewhat hastily concludes that what lies at the heart of these ideas in Husserl and Kierkegaard (and in existentialism generally) is in fact what he calls "philosophical suicide".[10] This occurs when, starting from the premise that nothing in the world has meaning or depth, they proceed to find meaning and depth in it. He thus criticizes the existentialists for "deify[ing] what crushes them".[11] Camus insists that his reasoning will not permit "such an abdication", and must begin and end with the absurd:

> My reasoning wants to be faithful to the evidence that aroused it. That evidence is the absurd. It is that divorce between the mind that desires and the world that disappoints, my nostalgia for unity, this fragmented universe and the contradiction that binds them together. Kierkegaard suppresses my nostalgia and Husserl gathers together that universe. That is not what I was expecting. It was a matter of living and thinking with those dislocations, of knowing whether one had to accept or refuse. There can be no question of masking the evidence, of suppressing the absurd by denying one of the terms of its equation. It is essential to know whether one can live with it or whether, on the other hand, logic commands one to die from it.[12]   (MS: 50; E: 134–5)

Having posited and accepted the absurd as an epistemic principle, Camus quickly poses what he considers to be the most important and urgent philosophical question to emerge from it: is life worth living? Or more accurately, if human existence is governed by the absurd, does the absurd dictate that we respond in one way or in another? Although it might seem that the absurdity of life is sufficient reason to deem it unworthy of effort, on the other hand, assuming that there is as little perfect coherence in death as there is in life, there is no clear choice between the two. Camus argues that we should keep the absurd alive rather than attempt to suppress it through philosophical suicide, or destroy it through physical suicide. He explains his reasoning as follows:

> Living an experience, a particular fate, is accepting it fully. Now, no one will live this fate, knowing it to be absurd, unless he does everything to keep before him that absurd brought to life by consciousness. Negating one of the terms of the opposition on which he lives amounts to escaping it. To abolish conscious revolt is to elude the problem. The theme of permanent revolution[13] is thus carried into individual experience. Living is keeping the absurd alive. Keeping

it alive is above all contemplating it. . . . One of the only coherent philosophical positions is thus revolt. It is a constant confrontation between man and his own obscurity. It is an insistence upon an impossible transparency. It challenges the world anew every second. Just as danger provided man with the unique opportunity of seizing awareness, so metaphysical revolt extends awareness to the whole experience. It is that constant presence of man in his own eyes. It is not aspiration, for it is devoid of hope. That revolt is the certainty of a crushing fate, without the resignation that ought to accompany it.

(*MS*: 53–4; *E*: 138)

Suicide, he says, is a "repudiation", an acquiescence to the absurd, while Camus would have us accept it without acquiescing to it.[14] Like the Kierkegaardian leap, such abdication is acceptance in the extreme. Suicide is not, therefore, for Camus an ultimate act of hubris, but is in fact a renunciation of all human values and indeed the possibility of human values. It is not the ultimate act of human freedom, but the renunciation of human freedom.[15] For Camus the absurd describes "a tension, born of a discrepancy between external reality and the human desire for familiarity", but this does not discount such things as the existence of beauty, friendship, health, satisfying work and creativity. While these values are contingent, a relative happiness remains possible, and "to commit suicide because of their relativity is to surrender all that is possible. . . . The *doxa* of life are a weave of beauty and ugliness, friendship and understanding, health and sickness, insight and opacity. It is a question of living with the mix and not succumbing to the temptation" to make an absolute value out of either hope or despair.[16]

Camus characterizes the struggle for human values in the light of the decision to affirm the ontological implications of the absurd as a struggle implying

> a total absence of hope (which has nothing to do with despair), a continual rejection (which must not be confused with renunciation), and a conscious dissatisfaction (which must not be compared to immature unrest). Everything that destroys, conjures away, or exorcises these requirements (and, to begin with, consent which overthrows divorce) ruins the absurd and devalues the attitude that may then be proposed.

The absurd has meaning, he says, "only in so far as it is not agreed to".[17] Already, Camus appears to be advocating a form of revolt in the face of the condition that seems to render life meaningless. Revolt here is an acceptance of the fact of the absurd (this, after all, is only to acknowledge the character of the human condition), but it is not a meek acceptance. Instead it is an acceptance filled with scorn, defiance and suffering. The incarnation of these responses is the mythical Sisyphus, condemned by the gods to "ceaselessly rolling a rock to the top of a mountain, whence the stone would fall back of its own weight": "Sisyphus, proletarian of the gods, powerless and rebellious, knows the whole extent of his wretched condition . . . the lucidity that was to constitute his torture at the same time crowns his victory. There is no fate that cannot be surmounted by scorn."[18]

However, we are still not clear on how we can move from the image of the solitary rebel to the concept of solidarity, which is necessary for revolt to have any political or social significance.[19] Ultimately, in fact, the only ethic possible at this point is a quantitative ethic, since in the absence of moral values the intensity and frequency of enjoyable experiences appears to be the only available determining standard with which to ascribe value to experience.[20] Accordingly, Camus suggests as illustrations or archetypes of absurd life Don Juan, the Actor and the Conqueror. Importantly, Camus makes it clear that these are not models to be emulated, but illustrations of an idea. Furthermore, these illustrations are not what they at first seem.[21] In Camus's account, Don Juan is a sexually omnivorous hero, but he ends his days contemplating nature from a secluded monastic cell, the Actor represents eternal liveliness (preferred to eternal life) and the Conqueror's greatest achievement is the overcoming of the self.[22] Indeed, the chief characteristic of the individual conscious of the absurd is his ability "to live in harmony with a universe without future and without weakness. This absurd, godless world is then peopled with men who think clearly and have ceased to hope" (*MS*: 85; *E*: 170). Camus even suggests that these absurd archetypes are united by "a metaphysical joy in enduring the world's absurdity".[23] It is never a question of overcoming the absurd, but only of "being faithful to the rules of the battle". "Conquest or play-acting, multiple loves, absurd revolt", says Camus, "are tributes that man pays to his dignity in a campaign in which he is defeated in advance" (*MS*: 86; *E*: 173). Significantly, as David Carroll points out, if "the awareness of the limitations of the human condition is characteristic of those who 'think clearly'," then it is not Don Juan, the Actor or the Conqueror but the Creator (who Carroll calls "the artist-writer") who is presented by Camus "as the figure who 'thinks' the most clearly of all".[24] "The absurd joy *par excellence*", says Camus, "is creation". Although artistic creation ultimately "has no more significance than the continual and imperceptible creation in which the actor, the conqueror and all absurd men indulge every day of their lives", these absurd archetypes know this in advance, and "their whole effort is to examine, to enlarge, and to enrich the ephemeral island on which they have just landed". It is in the context of this "absurd joy" derived from lucidity that we should consider the paradoxical statement with which *The Myth of Sisyphus* concludes, that "one must imagine Sisyphus happy". Although Camus tells us that Sisyphus's scorn of the gods and his fruitless task accomplish "nothing", "the 'nothing' he accomplishes each time he pushes his rock up to the very top of the hill", suggests Carroll, "is in fact the 'something' of art".[25]

This determination to reject suicide, to hold jealously to the absurd condition, to imagine Sisyphus happy, may seem to have brought us to the conclusion of our investigation of the absurd. It has, after all, answered the question with which *The Myth of Sisyphus* was ostensibly concerned – "does the absurd dictate death?" – by positing the "absurd hero" of a smiling Sisyphus filled with scorn for the gods, and committed to his fate. However, there remain at least two outstanding questions. First, notwithstanding Camus's own insistence that the absurd "does not liberate; it binds", that it "does not authorise all actions", that "'everything is permitted' does not mean that 'nothing is forbidden'", it is not at all clear that he has established any basis on which to insist upon limits to the so-called "ethic of quantity" realized by the absurd archetypes (*MS*: 16, 108, 65, 69, 75; *E*: 103, 196, 149–50, 154, 159). As "ridiculous" as Camus may have thought such suggestions, it is unclear what legitimate grounds can be found in *The Myth of Sisyphus* for rejecting Don Juan, the Conqueror or the Actor as models worthy of emulation.[26] Despite his protestations to the contrary, it seems that consequent on the absurd the task of the lucid individual, free of "all feeling of responsibility", "is not to live well in a moral sense – for the absence of moral values renders this meaningless – but *vivre à plus*, replacing the quality of experience by their quantity" (Thody 1961: 52–3). Second, we are still not clear on how we can progress from the image of Sisyphus as a solitary rebel towards some form of solidarity, necessary for revolt to have any political or social significance. One might even say that if we cannot rescue Sisyphus from his solipsistic exile, his revolt against the gods is of no real significance whatever.

In attempting to respond to these important questions it is necessary to pay close attention to a brief note appearing at the beginning of the published version of *The Myth of Sisyphus* (but absent from the manuscript).[27] Prompted, says Camus, by "certain personal experiences", he feels it necessary to explain that the absurd, "hitherto taken as a conclusion, is considered in this essay as a starting point". Accordingly, he suggests that "it may be said that there is something provisional in my commentary" and that the position the essay entails cannot be "prejudged". "There will be found here", Camus insists, "merely the description, in the pure state, of an intellectual malady" in which "no belief is involved" even "for a moment" (*MS*: 10; *E*: 97). In 1951, shortly before the publication of *The Rebel*, Camus made much the same point more clearly:

> This word "absurd" has had an unhappy history, and I confess that now it rather annoys me. When I analyzed the feeling of the absurd in *The Myth of Sisyphus*, I was looking for a method and not a doctrine. I was practising methodical doubt. I was trying to make a "tabula rasa", on the basis of which it would be then possible to construct something. If we assume that nothing has any meaning, then we must conclude that the world is absurd. But does nothing have a meaning? I have never believed that we could remain at this point. Even as I was writing *The Myth of Sisyphus* I was thinking about the essay on revolt that I would write later on, in which I would attempt, after having described the different aspects of the feeling of the absurd, to describe the different attitudes of the man in revolt. (This is the title of the book I am completing.) And then there are new events that enrich or correct what has come to one through observation, the continual lessons life offers, which you have to reconcile with those of your earlier experiences. This is what I have tried to do . . . though, naturally, I still do not claim to be in possession of truth.[28]

It is important to note that this does not constitute a refutation of the idea of the absurd as developed in *The Myth of Sisyphus*. Although dismissive of the idea that "nothing has any meaning" (which, properly speaking, is nihilism), it reaffirms the absurd as a "method", as a methodological deconstruction of commonplace assumptions, including those regarding morality and politics. In *The Rebel* Camus states that although "considered as a rule of life" the absurd is contradictory, the "greatness" of those philosophers and artists concerned with the absurd "is measured by the extent to which they have rejected the complacencies of absurdism in order to accept its exigencies".[29] The absurd is a method and not a doctrine, but its recognition remains a first necessary step in the development of properly human values.

However, although his antipathy to nihilism (the belief that all values are baseless and that nothing can be known) is evident from even a cursory glance at Camus's writing in the period (notably, as we shall see in later chapters, in his political journalism), it was not until the publication of *The Rebel* in 1951 that Camus presented a theoretical response to some of the unanswered questions in *The Myth of Sisyphus*. Certainly in Camus's other works contemporary with *The Myth of Sisyphus* (*The Outsider*, *Caligula* and *Cross Purpose*) there is no theoretical attempt to respond to these questions, and instead he seems to concentrate in these works on certain implications of the absurd. Nevertheless, as David Carroll has shown, Camus's depiction of Sisyphus betrays a distinct awareness of precisely what Camus's absurd reasoning cannot yet permit: political solidarity. For although Sisyphus's conscious lucidity may be that of the absurd artist (and his happiness the absurd artist's "absurd joy"), "the physical effort necessary to accomplish his task resembles more closely the labour of the worker", a subject on which Camus will reflect in *The Rebel* (Carroll 2007b: 64). Explaining the gods' punishment of Sisyphus, whom he calls the "proletarian of the gods", Camus notes: "they had thought with some reason that there is no more dreadful punishment than futile and hopeless labour". Indeed, Camus interrupts his retelling of the myth of Sisyphus to make the comparison explicit: "The workman of today works every day in his life at the same tasks and this fate is no less absurd" than that of Sisyphus (*MS*: 107–9; *E*: 195–6). As Carroll suggests, whereas Camus "says nothing more as to where such a proletarian consciousness could lead in the case of the worker . . . especially if he were to join with others in active protest and then resistance", the reason for this can be seen in the image of the solitary Sisyphus, who has no awareness of "class or collectivity". But of course, as Camus himself insists, his version of the myth of Sisyphus "is only a starting point – a possible origin for another form of history (or histories)". Although Sisyphus is the "absurd hero" of *The Myth of Sisyphus*, and "Camus makes Sisyphus's lucidity about his condition and his scorn for his tormentors indications of his 'victory' over both", Sisyphus's victory remains "individual and psychological, not collective and historical". Sisyphus's happiness "is a sublime joy . . . but no sense is given in the essay that he is anticipating joining with others" (Carroll 2007b: 65). Nevertheless, Camus's own personal political commitments (his joining of the French Resistance in 1943, quickly becoming editor-in-chief of the clandestine

Resistance newspaper *Combat*), clearly suggest that his account of Sisyphus's scorn-filled revolt against the gods can be read as a first definite step towards a more general conception of political and social commitment and resistance.[30]

The Outsider

> Lying is not only saying what isn't true. It is also, in fact especially, saying more than is true and, in the case of the human heart, saying more than one feels.
>
> (*TO*: 118; *TRN*: 1928)

Published, like *The Myth of Sisyphus*, in 1942 in Nazi-occupied Paris, *The Outsider* is a first-person narrative describing the life of a young *pied-noir* or European Algerian named Meursault. The novel is based around three important events: the funeral of Meursault's mother, during which he displays a disconcerting lack of emotion; his killing of an unnamed Arab under fairly obscure circumstances; and Meursault's trial and impending execution. The story culminates in the hero being condemned to death, and concludes with him confronting his fate at the guillotine. The first thing to note in approaching this frequently obscure novel is that *The Outsider*, *The Myth of Sisyphus* and *Caligula* (the last of which is discussed below) have an unusual mutual intimacy. Indeed, Camus had originally intended to have them published together in a single volume.[31] Accordingly, although we do not of course read them as a single text, if we are to read *The Outsider* as a novel of ideas, then the severe limits imposed on the meaning of the absurd in *The Myth of Sisyphus* need to be taken into account.

For Camus, Meursault is the absurd hero *par excellence*. His impending execution has nothing whatever to do with his killing of the forever-unnamed Arab. He was killed because of his social non-conformity, exemplified by his failure to express conventional grief after the death of his mother. Camus insists that at the heart of this non-conformity is a refusal to lie, noting that "lying is not only saying what isn't true. It is also, in fact especially, saying more than is true and, in the case of the human heart, saying more than one feels".[32] This affirmation of Meursault's exemplary honesty is the focus of my consideration of the novel, not only because it is affirmed in the context of the absurd, but also because it is central to one of the most influential critiques of *The Outsider*, that of Conor Cruise O'Brien.

For Cruise O'Brien, far from portraying any kind of philosophical or political truth, the novel in fact promotes a nefarious fiction about colonial Algeria: "What appears to the casual reader as a contemptuous attack on the court is not in fact an attack at all: on the contrary, by suggesting that the court is impartial between Arab and Frenchman, it implicitly denies the colonial reality and sustains the colonial fiction", the "fiction" being that a Frenchman in Algeria who had killed an Arab would be convicted in a court, a fiction that Cruise O'Brien argues is "vital to the status quo", to the legitimacy of the French colonial domination of Algeria.[33] The allegation of dishonesty in this depiction of "impartial" justice in Algeria places

Cruise O'Brien in the company of critics such as Henri Kréa and Pierre Nora, for whom Meursault's act is "the subconscious realisation of the obscure and puerile dream of the 'poor white' Camus never ceased to be", and for whom Camus was, like other *pieds-noirs*, "consciously frozen in historical immobility", "unable to confront", adds Cruise O'Brien, "the problem of the European–Arab relation".[34]

However, there is a far greater weight of evidence to support the inclination of his "casual reader" than Cruise O'Brien admits. I hope to show that a very strong case can be made, by a careful reader, in favour of the view that Meursault was indeed convicted and executed for failing to behave in a socially conventional fashion at the funeral of his mother. This becomes immediately clear when Meursault is first arrested after the killing: initially, in fact, "nobody seemed very interested in my case", and it was only later on, once they discovered his behaviour at a time when convention dictated Meursault should be publicly mourning his mother's death, that people began to "eye [him] with curiosity" (*TO*: 63; *TRN*: 1171). Later still, when, in bewilderment at the way that his trial is being conducted, Meursault's lawyer asks whether his client is being accused of burying his mother or killing a man, the prosecution replies that the two cannot be dissociated: "Yes . . . I accuse this man of burying his mother like a heartless criminal."[35] According to this interpretation, an interpretation supported, as we shall see, by the character of much of his contemporary political journalism, Camus was actually suggesting that a European Algerian was more likely to be condemned to death for failing to express himself according to social convention than he would be for killing an Arab. It is in this context, too, that we must consider the Arab's continued anonymity.

Cruise O'Brien suggests that it is Meursault's dishonesty rather than his honesty that is proved by close reading of the novel: he argues, for example, that Camus's hero lies when he writes a letter for his neighbour Raymond, designed to "deceive" his Arab girlfriend "and expose her to humiliation".[36] The only thing that Meursault refuses to lie about, Cruise O'Brien insists, is his own feelings. While this observation is in many respects correct, as Joseph McBride has argued, Cruise O'Brien's judgement is undermined by his failure to appreciate the context in which Camus affirms Meursault's honesty (McBride n.d.: 55). Meursault is honest within the context of the absurd; he is as honest as the absurd will allow. He is honest when he feels he can speak in honesty – that is, ultimately, in relation to his own feelings.[37] The absurd disallows him the possibility of constructing criteria for determining good and bad, right and wrong, in other more inclusive or social contexts. Meursault's perceived dishonesty amounts only to his refusal to accept that there are objective criteria for determining a scale of moral values. When Camus spoke of Meursault's honesty, it was this kind of honesty that he had in mind. Furthermore, while Meursault is no more an exemplar of moral behaviour than Sisyphus or Don Juan, he does exhibit a kind of honesty that, as we shall see, is conspicuously absent from most of the other, ostensibly reputable, characters in the novel.

Cruise O'Brien's failure to take Meursault's reasoning into account is exemplified in the very episode in which he argues that Meursault's dishonesty is most apparent: the writing of a letter for his neighbour Raymond, a letter designed to trick

Raymond's girlfriend into a humiliating trap. Meursault states: "I wrote the letter. I did it rather haphazardly, but I did my best to please Raymond because I had *no reason not to please him*."[38] He lacked the moral grounds required for him to refuse Raymond's request. Clearly then, had he refused, he would have done so on the grounds of moral beliefs he didn't actually possess. Such a refusal, Camus implies, would have been dishonest, since lying is "in fact especially, saying more than is true and, in the case of the human heart, saying more than one feels".[39] Once we situate Meursault within the context of the absurd we can begin to see that the "lies" he tells are less a consequence of dishonesty than a consequence of stubborn honesty in the midst of the moral equivalence apparently consequent on the absurd.

Other, more direct, examples of Meursault's honesty can be seen early in the second part of the novel. For example, he notes that when he was first arrested, "I was put in a room with several other prisoners, most of them Arabs. They laughed when they saw me. Then they asked me what I'd done. I told them that I'd killed an Arab and there was silence."[40] Indeed, Meursault expresses a strong (albeit potentially pathological) sense of honesty when he reads on a piece of paper discovered in his cell of the murder of a man by his mother and sister. The man had been in disguise; his mother and sister killed themselves when they discovered what they had done. Meursault's response is intriguing: "I decided that the traveller had deserved it really and that you should never play around."[41] For Camus, Meursault represents the modern Sisyphus, the authentic man in a world bereft of transcendent meaning.[42] He is the one who lives the absurd in revolt, a revolt that demands not only that he live with a jealous love for physical, sensory existence, but also that he take all actions as morally equivalent (McBride n.d.: 58).

This interpretation of *The Outsider* is further endorsed if we shift our attention from the often obscure psychology of Meursault and consider the novel's depiction of Meursault's confrontation with society as a whole in the context of the absurd (the "absurd" understood primarily as an epistemological claim, a claim regarding the sorts of things we can say we know). Adjusting the focus of our reading of the novel in this way, away from Meursault (whose status as Sisyphean absurd hero Camus affirms[43]) and onto the depiction of his relationship with society in general, our attention is drawn to events surrounding two central points in the novel: the wake and funeral of Meursault's mother and, especially, Meursault's trial (the wake itself at one point seems to take the form of a trial, Meursault noting that "at one point I had the ridiculous impression that [the other mourners] were there to judge me") (*TO*: 15; *TRN*: 1130). In both of these cases, Meursault's lucidity and honesty are seen to come into conflict with the dishonesty of society in general. From the perspective of the absurd, these two events, paradoxically, could be said to have greater significance than the killing of the unnamed Arab. The killing of the unnamed Arab, I suggest, serves both as a formal necessity, so that Meursault *could* stand trial, and as a powerful criticism of the inherent racism of French-Algerian justice, where an individual kills an Arab but is executed for failing to cry at his mother's funeral.

The opening lines of *The Outsider*, "Mother died today. Or maybe yesterday, I don't know", are probably among the most famous in modern literature, and tend to be interpreted as evidence of Meursault's jaded indifference, stoic or not, to normal emotional and moral behaviour. However, although there is certainly some justification to this interpretation, what tends to be overlooked is that Meursault's jarring statement is a direct result of the perfunctory telegram sent by the retirement home where Mme Meursault had lived for the previous several years: "Mother passed away, Funeral tomorrow. Yours sincerely." As Meursault explains, "That doesn't mean anything. It might have been yesterday" (*TO*: 9; *TRN*: 1125). This subtly constructed passage should make us wary of arriving too quickly at conclusions regarding the character of Meursault. It should also make us wary of arriving too quickly at conclusions regarding those characters with whom Meursault comes into contact. Indeed, if we are to accept Camus's claims regarding Meursault's martyrdom for the truth, then we cannot ignore the degree to which the society that condemns Meursault is constructed upon deceit and lies. This dishonesty, and the extent to which, for Camus, it is associated with religious belief, becomes apparent early in the novel when Meursault arrives at the retirement home, and the home's director tells Meursault that his mother "apparently often mentioned to her friends that she wished to have a religious funeral. I've taken it upon myself to make the necessary arrangements. But I thought I should let you know." Meursault notes, "I thanked him. Though she wasn't an atheist, mother never had given a thought to religion in her life" (*TO*: 11–12; *TRN*: 1127).

This form of dishonesty, and Meursault's confrontation with it, become far more pronounced after his arrest. If we regard the absurd as primarily a claim regarding the severe limits on human knowledge, we shall see that from the perspective of the absurd perhaps the most interesting episode in the novel is that of the judicial process, culminating in Meursault's trial. Heroically absurd, Meursault comes into conflict with the false positivism of both the state and its proxy, the court.[44] The trial stages a confrontation between the simple and direct language of Meursault, who regularly admits to uncertainty and never admits to more than he knows, and the false and bombastic language of the state.[45] As a confrontation between, on the one hand, conventional and institutional law and morality, and, on the other, the absurd, where law and morality rather than the absurd appear to embody injustice, it is worth looking at more closely.

Meursault's claims during his trial that he "hadn't intended to kill the Arab" and that "it was because of the sun" will provoke only laughter in the courtroom, but for the investigating magistrate, who questions Meursault before the trial commences, only one aspect of his confession "didn't make sense" (*TO*: 99, 68; *TRN*: 1196, 1173). Why, he wanted to know, after shooting the Arab once, did Meursault pause and then shoot the lifeless body four more times? It quickly becomes clear that this interests the magistrate (as, indeed, it will interest the state's prosecution) far more than why Meursault shot the Arab the first time. Indeed, it seems to interest them far more than the fact *that* he shot the never-named Arab at all. (Meursault himself seems to hint that these four gratuitous shots, rather than the killing of the Arab itself, are the reason for his own impending execution.[46]) When Meursault replies that the magistrate was wrong to insist on this point, that it didn't matter that much, the magistrate immediately interrupts him and his real concern is exposed. He is clearly not interested in the crime of which Meursault has been accused, but in his non-conformism, his atheism and, especially, his lack of religiously inspired remorse and guilt:

> he interrupted me and pleaded with me one last time, drawing himself up to his full height and asking me if I believed in God. I said no. He sat down indignantly. He told me that it was impossible, that all men believed in God, even those who wouldn't face up to Him. That was his belief, and if he should ever doubt it, his life would become meaningless. "Do you want my life to become meaningless?" he cried.

For the magistrate, who at one point brandishes a crucifix in Meursault's face, exclaiming "I am a Christian. I ask him to forgive your sins. How can you not believe that he suffered for your sake?" Meursault becomes "Mr Antichrist". For Camus, he represents "the only Christ we deserve".[47]

The state prosecutor, similarly, ignores the actual killing for which Meursault supposedly stands accused, and instead accuses him of being "morally responsible for his mother's death".[48] This compounds the growing sense that Meursault will be condemned to death because of his social non-conformism, and further highlights the sense that the actual killing for which Meursault is supposedly standing trial is of no consequence whatever to the court. Claiming to have "peered into" Meursault's soul, "he said the truth was that I didn't have one, a soul, and that I had no access to any humanity nor to any of the moral principles which protect the human heart". The prosecutor insists that in the case of Meursault "the wholly negative ethic of tolerance must give way to the stricter but loftier ethic of justice. Especially when we encounter a man whose heart is so empty that it forms a chasm which threatens to engulf society." He declares that Meursault had "no place in a society whose most fundamental rules [he] ignored" and calls "with a sense of urgent and sacred duty", with a feeling of "horror . . . at the sight of a man in whom I see nothing but a monster" and with "an easy mind", "for this man's head".[49] This febrile reasoning, grounded in "horror at [his] insensitivity", further permits the prosecutor to accuse Meursault of being "guilty of the murder which this court is to judge tomorrow" (a case of alleged parricide), while, it should be noted, neglecting all mention of the actual killing of the Arab for which Meursault was arrested.[50] Certainly whatever the prosecutor may have thought of Meursault's killing of the Arab, it was clearly not *that* crime to which he was referring when he accused Meursault of a crime equivalent to "parricide". As the trial scene progresses, the reader becomes increasingly aware that the prosecutor, sated with his own self-righteousness, represents a society with the power to send Meursault to his death for his non-conformity, for his refusal to lie, to say "more than is true", and indeed that it will.

Meursault's defence lawyer articulates an attitude essentially identical to that of the prosecution. This becomes evident from their first meeting, in Meursault's prison cell:

> "Let's get straight on with it." He sat down on the bed and explained that some investigation had been made into my private life. It had been discovered that my mother had died recently in a home . . . the magistrates had learned that I'd "displayed a lack of emotion" on the day of my mother's funeral . . . "it matters a great deal. And the prosecution will have a strong case if I can't find anything to reply." (*TO*: 64; *TRN*: 1172)

Initially he is concerned by Meursault's unwillingness to recite conventional platitudes of grief and sorrow, but his attitude quickly turns to contempt when Meursault refuses to lie: "he asked me if he could say that I'd controlled my natural feelings" on the day of his mother's funeral. "I said, 'No. because it's not true.' He looked at me in a particular way, as if he found me slightly disgusting."[51] The lawyer's disgust seems motivated less by Meursault's behaviour at his mother's funeral than by his apparent unwillingness to lie, to follow his lawyer's implicit advice and say what he knew to be untrue in order to improve his chances in court. This sense that the defence is playing the same "game", which Meursault alone refuses to play, is confirmed when, rather than object to it, his lawyer apes the spurious reasoning of the prosecution, claiming that he too had peered into Meursault's soul, and indeed claiming for himself greater talent in metaphysical divination than his colleague: "in fact I read it like an open book". Meursault himself comments at this point: "with all these long sentences and the endless days and hours that people had been talking about my soul, I just had the impression that I was drowning in some sort of colour-less liquid" (*TO*: 118, 100–101; *TRN*: 1920, 1197).

In the testimony of the warden from the nursing home where Mme Meursault died we begin to see a more explicit form of dishonesty: "He was asked whether mother used to complain about me and he said yes but that his inmates had rather a habit of complaining about their relatives. The judge asked him to specify whether she used to reproach me for having sent her to a home and the warden again said yes. But this time he didn't add anything."[52] The significance of Meursault's last comment becomes clear when we remember the warden's words of consolation at the beginning of the novel:

> You've no need to justify yourself, my dear boy. I've read your mother's file. You weren't able to look after her properly. She needed a nurse. You only have a modest income. And all things considered, she was happier here . . . you're a young man, a different generation, and she must have been bored living with you. (*TO*: 10–11; *TRN*: 1126)

The warden's testimony in court is clearly motivated by a desire to be seen to be on the side of the society that condemns Meursault, just as his desire to satisfy social convention motivates him to arrange a religious funeral for Mme Meursault, who, as we have seen, "had never given a thought to religion in her life" (*TO*: 12; *TRN*: 1127). Stating that he had been surprised by Meursault's "calmness", the warden goes on to explain that Meursault "hadn't wanted to see [his] mother", that he "hadn't cried once", that he had "left straight after the funeral without paying [his] respects at her grave" and that he did not know his mother's age. This testimony is sufficiently effective for the state's prosecutor to deem it unnecessary to add to it through cross-examination (*TO*: 86–7; *TRN*: 1186–7). However, as effective as it may have been in condemning Meursault in the eyes of the jury, the warden's testimony is false in at least one critical respect. Whereas he claims that Meursault did not wish to see his mother, the careful reader will have noticed that in fact immediately upon his arrival at the home, Meursault makes exactly this request and that, crucially, his request is denied on the grounds that he must first see the warden.[53]

Perhaps the most dramatic of these encounters is with the prison chaplain, who tells Meursault, towards the end of the novel, of his "certainty" regarding the success of his appeal against his sentence (curiously, he also admits to Meursault on the same occasion that he "knows nothing about" his appeal) (*TO*: 113, 111; *TRN*: 1206, 1205). The chaplain informs Meursault that he is "burdened with a sin from which [he] must free [himself]". Meursault replies that he "didn't know what a sin was", that he had "simply been told that [he] was guilty": "I was guilty and I was paying for it and there was nothing more that could be asked of me" (*TO*: 113; *TRN*: 1206–7). Meursault's blank refusal of the chaplain's proffered consolations prompt the priest to add: "I'm on your side. But you can't see that because your heart is blind. I shall pray for you." Meursault responds with an explosion of anger, insulting the priest and telling him that he did not want his prayers: "I was pouring everything out at him from the bottom of my heart in a paroxysm of joy and anger." What Meursault objects to, far more than the religious platitudes themselves, is the certainty they imply: "He seemed so certain of everything, didn't he? And yet none of his certainties was worth one hair of a woman's head" (*TO*: 115; *TRN*: 1208). Here too, more than ever before, Meursault clearly represents the absurd hero, exhibiting the same wild courage and rebellious scorn in accepting his fate that we saw in Sisyphus.

What is increasingly apparent in each of these cases, from the magistrate to the chaplain, is that beyond their religiously inspired and often violent indignation, beyond even the fact that the actual crime for which Meursault stands accused is almost completely ignored, is a level of certainty that Meursault finds incomprehensible and Camus evidently finds, in the context of the absurd, unjustifiable. This analysis may then lead us to reflect on the differences between the crime that the state commits in executing a man for non-conformity and the crime Meursault commits in killing the unnamed Arab. It seems that the chief difference is that although Meursault is certainly responsible for the death of the Arab, his was a totally unpremeditated act, whereas, in stark contrast, the execution of Meursault is committed by the machinery of the state, by culturally specific mores dressed up as objective moral principles. Nevertheless, although Meursault was executed by the state for not crying at his mother's funeral, Camus nowhere suggests that Meursault was not *responsible* for the death of the Arab.[54] Several critics appear to suggest that the killing of the unnamed Arab was in some way "excusable", and more generally, there frequently appears to be a temptation to interpret Camus's claim that Meursault was killed for failing to cry at his mother's funeral as itself implying that the court had no good reason to try Meursault for killing an Arab.[55] Meursault was condemned to death for not crying at his mother's funeral, but this clearly does not itself imply that he should not have been tried in a court for the killing of the Arab. This point should become clearer when we consider the suggestion in *The Myth of Sisyphus* that to "a mind imbued with the absurd . . . there may be responsible persons but there are no guilty ones, in its opinion".[56] Unsurprisingly, then, Meursault's understanding of "guilt" is associated explicitly with the judgement of society, which suggests that for Meursault guilt itself is socially constructed. We note that it is only after the warden and caretaker testify against him, citing his failure to cry at the funeral, his failure to pay respects at his mother's grave, the fact that he slept, smoked and drank coffee during her wake, that Meursault comments, "I stupidly felt like crying because I could tell how much all these people hated me", and "for the first time I realised that I was guilty".[57] Later, during the prosecution's summing-up – a summing-up in which the actual killing continues to be largely overlooked in favour of the events surrounding his mother's funeral – Meursault complains that he cannot understand "how the qualities of an ordinary man could be used as damning evidence of guilt".[58] In contrast, on several occasions Meursault does indicate an understanding of the concept of responsibility. Although his understanding of responsibility (or fault) is evoked in association with his mother's death, and while he admits to feeling "a certain kind of annoyance" rather than regret for what he had done, I also think that Meursault would have recognized his responsibility for the death of the unnamed Arab (*TO*: 9, 10, 15, 23, 24, 69; *TRN*: 1125, 1126, 1130, 1136, 1137, 1174).

Whereas many critics, such as Conor Cruise O'Brien, perceive a distinct indifference in the character of Meursault, the novel itself repeatedly reminds us of the simple pleasures in which he found joy: "I was assailed by memories of a life which was no longer mine, but in which I had found my simplest pleasures: the smells of summer, the part of town that I loved, the sky on certain evenings, Maria's dresses and the way she laughed."[59] Indeed, far from proclaiming an ethic of indifference, Camus believed that *The Outsider* had, as well as the obvious "metaphysical" or absurd meaning, a "social" meaning.[60] The "social" meaning Camus claimed for the novel relates to its comment on the forces of social conformity, on the death penalty, but also, as I have argued, on the judicial system in Algeria, which he suggests was more concerned with a *pied-noir* not crying at his mother's funeral that with his killing of an Arab. Nevertheless, it seems that to a large extent this social sense was obscured, though perhaps not suffocated, by the sheer metaphysical weight of the novel's pervasive absurdity. This is not to agree with Cruise O'Brien, who claims that the novel may posit Meursault as a metaphysical rebel – a rebel against Christian cosmogony or indeed any idea of the supernatural – but that this "is in no sense a revolt against the values of Camus' culture" (Cruise O'Brien 1970: 31). Quite to the contrary, the novel is about how a fundamentally sincere and honest man becomes a mortal victim of the state judicial system not because he refused to tell the truth, but because he refused to lie. *The Outsider* is a plea for the rights of the individual against social conformity and against the state – in a very profound way, despite its status as absurd novel *par excellence*, it can be seen as a restatement of classical liberalism. *The Outsider* is concerned almost exclusively with constructing a model of what the confrontation with the absurd may look like in a social or political context. Camus is concerned with developing a fictional image of the ontological position dictated by the absurd.[61] Accordingly, although there is a clear dimension of social criticism in the novel, there is no *positive* ethic, no ethic beyond the basic principle of sincerity. The austere dignity of Meursault confronting his death, his complete refusal of hope and despair, is Camus's negative ethic. The question remains, however, whether there is anything to stop Meursault, as the absurd hero *par excellence*, unflinching in the face of the apparent meaninglessness of human existence, from becoming a nihilist. This is the question that is pursued in *Caligula*.

Caligula

And yet – since this world is the only one we have, why not plead its cause?
(*COP*: 46; *TRN*: 25)

Camus seeks to create in *Caligula* the historical *Homo absurdus*, not simply to complement the fictional and mythical absurd heroes of *The Outsider* and *The Myth of Sisyphus*, but also to represent the very real implications that may result from the absurd once it has left the rarefied air of fiction or myth to firmly take its place in history.[62] Whereas the novel and essay, which precede by two years the play in its published form, tend to focus on the radical uncertainty consequent on the absurd, in *Caligula* the focus is firmly on its possible social and political implications. The paradox of Meursault, as both absurd hero and assassin, is pursued in greater detail in the play, through the exchanges between the Emperor Caligula and his chief adversary, Cherea, exchanges in which we see conscious awareness of the absurd leading to both a nihilistic penchant for murder and a will to resist precisely that tendency. It is in this context that a politics of revolt is seen to emerge from the exigencies of the absurd.

The play opens at the apex of a political crisis precipitated by the death of the emperor's sister and mistress, Drusilla. Caligula has been emperor for about one year, and we are told that, as an emperor, "he was perfection itself" (*COP*: 36; *TRN*: 10). The young poet Scipio, who will take part in the assassination of Caligula at the play's end, notes that the emperor had "been very good to me . . . I shall never forget some of the things he said. He told me life isn't easy, but it has consolations: religion, art, and the love one inspires in others. He often told me that the only mistake one makes in life is to cause others suffering. He tried to be a just man" (*COP*: 42; *TRN*: 19). However, Caligula's character appears transformed by the death of Drusilla. In fact, Caligula claimed to be less affected by her death itself than by "the truth" her death revealed: a "childishly simple, obvious, almost silly truth, but one that's hard to come by and heavy to endure", the truth that "men die, and they are not happy" (*COP*: 40; *TRN*: 16). Drusilla's death, and his irrational desire to recover her, provokes in Caligula a sudden awareness of the absurd, "that divorce between the mind that desires and the world that disappoints" (*MS*: 40; *E*: 135).

Alone among Camus's absurd works, *Caligula* directly addresses the question of whether or not the absurd necessarily results in nihilism.[63] We see in Caligula all the characteristics of the absurd rebel – he exhibits the same courage and lucidity as Sisyphus or Meursault. But we also see, apparently derived from the same reasoning, an unquenchable thirst for murder and tyranny. Camus's awareness that the absurd (specifically, the moral indifference apparently consequent on the absurd) may force itself onto the stage of history with more sinister and bloody consequences than might have been imagined in *The Myth of Sisyphus* is clearly in evidence here. Caligula's authority as Roman Emperor gives him unique privileges. When he exclaims, "I'm surrounded by lies and self-deception. But I've had enough of that; I wish men to live by the light of truth. And I've the power to make them do so", he has the power to "make" the whole world "discover" the absurd (*COP*: 41; *TRN*: 16). However, while Caligula may be "a lunatic absolutist", Camus makes it clear that the emperor is also an idealist (Freeman 1971: 38). He is like Meursault, absolved of hope and brutally honest. He is like Sisyphus, whose scorn defies the gods. But he is also Caesar, with a veto on the lives of all of his people.[64] Camus has made considerable effort to enlist our sympathy for Caligula, but ultimately, he wants us to react, like Cherea, who leads the eventual assassination of Caligula, by believing what the emperor says to be *true* but *wrong*.[65]

Reflections on the meaning and significance of the absurd in the play are confined primarily to the lines of its anti-hero Caligula and his main antagonist Cherea. Crucially, although Cherea alone confronts the reasoning behind Caligula's nihilism, it is clear that he too understands, or recognizes, the absurd. A moderate, an advocate of compromise, his significance to the meaning of the text grows as the need for action grows. He claims that what he wants is to live and to be happy, and that neither "is possible if one pushes the absurd to its logical conclusions". Accordingly, although he finds Caligula's murderous philosophy "logical from start to finish", he rejects both the philosophical and political implications that Caligula draws from the absurd (*COP*: 82–3, 53; *TRN*: 78, 35). In a key exchange in the play, Cherea confronts Caligula's nihilistic assertion that "I believe that all [actions] are equivalent" with a qualitative ethic: "I believe that some actions are more admirable [*plus belles*] than others."[66] This assertion marks a clear departure from the "ethic of quantity" posited in *The Myth of Sisyphus*.[67] Although Cherea does not say (or cannot say) that some actions are simply "better" than others, although he discriminates between actions using a primarily aesthetic term, this does not mean that the distinction is *merely* aesthetic.

Although only Caligula and the ineffectual patricians actually pretend to talk about morality itself, it is clear that Cherea's objection to Caligula is based on his objection to the nihilistic implications the emperor has drawn from the absurd.[68] Whether or not this objection is "moral" is moot. Cherea makes it clear that what he objects to in Caligula is not his tyranny over the patricians (his taking of their money, even their lives) but his nihilism. If he takes part in the assassination of Caligula, he does so "to combat a big idea – an ideal, if you like – whose triumph would mean the end of everything". "What's intolerable", he says, "is to see one's life being drained of meaning, to be told there's no reason for existing. A man can't live without some reason for living . . . all I wish is to regain some peace of mind in a world that has regained a meaning. What spurs me on is not ambition but fear, my very reasonable fear of that inhuman vision in which my life means no more than a speck of dust." Cherea's rejection of Caligula's nihilism clearly implies the recognition of a value to human life. This ability to distinguish qualitatively becomes more evident when Cherea asks Scipio to join the conspiracy: "this killing", he says, "needs honourable men to sponsor it" (COP: 53–4, 86*; TRN: 34–5, 82). Indeed, when Scipio (whose father Caligula has tortured and killed) protests that he feels too close to Caligula to partake in the assassination, Cherea's sense of scandal becomes even more apparent: "[Caligula] has taught you to despair. And to have instilled despair into a young heart is fouler than the foulest crimes he has committed up to now. I assure you, *that* alone would justify me in killing him out of hand" (COP: 87; TRN: 84). At the heart of the play is a dialogue between Cherea and Caligula, in which the former tells the emperor both that "I understand you far too well", and that he regards him as "noxious and cruel, vain and selfish . . . a constant menace". He explains his objection to Caligula's nihilism thus:

> I like, and need, to feel secure. So do most men. They resent living in a world where the most preposterous fancy may at any moment become a reality, and the absurd transfixes their lives, like a dagger in the heart. I feel as they do. I refuse to live in a topsy-turvy world. I want to know where I stand, and to stand secure . . . my plan may not be logical but at least it's sound . . . I'll be no party to your logic. I've a very different notion of my duties as a man.

He tells Caligula, "I understand, and to a point, agree with you," but he adds, "but you're pernicious, and you've got to go" (COP: 82, 83; TRN: 77–8, 79).

In a recent essay, Colin Davis (2007) claims that in this confrontation Caligula and Cherea "articulate the ethical impasse at the heart of the philosophy of the Absurd" and suggests that several of Camus's subsequent works "can be seen as repeatedly re-staging" the same quarrel.[69] While I think the observation that this confrontation echoes across Camus's works is astute, it seems something of an exaggeration to consider the confrontation an "impasse". The ethical subtext of *Caligula* is not as ambiguous as Davis suggests, for while Cherea may eschew specifically moral language, this does not mean that his objection to Caligula is without any moral content. Although the ethic Cherea defends has yet to be defined in anything like a satisfactory way, this does not mean that there is no ethic at all in Cherea's objection to the implications Caligula has derived from the absurd. In any event, whether or not we want to call this objection a moral objection is less significant than the fact that Cherea clearly rejects the conclusions Caligula has drawn from the absurd. This same exaggeration also leads Davis to the view that the assassination of Caligula "continues the sequence of murders that it is intended to terminate". When Caligula himself may be killed at the end of the play, says Davis, "the principle of senseless violence which he embodies is implemented again in the very moment of his death" (Davis 2007: 115–16). However, it is clear that the killing of Caligula is markedly different from those senseless murders perpetrated by or on behalf of the emperor that precede it. Indeed, as I show in a later chapter, the details of the assassination of Caligula in Camus's play, and the ways in which they differ from the account in Suetonius, indicate that although he placed severe limits on what he considered to be justifiable violence, he nonetheless considered the killing of the emperor morally legitimate. In marked contrast with the numerous killings perpetrated or sanctioned by Caligula on the basis of the absurd, this particular act constitutes explicit evidence that Camus rejects some potential implications of the absurd (and also that he would advocate violent struggle against such implications). Indeed, the assassination of Caligula marks an extremely significant point in the development of Camus's thinking – both with respect to what can be considered a legitimate response to the absurd and with respect to the idea of legitimate revolt, which he will examine in detail in *The Rebel*.

Although it is clear, especially in his killing of Caligula, that Cherea rejects the ethic of quantity tentatively posited in *The Myth of Sisyphus* and embraced by the emperor, he does not yet posit, at least in any recognizable way, an alternative.[70] Instead, what we find articulated here is a negative reaction to the implications derived from the absurd by Caligula, a negative reaction similar to the refusal Camus will identify in *The Rebel* as being at the beginning of all revolt. By replacing the "benign indifference of the universe" suggested in *The Outsider* with the tyrannical excesses of Caligula as a dramatic backdrop, Camus forces a confrontation between the absurd and nihilism. To the extent to which the characters in *Caligula* rebel against Caligula's ethic of destruction, the ethic implicit in the assassination can be said to be qualitative: Caligula's "freedom", as he himself appears to suggest at the play's end, wasn't "the right one". One may suggest that this ethic seems inadequate, and Cherea's revolt against Caligula, based on an objection that he himself admits may not be "logical", seems to leave a great deal to be desired (*COP*: 103, 82; *TRN*: 108, 78). However, it can be argued that the scope of the absurd trilogy was more limited than this, and that the primary concern of these texts has been to examine the absurd and discover its exigencies. In *Caligula* Camus asks whether the absurd leads inexorably to nihilism, and through the character of Cherea (and, to a lesser extent, Scipio) he suggests that it does not. Despite being, like Caligula, conscious of the absurd, Cherea appears to discern a communal ethic of human solidarity in the face of the absurd, which Camus will examine in greater detail in *The Plague* and, especially, *The Rebel*.[71] However, although *Caligula* suggests there is a need for an affirmative ethic to match the epistemological deconstruction wrought by the absurd method, the play itself makes little if any progress towards defining such an ethic, and suggests only, as a first step, that the absurd does not itself "dictate death" (*MS*: 16; *E*: 103).

Between nihilism and hope

> Where lay the difference? Simply that you readily accepted despair and I never yielded to it.   (*RRD*: 27; *E*: 240)

In 1942, in *The Myth of Sisyphus*, Camus had already asserted that he was interested "not so much in absurd discoveries as in their consequences", and he asks whether the absurd requires that one "die voluntarily" or that one "hope in spite of everything" (*MS*: 22; *E*: 109). We have seen that he rejects the idea that the absurd itself leads to suicide, and accordingly, we can say that he rejects the idea that the absurd may require that one "die voluntarily". However, his attitude to the possibility of hope seems far from optimistic. In "Hope and the Absurd in the Work of Franz Kafka", originally written as part of *The Myth of Sisyphus* but not published until 1948, Camus claims that Kafka reintroduces hope into a world where hope is absent, and identifies this hope with Kierkegaard's "philosophical suicide" (for Kierkegaard, Camus notes, "earthly hope must be killed; only then can we be saved by true hope").[72] Kafka "refuses his god moral nobility, evidence, virtue, coherence", Camus says, "but only the better to fall into his arms". In Kafka's works, "the absurd is recognized, accepted and man is resigned to it, but from then on we know that it has ceased to be the absurd. Within the limits of the human condition, what greater hope than the hope that allows an escape from that condition? As I see once more, existential thought in this regard (and contrary to current opinion) is steeped in a vast hope." But in that leap that characterizes all existential thought, Camus asks, "how can one fail to see the mark of a lucidity that repudiates itself?" In this way, Camus sees Kafka as guilty of the same philosophical suicide he diagnosed in the works of the existentialists discussed elsewhere in the essay. He identifies in Kafka, as he had already identified in the existentialists, "an attempt to recapture God through what negates Him, to recognize Him not through the categories of goodness or beauty, but behind the empty and hideous aspect of His indifference, of His injustice and of His hatred" (*MS*: 121, 119–20; *E*: 209, 207).

    All of this seems to warn us against seeking, or claiming to have found, hope in the absurd works of Camus, for here hope seems to imply a quest for or a belief in the eternal in which lucidity repudiates itself. However, although Camus states that lucid awareness of the absurd "implies a total absence of hope", he also insists that this total absence of hope "has nothing to do with despair", and as such, his approach to the possibility of hope in the context of the absurd should be looked at carefully.[73] Hope that is "an attempt to recapture God" is, it seems, a very specific type of hope, and repudiation of such hope does not seem to involve a repudiation of what could be called "finite" hope, a type of hope that I will suggest is present in all of Camus's works (with the possible exception of *The Misunderstanding*).[74] Certainly Camus rejected the religiously inspired "infinite" hope he identified in Kafka and Kierkegaard. But we must consider what lucidity reveals to him in relation to "finite" hope, and what ethic, if any, this might prescribe. On several occasions, Camus spoke of his pessimism in relation to "the human condition" and of his optimism in relation to "man".[75] Similarly, while we can say that neither Meursault nor Cherea finds a reason to hope in their absurd condition, we can also find in Camus's absurd works evidence to suggest that hope may be found, or nurtured, in the relations between men – as is suggested in the actions of the conspirators in *Caligula* and, as we shall see, in *The Plague*. Already, in *The Myth of Sisyphus*, Camus had suggested a distinction:

> There is hope and hope. To me the optimistic work of Henri Bordeaux seems peculiarly discouraging. This is because it has nothing for the discriminating. Malraux's thought on the other hand is always bracing. But in these two cases neither the same hope nor the same despair is at issue.   (*MS*: 120; *E*: 208)

Here, Camus is explicitly calling for a distinction between two forms of hope. Whereas he associates certain expressions of hope with Kierkegardian philosophical suicide, a type of hope we could perhaps call "infinite" hope, it seems clear that Camus had in mind the possibility of there being another type of hope – a kind of hope that, although not permitting an escape from the absurd confrontation between the individual and his world, nevertheless has philosophical or ethical significance for "finite" humankind living in lucid awareness of the absurd. This, by necessity, is a finite hope, a mundane hope in an unsponsored universe. Absurd hope is lucid hope, a hope tempered by an awareness of the limits to human comprehension and by a stubborn refusal to transgress the limits discerned through conscious awareness. From this perspective, when Camus states that "the absurd is the contrary of hope" or that the struggle with the absurd "implies a total absence of hope (which has nothing to do with despair)", he is referring to "infinite" hope (*MS*: 37, 34; *E*: 124, 121). For Camus, what I have called "finite" hope seems to emerge out of the resistance to both "infinite" hope, which he finds in Kierkegaard, and nihilism, exemplified by Caligula. Furthermore, it allows for the lucid understanding of the absurd human condition. Such "finite" hope maintains Sisyphean scorn (later to become rebellion) and keeps both "infinite" hope and despair at bay.[76]

Nevertheless, the questions prompted by Camus's absurd analysis remain. Are the cruelties of Caligula no less justified than acts of kindness or justice in an absurd world? Is there any intelligible difference between the lucidity of the absurd vision and the horror of the nihilistic proclamation? Is the absurd nihilistic? Camus certainly attempts to set a *limit* to the implications of the absurd, and had claimed as early as 1938, reviewing Sartre's novel *Nausea*, that the "realisation that life is absurd cannot be an end in itself but only a beginning" (*SEN*: 167–9; *E*: 1417–19). Where "nihilism is not only despair and negation but, above all, the desire to despair and negate", the absurd, in contrast, we are told, "does not liberate, it binds. It does not authorize all actions"; it "merely confers an equivalence on the consequences of those actions". It "does not recommend crime, for this would be childish, but it restores to remorse its futility" (*R*: 57–8; *E*: 467; *MS*: 65; *E*: 149–50. Cf. *R*: 57–61, 100–104; *E*: 467–71, 508–11). Although Camus may have insisted upon the conceptual integrity of the absurd, and its distinction from nihilism, his success in this endeavour may seem questionable. Ultimately, "everything is permitted" may indeed seem to imply that "nothing is forbidden". However, whereas nihilism is the deliberate and eternal negation of all values, the absurd is seen at least to admit the possibility of value. Camus objects to the transcendent truth that Kierkegaard, for example, embraces in order to escape the absurd, but this objection does not preclude the possibility of the creation of human or mundane values. The actions of the conspirators in *Caligula*, especially, seem to suggest that nihilism is not a necessary consequence of the absurd.[77] In this play in particular, Camus certainly does seem to suggest that *relative* values may well be defensible. But on what grounds could such a non-absolutist ethics be based?[78]

That principle, as we have seen in *Caligula* and will see more clearly in *The Plague* and elsewhere, is the principle of human solidarity. "I have no concern with ideas or with the eternal", Camus explains in *The Myth of Sisyphus*; "the truth that comes within my scope can be touched with the hand". The nexus of this mundane truth is, for Camus, in human relationships: there is, he says, "but one luxury for [the absurd hero] – that of human relations". Human solidarity is for Camus the fundamental link between the absurd and revolt.[79] Because awareness of the absurd is based on the individual consciousness and its relation to the world in which it finds itself, Camus's absurd hero is, at least initially, a necessarily solitary figure: consider the solitary exile of Meursault, Caligula and Sisyphus. Furthermore, it is this apparent solipsism, rather than the rejection of transcendence, that appears to present a major obstacle to the development of an ethic based upon the absurd (which Camus terms "revolt"). However, in Camus's analysis, the absurd subject, meditating on his condition, realizes at last that his condition is the common human condition, and crucially, this recognition gives rise to a solidarity that saves the individual conscious of the absurd from both solipsism and the temptation towards nihilism. "In absurdist experience", Camus says at the beginning of *The Rebel*,

> suffering is individual. But from the moment when a movement of rebellion begins, suffering is seen as a collective experience. Therefore the first progressive step for a mind overwhelmed by the strangeness of things is to realise that this feeling of strangeness is shared with all men and that human reality, in its entirety, suffers from the distance which separates it from the rest of the universe . . . this evidence lures the individual from his solitude. It founds its first value on the whole human race. I rebel – therefore we exist.
>
> (*R*: 22; *E*: 431–2)

2 | CAMUS AND *COMBAT*

In our daily trials rebellion plays the same role as does the "cogito" in the realm of thought: it is the first piece of evidence. But this evidence lures the individual from his solitude. It founds its first value on the whole human race. I rebel – therefore we exist.[1]

Camusian rebellion and political engagement

In Chapter 1 I discussed the absurd as manifest in *The Outsider*, *The Myth of Sisyphus* and *Caligula*, and sought to show that, at least theoretically, the absurd was not in conflict with a certain form of rebellion or revolt. Indeed, it was argued that a certain form of revolt, a revolt premised on "the human condition" (if not, as Camus appears to suggest in *The Rebel*, a "human nature") and solidarity, is seen to be at least a plausible consequence of the absurd.[2] In this chapter I examine Camus's political writing from the period between the publication of *The Myth of Sisyphus* and the publication of *The Rebel*, and detail the degree to which these works are consistent with the dictates of the absurd as defined in Chapter 1.

Tony Judt has claimed that Camus was "an unpolitical man", and to a certain extent, and from a certain perspective, this was probably the case. After all, aside from two years in the Communist Party in the mid-1930s, he remained assiduously independent of party affiliation throughout his life. However, given that his opinion of party politics was formed in large part, first, by the abandonment of Algerian Muslims by the Communist Party for political reasons in 1937 and, secondly, by the failure of the disparate non-communist groups to cohere into a viable political force in the wake of the Second World War, we should be careful not to rush to judgement regarding Camus's relationship with politics. Although Judt does not want to say that Camus was indifferent to public affairs or political choices, he does argue that Camus was "by instinct and temperament an *unaffiliated* person . . . and the charms of engagement . . . held little appeal for him" (Judt 1998: 104). However, it might be suggested here that Judt comes close to conflating political engagement with party affiliation. Camus, as Judt observes, viewed politics from a fundamentally moral perspective, but the implication that morality and politics were mutually exclusive is precisely the implication against which much of Camus's writing, especially his journalism, was directed. Camus did generally eschew party-political involvement (the one possible exception, discussed later on, was his support of Mendès-France after the outbreak of war in Algeria in 1954), and he once suggested that the only political party he would be comfortable joining would be one made up of "those who are not sure they are right" (*E*: 383–4). However, his record of independent political engagement is unquestionable, and, significantly, it parallels his disillusionment with party politics. It began early on in Camus's life, with his expulsion from the Communist Party in 1937. He was thrown out of the party because of his insistence that the institutionalized immiseration of the Muslim majority in Algeria was a cause for which the communists should continue to fight, after a change of policy directed by Moscow saw the communists actively support a French government policy of suppression and imprisonment against Arab nationalists, the same nationalists to whose cause they had not long before rallied. This experience may have made Camus wary of party affiliation, but he could hardly be said to have retired from politics altogether, for he continued to draw attention to the same injustice in the pages of the left-wing newspaper *Alger républicain*. It was the forced closure of this newspaper in 1940 by the colonial government that eventually led to Camus's move to Paris, where his work as a political journalist, as we shall see, achieved its full expression in the pages of the underground resistance newspaper *Combat*.

Letters to a German Friend

> I . . . chose justice in order to remain faithful to the world. I continue to believe that this world has no ultimate meaning. But I know that something in it has a meaning and that is man, because he is the only creature to insist on having one. This world has at least the truth of man.   (*RRD*: 28; *E*: 241)

Coinciding with his joining *Combat*, Camus began to write and publish, again clandestinely, his *Letters to a German Friend*.[3] These four polemical pieces, written in the guise of letters from an ally of the French Resistance to an ally of the Nazis, can be read as a development of the ideas already expressed in *Caligula*, perhaps even as letters from Cherea to Caligula. The experience of Nazi Occupation and indeed the very existence of Nazism itself required Camus to address with greater urgency the questions already raised in *Caligula* regarding the possibility, without the support of God or a regime of absolute values, of establishing an ethical code strong enough to both refute nihilism (of which Camus saw Nazism as exemplary) and justify political action. Camus's answer to the question was affirmative, and aside from some earlier indications in *Caligula* itself, *Letters to a German Friend* constitutes his first substantial move away from describing the absurd, towards dealing directly with its ethical and political consequences.[4] The peculiar form, that of letters from Camus to a (fictional) German with whom he is familiar and with whom he had in the past a great deal of sympathy, serves to highlight the extent to which the correspondents had a common intellectual background.[5] Nevertheless, as Richard Kamber has pointed out, there is no doubt that, having to choose between a "totalitarian society in which everything is subordinated to national destiny" and a "pluralistic society in which humane values and independent thinking are respected", Camus is confident about which is right, and "there is no hint that he cannot judge who is right and who is wrong" (Kamber 2002: 70).

However, it is also important not to exaggerate the ease with which Camus arrived at this conclusion, or the moral transparency of the conclusion and its cor-relatives: " 'What is truth?' you used to ask. Of course we still don't know, but at least we know what falsehood is, that is, just what you have taught us" (*RRD*: 14*; *E*: 228). Indeed, as he did with Caligula and Cherea, Camus goes to considerable lengths to point out the extent to which the correspondents had been in agreement. The first letter opens with a reminiscence of a claim the German "friend" had made in 1938: "The greatness of my country is beyond price. Anything is good that contributes to its greatness. And in a world where everything has lost its meaning, those who, like us young Germans, are lucky enough to find a meaning in the destiny of our nation must sacrifice everything else." However, rather than reply as might have been expected, Camus's letter continues thus: "I loved you then, but at that point we diverged. 'No,' I told you, 'I cannot believe that everything must be subordinated to a single end. There are means that cannot be excused'." Camus repeatedly asserts this common intellectual origin to both Nazism and his resistance: "both you and we started out from the same solitude, . . . you and we, with all Europe, are caught in the same tragedy of the intelligence" (*RRD*: 5, 30; *E*: 221, 242).

Notwithstanding this "same solitude", this "same tragedy of the intelligence", Camus derived very different conclusions to those of his fictional interlocutor. "For a long time", he writes, "we both thought that this world had no ultimate meaning [*raison supérieure*] and that consequently we were cheated. I still think so in a way. But I came to different conclusions from the ones you used to talk about, which, for so many years now you have been trying to introduce into history." The advent of Nazism led Camus to reflect on whether "if I had really approved of your reasoning, I ought to approve what you are doing". He argued that the conclusion his Nazi interlocutor derived from the absurd (in this context, the lack of "ultimate" mean-ing) was nihilistic: "you therefore deduced the idea that everything was equivalent and that good and evil could be defined according to one's wishes", that "in the absence of any human or divine code the only values were those of the animal world – in other words, violence and cunning" and that "the only pursuit for the individ-ual was the adventure of power and his only morality, the realism of conquests" (*RRD*: 27; *E*: 240).

Camus confessed that "believing I thought as you did", he "saw no valid argument to answer you except a fierce love of justice, which, after all, seemed to me as unrea-sonable as the most sudden passion." However, there was a difference: "simply that you readily accepted despair and I never yielded to it, . . . that you saw the injustice of our condition to the point of being willing to add to it, whereas it seemed to me that man must exalt justice in order to fight against eternal injustice, create happiness in order to protest against the universe of unhappiness". Freeing himself from his despair "by making a principle of it", the Nazi was willing "to destroy man's work and to fight him in order to add to his basic misery". In contrast, Camus desired merely "that men rediscover their solidarity in order to join the fight against their revolting fate". From "the same principle", he noted, "we derived quite different codes". His interlocutor finally chose to abandon lucidity (which had in any event become, for him, a matter of "indifference"), and chose "injustice". Camus, on the other hand, "chose justice in order to remain faithful to the world". Although continuing to believe "that this world has no ultimate meaning", he asserted that man, at least, has meaning, "because he is the only creature to insist on having one. This world has at least the truth of man", even if this truth has "no justification but man". Accordingly, whereas Camus "started out from the same solitude", caught in the "same tragedy of the intelligence" as his interlocutor, he discovered a means to affirm solidarity, thereby helping "to save man from the solitude to which you wanted to relegate him".[6]

It may appear, as it did to Philip Thody, for example, that Camus's arguments here are more emotive than philosophical, that ultimately "they come down to saying that because a man wants a thing then it must exist" (Thody 1961: 81). However, although the letters are clearly emotive in both tone and content, they should not be dismissed too quickly. Camus, after all, is not arguing that if humankind wants an ethical order, then such an order must exist, but rather that if humankind wants an ethical order, it is capable of creating one. The validity of such an interpretation appears to find support in an article written by Camus around the time that he was completing the fourth and final letter: "Nothing is given to man", he writes, "and the little they can conquer is paid for with unjust deaths. But man's greatness lies elsewhere. It lies in his decision to be greater than his condition. And if his condition is unjust he has only one way of overcoming it, which is to be just himself" (RRD: 39–40; E: 258).

If we interpret the absurd as a kind of epistemological scepticism, we can see why Camus would have found the idea of an absolutist transcendent ethic impossible. However, what we see in Letters to a German Friend is the suggestion that it is still possible, even within the strictures imposed by the absurd, to recommend an ameliorative ethic. Furthermore, Letters to a German Friend is a dramatic example of dialogue that affirms one's enemy even while opposing him, respecting in him the humanity he fails to respect, or even acknowledge, in others (Friedman 1967: 258). This involves overcoming hatred and moral cynicism without weakening one's determination to resist and oppose the forces that inculcate that hatred and moral cynicism. Essentially, we see in Letters to a German Friend the positing of human solidarity as the basis for an ethics, an ethics that Camus envisages without revising any of his earlier claims regarding the absurd (this latter point is highlighted in a striking way by his admission in *Letters to a German Friend* to having shared some of the assumptions behind the nihilism of the Nazis). The summary of Thomas Busch seems especially helpful in this context:

> The argument [of *Letters to a German Friend*], if translated into the terms of *The Myth*, would have this logic: I experience the absurd (my unfamiliarity with the universe); I feel cheated, wronged; this implies that I ought not to be cheated and that *my* desires should be fulfilled, not frustrated; thus I will be a rebel against the absurd by trying to match *my* desires with reality in the form of living as intensely as I can. But this form of the argument would not generate the conclusion that Camus requires to separate himself from his German friend. The argument will work to Camus's purpose only if my experience of the absurd, and my experience of being cheated, can lead to the further step that *all people's* desires, not just my own, ought to be fulfilled, which will produce then the conclusion that the absurd should be diminished not just in my life, but in all lives. The argument will work only if there is some sort of identity or important linkage established between my life and others' lives. This is what subsequent works, *The Plague* and *The Rebel*, seek to accomplish.[7]

Read in the context of the absurd, *Letters to a German Friend* displays a conscious effort, motivated by the experiences of occupation and resistance, to move beyond a discussion of the absurd itself to a discussion of the possibility of ethics. More than ever before, the absurd is clearly a "starting point". It is nevertheless important to stress that *Letters to a German Friend* represents not a change in Camus's thinking, but a change in the focus of his attention.

Camus and *Combat*

The epigraph Camus chose for the fourth letter in *Letters to a German Friend*, from Senancour's *Obermann* (itself written as a series of letters), summed up his thinking at this time: "Man is mortal. That may be; but let us die resisting; and if our lot is complete annihilation, let us not behave in such a way that it seems justice!"[8] The fundamental insight we see in both *Letters to a German Friend* and Camus's writing in *Combat* is that the image of Sisyphus is only an inaccurate image of the human condition in that he is solitary, an insight reflected in the use, almost without exception, of "we" rather than "I" in both *Letters to a German Friend* and the *Combat* articles. The transposition of Sisyphus's revolt against the gods onto the experience of the resistance of the French against Nazism, although it encouraged Camus to see Sisyphus's revolt as no longer solitary, must also have given Camus's journalistic voice a particularly appealing timbre. Much of his journalism in *Combat* focused on two themes: the need for a new kind of politics in France (reflected in *Combat*'s banner: "from Resistance to Revolution") and, perhaps surprisingly, the need for a purge of those who collaborated with the Nazis during the war. Indeed, the new kind of politics envisioned, a consciously moral politics, was first articulated in his attitude to the purge of intellectuals after the war.

In the period immediately following the liberation of France, Camus was among the many intellectuals and writers to advocate harsh and swift justice in cases involving those who had collaborated with the Nazis. He envisaged a new France emerging out of the experience of occupation, liberated from the shame of defeat and collaboration. Writing at the end of August 1944, while France was still being liberated, he asks, "Who would dare speak here of pardon?" (*CC*: 21*; *CAC8*: 158). In October he wrote an editorial in *Combat* that reflected his thinking at this point in time: "France is carrying in her midst a foreign body, a minority of men who harmed her in the past and harm her still today. These are men of betrayal and injustice. Their very existence poses a problem of justice, since they are part of the living body of the nation and yet they must be destroyed."[9] Similarly, writing in the communist *Les Lettres Françaises*, Camus declared his approval, "without hate, but without pity", of the execution of Pierre Pucheu, who had been a minister in the collaborationist Vichy government (*E*: 1468–70).

Although Camus was soon to recoil from this position, in favour of a more compassionate stance, his thinking at this time is worth examining and is well represented in a series of editorial exchanges that took place between himself and François Mauriac in the post-war period.[10] Divided by age, religion and class, Camus and Mauriac acted as the moral voices of their respective communities in the crucial post-war period. Whereas Mauriac was inclined to invoke Divine Justice as an argument for clemency in the treatment of collaborators, Camus, having no recourse to such faith, advocated human justice "with all of its terrible imperfections". In late 1944 the two clashed publicly over the conduct of the purges. Mauriac argued that the current purge was not only inherently troubling, in that it was more concerned with retribution than justice, it was also in danger of poisoning the new state before it had been properly constituted. In a claim bound to be controversial, he said that it would be better for the guilty to escape than for the innocent to be punished. God, he assured his readers, would ensure that justice was served. Camus, not being a Christian, could have no faith in Divine Justice. He insisted that crimes against humanity must be met with human justice: "And we have chosen to embrace human justice, with its terrible imperfections, while seeking anxiously to correct it, by clinging desperately to honesty" (*CC*: 89–90; *CAC8*: 289).

Early in the following year, Mauriac wrote an article entitled "Contempt for Charity", referring to Camus as "our young master" who had attacked those writers thought to have collaborated "from a great height, the height, I imagine, of his future oeuvre".[11] Four days later Camus replied:

> Whenever I used the word justice in connection with the purge, M. Mauriac spoke of charity. So singular is the virtue of charity, moreover, that in calling for justice I seemed to be pleading on behalf of hatred. To hear M. Mauriac tell it, it truly seems that in dealing with these mundane matters we must make an

absolute choice between the love of Christ and the hatred of men. Surely not! . . . I shall join M. Mauriac in granting open pardons when Vélin's parents and Leynaud's wife tell me that I can. But not before. Never before, so as not to betray, for the sake of an effusion of the heart, what I have always loved and respected in this world, the fount of man's nobility, which is loyalty.[12]

At this point Camus was not saying anything exceptional, and a number of other left-wing intellectuals were expressing many of the same views. However, within a few weeks of writing the above article, Camus was already beginning to express doubts about the very justice of the summary trials and executions sanctioned by the Conseil National des Ecrivains and other "progressive" groups, and his right-eousness was quickly turning to horror at the sight of the bloody fury of the purge.[13] Accordingly, a little over two weeks after defending himself against Mauriac, and just over three months after calling for pitiless, swift and all-embracing justice to be served, he signed a letter appealing for clemency in the case of Robert Brasillach, probably the most notorious of those intellectuals and artists who collaborated with the Nazis.[14] Camus explained to Marcel Aymé, who had solicited his signature, that he had signed the petition, not for Brasillach (whom he "despised with all [his] strength"), but because of his opposition to the death penalty.[15]

By August 1945 Camus's view of the purge had transformed utterly: "the word 'purge' is bad enough", he protested; "the thing itself has become odious". He began to perceive the extent of the discrepancies between the purge as he had imagined and defended it and the purge as it actually functioned, the gulf between the liber-ated France he had hoped for and the France taking shape before him. Rather than uniting the nation around a clear understanding of justice and individual guilt, responsibility as well as community, the purge had the effect of inculcating in people exactly the sort of moral cynicism and partisan self-interest that it was sup-posed to banish. The purge has, he says, failed completely.[16]

Two further factors would probably have influenced Camus in his disenchant-ment with the purge. First, there was, in May 1945, the ruthless suppression of the rioting of indigenous Muslims in and around the Algerian town of Sétif, an experi-ence that would probably have suggested to Camus that, notwithstanding its own recent experience of occupation and domination, France was no more sensitive to its own colonialism than it had been before the war. Secondly, in the summer of 1945 he began preparations for his introduction to a collection of poems by René Leynaud, a close friend and *Combat* colleague who was arrested and executed by the Nazis in 1944.[17] Camus became increasingly aware that the France that Frenchmen were creating for themselves out of the crucible of the purge was one that would have appalled men like Leynaud, who had fought and died to defend their country against oppression. His dismay at the highly partisan ways in which the purge was manifesting itself, and his regret at his own initial support, was pithily expressed in his introduction to the poet's book: "Truth needs witnesses. Leynaud was one of them, and this is why I miss him today. With him here I saw more clearly, and his death, far from making me better, as the books of consolation say, made my revolt more blind. The finest thing I can say in his favour is that he would not have followed me in that revolt."[18]

Although the two intellectuals had radically different backgrounds and hopes for France, Camus's position throughout this period was drawing nearer to that of Mauriac. His dismay at the ways in which the purge had come to be used to satisfy political and personal agendas, suffocating any hope of a political rebirth of France as a great and just nation, struck a chord with Mauriac's claim that of all possible purges, this was the worst, in that it was corrupting the very hearts and minds of the French people (Judt 1998: 112). The proximity of their positions was made explicit the following year, when in a talk given at the Dominican community at Latour-Maubourg, Camus said that despite some of the excesses of language on the part of Mauriac, he had never stopped meditating on his words and he now felt that in relation to the specific issue of the purge, he himself had been wrong and Mauriac right.[19] However suspicious Camus became of the intellectual landscape of which he had become a part, however much he despaired of the contemporary political climate, his instincts remained assiduously humanist. In the pages of *Combat*, this humanism began to contrast itself with what he referred to as "political realism", the increasingly prevalent view that morality had no place whatever in the political domain.

It was such political realism, Camus contends, that convinced erstwhile opponents of fascism to support collaborationist Pétain: "in politics", Camus says, "realism is always right, even if it is morally wrong".[20] However, Camus does not identify this penchant among collaborators only. A few weeks later he warns against realism playing a role in the creation of a new democratic France. "Our idea", he writes, "is that the reign of justice must be ensured in the economic sphere while freedom is guaranteed in the political sphere." Fundamentally, what *Combat* "[wants] for France is a collectivist economy and liberal politics". A collectivist economy, without which "liberal politics is a fraud", will take privilege away from capital "in order to grant it to labour". At the same time, "without constitutional guarantees of political liberty", the collectivist economy "risks absorbing all individual initiative and expression". In order to avoid "adding a purely human injustice to the profound miseries of our condition", a "true people's democracy" with a collectivist economy and guaranteed political liberty at its heart must be instituted "without delay". However, he also insists that not all means can be used in pursuit of this end:

> We believe that the difficult equilibrium we are seeking cannot be achieved without unremitting intellectual and moral honesty, which alone can provide the necessary clarity of mind. We do not believe in political realism. Lies, even well intentioned lies, separate men from one another and relegate them to the most futile solitude. We believe that, on the contrary, men are not alone and that when faced with hostile conditions, their solidarity is total. Anything that serves this solidarity and reinforces this communion, hence anything that involves sincerity, is just and free.

That is why we believe that political revolution cannot take place without moral revolution, which goes hand in hand with it and establishes its true dimensions. (*CC*: 55–6; *CAC8*: 223–4)

Camus was concerned to stress the democratic and ameliorative character, rather than the allegedly "scientific" character, of socialism. Indeed, he treated this as a defining distinction between two forms of socialism. The first "form" he associates with the pre-war doctrine of socialist parties in Europe, which "rests on optimism and invokes the love of humanity to exempt itself from serving human beings, the inevitability of progress to evade the question of wages, and universal peace to avoid necessary sacrifice". This form of socialism, says Camus, "is accomplished mainly on the sacrifices of others. Those who preach it never commit themselves." In contrast, Camus recommends an alternative conception of socialism, one that "does not waste its breath with talk of progress, yet it is convinced that man's fate is always in man's hands. It does not believe in absolute and infallible doctrines but in obstinate and tireless if inevitably halting improvement of the human condition."[21] It is precisely an explication of the principles of such an ameliorative socialism that, we shall see, is undertaken in *The Rebel*.

This perspective went on to inform one other crucial aspect of *Combat*'s political agenda: its relationship with the Communist Party. In an editorial from October 1944, Camus reaffirms *Combat*'s stated view that "anti-communism is the first step toward dictatorship", explaining that "while we are not in agreement with the philosophy or practical ethics of Communism, we vigorously reject political anti-Communism because we know what inspires it and what its unavowed aims are". Although *Combat* shares "most of our [communist] comrades' collectivist ideas and social programme, their ideal of justice, and their disgust with a society in which money and privilege occupy the front ranks", it rejects the communists' "very consistent philosophy of history" and the "political realism" they derive from it. For the communists, says Camus, this political realism constitutes "the primary method for securing the triumph of an idea shared by many Frenchmen". However, he insists, on this question "we very clearly differ. As we have said many times, we do not believe in political realism." Camus, we remember, has an especially bitter memory of this realism, as manifested in the abandonment by the French communists of the cause of Algerian Muslims in 1937. Although respecting the considerable authority the communists enjoyed as the primary political representative of the working class, *Combat* seeks not to "reinvent the country's politics from top to bottom", but to undertake a "very limited experiment: to introduce the language of morality into the practice of politics by means of simple, objective criticism".[22]

By 1945 it had become clear to Camus with respect to the conduct of the purge in particular and the political character of post-war France in general that his hopes for a morally conscientious politics had ended in failure. In fact, although it is generally thought that Camus continued to write for *Combat* until his departure from the newspaper in 1947, his editorial from August 1945, in which he claimed that the purge was "completely discredited" and "odious", proved to be among the last he published in *Combat* for more than twelve months. Significantly, in this article he attributes the "complete" failure of the purge to the fact that "politics got mixed up in it, with all its varieties of blindness" (*CC*: 250; *CAC8*: 595). Clearly for Camus this blindness was endemic in French politics, for two days after that editorial he wrote that although a year had now passed since the liberation of France, *Combat's* attempt to "make dialogue possible" between the various political factions including Christians and communists "had ended in abject failure". In his final editorial from this period, he reiterated the same view, that cooperation between political parties is essential for the economic survival of France, but hardly gives the impression that he believes such cooperation is possible.[23] Shortly thereafter, writing to Pascal Pia, a colleague at *Combat*, Camus made it clear (albeit privately) that he also believed *Combat* held some responsibility for the lack of political clarity in France. Asking that Pia accept his decision to "withdraw completely" from *Combat*, he made the following observation about the content of some recent issues of the newspaper: "One cannot, after having published three marked and acerbic antiparliamentarian editorials, solemnly ask the reader not to fall into the trap of antiparliamentar-ianism. One cannot, after publishing three opinion pieces of un-nuanced anti-Communism, call on the other hand for power for the Communists, at least not without leaving oneself open to the worst interpretation."[24] Evidently he considered *Combat's* modest proposal, the introduction of "the language of morality into the practice of politics", to have ended in failure, and thought that *Combat* itself was in part responsible.[25]

"Neither Victims nor Executioners"

In a notebook entry from October 1946 Camus gives an unusually detailed sum-mary of an exchange between himself, Arthur Koestler and Sartre. Two especially interesting passages are juxtaposed and are reproduced in quotation marks (con-noting their literal accuracy). The first of these is from Camus, wherein he reaffirms his conviction regarding the need to introduce morality into politics: "Don't you think that we are all responsible for the absence of values? And that if all of us who come from Nietzscheism, from nihilism, or from historical realism said in public that we were wrong and that there are moral values and that in the future we shall do what has to be done to establish and illustrate them, don't you think that this might be the beginning of hope?" This affirmation of moral value is immediately fol-lowed by this assertion attributed to Sartre: "I cannot turn my moral values solely against the USSR. For it is true that the deporting of several million men is more serious than the lynching of a Negro. But the lynching of a Negro is the result of a situation that has been going on for a hundred years and more, and that represents in the end the suffering of just as many millions of Negroes over the years as there are millions of Cherkess deported" (*NB2*: 145–6*; *C2*: 186).

Sartre's opinion regarding the relation between politics and morality (which is discussed at length in a later chapter) is here informed by an essay by his friend and colleague, Maurice Merleau-Ponty, entitled "Le Yogi et le Prolétaire", which had just been published in their journal *Les Temps modernes*. The significance of this essay in Sartre's political development can hardly be overstated, as he himself praised the essay, in its complete published form, for having released him from political "immobility" (Sartre 1965: 253). However, it was to have, as we shall see, an equal and opposite effect on Camus. The growing tension between Camus and several of his erstwhile colleagues came to a head a few weeks later when, at the apartment of Boris Vian, Camus accused Merleau-Ponty of having written an apologia for Stalinist terror. Merleau-Ponty argued that politics was inevitably immoral and that no political regime was innocent of violence. He alleged that the question that really concerned him in his essay was whether communist violence could help to humanize humanity: he believed that it could. Sartre defended Merleau-Ponty's position, and Camus angrily left the apartment. Camus and Sartre (who remained closely associated in the popular mind) would not meet again for another five months.[26]

The purpose of *Humanism and Terror*, the title under which Merleau-Ponty's serialized essay was published in book form, is to investigate the role of violence in history.[27] He argues that despite the evident failings in the USSR (which is not, he says, "the proletarian light of History Marx once described"), there is no viable political alternative to Marxism's rational account of human history.[28] And indeed, despite its pretensions, despite the horror it exhibits at the reports of violence perpetrated by the communists, Western liberal society is also marked by violence – most clearly in its long and bloody history of colonial domination. Given that liberal democracy is pervaded by violence at least to the same extent as revolutionary communism, the task Merleau-Ponty sets himself in *Humanism and Terror* is to examine the question of "whether communist violence was, as Marx thought, 'progressive'". "We do not have a choice", he says, "between purity and violence but between different kinds of violence. Inasmuch as we are incarnate beings, violence is our lot ... Violence is the common origin of all regimes. Life, discussion, and political choice occur only against a background of violence. What we have to discuss is not violence, but its sense or its future."[29] In order to properly understand violence, Merleau-Ponty contends, it is necessary to locate it "in the logic of a situation, in the dynamics of a regime, and into the historical reality to which it belongs, instead of judging it by itself according to that morality mistakenly called 'pure' morality" (Merleau-Ponty 1969: 1–2). For Merleau-Ponty "*the* question is where a form of violence fits in the [meaning] of history, and whether it carries with it the promise of the negation of future violence" (Roth 1988: 50).

Although for Merleau-Ponty history "will give us the final word as to the *legitimacy* of a particular instance of violence", this does not mean that he shares the view of history as "the inevitable and esoteric process of change". He rejects such simplistic "deification of History", considering it a caricature of Marxism, and claims instead that Marx held that "it is *we* who make our own history". History is the sum of our efforts "to create a world in which we can live in mutual recognition". However, this does not help to answer the question of how we can know the meaning of history, and more particularly, how we can discern the legitimacy of violence, whether it is "progressive". Merleau-Ponty's answer to this question is that we cannot know the answer unless history is over, and that "the decision to be a revolutionary or, more accurately, the effect of living within a revolutionary historical period implies a will to create a radically new future on the basis of present action, but there is no guarantee either of the success of this action or of its legitimacy".[30] However, this is not to affirm the legitimacy of all action that calls itself revolutionary, and the legitimacy of revolutionary violence depends, thinks Merleau-Ponty, on its adherence to the "logic of development" contained within the Marxist theory of history. It is exactly this "logic of History" that distinguishes Marxism from "vulgar relativism" and "other authoritarian politics".[31] Revolutionary violence consistent with this "logic of History" will be vindicated in the future "by a way of life in which violence will no longer be necessary" (Roth 1988: 52).

However, as Michael Roth notes, the "great gap" in the reasoning of *Humanism and Terror*, "the unasked question whose absence is at the centre of the book", is "where this logic of history is to be found or derived" (Roth 1988: 54). Merleau-Ponty is, however, untroubled by this absence and entirely persuaded of the Marxist view, as is everywhere reflected in his essay: "The revolution takes on and directs a violence which bourgeois society tolerates in unemployment and in war and disguises with the name misfortune. But successful revolutions taken altogether have not spilled as much blood as the empires. All we know is different kinds of violence and we ought to prefer revolutionary violence because it has a future of humanism."[32] Furthermore, based on this logic, Merleau-Ponty argues:

> it should be observed that the categories of "ends" and "means" are entirely alien to Marxism. An end is a result to come which one proposes for oneself and seeks to realise. It ought to be superfluous to recall that Marxism very consciously distinguishes itself from utopianism by defining revolutionary action not as the adoption of a certain number of ends through reasoning and will, but as the simple extrapolation of a *praxis* already at work in history, of a reality that is already committed, namely, the proletariat. It is not a question of representing a "society of the future".[33]

In November 1946, coinciding with his dispute with Merleau-Ponty, with the serialized publication of *Humanism and Terror* and almost exactly a year after last writing for *Combat*, Camus returned to the newspaper with a series of articles, collectively titled "Neither Victims nor Executioners", in which he articulates his vision of a moral politics, already loosely defended in those early articles from 1944 and 1945.[34] More immediately, Camus's articles can be read as a response to *Humanism and Terror*: we will see that criticism of precisely Merleau-Ponty's concept of the "logic of History", his treatment of the question of ends and means and his denial of the utopian character of Marxism are all at the heart of "Neither Victims nor Executioners".[35]

The twentieth century, says Camus at the beginning of this series of articles, the epoch in which scientific investigation has culminated in the atom bomb, is the "century of fear". "The years we have just gone through", he says, "have killed something in us. And that something is simply the old confidence that man had in himself, which led him to believe that he could always elicit human reactions from another man if he spoke to him in the language of a common humanity. . . . Mankind's long dialogue has just come to an end. And naturally a man with whom one cannot reason is a man to be feared." The resultant "conspiracy of silence" has served only to further polarize existing camps:

> "You shouldn't talk about the Russian culture purge – it would play into the hands of the reactionaries." "Don't mention the Anglo-American support of Franco – it would play into the hands of Communism." . . . We suffocate among people who think they are absolutely right, whether in their machines or in their ideas. And for all who cannot live without dialogue and the friendship of other human beings, this silence is the end of the world.

Camus suggests that there are many who "doubt that socialism has been realised in Russia or liberalism in America" and "who grant each side the right to affirm its truth but refuse it the right to impose that truth by murder, individual or collective". However, if the voice of this opposition (which Camus seems to locate primarily, if not exclusively, in Europe) is to be heard, they must clarify what it is that they want "and proclaim it directly and boldly enough to make their words a stimulus to action". The first issue upon which this opposition must achieve clarity relates to political violence. Furthermore, to reject the theoretical sanctioning of violence, he says, "automatically" commits one to a series of consequences (*CC*: 257–60*; *CAC8*: 608–13).

Before discussing these consequences, he first insists that such a refusal of the theoretical justification of violence does not amount to pacifism. It does not imply that violence may never be the appropriate response to a specific state of affairs, nor does it imply the utopian aspiration to "a world in which people don't kill one another (we're not that crazy!)". Instead we should aspire to a world in which "murder" is not given theoretical legitimacy. Although it would be "completely utopian to want people to stop killing people", "a much sounder utopia is that which insists that murder be no longer legitimised". Indeed, implicitly rejecting Merleau-Ponty's claim that Marxism was not utopian, Camus claims that both Marxist and capitalist ideologies are utopian to a far greater extent, in that they are both "based on the idea of progress", and are "both certain that the application of their principles must inevitably bring about a harmonious society", a society in which violence will no longer be necessary. Furthermore, he adds, in their ready use of violence in the cause of an imagined non-violent future, "they are both at the moment costing us dearly".

In reality, thinks Camus, the struggle of the next few years (by which he means what will become known as the Cold War) will not be between the forces of utopia and the forces of reality, "but between different utopias". Ultimately, then, he says, it comes down to choosing the "least costly" among these competing utopian visions. Subsequent articles in this series will attempt "to define the conditions for a political position that is modest – i.e., free of messianism and disencumbered of nostalgia for an earthly paradise" (*CC*: 260–61*; *CAC8*: 613).

Favouring what he calls elsewhere a form of "liberal socialism", which "tends to invoke the French collectivist tradition that has always made room for individual freedom and that owes nothing to philosophical materialism", in these articles Camus claims for himself a position independent of both US-inspired free-market capitalism and Soviet-inspired communism (*CC*: 121; *CAC8*: 349). Although the latter, far more than the former, tends to be the object of his criticism in "Neither Victims nor Executioners", this can be explained, at least in part, by the degree to which these articles constitute a response to Merleau-Ponty's *Humanism and Terror*. Indeed, despite Merleau-Ponty's insistence that the terms "ends" and "means" were "entirely alien" to Marxism, Camus attributes to both Nazism (the "state of terror in which we have lived for the past ten years") and Marxism the same fundamental supposition: that "the end justifies the means". This principle, Camus argues, can only be accepted if the efficacy of an action is taken to be an absolute end, such as is found in nihilism (here, the view that everything is permitted and that success is all that matters) and in those ideologies that make of history an absolute (first Hegel, then Marx, "the end being a classless society, everything is good that leads to it"). Such a problem, Camus argues, currently confronts French socialists. Having experienced at first hand the "violence and oppression, of which they had hitherto only a theoretical idea", they now "have to ask themselves whether, as their philosophy requires, they would consent to use that violence themselves, even as a temporary expedient and for a quite different end". As evinced in the recent Socialist Party Congress, where the humanism of Léon Blum clashed with the Marxism of Guy Mollet, the French socialists had begun to concern themselves more directly with such moral questions.[36] However, says Camus, although the chief task of the Party Congress was to reconcile "a morality superior to murder" with "the determination to remain faithful to Marxism", such a reconciliation is in fact impossible, since "one cannot reconcile what is not reconcilable". Again alluding to Merleau-Ponty, Camus argues that "if it is clear that Marxism is true and there is logic in History, then political realism is legitimate"; however, if the moral values now extolled by the socialists are legitimate, "then Marxism is absolutely false since it claims to be absolutely true".[37]

For Camus, the best hope of creating such a modest politics seems to be with the socialists, and he berates them for their continued attachment to Marxism as an absolute tenet of faith: "the Communists have a solid logical basis for using the lies and the violence which the Socialists reject, and the basis is that very dialectic which the Socialists want to preserve". The political consequences of this theoretical incoherence, says Camus, are clearly visible in the most recent elections (in which the

Socialists came third after the Communists and the Christian Democrat MRP). Ultimately the Socialists will be forced to "either admit that the end justifies the means, in which case murder can be legitimised; or else they will reject Marxism as an absolute philosophy, confining themselves to its critical aspect, which is often valuable". If the Socialists choose the former, their contradictions, their "moral crisis", will be resolved; if they choose the latter, "they will exemplify the way our period marks the end of ideologies, that is, of absolute utopias". Choosing to reject Marxist historical messianism will make it necessary to "choose a more modest and less costly utopia" (*CC*: 263–4*; *CAC8*: 619–21).

Although there had been, since the liberation of France in August 1944, a great deal of sincere talk about revolution, sincerity, Camus notes, "is not itself a virtue". Indeed, certain manifestations of sincerity "are so confused that they are worse than lies". In truth, he says, the concept of revolution "obviously lacks meaning in present historical circumstances". This is the case for two reasons. First, the "repressive apparatus of a modern state", its military power, requires a similar power among the would-be revolutionaries: "1789 and 1917 are still historic dates, but they are no longer historic examples". Secondly, changes in the economic and political relations between nations and their peoples mean that a national revolution is unlikely: "we can no longer be revolutionary all by ourselves, since there no longer exists any policy, conservative or socialist, which can operate exclusively within the borders of a single nation". It was once believed that such a world revolution "would be brought about by the conjunction or the synchronisation of a number of national revolutions – a kind of totting up of miracles", but now it is possible only to conceive of "the extension of a revolution that has already succeeded". This is one interpretation of Stalin's policies in Europe (the other, Camus says, is "to refuse Russia the right to speak in the name of revolution"). However, "since the conservative force – in this case, the United States – is equally well armed, clearly the idea of a revolution has now been replaced by that of ideological warfare". Conceiving revolution in this way, as the definitive triumph of one superpower over the other, requires that "we use a little imagination about what this globe, where already thirty million fresh corpses lie, will be like after a cataclysm which will cost us ten times as many" (*CC*: 264–6*; *CAC8*: 621–4).

If the revolution as traditionally conceived can therefore only bring destruction on a hitherto unknown scale, and if we agree that this outcome is not a desirable one, even in the name of a future utopia, then the choices remaining, the choices with which we are faced, are either: (a) the defence of the status quo, "which is a completely utopian position insofar as it assumes that history is immobile"; or (b) the effort to "give new content to the word 'revolution', which means assenting to what I will call a relative utopia". Those who want to change the world effectively, says Camus, "have to choose among carnage, the impossible dream of bringing history to an abrupt halt, or the acceptance of a relative utopia that leaves some chance to action and humankind".[38]

Whatever form such a relative utopia might take, Camus insists, it will have to be internationalist. There seem to Camus two alternative methods for the realization of this "international revolution . . . in which the resources of men, of raw materials, of commercial markets and cultural riches may be better distributed". The first of these, whereby an international order is imposed from above "by a single state more powerful than the others", could be achieved only by the USSR or the USA. Camus finds this conception of a new international order "repellent", not simply because he is a European and a Mediterranean (we will see in a later chapter the significance for Camus of his culturally plural Mediterranean identity), but because such unification could be achieved only by war, or at the very least with the extreme risk of war, a war that would "leave humanity so mutilated and impoverished that the very idea of a world order would become anachronistic". Given the accelerating growth in warfare technology (a fact Marx, despite his repute in discerning the "meaning of History", never imagined), even if such an international order were desirable, "the means employed to attain it represent so enormous a risk and are so disproportionate to the slender hopes of success" that we must refuse to run the risk. The second possibility of achieving international consensus is through "international democracy". Although "everybody at the UN" may be talking about international democracy, and its meaning may appear self-evident, it is worth talking about plainly because "the most self-evident truths are also the ones most frequently distorted". Although democracy is "a form of society in which the law has authority over those governed, the law being the expression of the common will as expressed in a legislative body", it is not clear that the form of government being created at the UN corresponds to this conception of democracy. Although they are indeed elaborating an international law, such law is being made and broken by governments. Rather than a manifestation of Camus's relative utopia, then, the UN either constitutes, or is in danger of constituting, "a regime of international dictatorship". The only solution to this state of affairs, the only way to achieve a viable system of international democracy, he argues, is to place international law above the will of individual governments. International law must therefore be the creation of a properly international parliament, one constituted by worldwide elections. Since such a parliament does not exist, says Camus, "the only option open to us is to resist this international dictatorship on an international level using means not in contradiction with the ends we seek" (*CC*: 267–8*; *CAC8*: 627–9).

While the need for such an international order grows, Camus suggests that contemporary political discourse is dominated by "anachronistic thinking". Entirely preoccupied with the "German question", the developing conflict between Russia and America, "the clash of empires which threatens us", is being ignored. Furthermore, Camus suggests, it is becoming increasingly likely that even this epochal ideological battle may be obscured, in the not too distant future, by the demise of colonialism and the concomitant demise in the dominance of the West. For this reason, "it would be better to anticipate this by opening the World Parliament to these civilisations, so that its law will truly become universal law and the order that it consecrates will truly become the world order". In this context he reiterates the view that the UN as presently constructed is inegalitarian, and he suggests that contemporary criticism of the UN is misguided in so far as it is preoccupied with the threat posed by the USSR's Security Council veto. As long as the majority at the UN continues to be a majority of ministers (appointed by governments) rather than directly elected public representatives, the USSR will continue to have the right to reject the will of the majority. However, once such a popularly constituted parliament is created, "each nation must obey it or else reject its law – that is, openly proclaim its will to dominate". Such proposals clearly seem utopian, but the only alternative to such internationalism, Camus thinks, is likely to be war, the direction in which "anachronistic thinking" is heading. Subverting, again, the polarizing discourse of "utopia or realism", he asserts that, although he is sceptical about the outcome of such proposals, "realism forces us to embrace that relative utopia" (*CC*: 268–70*; *CAC8*: 630–33).

Accordingly, the "only real issue is the creation of an international order, which will finally bring about lasting structural reforms tantamount to a revolution". Domestic politics "can be judged only in terms of what it does or does not contribute to the creation of an international order based on justice and dialogue". Domestic political discourse must also be evaluated from this internationalist perspective. Accordingly, although every month thirty editorials in the conservative *Aube* might range themselves against thirty editorials in the communist *Humanité*, the papers themselves and the political parties they defend all supported the annexation of La Brigue and Tende by France and are therefore, Camus says, "accomplices in the destruction of international democracy". "Whatever their reasons", Camus says, both Christian Democrat MRP and Communist leaders Georges Bidault and Maurice Thorez "opted for the principle of international dictatorship". Politically, this is not realism, it is utopianism, and utopianism of the worst kind. Because the political crisis is global in scale, so must be the response, and accordingly, "we must minimise domestic politics". In the face of such a discredited politics, individuals must "draw up among themselves, within frontiers and across them, a new social contract which will unite them according to more reasonable principles". Such groups could be formed, nationally, on the basis of labour organizations, and, internationally, on the basis of intellectual organizations (*communautés de réflexion*). These labour organizations, through mutual agreement and cooperation, would help as many as possible to solve their material problems, while the intellectual organizations "would try to define the values by which this international community would live", and would "plead its cause at every opportunity". More precisely, the purpose of these intellectual groups "should be to meet the confusions of terror with clear language and at the same time to set forth the values that a world at peace will find indispensable". Evoking the same moral politics and the same disenchantment with political realism that he had in *Combat*, he suggests that the first objective of such a group "could be to formulate an international code of justice whose first article would abolish the death penalty everywhere and to give a clear statement of the principles necessary for any civilisation based on dialogue". Such individuals would "refuse all the advantages of society as they find it today and accept only the duties and responsibilities that tie them to others", and would "devote themselves to orienting education, the press and public opinion towards the principles outlined here". Far from being utopian, such people would be acting in accordance with "the most genuine realism". Possessing "the courage to give up, for the present, some of their dreams, so as to grasp more firmly the essential point, which is to save lives", such people would be acting as "honest realists".[39]

The need for such "honest realism" is clear, Camus says, for, alluding again to Merleau-Ponty, "we are being torn apart by a logic of History". Nevertheless, recognizing that "we cannot escape from history, since we are in it up to our necks", he insists that we can still endeavour to struggle within history to preserve that part of humankind which is not reducible to history. It is not a question of trying to obstruct the movement of a world "on a course governed by the laws of power and domination", for such efforts would prove laughable; it is merely a question of asking ourselves what will happen if that experiment fails, if the "logic of History on which so many now rely" proves to be faulty.[40]

Although from the perspective of the present it may be difficult to see beyond the apparent naivety of this view, it is important to note that this was not mere rhetoric for Camus. In 1948 and 1949 he was at the centre of the formation of the short-lived Groupes de Liaison Internationale, whose aims, according to its manifesto (written by Camus) were, first, the provision of material aid to victims of totalitarian tyranny and, secondly, the dissemination of information highlighting the existence of "non-conformist" Americans and dissident Soviets. "It is not a question", the manifesto claims, "of choosing between the two societies, though we recognise that American society represents the lesser evil. We do not have to choose evil, even the lesser."[41] Similarly, in 1947 he drafted an essay condemning a recent speech and declaration by President Truman, calling them "two deadly errors", "defining a politics of *blocs* which risks opening the way for war".[42] A pronounced sympathy for anarchism and anarcho-syndicalism also saw Camus publish articles and otherwise support newspapers and journals including *Témoins* (whose editorial board he joined), *Le Libertaire*, *Le Monde Libertaire*, *La Révolution Prolétarienne* and *Solidaridad Obrera*.[43] Similarly, his internationalism led him to vocally support the American GI Gary Davis, who in 1948 returned his passport in protest against the Cold War and, declaring himself a "world citizen", claimed what he called "global political asylum" at the UN's temporary headquarters in Paris. Although his jejune theatricality was not lost on Camus, Davis nevertheless enacted just the kind of commitment "Neither Victims nor Executioners" had advocated (he gave up many privileges by renouncing his American citizenship). Furthermore, Davis's self-proclaimed status as "world citizen" had symbolic importance for Camus, especially after his attempt to speak at the UN's temporary headquarters resulted in his arrest.[44]

In marked contrast to Camus, Sartre was "in complete agreement with the Communists" and believed that "that the Gary Davis affair was nothing but hot air" (de Beauvoir 1968: 180, cf. 271). Asked his opinion of Davis's World Citizen Movement, Sartre criticized "the utopian idealism of the project to form a world government" and attacked "their misunderstanding of economic, social and political factors, as well as [their] short-range goals". He pointed out "that their refusal to make concrete and immediate commitments can only win them the ear of 'certain upright, uneasy, mobile, and idealistic circles of the petty bourgeoisie and the middle classes who have no political experience'", and was particularly scathing of "their moralising attitude", asking "Doesn't your peace resemble the Kantians' categorical imperative which is so pure and uncompromising that, as Kant himself recognised, no one on earth has ever followed it?"[45]

Furthermore, not only did Sartre claim that *Humanism and Terror* had released him from political immobility; he was quick to form an inversely proportionate opinion of "Neither Victims nor Executioners". The December issue of his journal *Les Temps modernes*, which would have appeared as Camus's articles were still appearing in the pages of *Combat* (the final article was published in November), was ironically titled "Both Victims and Executioners", and contrasted starkly with the theme of Camus's editorials. Whereas Camus insisted that we ought to refuse all theoretical legitimization of violence and campaign on behalf of international democracy, the subject of the *Les Temps modernes* editorial was the reality of French government policy in Indochina, which it compared to the Nazi occupation of France.[46] Some months later, in his celebrated essay "What Is Literature?", Sartre returned to the same point, and without naming Camus noted "the publication of a rather brilliant article saying that it was necessary to refuse any complicity with violence wherever it came from" in a newspaper that "had to announce the very next day the first skirmishes of the Indo-Chinese War".[47] Rejecting the idea (Camus's idea) that "we must be systematically opposed to the use of violence", Sartre argued that although violence "under whatever form it may show itself, is a setback", "it is an inevitable setback because we are in a universe of violence; and if it is true that recourse to violence against violence risks perpetuating it, it is also true that it is the only means of bringing an end to it". Echoing Merleau-Ponty in *Humanism and Terror*, he went on to address directly this writer who had opposed violence systematically:

> I should like to ask the writer today how we can refuse to participate indirectly in all violence. If you say nothing, you are necessarily for the continuation of the war [in Indochina]; one is always responsible for what one does not try to prevent. But if you got it to stop at once and at any price, you would be at the origin of a number of massacres and you would be doing violence to all Frenchmen who have interests over there. I am not, of course, speaking of compromises, since war is born of compromise. Violence for violence; one must make a choice, according to other principles . . . it is incumbent upon the writer to judge the means not from the point of view of an abstract morality, but in the perspectives of a precise goal which is the realisation of a socialist democracy.[48]

Neither was this the first time Sartre had displayed impatience with Camus's lack of political realism. Prompted probably by an essay from 1945 in which Camus had sought to distinguish between revolt and revolution (ideas that would achieve their full expression in *The Rebel*), in an essay from 1946 discussing Baudelaire Sartre insisted:

> The revolutionary wants to change the world; he transcends it and moves toward the future, towards an order of values he himself invents. The rebel [*le révolté*] is careful to preserve the abuses from which he suffers so that he can go on rebelling against them. . . . He does not want to destroy or transcend the existing order; he simply wants to rise up against it. The more he attacks it the more he secretly respects it. In the depths of his heart he preserves the rights which he challenges in public. If they disappeared, his own *raison d'être* would disappear with them.[49]

Although neither Sartre nor Merleau-Ponty responded to "Neither Victims nor Executioners" directly, when the series of articles was reprinted in November 1947, a year after their original publication, Emmanuel d'Astier de la Vigerie, editor of the crypto-communist *Libération* and member of the French National Assembly, did respond. D'Astier insisted that before one could proclaim oneself neither victim nor executioner, it was necessary to "wrest the victim from the executioners" (this was the title of his response). In other words, for d'Astier it was necessary to recognize the legitimate role violence would play in the creation of a political scenario in which it was at last possible to refuse the status of either victim or executioner. Sartre's implicit criticism was made explicit by d'Astier: "you shun politics and take refuge in morality" (quoted in McCarthy 1982: 236). By refusing violence any theoretical legitimacy – and that was the central argument of "Neither Victims nor Executioners" – he was an accomplice of the right, an apologist for the status quo.[50]

Camus's response to d'Astier was taken up primarily with refuting the accusation of pacifism and with reasserting more forcefully than before his objections to theoretical defences of political violence:

> I have never argued in favour of [non-violence] . . . I don't think one answers blows with a blessing. I believe that violence is inevitable, the years of Occupation taught me that. To be honest, during that time there were terrible acts of violence which caused me no problems. I will not therefore say that all violence must be suppressed, which although ideal, is utopian. I claim only that we must refuse all attempts to theoretically legitimise violence, whether as an absolutist *raison d'Etat* or in the interests of a totalitarian philosophy. Violence is at the same time unavoidable and unjustifiable. I believe that it is necessary to preserve its exceptional character and to restrict it to certain limits. Therefore, I preach neither non-violence, which I know to be impossible, nor, as my detractors suggest, do I advise sanctity: I know myself too well to believe in pure virtue. In a world where people are occupied with opposing arguments defending the use of terror, I believe it is necessary to impose a limit to violence, to confine it when it is inevitable, to limit its terrifying

effects by restricting its excesses. I have a horror of comfortable violence. I have a horror of those whose words exceed their actions. It is on this basis that I distance myself from several of our great minds for whose appeals to murder I will cease feeling contempt only when they themselves take up the executioner's gun.

At the beginning of your article you asked me why I had sided with the Resistance. Such a question has no meaning for some men, of which I am one. I could not imagine being anywhere else, that is all. I thought then, and I think now, that one cannot be on the side of the concentration camps. I understood at that moment that I despised violence less than I did the institutions of violence.[51]

The vehemence with which Camus attacked d'Astier's argument might suggest that he had more than the author in mind.[52] And indeed the text itself suggests that it was also addressed to Merleau-Ponty, and perhaps Sartre (who, as we have seen, had also suggested that Camus was a pacifist). Roger Quilliot and Maurice Weyembergh both identify an allusion to Merleau-Ponty in Camus's assertion that "even if the violence you recommend were more progressive, as claim our philosopher-spectators, I would still say that it must be limited".[53] Indeed, the title of Camus's response alone, "Where Is the Mystification?", evokes not so much d'Astier's essay as those of Merleau-Ponty and Sartre, who, at this time, were suggesting that there was a "mystification" at the heart of anti-communist liberalism, a mystification that ascribes violence to Marxism and only progress to itself.[54] Addressing precisely this argument, Camus spoke of "that mystification which aims to convince us that a politics of power, of whatever kind, can lead us to a better society where social freedom will at last be realised". Such a politics of power, says Camus, "signifies preparation for war".[55] "You say that, in order to put an end to war, it is necessary to put an end to capitalism. I'm quite willing to accept that. However, in order to do away with capitalism, you will have to wage war against it. This is absurd, and I continue to believe that you do not fight the bad with the worse, but with the less bad." "In truth, despite your declarations," Camus insists, "justice is no longer at issue. What is at issue is a prodigious myth of the divinisation of mankind, of domination, of the unification of the world through human reason alone. What is at issue is the conquest of totality, and Russia considered the instrument of this messianism without God. Of what significance is justice, the lives of generations, human misery, compared to this excessive, overweening mysticism [*ce mysticisme démesuré*]? Strictly speaking, none at all." "Every false idea ends up with bloodshed", he continues, "but it is always somebody else's blood. This explains why certain of our philosophers feel at ease saying anything at all." Alluding again, perhaps, to Merleau-Ponty's talk of the "logic of History" in *Humanism and Terror*, Camus suggests that from a certain perspective these self-proclaimed orthodox Marxists "are no longer of this world", and exist instead in "logic". And it is in the name of this logic, says Camus, that for the first time in the intellectual history of France, writers on the avant-garde "have applied their intelligence to the justification of the executioners [*les fusilleurs*], forsaking protest in the name of those who are clearly the victims [*les fusillés*]" (*E*: 360–62).

In this way Camus rejects accusations of pacifism, utopianism, but he also reaffirms his rejection of Marxism as an "absolute philosophy", while recognizing the value of its "critical aspect" (*CC*: 264*; *CAC8*: 620–21). He hoped, he told Roger Quilliot, that the French socialists would "repudiate dialectical materialism as an absolute principle of explication as we are unwilling to accept with light hearts its ineluctable consequences", while at the same time affirming that "the Marxist critique of bourgeois society is our particular arsenal" (*E*: 1579–80). Accordingly, Ronald Aronson's claim that by this time Camus was asserting that "Marxism equalled murder but capitalism and colonialism did not" seems without much justification.[56]

The Plague[57]

> Those deprived of grace simply have to practise generosity among themselves. As far as the believers are concerned, they lack nothing, they are provided for; or at least they act as if that were the case. We, on the other hand, lack everything but the fraternal hand.[58]

Camus's rejection in "Neither Victims nor Executioners" of what he considered to be Marxist prophecy and utopianism was undergirded by his conception of the absurd – indeed, the articles can be read as a first detailed attempt at defining a moral politics consistent with the absurd. *The Plague* (1947) articulates a politics of moderation similar to that found in "Neither Victims nor Executioners", though in the novel it is conventional Christianity, rather than orthodox Marxism, that serves as a conceptual foil. For this reason Camus considered *The Plague* his most anti-Christian work.[59] Before we consider this aspect of the novel, however, it is worth considering what is perhaps its most controversial characteristic: its symbolic representation of Nazism as a plague.

Because *The Plague* was read, loosely, as an allegory of Nazi occupation (not least because in France the Nazis were known as *la peste brune*) some critics, including Sartre and de Beauvoir, were highly critical of what they saw as Camus's failure to situate the "plague" in a historical or political context, thereby implicitly positing the plague as "natural".[60] At the very least, they felt that the novel should have laid the responsibility for the plague on the shoulders of certain individuals. Immediately after its publication Sartre was vaguely complimentary, describing the novel as "a good example of a unifying movement which bases a plurality of critical and constructive themes on the organic unity of a single myth", and a few months later *Les Temps modernes* devoted two articles to Camus's novel, by Etiemble and Jean Pouillon.[61] Although both reviews were, in general, politely sympathetic, Pouillon suggested that *The Plague* placed responsibility for the occurrence of evil outside mankind, and would therefore be met with hostility by Marxists. Such hostility eventually manifested itself in the criticism of both de Beauvoir and Sartre themselves. De Beauvoir claimed that "to treat the Occupation as the equivalent of a natural calamity was merely another means of escaping from History [*sic*] and the real problems" (de Beauvoir 1968: 138). As we shall see in the analysis of the angry debate between Sartre and Camus that followed the publication of *The Rebel*, Sartre and his associate, Francis Jeanson, interpreted *The Plague* in very much the same way. Sartre alleges that Camus was inclined to blame human misery and oppression on "the absurdity of the world" rather than individuals and their actions.[62] Years later, Sartre was to repeat the point with less circumspection: "When I think of Camus claiming . . . that the German invasion was like the plague – coming for no reason, leaving for no reason – *quel con*, what a shmuck! The German invasion was an invasion of *men*, and it was eventually defeated by *men*."[63] Even Roland Barthes, who might have been thought a more subtle reader, found in *The Plague* an "antihistoric moral and a politics of solitude".[64] This same argument occasionally resurfaces among Camus's more recent critics as well. Susan Dunn, for example, asserts that the novel treats Nazism "in terms of a nonideological and nonhuman plague" (Dunn 1994: 150). Camus's response to Barthes functions as a riposte to the others as well. Although he wanted *The Plague* to be read "on a number of levels", Camus claims that it is nevertheless the case that the novel has as its "obvious content the struggle of the European resistance movements against Nazism" (*SEN*: 220; *TRN*: 1965). This is borne out, he suggests, by the simple fact that a long passage from the novel had been published during the Occupation in a collection of Resistance texts.[65] Camus further insists that "compared to *The Outsider*, *The Plague* does represent, beyond any possible discussion, the movement from an attitude of solitary revolt to the recognition of a community whose struggles must be shared. If there is an evolution from *The Outsider* to *The Plague*, it is towards solidarity and participation" (*SEN*: 220; *TRN*: 1965–6). In a notebook entry from about the time *The Myth of Sisyphus* was being published, he notes:

> [*The Outsider*] describes the nakedness of man facing the absurd. *The Plague*, the basic equivalence of individual points of view facing the same absurd. It's a progress that will become clearer in other works. But in addition *The Plague* shows that the absurd *teaches nothing*. It's a definitive progress.
> (*NB2*: 24; *C2*: 36. Cf. *NB2*: 20; *C2*: 31)

Of course Camus did not attribute Nazism to a non-human force, and there is perhaps some justice in Tony Judt's suggestion that the "acerbity of their attacks" on *The Plague* may have been partly motivated by the critics' knowledge of the extent of Camus's activism during the Nazi Occupation (Judt 1998: 106). Notwithstanding its deliberate ambiguity, *The Plague* nowhere suggests that the plague of Nazism was a naturally occurring phenomenon. Far from thinking of Nazism as a phenomenon "coming for no reason, leaving for no reason", as Sartre suggested, as he points out in *Letters to a German Friend*, Camus considered it a form of deliberately chosen nihilism, and in this essay he differentiates between himself and his Nazi interlocutor precisely on the basis of their respective choices: "you saw the injustice of our condition to the point of being willing to add to it, whereas it seemed to me that man must exalt justice in order to fight against eternal injustice, create happiness in order to protest against the universe of unhappiness" (*RRD*: 27–8*; *E*: 240). Furthermore, as Ronald Aronson has noted, *The Plague* "was not at all a reflection on the causes of the pestilence, whether human or natural, but, rather, the story of the collective spirit of combating it" (Aronson 2004: 56). As early as 1942, when ideas for the novel began to germinate, Camus had a clear sense of what the symbol of the plague was to represent:

> I want to express by means of the plague the suffocation which we have all suffered and the atmosphere of threat and exile in which we all lived. I want at the same time to extend that interpretation to the notion of existence in general. The plague will give the image of those who in this war were limited to reflection, to silence – and to moral anguish.   (*NB2*: 53–4; *C2*: 72)

As we have seen in the discussion of *Caligula*, the struggle against the absurd involves not just metaphysical Sisyphean scorn, but also, and especially, a determined rebellion against human systems that give the absurd social and political extension. Although it can never be a question of "transcending" the absurd (the human condition is characterized by the absurd, and to speak of transcending the human condition is necessarily erroneous), as *Letters to a German Friend* suggests, the fact of the absurd requires one to choose between complicity with it and resistance against it (see Glicksburg 1963: 60). This resistance is premised not on a hope of evading, transcending or triumphing over the absurd, but on the simple assumption that one should not add to the absurdity by conceding to it. This point is clearly expressed in *The Plague*, where we see solidarity and resistance, but also the awareness that the plague can never be completely vanquished. The novel's protagonists are conscious that their struggle is against human suffering, and is not an effort to overcome it. Dr Rieux, the novel's chief protagonist and narrator, refers to the struggle against the plague as an "interminable defeat" (*TP*: 108*; *TRN*: 1322):

> he knew that the tale he had to tell could not be one of a final victory. It could be only the record of what had had to be done, and what assuredly would have to be done again in the never ending fight against terror and its relentless onslaughts, despite their personal afflictions, by all who, while unable to be saints but refusing to bow down to pestilences, strive their utmost to be healers.   (*TP*: 251–2; *TRN*: 1473–4)

Whereas in the pages of *Combat* Camus's ameliorative politics was contrasted with the messianic pretensions of contemporary French Marxism and Stalinism, in *The Plague* that same politics is contrasted with Christianity. Generally Camus's attitude to Christianity can be said to be sympathetically ambivalent, and although he may have considered *The Plague* to be his "most anti-Christian" work, in 1948 he claimed that among his intentions when writing it "was to do justice to the Christian friends whom I met during the occupation and with whom I joined in a just fight".[66] In 1946, a few months before the publication of the novel, he told a group of Dominicans in Paris: "I am your Augustine before his conversion. I am debating the problem of evil, and I am not getting past it."[67] What Camus seems to have meant here, as *The Plague* appears to illustrate, is that he finds the Christian response to the fact of human suffering unacceptable. This becomes particularly evident in the exchange between the characters of Rieux and the Jesuit priest Fr Paneloux immediately following the slow and tortured death of a child from the plague. For the priest, the child's death "is revolting because it passes our human understanding". "But", he adds, "perhaps we should love what we cannot understand." When Rieux objects that he could never "love a scheme of things in which children are put to torture", Paneloux replies "I've just realised what is meant by 'grace'." The doctor readily admits to being without grace, and suggests to the priest that "beyond blasphemy and prayers" they were working together for a common cause, and that, at the time, was "the only thing that matters".[68] Notwithstanding this solidarity, however, the clear distance between Rieux and Paneloux remains a dominant theme throughout the novel. The doctor, for example, at one point asks "since the order of the world is shaped by death, mightn't it be better for God if we refuse to believe in Him and struggle with all our might against death, without raising our eyes towards heaven where He sits in silence?"[69] Paneloux, in contrast, even after witnessing the death of the child, exhorts his parishioners to accept the child's suffering, since it is God's will. Further, he says, this acceptance of God's will has nothing to do with "mere" humility; it involves a humiliation fully assented to. Indeed, since it was God's will that a child die in agony from the plague, the people of Oran should will it too. The choice thus facing a Christian in Oran is "to believe everything, so as not to be forced into denying everything" (*TP*: 184; *TRN*: 1401).

To the extent to which Paneloux's sermons articulate a Christian ethics, their justification of the scandal of the plague indicates the depths to which they are opposed to the modest morality of solidarity in suffering we find in *The Plague*. Paneloux preaches the renunciation of the self to the will of God, but for Camus this self-renunciation is no more that a renunciation of the individual's ability to alleviate the extent of human suffering; it is ultimately an act of philosophical suicide, such as is described in *The Myth of Sisyphus*. It is in this specific sense that *The Plague* is the most anti-Christian of his books. Furthermore, we can see in this light that Camus's objections to Christianity, as outlined in *The Plague*, are not dissimilar to his objections to Marxism, as outlined in "Neither Victims nor Executioners". Camus evidently found just such an exhortation "to believe everything, so as not to be forced into denying everything" at the heart of contemporary Marxism as well. Paneloux's appeal to Divine Mystery in the context of human suffering had, for Camus, a great deal in common with the Marxist appeal to "History". In his notebooks a few months after the publication of *The Plague*, Camus writes that Marxism is no less a revealed religion than Christianity, the difference being that for Marxists the Revelation will happen only at the end of history.[70] Indeed, as we shall see in the next chapter, in *The Rebel* Camus treats Christianity and Marxism as two sides of the same messianic coin, and although he considered both to possess remarkable virtues, he believed that as universal ideologies they were both morally and politically ruinous.

3 | *THE REBEL*

Introduction

Philosophically, *The Rebel* is Camus's most important book. Although it is much maligned and frequently ignored, the fact that Camus spent more time writing it than any other book, combined with the fact that we find in the essay the most detailed articulation, indeed the culmination, of many of the ideas we have examined in previous chapters, justifies a more careful scrutiny than it usually receives. Such scrutiny is given further justification, I believe, precisely by the degree and extent of the critical hostility the essay engendered among Camus's contemporaries.[1]

Contrary, perhaps, to our expectations, and certainly contrary to some of the relevant scholarship, what is to be found at the beginning of *The Rebel* is a reassertion of the fact of the absurd, as described in *The Myth of Sisyphus*.[2] Although Camus does assert at the beginning of *The Rebel* that "the absurd, considered as a rule of life is . . . contradictory", that the absurd is a "point of departure, a criticism brought to life – the equivalent, in the plane of existence, of systematic doubt", as we have already seen, this awareness was already present in *The Myth of Sisyphus*, where "the absurd, hitherto taken as a conclusion, is considered . . . as a starting point" (*R*: 9, 8, 10; *E*: 418, 417, 419; *MS*: 10; *E*: 97). Clearly, Camus, like other "great explorers in the realm of absurdity", had early on "rejected the complacencies of absurdism in order to accept its exigencies" (*R*: 9; *E*: 418). Those complacencies relate broadly to nihilism, manifested in *The Rebel* in the juvenile posturing of Rimbaud: his extolling of crime, his complaint that life was "a farce for the whole world to perform".[3] The exigencies of the absurd refer to the challenge posed by the absurd to the supposed rationality of our moral and political beliefs, the "absurd condition" conceived as the "human condition". The absurd, Camus affirms in the introduction to *The Rebel*, "has wiped the slate clean", has undermined our most cherished assumptions about our knowledge of the world, leaving us in a political and moral "blind alley". However, notes Camus, absurd reasoning does not end there, and he is determined to show that accepting the exigencies dictated by the absurd does not lead to nihilism: "I proclaim that I believe in nothing and that everything is absurd, but I cannot doubt the validity of my proclamation and I must at least believe in my protest" (*R*: 10; *E*: 419).

Although such "exigencies" are substantially in evidence in *The Myth of Sisyphus*, in the scorn-filled lucid revolt of its eponymous hero, the nihilistic "complacencies" are entirely absent, as we see reflected in Camus's markedly sober claim that the absurd "is lucid reason noting its limits" (*MS*: 49; *E*: 134). Similarly, in a 1955 preface to *The Myth of Sisyphus* Camus declared, "this book declares that even within the limits of nihilism it is possible to find the means to proceed beyond nihilism . . . I have progressed beyond several of the positions which are set down here; but I have remained faithful, it seems to me, to the exigency which prompted them" (*MS*: 7). Accordingly, I think we can say that the absurd was never intended to serve as a "rule of life" for Camus, and therefore there are good reasons, at least, for supposing a continuum in the intellectual trajectory of both essays. As an assertion of ontological scepticism, I think the absurd remained a central theme of Camus's writing, and continued to be expressed, for example, in his assertion that he was not a philosopher because he hadn't "sufficient faith in reason", and in his rejection in *The Rebel* of the "historical reason" of Marx and his intellectual successors (including Sartre).[4]

Although the politico-historical context had changed radically in the years between the publication of *The Myth of Sisyphus* and *The Rebel*, and the questions that concern Camus in the latter essay have to do, in particular, with ideologies of political violence and the contemporary penchant for them, Camus neither refutes nor revises the positing of the absurd found in *The Myth of Sisyphus*.[5] In fact, what he does at the beginning of *The Rebel* is ask whether, in the light of the absurd, political violence is a problem at all, or whether indeed it should properly be a matter of indifference to a lucid mind conscious of the absurd. Indeed, at the beginning of *The Rebel* he suggests that, at first, awareness of the absurd appears to make political violence at least a matter of indifference. Ultimately, however, Camus finds that the absurd does not make violence a matter of unconcern, and the key to this conclusion is the recognition that the fate of Sisyphus is the human fate: "The first progressive step for a mind overwhelmed by the strangeness of things is to realise that this feeling is shared with all men and that human reality, in its entirety, suffers from the distance which separates it from the rest of the universe." As we have seen, for Camus this recognition ultimately gives rise to a sense of solidarity. The absurd premise implies that human life is the only indubitable value, since it is this that makes the absurd encounter possible. And "from the moment that life is recognised as good, it becomes good for all men" (*R*: 5, 22, 6; *E*: 415, 432, 416). Camus's investigation of the problem of political violence begins with this realization that the absurd condition is the human condition, that it describes not just the experience of the individual in whose consciousness the recognition of the absurd necessarily begins, but the character of all human experience. This recognition permits an important reorientation of the absurd premise, a reworking that permits the emergence of the ethics of revolt.[6]

He asks whether this datum regarding "the value of a life like mine" gives us any insight into the contemporary era and the problem of political violence. In order to investigate this question further he sketches an outline of what he believes are the motives behind political violence, the factors that motivate an individual to revolt. The rebel is first and foremost one who refuses, who says "no". But, Camus observes, this refusal is also affirmative, because the declaration implies a discourse of value: the rebel must revolt in the name of something. The instant that the slave, or any human being who becomes aware of the weight of oppression on his shoulders, realizes that his master has exceeded certain limits, has trespassed upon certain rights that the slave holds to be inalienable, revolt is born. The rebel affirms the existence of a value, which must be recognized by both slave and master, and a limit to the absolute freedom the master assumes that he should enjoy. "The slave who opposes his master", says Camus, "is not concerned . . . with repudiating his master as a human being" – "he repudiates him as a master". "If men cannot refer to a common value, recognised by all as existing in each one, then man is incomprehensible to man" (R: 23; E: 435). Accordingly, although the act of revolt is, explicitly, the assertion of a limit that must not be transgressed by the master, it is also, implicitly, an acceptance on the part of the slave not to transgress that limit either (in other words, the slave's revolt is a refusal of both servitude and oppression). Having established this, Camus is able to assert that the solidarity of humankind is based upon revolt, "and revolt, in its turn, can only find its justification in this solidarity".[7] Accordingly, these two mutually generating values of revolt and solidarity present the basis for an ethical understanding of legitimate political action:

> We have, then, the right to say that any rebellion which claims the right to deny or destroy this solidarity loses simultaneously its right to be called rebellion and becomes in reality an acquiescence in murder. In the same way this solidarity, except in so far as religion in concerned, comes to light only on the level of rebellion. And so the real drama of revolutionary thought is announced. In order to exist, man must rebel, but rebellion must respect the limit it discovers in itself – a limit where minds meet and, in meeting, begin to exist. Rebellious thought cannot therefore dispense with memory: it is a perpetual state of tension. In studying its actions and its results, we shall have to say, each time, whether it remains faithful to its first noble promise or if, through indolence or folly, it forgets its original purpose and plunges into a mire of tyranny or servitude.   (R: 22; E: 431)

This account of the origin of revolt will acquire a particular significance later on, when Camus examines the importance in the history of rebellion of Hegel's account of the relation between the Master and the Slave. For now, let us note that in concluding the introductory section of *The Rebel*, Camus summarizes the discussion thus far as a movement from the awareness of suffering as a solitary experience to the recognition of that suffering as being common to all. This is the first step away from the solipsistic exile of Sisyphus. He likens this recognition of a common human condition to Descartes's *cogito*, the first principle on which it is possible to build a positive ethics: "In our daily trials rebellion plays the same role as does the 'cogito' in the realm of thought: it is the first piece of evidence. But this evidence lures the individual from his solitude. It founds its first value on the whole human race. I rebel – therefore we exist."[8]

Metaphysical rebellion

The Rebel argues that the history of political or historical rebellion is to a large extent the history of the forgetting of the initial impulse that motivated it: "The slave begins by demanding justice", Camus says, "and ends by wanting to wear a crown" (*R*: 25; *E*: 437). Revolutionary action has in most instances, he says, culminated in the denial of the principles that initially motivated it. However, this is not to say that revolution is the antithesis of rebellion (a false polarization to be found in much of the negative criticism directed at *The Rebel*). As David Sprintzen argues, for Camus, rebellion is merely "a vague yearning if it does not give birth to a revolutionary development in which the structures of exploitation are transformed", but at the same time, "the revolutionary transformation of society . . . only promises further and even greater humiliation if it is not guided by the spirit and concerns of rebellion".[9] Camus observes that the modern rebel has lost sight of the relativity of all revolt. Whereas originally the rebel does not deny God, but talks to him "as an equal", he ends up wanting to replace Him. "When the throne of God is overturned, the rebel realises that it is now his own responsibility to create the justice, order and unity that he sought in vain within his own condition and in this way to justify the fall of God." Thus begins the desperate effort to create "at the price of crime and murder if necessary, the dominion of man" (*R*: 25; *E*: 437). Having turned from God and the Church, accusing it of denying man what was rightfully his, the revolutionary, in turn, creates his own church, complete with its own set of dogmas or absolute truths, idolizing either history or a future vision of man himself.

Crucially, Camus insists that these consequences do not derive inevitably from rebellion itself. He asserts that rebellion is travestied "to the extent that the rebel forgets his original purpose, tires of the tremendous tension created by refusing to give a positive or negative answer, and finally abandons himself to complete negation or total submission". Thus murder and enslavement became legitimate political weapons in the attempt to establish the reign of the New Church. Having forgotten the first generous impulse inherent in revolt, the rebel goes on to become the doctrinaire revolutionary whose blind pursuit of utopia leads to a uniquely modern form of horror. Thus "the philosophy of revolt cannot do without memory" (*R*: 25, 22; *E*: 437, 431; see also *R*: 87; *E*: 496). The rebel must retain the memory of the slave's former servitude and the generous impulse that motivated his initial revolt, enabling him to conceive of his action in relation to the absurd human condition, the consciousness of which will enable a more capacious form of revolt to emerge. The utopian ends posited by modern revolutionaries (utopian ends that, says Camus, true "rebellion does not demand") justify *prima facie* any means. This total-itarian pathology is a travesty of rebellion (*R*: 47; *E*: 457).

Having provided this outline of what Camus calls "the initial progress that the spirit of rebellion provokes in a mind originally imbued with the absurdity and apparent sterility of the world", he then proceeds to analyse what he calls meta-physical rebellion, "the movement by which man protests against his condition and against the whole of creation", doing so with a juxtaposition of two archetypal meta-physical rebels, Prometheus and Cain. According to Camus, Prometheus exhibits all the standard characteristics of a rebel or revolutionary, such as "the fight against death ('I have delivered man from being obsessed by death'), Messianism ('I have instilled blind hopes into men's minds') and philanthropy ('Enemy of Zeus . . . for having loved mankind too much')". However, the Greeks, says Camus, were never vindictive and "in their most audacious flights they always remain faithful to the idea of moderation, a concept they deified" (he notes that in Aeschylus's drama *Prometheus the Firebringer*, the rebel was eventually pardoned). Accordingly, we see that Prometheus does not "range himself against all creation, but against Zeus, who is never anything more than one god among many . . . Prometheus himself is a demigod". Hence the myth of Prometheus is not an illustration of ultimate hubris or of "a universal struggle between good and evil", but instead describes "a dispute about what is good" (*R*: 22, 23, 26–7; *E*: 43, 435, 438–9).

At the heart of modern rebellion, says Camus, is a simplified binary view of the world, which is anathema to the Greek spirit. In the Greek view there were not gods on the one side and mankind on the other, but a series of stages between one and the other. Although modern revolutionary ideology is Manichaean, interpreting the world in terms of good and evil, innocence and guilt, for the Greeks such a per-spective would be alien. In their universe "there were more mistakes than crimes, and the only definitive crime was excess". Indeed, Camus suggests that rebellion in the modern sense is dependent on the idea of a personal god who has created, and is therefore responsible for, everything: "in the Western World the history of rebel-lion is inseparable from the history of Christianity". Accordingly, in contrast to Prometheus, Camus considers Cain, whose act of rebellion, the killing of Abel, "coincides with the first crime" (*R*: 28, 32; *E*: 440, 443). Cain is the first nihilist, the first to negate all value, whether social or spiritual, mundane or transcendent. Whereas Prometheus, by stealing fire from the gods and giving it to humankind, rebelled against Zeus in the name of human values, Cain's revolt is an attack both on God and the values of human life. The history of rebellion, as we are experiencing it today, says Camus, "has far more to do with the children of Cain than with the disciples of Prometheus".[10] That is to say that the nexus of modern rebellion is found in an act of murder, in crime, rather than in "a dispute about what is good" (*R*: 27; *E*: 439).

After juxtaposing the two contradictory models of metaphysical rebellion, Prometheus and Cain, Camus proceeds to examine, at considerable length, three illustrative examples of modern metaphysical rebellion: the Marquis de Sade, the character of Ivan Karamazov in Dostoyevsky's novel *The Brothers Karamazov* and Nietzsche. He finds that each begins at the same point, bearing "the same ravaged countenance: the face of human protest".[11] However, although each act of metaphysical revolt begins as an act of protest against the human condition, and as an effort to "construct a purely terrestrial kingdom where their chosen principles will hold sway", "their conclusions have only proved disastrous or destructive to freedom from the moment they laid aside the burden of rebellion, fled the tension that it implies, and chose the comfort of tyranny or servitude". There are two general ways in which metaphysical revolt can betray its original impulse. Like Sade, it may deify "the total rejection, the absolute negation of what exists", or like Nietzsche, it may "blindly [accept] what exists and gives voice to absolute assent". Revolt motivated by hatred of the creator can become hatred for creation or a defiant love of what exists. But in both cases it ends in murder, "and loses the right to be called rebellion. One can be nihilist in two ways, in both by having an intemperate recourse to absolutes." Anticipating a later and more comprehensive discussion of legitimate violence, Camus hints at his conclusion in this regard: "Apparently there are rebels who want to die and those who want to cause death. But they are identical, consumed with desire for the true life, frustrated by their desire for existence and therefore preferring generalised injustice" to what they consider to be "mutilated justice". "At this pitch of indignation", says Camus, "reason becomes madness" (*R*: 100–102; *E*: 508–10).

Far from reflecting an amelioration in the extent of human suffering, the modern history of metaphysical rebellion has consisted "in gradually enlarging the stronghold where, according to his own rules, man without God brutally wields power". Henceforth, metaphysical rebellion retains of its original movement only the will to power: "In principle, the rebel only wanted to conquer his own existence and to maintain it in the face of God. But he forgets his origins and, by the law of spiritual imperialism, he sets out in search of world conquest . . . Man, on an earth that he knows is henceforth solitary, is going to add, to irrational crimes, the crimes of reason that are bent on the triumph of man" (*R*: 102–4; *E*: 510–11).

Historical rebellion

What he calls historical rebellion, the same rebellious impulse manifest on the stage of history, and the "logical consequence of metaphysical rebellion", is the subject of the next, and perhaps most important, section of *The Rebel*. Unsurprisingly, Camus finds the history of modern historical rebellion pervaded by the same "forgetfulness of origins" he perceived in modern metaphysical rebellion. He argues that historical rebellion is rooted in an appeal to the values of freedom and justice: freedom being the "motivating principle of all revolutions", without which "justice seems inconceivable to the rebel's mind". Yet although justice at first seems impossible without freedom, "there comes a time when justice appears to demand a suspension of freedom. Then terror, on a grand or small scale, makes its appearance to consummate the revolution."[12] What then of the future of rebellion if the values that motivate it themselves appear to be mutually contradictory?

Just as the study of modern metaphysical revolution began with Sade and the death of God, the enquiry into modern historical rebellion (what Camus here calls "our real inquiry") begins with Sade's contemporaries, the French revolutionaries, and with regicide (*R*: 108; *E*: 518). Noting Michelet's view of the French Revolution as a struggle between divine grace and justice, Camus observes that revolutionary justice in 1789 has something crucial in common with the grace it sought to replace: "it wants to be total and to rule completely". This new religion of justice found its clearest articulation in Rousseau's *The Social Contract* (1762). Before Rousseau, says Camus, "God created kings, who in their turn created peoples"; after *The Social Contract*, peoples created themselves, and then they created kings. Power is no longer either arbitrary or bequeathed by God, but derives its existence through general consent. In Rousseau, political society is understood in terms of the complete and voluntary subjection of the individual will to the collective general will. The collective general will is understood by Rousseau to constitute the sole source of legitimate sovereignty and to be something that can only work for the general good: "This political entity, proclaimed sovereign, is also defined as a divine entity. Moreover, it has all the attributes of a divine entity. It is, in fact, infallible in that, in its role of sovereign, it cannot even wish to commit abuses" (*R*: 114–17; *E*: 523–4). Adherence to this collective will is in the interests of everyone, is indeed what each individual wants: if we are coerced in its name, we are merely, in Rousseau's terms, being "forced to be free" (Rousseau 1968: 64). Therefore, although *The Social Contract* appears to herald a new era of humanism, it in fact establishes another Church, evident from the preponderance of terms such as "absolute", "sacred" and "inviolable" in the book. "We are witnessing", says Camus, "the dawn of a new religion with its martyrs, its ascetics and its saints." Symbolically, the clearest expression of this excess was in the execution of the King: "in order that 1789 shall mark the beginning of the reign of 'Holy Humanity' and of 'Our Lord the human race', the fallen sovereign must first of all disappear. The murder of the King-Priest will sanction the new age – which endures to this day."[13] Camus, of course, was not a monarchist.[14] He claimed only that the execution (as opposed to the deposition) of the King was carried out in the name of principles no less fanciful than those by which the King himself had ruled. The regicide proved that the social hierarchy the revolution purported to destroy had in fact only been inverted. At the very moment that the inviolability of the King is denied, the inviolability and transcendence of the general will is proclaimed. The King, as the embodiment of truth, is being executed in the name of the people, as the embodiment of truth. In the view of the

Revolutionaries, citizens are inviolable and sacred and can only be constrained by the law, which is an expression of their common will. The King alone does not benefit from this particular inviolability or by the assistance of the law, "for he is placed outside the contract" (*R*: 118–19; *E*: 527). This exclusion of the King is made explicit in Saint-Just's own words, spoken at the trial of the King: "I shall undertake, citizens, to prove that the king can be judged, that the opinion of Morrison which would respect [his] inviolability and that of the committee which would have him judged as a citizen are equally false, and that the king ought to be judged according to principles foreign to both" (Walzer 1992: 121).

The concept of the general will, furthermore, not only excludes its obvious ideological opponents (such as the King). Given the popular desire to see the King pardoned, the equation of the general will with the regicide only survives by the introduction of a distinction between the general will and the "will of all", where the former represents the "common interest" and the latter represents "private interest", and as such is merely "the sum of individual desires", something of obviously less importance than the common interest from the revolutionary perspective (Rousseau 1968: 72). For Rousseau everyone wills the "general will", even when they are compelled by others to accept it. Transposed onto revolutionary justice we find the emergence of "the era of formal morality", where because, according to the Declaration of the Rights of Man, "the law is the expression of the general will" (Article 6), "every form of disobedience to law" is seen to derive "not from an imperfection in the law, which is presumed to be impossible, but from a lack of virtue in the refractory citizen. . . . A principle of infinite repression, derived from this very doctrine, is then established (*R*: 123; *E*: 531–2). Revolutionary justice, expressed through the general will, becomes totalitarian. It might be objected that Rousseau's concept of the general will cannot legitimately be used to defend revolutionary "infinite repression", but it should be stressed that Camus's interest is not as much with the thought of Rousseau himself as with the Rousseau of Saint-Just, and Saint-Just certainly believed he owed a great deal to Rousseau.[15]

Camus's conclusion is simple: "Morality, when it is formal, devours." The evidence he provides to support this claim is found in the advent of the revolutionary "Terror", designed to quash dissent: "Factions divide the sovereign [understood in the Rousseauean sense of a society acting in accordance with the general will]; therefore they are blasphemous and criminal . . . Saint-Just exclaims 'Either the virtues or the Terror'." At the beginning of the revolution Saint-Just and Robespierre opposed the death penalty, indeed Saint-Just sought to establish a form of justice that did not attempt to "find the culprit guilty, but to find him weak", and imagined a "republic of forgiveness, which would recognise that though the fruits of crime are bitter, its roots are nevertheless tender".[16] However, by the time of the Terror, on the basis of guaranteeing "freedom", "the draft constitution presented by the Convention already mentions the death penalty". Analysing Saint-Just's intellectual trajectory, Camus concludes that "Absolute virtue is impossible, and the republic of forgiveness leads, with implacable logic, to the republic of the guillotine."[17]

It is thus that the Revolutionaries finally arrive at the justification of crime, a crime Camus refers to as state terrorism.[18] Like all other rebellions, Saint-Just's rebellion is based upon a demand for "unity".[19] But his demand has become excessive, and no voice even nominally opposed to that unity can be tolerated. Hence Saint-Just declares what Camus calls "the major principle of twentieth century tyrannies": "A patriot is he who supports the Republic in general; whoever opposes it in detail is a traitor."[20] For the Revolutionaries, when neither reason nor the free expression of individual opinion succeeds in inculcating a sense of unity, then there is no choice but to impose unity on an unwilling populace. Dissent is forbidden; the people, in Rousseau's words, will be "forced to be free".[21] "The law still reigns supreme", concludes Camus, "but it no longer has any fixed limits" (*R*: 131; *E*: 539).

The successors to the French Revolutionary movement proved, according to Camus, even less scrupulous. Whereas the regicide was supposed to inaugurate the era of absolute formal virtue grounded in Rousseau's "general will", it actually instituted a regime that "simply made use of this frame of reference as an alibi, while employing, on all occasions, the opposite values. By its essential corruption and disheartening hypocrisy, it helped to discredit, for good and all, the principles it proclaimed." "Its culpability in this regard", says Camus, "is infinite" because the revolutionary "religion of virtue", through its violent excess, served to discredit virtue itself, thereby heralding a new era in which "reason will start to act without reference to anything but its own successes". At the heart of this new era was Russian communism, which inaugurated what Camus calls the "reign of history", which in a definitive insult against the original impulse of revolt, "denies all morality". The Jacobin revolution, which, Camus says, sought to institute the religion of virtue in order to establish unity upon it, is succeeded only by the era of cynical revolutions, which, whether of the Right or Left, seek only to institute the religion of man: "All that was God's will henceforth be rendered to Caesar" (*R*: 132; *E*: 540).

Hegel

Camus locates the foundation of this revolutionary attempt to make the "City of God" coincide with the "City of Humanity" in Hegel, and ascribes his "undeniable originality" to "his definitive destruction of all vertical transcendence". For the abstract universal reason of the Jacobins and Rousseau, Hegel posits "a less artificial but more ambiguous idea: concrete universal reason". Until this point, says Camus, reason had "soared above the phenomena which were related to it", but Hegel sought to introduce reason "into the stream of historical events, which it explains while deriving its substance from them" (*R*: 142, 133; *E*: 550, 541). Jeffrey Isaac points out that this interpretation of Hegel "glosses" Nietzsche's criticism that:

> Hegel has implanted in a generation that he has thoroughly penetrated the worship of the "power of history" that turns every moment into a sheer gaping at success, into an idolatry of the actual . . . If each success is comprised by a "rational necessity", and every event is the victory of logic or the "Idea", then – down on your knees quickly, and let every step in the ladder of "successes" be

revered! What? There are no more ruling mythologies? What? Religions are becoming extinct? Look at the religion of the power of history, and the priests of the mythology of Ideas with their scarred knees![22]

For Camus, Hegel did not simply reduce reason to history; he also endowed reason with "a lack of moderation". Truth, reason and justice were "abruptly incarnated in the progress of the world", and crucially, these values "ceased to be guides" and instead became "goals". Furthermore, in the historically ordained pursuit of these goals, "no pre-existent values can point the way". In fact, says Camus, Hegel goes to some lengths to show that moral conscience, by being so banal as to obey preconceived ideas of justice and truth, naively assumed to exist independently of the world, jeopardizes the advent of these values. "The rule of action has thus become action itself – which must be performed in darkness while awaiting the final illumination". Reason, he says, "annexed by this form of romanticism", is nothing more than an "inflexible passion".[23] The ends have remained the same: Hegel, like his revolutionary predecessors, seeks truth, reason and justice. However, in Hegel we see a striking, even disturbing, increase in ambition. Reason aspires not to understanding but to conquest:

> Just as Darwin replaces Linnaeus, the philosophers who supported the doctrine of an incessant dialectic replaced the harmonious and strict constructors of reason. From this moment dates the idea (hostile to every concept of ancient thought, which, on the contrary, reappeared to a certain extent in the mind of revolutionary France) that man has not been endowed with a definitive human nature, that he is not a finished creation but an experiment, of which he can be partly the creator. With Napoleon and the Napoleonic philosopher Hegel, the period of efficacy begins. Before Napoleon, men had discovered time and the universe; with Napoleon, they discovered time and the future in terms of this world; and by this discovery the spirit of rebellion is going to be profoundly transformed. (*R*: 134; *E*: 542)

Although Camus suggests that evidence can be found in Hegel's writings themselves to contradict this interpretation, it is nevertheless this interpretation that interests him, because it is in this account that, he claims, the revolutionaries of the twentieth century found the ideological weapons "with which they definitively destroyed the formal principles of virtue". Consequently, all that has been preserved of Hegel in the twentieth century is his vision of "a history without any kind of transcendence, dedicated to perpetual strife and to the struggle of will bent on seizing power". Prior to the French Revolution divine transcendence served to justify the arbitrary action of the King. After the Revolution, the Jacobins used the transcendent character of the formal principles of reason and justice to justify a regime that was neither reasonable nor just. Finally, through this interpretation of Hegel, there emerges the idea that transcendence must be purged from the world: "The hatred of formal virtue – degraded witness to divinity and false witness in the service of injustice – has remained one of the principal themes of history today. Nothing is pure: that is the cry which convulses our period" (*R*: 135; *E*: 543).

In assessing the merits of this criticism it is important to note that the focus of Camus's attention here is less on Hegel himself than on the massively influential interpretation of Hegel presented by Alexandre Kojève (just as it had been on the Rousseau of Saint-Just, rather than on Rousseau himself).[24] Kojève's reading of Hegel, which has been called "the secret to contemporary French thinking about history", emphasized a Marxist interpretation of Hegel's account of the Master and the Slave as a dialectic of human history (Roth 1988: 94). According to Kojève's Hegel, "to speak of the 'origin' of Self-Consciousness is necessarily to speak of a fight to the death for 'recognition.' Without this fight to the death for pure prestige, there would never have been human beings on earth." Human reality, he argues, "is constituted only in the fight for recognition", and "the truth of man, or the revelation of his reality, therefore, presupposes the fight to the death".[25] Without being willing to engage in this "fight to the death" we remain, according to Hegel (or, at least, Kojève's Hegel), on the level of "animal" being. Hegel characterized human reality, therefore, as one of conflict between the Master and the Slave. Although the human struggle is "to the death", it in fact desires not the death of the other, but recognition as "Master" by the Other (and the Other's self-recognition as the Master's Slave). "The Slave", says Kojève, "is the defeated adversary, who has not gone all the way in risking his life, who has not adopted the principles of the Master: to conquer or to die." The Slave has accepted a life "granted to him by another", has "preferred slavery to death, and that is why, by remaining alive, he lives as a slave". It is at this point that the Marxian character of Kojève's interpretation of Hegel is most apparent. Conceptualizing the Master–Slave dialectic in terms of the relations between capital and labour (or "work"), Kojève argues that in Hegel "Work 'appears' for the first time in Nature in the form of slavish work imposed by the first Master on the first Slave." However, in this context the only "evolution" the Master experiences "is purely external or 'material' and not truly human", and, furthermore, "only the Slave can *want* to cease to be what he is (i.e. a Slave)". Ultimately, the working Slave must again take up the fight for prestige, "for there will always be a remnant of Slavery in the worker as long as there is a remnant of idle Mastery on earth". Thus we arrive at the end of History: "It is in and by the final Fight, in which the working ex-Slave acts as combatant for the sake of glory alone, that the free Citizen of the universal and homogenous State is created; being both Master and Slave, he is no longer either the one or the other, but is the unique 'synthetical' or 'total' Man, in whom the thesis of Master and the antithesis of Slavery are dialectically 'overcome'."[26]

If we contrast Kojève's Hegelian account of the Master–Slave dialectic with the account of the slave's revolt discussed by Camus earlier, the extent to which he objects to the Hegelian schema becomes immediately evident. Whereas for Camus the legitimacy of the slave's revolt is dependent upon its guaranteeing the relative rights of both the master and the slave, in Hegel this solidarity is replaced with a dialectic of domination and submission. Camus sees in this dialectic what he calls "the thought that will inspire our revolutions", the idea that "the supreme good does not, in reality, coincide with existence". Instead, in the wake of the destruction of "vertical transcendence" and the affirmation of the Master–Slave dialectic, the supreme good at last coincides with the future. In this way, according to Camus, Hegel has deified history. This "deification of history", says Camus, permits Hegel the following perspective: "This is truth, which appears to us, however, to be error, but which is true precisely because it happens to be error. And for proof, it is not I, but history, at its conclusion, that will furnish it."[27] Such a viewpoint, Camus surmises, can permit one of only two attitudes: "either the suspension of all affirmation until the production of proof" or "the affirmation of everything, in history, which seems dedicated to success – force in particular". Both of these attitudes, Camus suggests, imply "nihilism", which he has defined already as "not only despair and negation but, above all, the desire to despair and negate", and describes in the present context as "a calumny of the present life to the advantage of a historical future in which one tries to believe" (*R*: 147, 57–8, 144n.; *E*: 554, 467, 552n.).

Camus's account of Hegel has received a certain amount of negative criticism, not least, as we shall see in a later chapter, from Sartre. However, such criticism tends to overlook the crucial fact that Camus was less concerned to critique Hegel than to critique his contribution to contemporary ideologies of political violence ("The day when crime arrays itself in the discarded attire of innocence, . . . innocence is called upon to justify itself. The intent of this essay is to accept this strange challenge"[28]). For this reason Camus's focus, as I have already noted, was less on Hegel himself than on the influence of Hegelian philosophy in the twentieth century, in particular the Hegel of Alexandre Kojève. The Sartre scholar William McBride, for example, has dismissed Camus's account of Hegel as "abominable from a scholarly standpoint", and supports this judgement by reference to Camus's claim that "first Hegel, and then the Hegelians, have tried, on the contrary, to destroy, more and more thoroughly, all idea of transcendence and any nostalgia for transcendence".[29] "At this point", says McBride, "the informed reader can only shake his or her head."[30] However, Camus's point (repeated in relation to Marx), that Hegel reduces all value to History, is, as we shall see, not quite as obviously wrong as McBride suggests.[31] Furthermore, as he makes clear elsewhere, Camus shared the view that although Hegel discounts transcendence, he replaces transcendence with immanence: "Hegel's undeniable originality lies in his definitive destruction of all vertical transcendence – particularly the transcendence of principles. There is no doubt that he restores the immanence of the spirit to the evolution of the world" (*R*: 142; *E*: 550). In this light we can say that Camus was asserting a view of Hegel that, far from being "abominable", indicated a certain familiarity with the material in question, for, despite McBride's assertion, there continues to be a debate in Hegelian studies as to whether his philosophy should properly be thought of as one of immanence or transcendence. As the debate "can be sustained indefinitely on a diet of suitable quotations", thankfully it need not concern us here, although the existence of the debate itself seems to undermine McBride's rather condescending criticism (McCarney 2000: 40). Secondly, and more importantly, given that it is Hegel as interpreted by Kojève that had such an influence on French Marxism, and therefore it is Kojève's

Hegel that interests Camus, it is important to note that Kojève himself declares in his lectures on Hegel a view entirely congruent with Camus's interpretation:

> the transcendent universal (God) . . . must be replaced by a universal that is immanent in the World. And for Hegel, this immanent universal can only be the State. What is supposed to be realised by God in the Kingdom of Heaven must be realised in and by the State, in the earthly kingdom. And that is why Hegel says that the "absolute" State that he has in mind (Napoleon's Empire) is the *realisation* of the Christian Kingdom of heaven.
>
> The history of the Christian World, therefore, is the history of the progressive realisation of that ideal State. . . . But in order to realise this State, Man must look away from the Beyond, look toward this earth and act only with a view to this earth. In other words, he must eliminate the Christian idea of transcendence. (Kojève 1980: 67)

Kojève later asserts baldly that Hegel's *Phenomenology* "ends with a radical denial of all transcendence".[32] McBride's characterization of Camus's account of Hegel as involving "massive distortions in the name of some higher Truth" is, then, wholly, and obviously, unfounded (McBride in *SCHC*: 240; the capitalization of "truth" in the text is McBride's). Although one might criticize Camus for basing his criticism of Hegel to a large extent on Kojève's lectures, as we have seen, it was precisely Kojève's Hegel that interested him because it was Kojève's Hegel that had such a profound influence on the intellectual milieu that was the object of study in *The Rebel*. The question of the accuracy of Kojève's interpretation of Hegel was not a question that could have properly concerned Camus in *The Rebel*.

Marx, history and state terrorism

This discussion of Kojève's Hegel lays a platform for Camus's analysis of Marxism. However, he first introduces the concept of "state terrorism". Notwithstanding their original intent (the achievement of freedom and justice), all modern revolutions, he says, "have ended in a reinforcement of the power of the State. 1789 brings Napoleon; 1848, Napoleon III; 1917, Stalin; the Italian disturbances of the twenties, Mussolini; the Weimar Republic, Hitler". These revolutions both liquidated the last remaining vestiges of divine right and professed, with ever-increasing audacity, their intention to create a City of Man and establish the reign of authentic freedom and justice. This "strange and terrifying growth of the modern State", says Camus, although "the logical conclusion of inordinate technical and philosophical ambitions, foreign to the true spirit of rebellion", is the nexus of the "revolutionary spirit of our time". The fascist states of Hitler and Mussolini were undoubtedly terroristic, but they were exemplary of what Camus calls "irrational terror". He suggests that the Fascists' "revolution" is something of a misnomer, for Hitler and Mussolini both "lacked the ambition of universality". Instead of deifying reason, they were "the first to construct a State on the concept that everything is meaningless and that history is only written in terms of the hazards of force".[33] However, although Fascism represents a clear subversion of the original rebellious momentum, its excesses are exceeded by those of Soviet communism, which "by its very origins, openly aspires to world empire". The ravages of Nazism, says Camus, were in fact greater than its real ambitions. Russian communism, in contrast, has appropriated that "metaphysical ambition" which, as we have seen, is the central concern of *The Rebel*: "the erection, after the death of God, of a city of man finally deified" (*R*: 186; *E*: 591–2). Camus intends to examine this "pretension" in detail in the next section, and so under the heading "State terrorism and rational terror", he begins one of the longest sections of the book, devoted to Marx and Marxism.

Camus had referred earlier to "the totalitarian revolution of the twentieth century", and although state terrorism was to take two distinct forms in the twentieth century, fascist and communist, for Camus properly speaking there was only *one* totalitarian revolution in the twentieth century – that which culminated in the creation of the USSR. Whereas fascism, Camus declares later on, represents "the exaltation of the executioner by the executioner", Russian communism represents "the exaltation of the executioner by the victims". Whereas the former "never dreamed of liberating all men, but only of liberating a few by subjugating the rest. The latter, in its most profound principle, aims at liberating all men by provisionally enslaving them all" (*R*: 174, 247; *E*: 579, 648). Therefore, for Camus, only the Soviet regime was, properly speaking, totalitarian. No doubt of comparable, if not equal, importance was the fact that whereas there were obviously no apologists for Nazi Germany in France in 1951, there were a significant number of French intellectuals (not only communist intellectuals) who were committed to defending the USSR. For both of these reasons, Ronald Aronson's complaint that under the rubric of "rational terror" Camus neglected to mention the Jewish Holocaust, French colonialism or Hiroshima seems oddly misplaced (Aronson 2004: 122).

Perhaps the most critical point to be made when considering Camus's treatment of Marxism in *The Rebel* is one that is frequently overlooked by critics. The focus of Camus's critique, as we shall see, is specifically on the Marxist theory of history. According to Marx, class struggle was at the heart of all economic and social development. Modern Western society was characterized by an especially exploitative class relationship – that between the capitalist (those who own capital) and the proletarian classes (those who "own" only their own labour). In Marx's analysis, in a capitalist society this class relation eventually becomes an impediment to continuing economic growth and efficiency, "primarily because the need to sell goods at a profit increasingly conflicts with the meagre purchasing power of the exploited masses".[34] As capitalism sinks further into this self-generated crisis, revolution becomes inevitable, as does, ultimately, the institution of a classless or communist society. Why this communist society would be immune to further social upheaval is never adequately explained and, instead, it is assumed that the absence of class contradictions would mean "the absence of all contradictions".[35] Marx and Engels considered this conception of objective historical necessity to be the chief characteristic distinguishing their own "scientific" socialism from the "utopian" socialism of their predecessors, for which they exhibited prodigious contempt.[36] For Camus this theory was not only intellectually suspect, given its status as the cornerstone of Soviet ideology; it also appeared to license what he called "rational state terrorism". This theory of history was of such importance to the coherence of Marxism as a whole that to believe it to be incorrect, as Camus did, necessarily implied the belief that Marxism as a conceptual system was incorrect. On the other hand, holding this view did not require Camus to reject everything Marx said as false. In 1944 he affirmed, as we have seen, that the political position of *Combat* after the liberation of France remained that "anti-Communism is the first step toward dictatorship". "We vigorously reject political anti-Communism", he says, "because we know what inspires it and what its unavowed aims are." *Combat*, he asserts, shares "most of our [communist] comrades' collectivist ideas and social programme, their ideal of justice, and their disgust with a society in which money and privilege occupy the front ranks". However, *Combat* rejects the communists' "very consistent philosophy of history" and the "political realism" they derive from it. In "Neither Victims nor Executioners", in 1946, Camus discusses the possibility of being socialist without being Marxist, and claims that socialists will have to choose: "Either they will admit that the end justifies the means, hence that murder can be legitimised, or else they will renounce Marxism as an absolute philosophy and limit their attention to the critical aspects, which are often still valuable."[37] Two years later, in a letter to his friend and editor Roger Quilliot, Camus writes:

> I am in agreement with you in regard to the precious critical lessons of Marxism, but I have arrived at the conclusion that the Marxist conception of the world is not only false but leads inexorably to murder . . . since we are talking about French Socialism, let me tell you, as a comrade, what hopes I had for it. I wanted it to speak clearly and say: "The Marxist critique of bourgeois society is our particular arsenal. However, we repudiate dialectical materialism as an absolute principle of explication as we are unwilling to accept with light hearts its ineluctable consequences."   (*E*: 1579–80)

It is unsurprising, then, that at the beginning of his discussion of Marx in *The Rebel* Camus states clearly that Marx's writings combined "the most valid critical method" with "a Utopian Messianism of highly dubious value", and argues that Marxism as an absolute philosophy should be rejected (something that is clearly not an "absolute rejection" of Marxism) (*R*: 188; *E*: 593). Notwithstanding this repeated reiteration of the nature and extent of his objection to Marxism, as we shall see in a later chapter, Camus was obliged to reiterate it in his letter to *Les Temps modernes* responding to the failure of Francis Jeanson to recognize this crucial distinction (along with much else) in his review of *The Rebel* (*SCHC*: 120; Camus 1952: 327). More recently, Ronald Aronson also ignores this crucial aspect of Camus's criticism of Marxism, even accusing Camus of having ignored "the socioeconomic concerns of Marxism". "To Camus", says Aronson, "Marxism was not about social change; it was nothing less – and nothing more – than a revolt that 'attempts to annex all creation'."[38] In any event, in the context of *The Rebel*, Camus is less concerned with defending Marxist critical method (which he believes was not static, but changed in relation to the nature of the bourgeois socio-economic environment) than with presenting a sustained critique of what he considered to be Marxist historical determinism: "Marxism and its successors", he says, "will be examined here from the angle of prophecy" (*R*: 189; *E*: 594).

Camus first approaches the Marxist theory of history by noting its striking similarity with Christian Messianism – the view of human history as one "unfolding from a fixed beginning toward a definite end, in the course of which man achieves his salvation or earns his punishment". One defining consequence of this historical vision is discernible in the attitude to nature, which for Marxists, as for Christians, is an object not for contemplation, but for transformation. This allows Camus to remind his reader that Marx's utopian vision was specifically a post-capitalist vision, at the heart of which was the most efficient exploitation of resources: "The most eloquent eulogy of capitalism was made by its greatest enemy. Marx is only anti-capitalist in so far as capitalism is out of date." Furthermore, Camus asserts that "Marx's scientific Messianism" itself has bourgeois roots. The idea of progress and the cult of technology and production are "bourgeois myths", wholly commensurate with the hopes and desires of the mercantile classes.[39] Indeed, notwithstanding the arguments of Kojève, such a belief in progress can, says Camus, be used to justify conservatism. Injustice in the present can be excused with the hollow consolation that the future belongs to the oppressed: "The future is the only kind of property that the masters willingly concede to the slaves." Although Camus recognizes that Marx "cannot pour enough scorn on bourgeois rational optimism", and its attendant notion of progress, "arduous progress toward a future of reconciliation nevertheless defines Marx's thought". "Hegel and Marxism" may have "destroyed the formal values that lighted for the Jacobins the straight road of [their] optimistic version of history", but they preserved "the idea of the forward march of history", which they confounded with social progress and declared necessary (*R*: 194–5; *E*: 599).

Although he claims that the roots of Marx's unified theory of history are bourgeois, Camus nevertheless acknowledges that the theory is also revolutionary: "At each level of production the economy arouses the antagonisms that destroy, to the profit of a superior level of production, the corresponding society" (*R*: 197; *E*: 602). For Marx, capitalism is the last of these antagonistic stages of production before the advent of communism.[40] Echoing the consensus view that Marx "inverted" Hegel, transforming idealism into materialism, Camus asserts that what Hegel "affirmed concerning reality advancing toward the spirit, Marx affirms concerning economy on the march toward the classless society". *Das Kapital*, says Camus, returns to the Hegelian dialectic of the Master and the Slave, but replaces self-consciousness with economic autonomy and the final reign of the Absolute Spirit with the advent of communism. According to Camus, Marxism conceptualizes man only in terms of his history and understands that history primarily, if not exclusively, in terms of economics. Marxists infer from the premise that man first seeks to secure his own subsistence the conclusion "that economic dependence is unique and suffices to explain everything" (*R*: 198, 200*, 199; *E*: 602, 605, 603–4). As the Marx scholar G. A. Cohen has it, "there is no history when nature is unusually generous".[41] In a certain sense, according to Camus, Marxists complete the movement begun by the Jacobins. The latter destroyed the transcendence of a personal God, "but replaced it by the transcendence of principles". Marx denies both the existence of God and the existence of any transcendent principles; he "destroys, even more radically than Hegel, the transcendence of reason and hurls it into the stream of history" (*R*: 200; *E*: 604).

Camus reiterates his admiration for Marx's criticism of the bourgeois society of his time, asserting that "his most profitable undertaking" had been to "reveal the reality that is hidden behind the formal values of which the bourgeois of his time made a great show". Marx's "theory of mystification", according to which the nature of bourgeois class society is misrepresented in the interests of its own preservation, is, according to Camus, "still valid, because it is in fact universally true" (although Camus also notes that it "is equally applicable to revolutionary mystifications"). The "extreme decadence brought about by the economy of prosperity" compelled Marx ("the incomparable eye-opener") "to give first place to social and economic relationships and to magnify still more his prophecy of the reign of man".[42] For Camus, it is in his ethical considerations that the greatness of Marx actually lies. Central to Marx's beliefs was a belief in the dignity of labour, and he "rebelled against the degradation of work to the level of commodity and of the worker to the level of an object". It is to Marx, says Camus, that we owe the idea that "when work is a degradation, it is not life, even though it occupies every moment of a life".[43] Camus suggests that the entire edifice of Marx's "purely economic explanation of history" can be understood as a reaction to the extent of economic inequality Marx witnessed. It was his sensitivity to social inequality that led him to interpret history primarily in terms of class conflict.[44]

For Marx, the era of bourgeois capitalism was marked by the greatest separation yet between the proletariat (who produce) and bourgeoisie (who control the means of production), and would be succeeded by the dissolution of all social classes and the reign of communism: "Marx says plainly that there will be no more classes after the revolution than there were Estates after 1789." However, just as the Estates disappeared without bringing class inequality to an end, it is not at all clear that after the Marxist revolution, classes will not be replaced by some other form of social antagonism. Yet the key to "Marxist prophecy lies, nevertheless, in this affirmation". This leads Camus to remind us again that the successful emergence of communism is understood as a specifically post-capitalist event. Thus Marx speaks of "the 'historic rights' of capitalism", as the source of human misery but also of human progress, and he "recommends tolerating the bourgeois State, and even helping to build it, rather than returning to a less industrialised form of production. The proletariat 'can and must accept the bourgeois revolution as a condition of the working class revolution'."[45] Marx is thus, in Camus's words, "the prophet of production", who on this precise point, though on no other, ignored social reality in favour of an abstract system: "Suffering is never provisional for the man who does not believe in the future. But one hundred years of suffering are fleeting in the eyes of the man who prophesies, for the hundred and first year, the definitive city."[46] Although his "prophecies are generous and universal", Marx's doctrine is restrictive, and his reduction of every value to historical terms "leads to the direst consequences" (*R*: 209; *E*: 614).

In this regard, Camus sees Marxism as consistent with the tradition of Christian millenarianism, which expressed little interest in ordinary theological or scriptural matters and was wholly concerned with the coming judgement day. A similar movement can be discerned in the history of Marxism, according to Camus. The Russian Revolution was understood as at least a partial realization of Marxist "prophecy", and it was believed that that first revolution would be succeeded by others across Europe. In 1919, for example, the Bolshevik leader Nikolai Bukharin declared his belief that "we have entered upon a period of revolution which may last fifty years before the revolution is at last victorious in all Europe and finally in all the world" (Ransome 1919: 54). Yet precisely the opposite happened, with the failure of the General Strike in France in 1920, the destruction of the revolutionary movement in Italy, the defeat of Béla Kun in Hungary and the short-lived Soviet Republic in Bavaria. In the face of such failure, it was proclaimed that Europe was not yet ready for revolution, but that there was no doubt about its eventual, inexorable arrival. Illustrating how "defeat can excite vanquished faith to the point of religious ecstasy", Camus quotes the German revolutionary, Karl Liebknecht: "At the crash of economic collapse whose rumblings can already be heard, the sleeping soldiers of the proletariat will awake as at the fanfare of the Last Judgement, and the corpses of the victims of the struggle will arise and demand an accounting from those who are bowed down with curses" (*R*: 212; *E*: 616).

And it is little wonder, says Camus, that the world revolution never came, for the world economy has changed over time to a point where Marx's predictions are no longer easily applicable. Marx's revolution could not come about because the social relations on which his revolution was premised have radically changed.[47] For Camus the primary reason for the failure of world revolution to materialize was a rapid transformation in economic and social relations, a transformation that, he suggests, flatly contradicts Marx. This is exemplified, for Camus, in the massive growth in the middle class, a consequence of the rapid growth in industrialization unforeseen by Marx. Therefore Marxist analysis is seen to be faulty not only in its predictive powers, but also in its analysis of actual social and economic relations. This failing is most apparent for Camus in the attitude of Marxism to the peasantry (as opposed to the urban working class). In its ambition to postulate a post-industrial utopia, Marxian socialism treated with little serious regard certain aspects of the economy, especially agriculture. This leads Camus to one of his most astute criticisms of Marxism: "in one of its aspects, the history of socialism in our times can be considered as the struggle between the proletarian movement and the peasant class. This struggle continues, on the historical plain, the nineteenth-century ideological struggle between authoritarian socialism and libertarian socialism, of which the peasant and artisan origins are quite evident." However, in the case of agriculture, this preference for the authoritarian "was to prove expensive for the kulaks who constituted more than five million historic exceptions to be brought, by death and deportation, within the Marxist pattern" (*R*: 213; *E*: 617). This analysis is shared by David Mitrany, whose *Marx Against the Peasant* was published in the same year as *The Rebel*:

> The Marxists were interested in production, the eastern reformers (Populists) were interested in the producers. It is significant that what in the West is significantly known as the Land question, in the East has always been spoken of as the Peasant question. For the sake of scientific production the Marxists accepted with equanimity, if not actually with eagerness, the destruction of the peasantry as a class. But in Eastern Europe, the whole social problem centred on the peasants, who had the greatest needs and numbers; a revolutionary movement which left them out of account would have neither hope nor scope.[48]

Furthermore, like the bourgeoisie, the Marxist believes in maximum productivity, but increasing productivity requires a concomitant increase in specialization. Accordingly, the Marxist plan "to abolish the degrading opposition of intellectual work to manual work" comes into conflict with the central demand to maximize production. Camus is not content to argue that Marx is merely contradictory on this point, and argues that the prioritization of production has led, in the words of Simone Weil, to a form of oppression comparable to oppression by armed force and oppression by wealth; that is, "oppression by occupation".[49] Weil's *La Condition ouvrière* (1951), says Camus, serves to highlight the "degree of moral exhaustion and silent despair" to which "the rationalisation of labour can lead" (*R*: 216; *E*: 620). For Camus, industrial socialism has done nothing essential to alleviate the conditions in which industrial workers have to work "because it has not touched on the very principle of production and the organisation of labour, which, on the contrary, it has extolled". Further, Camus argues that the Marxist exaltation of production went unopposed only because, in the wake of the Paris Commune, "the only socialist tradition that could have opposed it had been drowned in blood". The Marxist historic justification of the workers' lot, indeed, has much in common with "the promise of celestial joys" offered by the millenarian Church in exchange for total personal sacrifice. Never "did it attempt to give him the joy of creation". The political form of society is no longer the issue of concern; instead it is the belief in a technocratic society on which capitalism and Marxian socialism are equally dependent.[50]

Camus concludes this consideration of Marxist doctrine with the assertion that, despite it pretensions to the contrary, Marxism is not in fact scientific, and at best, it can be said to have "scientific prejudices". If Marxist theory is determined by economics, "it can describe the past history of production, not its future, which remains in the realm of probability. The task of historical materialism can only be to establish a method of criticism of contemporary society." An ironic consequence of declaring Marxism scientific has been the denial of all science that appears to disprove Marx. Marx declared to Engels that Darwinian theory constituted the very foundation of their method; hence, in order to defend Marxism it has been necessary, says Camus, to refute all biological discoveries that might contradict Darwin. Once Western scientists began to question the doctrines of determinism, it became necessary "to entrust Lyssenko with the task of disciplining chromosomes and of demonstrating once again the truth of the most elementary determinism". Indeed, Camus asserts, "Marxism is only scientific today in defiance of Heisenberg, Bohr, Einstein, and all the greatest minds of our time".[51] He notes, in passing, Roger Caillois's remark that Stalinism rejects quantum theory, but makes use of atomic science, which is derived from it, and concludes that Marxism is clearly in conflict "with its two principles, economy and science", and as a result is "no more founded on pure reason than were the ancient faiths".[52]

Finally, not only is Marxist "scientific socialism" apparently refuted by economic and scientific realities; Camus suggests that if the Marxist dialectical interpretation of history is to have any meaning whatever it cannot predict an end to history. A society based upon class may well be replaced with a classless society, but to declare that it will be replaced with a society without any similar antagonism is, according to Camus, logically flawed: "From our point of view, it is only nihilism – pure movement that aims at denying everything which is not itself . . . The end of history is not an exemplary or perfectionist value; it is an arbitrary and terroristic principle" (R: 224; E: 628).

Notwithstanding these criticisms of Marxism, Camus argues that "Marx himself never dreamed of such a terrifying apotheosis" as has been achieved under Stalin (we should remember that The Rebel was published in 1951, when Stalin was still very much in power).[53] Neither, Camus claims, did Lenin imagine the form Marxism would take after the Russian Revolution, even though he was himself responsible for taking "a decisive step toward establishing a military Empire".[54] Although he did not equal the depredations of Stalin, Lenin believed, says Camus, "only in the revolution and in the virtues of expediency". In Left-Wing Communism: An Infantile Disorder, he claims: "One must be prepared for every sacrifice, to use if necessary every stratagem, ruse, illegal method, to be determined to conceal the truth, for the sole purpose of penetrating the labour unions . . . and of accomplishing, despite everything, the Communist task."[55] Given this cult of efficacy, it is unsurprising that Lenin endeavoured to abolish the "sentimental" and "moral" forms of revolutionary action, attacking reformism for "dissipating revolutionary strength" and the Socialist Revolutionaries, whose "scrupulous" terrorism will be discussed in the next chapter, for being both "exemplary and inefficacious". Lenin's point of view, in order to be understood, says Camus, "must always be considered in terms of strategy", his strategy being the preservation, at all costs, of the Bolshevik Revolution. It is only in this light, argues Camus, that we can make sense of the glaring contradictions in Lenin's pamphlet The State and Revolution. In it he does not merely play lip service to Engels's talk of the "withering away of the State"; he presents a philosophical exposition of the event: "As soon as there is no longer a social class which must be kept oppressed . . . a State ceases to be necessary. The first act by which the [proletarian] State really establishes itself as the representative of an entire society – the seizure of the society's means of production – is, at the same time, the last real act of the State." The dictatorship of the proletariat is thus necessary for two reasons: first, to suppress what remains of the bourgeois class; secondly, to bring about the social-ization of the means of production. "Once these two acts are accomplished", says Lenin, the state "immediately begins to wither away." However, in the same pam-phlet Lenin also justifies the preservation, even after the socialization of the means of production, and without any predicted end, of "the dictatorship of a revolutionary faction over the rest of the people". The pamphlet, argues Camus, makes continual references to the Paris Commune, yet "flatly contradicts the . . . federalist and anti-authoritarian ideas that produced the Commune". The reason for this is clear: Lenin, the strategist, "had not forgotten that the Commune failed". Later in the same pamphlet, and without any justification, Lenin asserts that power is necessary to crush the resistance of the bourgeois but also "to direct the great mass of the popu-lation, peasantry, lower middle classes, and semi-proletariat, in the management of the socialist economy". This is clearly very far from the provisional, transitional communist state envisaged by Marx and Engels. Accordingly, says Camus, already in these ideological formulations of Lenin can be found the contradiction in which contemporary Stalinism is mired: either the Soviet regime has realized that

> the classless socialist society, and the maintenance of a formidable apparatus of repression is not justified in Marxist terms, or it has not realised the class-less society and has therefore proved that Marxist doctrine is erroneous and, in particular, that the socialisation of the means of production does not mean the disappearance of classes. Confronted with its official doctrine, the regime is forced to choose: the doctrine is false, or the regime has betrayed it.
>
> (*R*: 227–30; *E*: 630–34)

The history of Russian communism, says Camus, "gives the lie to every one of its principles". It has been marked, from Lenin to Stalin, by an internecine struggle "between the workers' democracy and military and bureaucratic dictatorship; in other words, between justice and expediency". Lenin secured the triumph of expe-diency over justice, and with his institution of the dictatorship of the proletariat "even after control by the masses has been achieved", he also secures the triumph of the totalitarian, as opposed to merely authoritarian, state over freedom: "Finally it is announced that the end of the [provisional dictatorship of the proletariat] cannot be foreseen and that, what is more, no one has ever presumed to promise that there will be an end. After that it is logical that the autonomy of the soviets should be contested, Makhno betrayed, and the sailors of Kronstadt crushed by the party."[56] Camus therefore sees in the history of Soviet communism nothing less than the sys-tematic destruction of the values he claims are at the heart of "historical rebellion": justice and freedom. The "dialectical miracle" proclaimed by the Soviet Union and its apologists is in reality "the decision to call total servitude freedom"; the history of the Russian Revolution, though it lays claim to justice, constitutes in reality a "procession of violence and injustice" (*R*: 234, 240; *E*: 637, 643).

Unity and totality

Camus had earlier claimed that rebellion "is, above all, a demand for unity". The rebel, he says, "obstinately confronts a world condemned to death and the impenetrable obscurity of the human condition with his demand for life and absolute clarity. He is seeking, without knowing it, a moral philosophy or a religion."[57] As we have seen, what the rebel discovers is the unity implied in the human condition itself:

> the first progressive step for a mind overwhelmed by the strangeness of things is to realise that this feeling of strangeness is shared with all men and that human reality, in its entirety, suffers from the distance which separates it from the rest of the universe . . . in our daily trials rebellion plays the same role as does the "cogito" in the realm of thought: it is the first piece of evidence. But this evidence lures the individual from his solitude. It founds its first value on the whole human race. I rebel – therefore we exist.

The rebel pursues unity not through religion or morality per se, but through the assertion of human solidarity based on a common human condition. This principle of human solidarity constitutes the basis of the unity desired by the rebel, a unity Camus sees articulated in syndicalism and in certain forms of social democracy, such as the Scandinavian model. Crucially, as becomes clear later on, according to Camus authentic rebellion ends up dropping its "demand" for unity in favour of an "approximation": "Uncompromising as to its means, it would accept an approximation as far as its ends are concerned" (*R*: 22, 290; *E*: 432, 694).

Camus's main purpose at this stage in *The Rebel* is not to investigate what political form "authentic" rebellion might take, but to articulate reasons why the contemporary Soviet regime is a travesty of these principles. He argues that the revolutionary tradition exemplified by Soviet ideology demands not "unity" but "totality", an idea derived from Hegel, which is "in effect, nothing other than the ancient dream of unity common to both believers and rebels, but projected horizontally onto an earth deprived of God", thereby creating a "horizontal religion".[58] "In reality", Camus says later on, "the purely historical absolute is not even conceivable". Grasping totality is impossible, he argues, since one lives in the midst of this totality. History, as an entirety, "could only exist in the eyes of an observer outside it and outside the world. History only exists, in the final analysis, for God." Accordingly, it is "impossible to act according to plans embracing the totality of universal history" and therefore any given historical enterprise can be only "a more or less reasonable or justifiable venture". It is primarily a risk, and as such, that historical enterprise "cannot be used to justify any excess or any ruthless and absolutist position" (*R*: 289*; *E*: 692–3).

The suggestion that "totality" was at the heart of the intellectual heritage of the Soviet Union could hardly be said to be controversial, as indeed the debate about the nature of this "totality" has been a recurring theme in Marxist scholarship, perhaps especially since it was identified by Kojève with the Marxian "end of history".[59] The Marx scholar Kevin Anderson (1995: 72) suggests that it was Lenin himself who first introduced this idea of totality into Marxist discourse. In any case, what was controversial about Camus's analysis was not his claim that communist ideology aspired to "totality", but his identification of this "totality" (or "totalization") as the millenarian or eschatological root of the "totalitarian" reality of the Soviet Union. The historicist perspective (*la pensée historique*) of this revolutionary tradition, says Camus, "was to deliver man from subjection to a divinity; but this liberation demanded of him the most absolute subjection to historical evolution. Then man takes refuge in the permanence of the party in the same way that he formerly prostrated himself before the altar."[60] Rebellion "in its original authenticity" does not justify "any purely historical concept". Its "demand is unity", whereas "historical revolution's demand is totality". Exemplified by the slave's refusal of the master in the name of a value he recognizes in both himself and the master, authentic rebellion "starts from a negative supported by an affirmative". "Historical revolution", on the other hand, "starts from an absolute negation and condemns itself to every form of servitude in order to fabricate an affirmation which it then postpones until the end of time." It is therefore, repeats Camus, nihilist.[61] The legacy of the Russian Revolution is maintained, Camus says, only by "denying, to the advantage of history, both nature and beauty and by depriving man of the power of passion, doubt, happiness, and imaginative invention – in a word, of his greatness". Perhaps the most interesting, if not most important, word here is "doubt". It is this doubt, the recognition of the possibility of error, that perhaps most clearly separates the pursuit of totality from the pursuit of unity. The former cannot countenance the possibility of error; for the latter it is the recognition of the possibility of error that characterizes its pursuit. We shall see in Chapter 4 that, for Camus, it is the doubt about the legitimacy of his actions, combined with the fact that this doubt does not prevent him from acting, that makes the socialist revolutionary terrorist Kaliayev "the purest image of rebellion" (*R*: 240, 173; *E*: 643, 579).

Whereas the authentic rebel is characterized by his refusal to recognize the right of the powerful to punish on the basis of their power alone, in its most recent manifestation rebellion has become nothing but a trial, with history alone as judge. Accordingly, Lenin and Stalin are considered innocent; Bakunin and Trotsky guilty; Beria, like so many others, says Camus, was first innocent and only later proven to have been guilty all along. The universe of the trial finally culminates in the perversion of fact and in generalized culpability. In order to support the regime, the individual must have precisely the sort of faith defined by St Ignatius in his *Spiritual Exercises*: "We should always be prepared, so as never to err, to believe that what I see as white is black, if the hierarchic Church defines it thus" (quoted in *R*: 242; *E*: 645). Further, culpability no longer requires any basis in fact – it consists simply in the absence of faith. Whereas in a capitalist regime an individual claiming neutrality "is considered objectively to be favourable to the regime", in totalitarian society neutrality is considered to be objectively hostile to the regime. In this way the history of modern revolution seeks to stifle any remnants of the original rebellious impulse. The characteristics that define Prometheus are to be found not in the leaders of the Russian Revolution or their descendants, but among their victims (R: 244–5; E: 646–7).

As we shall see in Chapter 5, both Sartre and his colleague Francis Jeanson argued that Camus's preference for "unity" over "totality" in *The Rebel* made of their former comrade what Hegel dismissively referred to as a "beautiful soul"; that is, someone who attempts to "achieve personal wholeness by escaping from the world".[62] However, Camus concludes his analysis of Marxist "teleological socialism" not by rejecting history, but by rejecting the Marxist idea of history; that is, the idea that history was following a discernible path with a definite end and that it was itself the only source of human values.[63] Indeed, at the same time that he rejects his conception of history, Camus also argues that to attempt to create values without reference to history amounts to "ratifying historical injustice and the sufferings of man", adding, "thought that is derived from history alone, like thought that rejects history completely, deprives man of the means and the reason for living". Far from surreptitiously endorsing bourgeois morality through a hysterical attack on revolution, Camus insists that authentic rebellion has "nothing but scorn for the formal and mystifying morality to be found in bourgeois society", although it also recognizes that legitimate rebellion cannot exist without either a moral or metaphysical rule with which to counterbalance "the historicist delusion" (*le délire historique*). The mistake of revolutionaries, thinks Camus, where they have travestied the original rebellious impulse, has been to extend that scorn for traditional formal morality "to every moral demand". This despite the fact that the very source of rebellion is, he insists, an ethical claim regarding limits "that is not formal but nevertheless can serve as a guide".[64]

The Rebel, says Camus, proposes neither "a formal morality nor a dogma. It affirms only that a morality is possible and that it is costly."[65] What, then, should be the attitude of the rebel? He cannot turn away from history and seek solace in an extemporal fantasy, but neither can he submerge himself in an imagined "tide of history", in pursuit of its supposed "true" direction. Further, if the rebel refuses to make a choice, or chooses inaction, he effectively chooses "silence and the suffering of others" (R: 287*; E: 691). Camus proceeds to examine revolt from the perspective of the two values he suggests are at its heart – freedom and justice – and argues that the values that motivate the rebel's actions, and that his actions are designed to defend, are never absolute. The rebel is not concerned with either absolute justice or absolute freedom:

> Absolute freedom is the right of the strongest to dominate. Therefore it prolongs the conflicts that profit by injustice. Absolute justice is achieved by the suppression of all contradiction: therefore it destroys freedom. The revolution to achieve justice, through freedom, ends by aligning them against each other.[66]

Although the demands for justice and freedom are to be found at the nexus of rebellion, the history of revolutions tends to show that the two values inevitably conflict, to the point where they could be judged incompatible. However, notes Camus, this contradiction only exists in so far as the two values are understood as absolute, as opposed to relative, values. If rebellion could found a philosophy, "it would be a philosophy of limits".[67] This idea of a "philosophy of limits" neatly evokes both the limit beyond which the rebel insists the master not pass, and the sense that the values on behalf of which the rebel rebels are not absolute values. Otherwise stated, political actions and doctrines are legitimate to the extent to which they refute absolutism and reflect the needs of individuals and communities in relation to their own particular political, social and economic circumstances. For example, the rebel opposes injustice "not because it contradicts an eternal idea of justice, but because it perpetuates the silent hostility that separates the oppressor from the oppressed. It kills the small part of existence that can be realised on this earth through the mutual understanding of men."[68] Camus implies that the ideologically inspired pursuit of utopia, witnessed, for example, in the Soviet Union, is both intolerant of difference, in respect of the ways humans are different, and intolerant of commonality, in respect of the ways humans are the same (that is, in respect of human nature or, at least, the human condition). Furthermore, these contrasting forces of sameness and difference suggest to Camus that neither man nor society is perfectible.[69] Conversely, the generosity of the initial rebellious impulse, and the sense of solidarity derived from it, renders the issue almost irrelevant (once one has accepted the premise that the value ascribed to political action should be determined by its ameliorative successes, rather than the exhortatory quality of its utopian fantasy). Camus's claim is that absolute justice and absolute freedom are unattainable, and that all that individuals can aspire to is a more or less accurate approximation to these values. But more radically, he is also suggesting that revolt is not itself a demand for these absolute values. A legitimate revolutionary act, "a revolutionary action which wishes to be coherent in terms of its origins", as I have already noted, must be "uncompromising as to its means" yet will accept "an approximation as far as its ends are concerned".[70] This he labels a philosophy "of limits" or "*la mesure*" (usually – and, for some, misleadingly – translated as "moderation").

In stark contrast with this philosophy of limits, the totalitarian mind contrives to introduce "by the promise of absolute justice, the acceptance of perpetual injustice, of unlimited compromise and of indignity". It similarly travesties the ideal of freedom. The errors of contemporary revolution, says Camus, "are first of all explained by the ignorance or systematic misconception of that limit" which is revealed by rebellion. "Nihilist thought", which includes Soviet communism, "neglects this frontier", and it finally results in the theoretical justification of "total destruction and unlimited conquest . . . rebellion with no other limits but historical expediency signifies unlimited slavery".[71] Rebellion coherent with its origins, in contrast, "itself only aspires to the relative and can only promise an assured dignity coupled with relative justice", it "supposes a limit at which the community of man is established", and its universe "is the universe of relative values". Camus suggests that a contemporary illustration of authentic rebellion can be found in French revolutionary syndicalism. Against the frequent objection of other left-wing groups that syndicalism is ineffectual, Camus argues that it is thanks to these revolutionary trade unionists that workers in France enjoy the forty-hour week. He identifies as a core characteristic differentiating syndicalism from authoritarian or "caesarean" socialism the fact that trade unionism "started from a concrete basis, the basis of professional employment (which is to the economic order what the commune is to the political order), the living cell on which the organism builds itself". Authoritarian socialism, in contrast, "starts from doctrine and forcibly introduces reality into it". Trade unionism is "the negation, to the benefit of reality, of bureaucratic and abstract centralism". In contrast, the Marxist revolution manifest in the Soviet Union "cannot, by its very function, avoid terror and violence done to the real. Despite its pretensions, it begins in the absolute and attempts to mould reality." Rebellion, inversely, "relies on reality to assist in its perpetual struggle for truth" and ultimately, "when it causes history to advance and alleviates the suffering of mankind, it does so without terror, if not without violence". This conflict between the origins of rebellion and its expression in the USSR is further exemplified, says Camus, in the early history of international socialism. The First International, he argues, was marked by the ceaseless struggle of German socialism to overcome the libertarian thought of the French, Spanish and Italians socialists.[72] Similarly, the era immediately after the October Revolution saw the imprisonment or liquidation of its "rebellious opponents", including the Socialist Revolutionaries (see Savinkov 1931; Steinberg 1935). Communist parties throughout Europe were implacable in their hostility to non-Marxist forms of socialism throughout the twentieth century. Nevertheless, despite the best efforts of the autocratic Marxists, libertarian, syndicalist and anarchist movements were never submerged completely. Since rebellion emerges as a direct consequence of suffering, the effort to suppress rebellion by force was inevitably to have the opposite effect.

Moderation, Camus hopes he has made adequately clear by now, does not condemn or preclude the possibility of rebellion. In fact, rebellion itself is precisely a demand for moderation, "and it demands, defends, and re-creates [moderation] throughout history and its eternal disturbances". Anticipating the argument that his advocacy of rebellion and legitimate violence is obscure and paradoxical, he asserts that "every undertaking that is more ambitious than this proves to be contradictory". As ambiguous as rebellion might be, it nevertheless avoids the stark contradictions Camus has identified in the murderous ideologies of the modern era: he insists that it is not his intention to present "formulas for optimism" in *The Rebel*, formulas for which, he says, "we have no possible use . . . in the extremities of our unhappiness". Instead, he proposes that the essence of *The Rebel* be considered as "words of courage and intelligence", which despite everything have the qualities of virtue. We can, he says, hope for no more than that. Rebellion involves the effort to "rectify in creation everything that can be rectified". Yet even by his greatest effort, the rebel "can only propose to diminish arithmetically the sufferings of the world", and although he appreciates that "the injustice and suffering of the world will remain", such suffering and injustice will never cease "to be an outrage" (*R*: 301–3; *E*: 704–6).

As we have seen, historically there have been two substantial expressions of rebellion: Christianity and Marxist materialism. Effectively, Christianity has responded to the rebel's protest with the promise of a future kingdom and eternal life, and suffering is usually explained in terms of a mystery which requires acceptance. It "postpones to a point beyond the span of history the cure of evil and murder, which are nevertheless experienced within the span of history". Contemporary materialism, likewise, explains suffering in terms of a future point in history, although in this instance the ideology tends to increase "the domain of historic murder". Both ideologies, in any case, demand faith; in both cases "one must wait" while "the innocent continue to die". Twenty centuries, says Camus, have passed, and the sum total of evil in the world "has not diminished [and] no paradise, whether divine or revolutionary, has been realised". Yet the human species still recognizes an injustice "inextricably bound to all suffering, even the most deserved in the eyes of men. The long silence of Prometheus before the powers that overwhelmed him still cries out in protest." These thoughts remind us that the most important characteristic of rebellion is the profession of solidarity at its heart. It is precisely this solidarity, argues Camus, that was to be found among those Catholic prisoners in Franco's Spain who refused Holy Communion "because the priests of the regime had made it obligatory in certain prisons. These lonely witnesses to the crucifixion of innocence also refused salvation if it must be paid for by injustice and oppression." This "tremendous generosity [*folle générosité*] is the generosity of rebellion". In contrast to ideologies that make a fetish of the future, for the rebel, "real generosity toward the future lies in giving all to the present" (*R*: 303–4*; *E*: 706–7).

The forgetting of that generosity, the replacement of living man with an abstraction, is the travesty of rebellion. Forgetful of its origins, contemporary revolutionary ideology "denies life, dashes toward destruction, and raises up the grimacing cohort of petty rebels, embryo slaves all of them who end by offering themselves for sale, today, in all the market places of Europe, to no matter what form of servitude". It "is no longer either revolution or rebellion but rancour, malice, and tyranny". The modern ideologists "forget the present for the future, the fate of humanity for the delusion of power, the misery of the slums for the mirage of the eternal city, ordinary justice for an empty promised land". They "no longer believe in the things that exist in the world and in living man" (*R*: 304–5; *E*: 707, 708). Yet the validity of an act of rebellion is dependent upon its eschewal of political myths or grand narratives in its justification:[73]

> Each time that [rebellion] deifies the total rejection, the absolute negation, of what exists it destroys. Each time that it blindly accepts what exists and gives voice to absolute assent, it destroys again. Hatred of the creator can turn to hatred of creation or to exclusive and defiant love of what exists. But in both cases it ends in murder and loses the right to be called rebellion. One can be nihilist in two ways, in both by having an intemperate recourse to absolutes.[74]

There is no doubt that Camus's presentation of what he calls "*la pensée de midi*" is primarily lyrical, and there is little attempt to support it with practical suggestions, beyond brief comments in relation to the possibility of a rejuvenation of syndicalism and a favourable appraisal of the Scandinavian model of social democracy. Nevertheless, it is not at all clear why we should expect so much from Camus in one book, least of all a book the declared purpose of which was to "face the reality of the present, which is logical crime, and to examine meticulously the arguments by which it is justified".[75] He may not have been as successful as we would have liked in transforming his essentially negative criticism of the history of revolutions into a practical description of how the excesses that travesty the rebellious momentum could be avoided, but to have achieved such a goal would be to have achieved something beyond the declared, relatively modest, scope of the essay.

However, as recalcitrant as Camus's ideas of limits and "*la mesure*" may be to systematic analysis (and I have no doubt that they are), some effort can be made to present his ideas in a clear fashion. This can be conveniently done by consideration of his account of freedom and justice, which is the most concrete extrapolation from a frequently nebulous discussion. He argues, as we have seen, that absolute freedom denies justice and that absolute justice denies freedom, and suggests that "to be fruitful, the two ideas must find their limits in each other".[76] In her analysis of these concepts, Annabel Herzog argues that Camus's political and moral concerns "never diverged from his aporetic attempt to reach an 'agreement' between two concepts that he regarded as incompatible: justice and freedom". This set of concerns led Camus, at least initially, "to an original – albeit rather hopeless – view of the human condition". Herzog argues that for Camus reconciliation between the demands of justice and freedom "could at least find a partial *solution* in art", since, "contrary to nihilist ideologies that 'divinize' human beings, and neglect the limits of the human condition, art takes reality into account, and only then does it attempt to make changes that provide a 'correction' of our condition". The political significance of this insight may seem limited to the point of irrelevance, but according to Herzog, it does define a particular role for the artist whose "political and moral function . . . is to insert contradictions and aporias into the public domain", thereby deflating or destabilizing the obnoxious certainties of the political and intellectual elite (Herzog 2005: 188, 196, 197). Herzog is surely correct to stress both the significant role the artist plays in the shaping of Camus's moral and political ideas, and the increased relevance of Camus to the current period of renewed political Manichaeism among terrorists and counterterrorists.[77] However, I think that her interpretation may overlook the extent to which Camus's concept of rebellion did not in fact demand absolute freedom and absolute justice (the "contradictory" values that are at the source of the aporia identified by Herzog), but sought a relative freedom and a relative justice, which are not in themselves incompatible. For this reason, it may be worth comparing it with the Greek concept of *sophrosyne*.[78]

Sophrosyne, which is usually translated as either "moderation" or "temperance", is one of the four cardinal virtues as defined by Plato in the *Republic* (the others being wisdom, justice and courage), and is said to relate to "the Greek tendency to interpret all kinds of experience – whether moral, political, aesthetic, physical, or metaphysical – in terms of harmony and proportion" (North 1966: 258). There are a number of more precise renderings that can be useful to present purposes. In Homer, for example, *sophrosyne* is associated with modesty and consciousness of one's limitations, and in Theognis of Megara it is seen as the absence of hubris (overbearing pride and presumption). Similarly, in Aeschylean tragedy, *sophrosyne* is consistently linked with a set of desirable qualities, including justice and freedom, and is opposed to arrogance, immoderate behaviour and other forms of hubris.[79] Significantly, as we have seen, in *The Rebel* Aeschylus's Prometheus replaces Sisyphus as the symbolic representative of humankind; Prometheus, in Camus's account, does not "range himself against all creation, but against Zeus, who is never anything more than one god among many" (and Prometheus himself is a demigod). Hence Camus argues that the myth of Prometheus is not an account of hubris, not a Manichaean account "of a universal struggle between good and evil", but is "a dispute about what is good" (*R*: 27; *E*: 439). Explicitly evoking the Hellenic sense of *la mesure*, in a later essay, "In defence of *The Rebel*", Camus claimed that

> *la mesure* is not therefore the casual resolution of contraries. It is nothing other than the affirmation of contradiction, and the firm decision to insist upon it in order to outlive it. What I call excess [*la démesure*] is that movement of the soul that passes blindly beyond the frontier where opposites balance each other in order to finally take its stand in drunken consent, the cowardly and cruel examples of which abound before our eyes.
>
> (*SCHC*: 213*; *E*: 1710)

Camusian revolt, exemplified in Prometheus, therefore finds its validity in its insistence upon *limits*. And these limits are grounded ultimately upon the consequences of the absurd: "The absurd", Camus noted in *The Myth of Sisyphus*, is "lucid reason noting its limits" (*MS*: 49; *E*: 134).

However strong these affinities with Hellenic thought may be, unsurprisingly Camus's talk of limits, moderation and so on has frequently been interpreted as clear evidence of his political inconsequence. The conspicuous absence from *The Rebel* of a clear alternative to the historicist thought it criticizes at such length has led many to interpret it as an essentially "unpolitical" work. Although the book was received with some considerable enthusiasm, notably in the anarchist and libertarian press, its fundamentally negative commentary on the contemporary history of revolution met with hostility from many of Camus's erstwhile comrades on the predominantly Marxist-Leninist left, most notoriously from Sartre's journal *Les Temps modernes*. Notwithstanding the enmity contained in his critique generally, Sartre was among a very few critics who recognized the intellectual coherence of *The Myth of Sisyphus* and *The Rebel*.[80] However, as we shall also see, in Sartre's estimation it is because of precisely this coherence, specifically because of the dependence of revolt on Camus's absurd premise, that his work inexorably evolved towards a sort of critical entropy that rendered it politically worthless. Sartre declared *The Rebel*, precisely in its political insignificance, to be the culmination of Camus's life's work. He not only sought to ridicule Camus's anxieties about Marxist historicism; he was particularly critical of his advocacy of a philosophy based on the idea of limits and moderation (*la mesure*), attributing it to "your internal difficulties" (*SCHC*: 132*; Sartre 1952: 334). Similarly, Francis Jeanson, who reviewed *The Rebel* in *Les Temps modernes*, claimed that, on the evidence of *The Rebel*, politically Camus was neither on the left nor the right but "up in the air" (*SCHC*: 188; Jeanson 1952b: 372). Although perhaps for different reasons, as we have already noted, Tony Judt also believed that Camus was essentially "unpolitical".[81]

Nevertheless, as Jeffrey Isaac has argued, it can be suggested that if Camus was unpolitical, he was unpolitical in a particularly interesting way, in that his refusal to "take sides" can be interpreted as the action of an "independent radical", as opposed to the chronic inaction of a Hegelian "beautiful soul" (*SCHC*: 265–7; Isaac 1992: 148–59). After all, Camus's critical independence was reflected not only in his criticism of teleological socialism, but also in his attitude to the political status quo generally, as can be seen from the repeated criticism of bourgeois "formal morality" we find in *The Rebel*, as well as in his affiliation with organizations such as the Groupes de liaison internationale and his support and writing for the revolutionary syndicalist newspaper *La Révolution Prolétarienne*. Isaac has pointed out that this perspective on Camus's political thought highlights a marked affinity with the more contemporary "antipolitical politics" of East European dissident intellectuals such as Václav Havel and George Konrád, who "have long abjured prevailing forms and strategies of political opposition, whether revolutionary or reformist", instead favouring "an antistatist politics driven by self-constituted and self-limiting political agents, associations of individuals confident in their capacity for creative opposition and profoundly aware of their own limits". With names such as Dialogue, Civic Forum, Solidarity and Democratic Forum, these dissident groups, notes Isaac, "seemed to incarnate the 'solidarity of chains' of which Camus wrote" (Isaac 1992: 248, 250, 252–3; cf. *R*: 281; *E*: 684). Havel, who after many years as a political prisoner became, in 1989, the first president of post-communist Czechoslovakia, claimed to favour "politics as practical morality, as service to the truth, as essentially human and humanly measured care for our fellow humans" (Havel 1987b: 155). In an interview in 1987, which clearly resonates with Camus's idea of "relative utopia", introduced in "Neither Victims nor Executioners" and pursued in *The Rebel*, Havel explains that although he has severe reservations about utopianism ("What is a concentration camp", he asks "but an attempt by utopians to dispose of those elements which don't fit in?"), he does not think that this should prohibit him from what his interviewer calls his "modest utopian scheming . . . for the strengthening of human qualities such as love, sympathy, tolerance, understanding, solidarity and friendship". He explains that there is a "fine difference between striving for particular ideals, and creating a blueprint for creating them. A utopia is really the materialisation of an ideal – and is obviously easier and more convenient to deal with. At the same time, it is more dangerous, because the moment that we put all our faith and trust in a specific project for implementing them, we lose touch with the ideals themselves."[82] Camus, according to Isaac, "saw that the dominant political agencies of our world – nation-states, bureaucracies, political parties – are remote, impervious to ordinary people and uninterested in ambiguity. And he saw that there is much to be said for a politics based largely on a *resistance* to such agencies rather than the pursuit of grand, and illusory, ideological objectives" (*SCHC*: 266). Similarly, the chief theoretician of antipolitics, George Konrád:

> A society does not become politically conscious when it shares some political philosophy, but rather when it refuses to be fooled by any of them. The apolitical person is only the dupe of the professional politician, whose real adversary is the antipolitician. It is the antipolitician who wants to keep the scope of government policy (especially that of its military apparatus) under the control of civil society. (Konrád 1984: 227)

Isaac suggests that although this new politics of civil society may have much to learn from traditional forms of political radicalism (such as democratic socialism), it is "absurd" to assert that this political movement "represents a 'loss of nerve', a 'full retreat' from the 'traditional role of the Western left as a critic of capitalism'".[83] Certainly for Camus such ideas, although marginalized in the history of political radicalism, remained discernible in certain concrete manifestations of revolt: he recognizes them in the Scandinavian model of social democracy, in revolutionary syndicalism in Spain and in France, and even in the terrorism of certain pre-Bolshevik Russian revolutionary organizations, such as the Socialist Revolutionaries.

Shortly after his violent dispute with Sartre over *The Rebel*, Camus drafted an essay in which he reiterates and defends several of its core arguments.[84] Centrally, he argues that *The Rebel* does not amount to a condemnation of revolution; instead it insists that revolution must not forget its origins: "Indeed I concluded . . . that in order to reject organised terror and the police, revolution needs to keep intact the spirit of revolt that has given it birth, just as revolt needs a revolutionary development [*prolongement*] in order to find substance and truth. Each, finally, is the limit of the other." Furthermore, he insists that *The Rebel* is a "condemnation [not] of history in the name of the individual", but of historicism, the subordination of the individual to history (*SCHC*: 212, 214; *E*: 1709, 1711). Indeed, although Camus repeatedly condemns historicism as a cruel and merciless mystification, he nowhere denies the individual's historicity (or "historical situatedness"). It is for this reason that William McBride is mistaken in his claim that "the nostalgia for transcendence . . . appears in its full splendour in *The Rebel*" (*SCHC*: 243). Camus makes no appeal whatever to transcendent values in *The Rebel*.[85] Instead, he argues that on the basis of a common humanity (something that is universal but not transcendent) it should be possible to create values, such values as come into being in the act of rebellion itself. It is the very absence of transcendence that informs his philosophy of "limits". Ronald Aronson (2004: 118) has suggested that there is something very "Sartrean" in this idea that revolt creates values. However, Camus recognizes that this desire to create values was also present in those expressions of revolt *The Rebel* explicitly criticizes, so the claim to create values is not unique to authentic or legitimate rebellion. What differentiates the activity of creating value in the context of authentic rebellion is that it is achieved by appeal to and in the context of relative values, such as relative justice and freedom, as opposed to what Karl Popper called the "Inexorable Laws of Historical Destiny" (Popper 1960: v).

Crucially, according to Camus, legitimate rebellion seeks neither absolute justice nor absolute freedom, but seeks to institute a regime of relative values, wherein relative justice and relative freedom can be enjoyed. In stark contrast, Soviet communism, which has appropriated the "metaphysical ambition" that is "the erection, after the death of God, of a city of man finally deified", is characterized by the deferral of freedom in the name of justice.[86] Specifically, Camus identified as the acme of this ideological hubris, this pursuit of totality, the historical materialism inaugurated by Marx, manifested in the Soviet Union and defended by its allies in the West. Although he sees much to admire in Marx, as we have seen, a large part of *The Rebel* constitutes a sustained critique of the Marxist theory of history, which he characterizes as the invocation of "History" to justify an indifference to the terrible human costs of radical political choices. Camus saw in Marx no insight into the "mechanism of History"; instead he saw Marxism as a millenarian act of "divinisation of history", anathema to the origins of revolt. He saw the tragedy of a radically desacralized society that had made itself, as Tony Judt has it, "an ersatz of religion and thus an object of its own adoration".[87] Camus insists that all our political aspirations should be relative or ameliorative, but as Isaac notes, this does not mean that "we ought not to have aspirations", only that our aspirations be undergirded by a sense of limits and moderation (*SCHC*: 264).

4 | CAMUS AND POLITICAL VIOLENCE

The scrupulous assassin

In the final section of *The Rebel* Camus asserts that since the beginning of its revolt against God, the "European mind" had believed that it had "all humanity as its ally". However, it subsequently became apparent to the rebel that if he were not to be defeated, he must also learn to fight against men. The dilemma of the rebel is thus posed in the following terms: "if they retreat they must accept death; if they advance they must accept murder. Rebellion, cut off from its origins and cynically travestied, oscillates, on all levels, between sacrifice and murder." Rebellion had originally pleaded the case of the innocence of man, but now "it has hardened its heart against its own culpability". Must we, as a consequence, "renounce every kind of rebellion", even if it means accepting a society weighed down with injustice or serving the interests of history even against the interests of man? Can the original, allegedly irrefutable rebellious proposition ("I revolt, therefore we exist") be reconciled with killing? The original moment of revolt assigned oppression a limit, "within which begins the dignity common to all men". It defined a "primary value", in that "it put in the first rank of its frame of reference" a point of contact between human beings, "which makes men both similar and united". It posited a profound solidarity and "compelled the mind to take a first step in defiance of an absurd world". How can this solidarity be reconciled with the problem of killing? On the level of the absurd, says Camus, the problem of murder would give rise only to "logical contradictions; on the level of rebellion it is mental laceration". For at this point, it is a question of deciding whether it is possible to kill someone "whose resemblance to ourselves we have just recognised and whose identity we have just sanctified". Having just "conquered solitude" by declaring the rebel's solidarity with humanity, "must we then re-establish it definitively by legitimising the act that isolates everything? To force solitude on a man who has just come to understand that he is not alone, is that not the definitive crime against man?"[1]

"Logically", says Camus, "one should reply that murder and rebellion are contradictory." In one clear sense, once the rebel has killed a master, he is no longer justified in using the term "community of men" from which he derives his justification. The rebel's justification is based on the common humanity of both master and slave; however, once he kills the master, he consecrates their "difference in blood". The rebel's act of killing, "intended to affirm him, thus brings an end to his existence". If it is not possible to speak of the solidarity of every man, then, for the rebel, it is not possible to speak of solidarity at all: "If we are not, then I am not"; if such solidarity is impossible so is such rebellion. "On the level of history, as in individual life, murder is thus a desperate exception or it is nothing. The disturbance that it brings to the order of things offers no hope of a future; it is an exception and therefore it can be neither utilitarian nor systematic as the purely historic attitude would have it." The only way that the rebel has to reconcile himself with his freely chosen act of assassination appears to be to accept with the same gravity his own death and sacrifice: "he kills and dies so that it shall be clear that murder is impossible [that is to say, morally impermissible]" (R: 281–2; E: 685–6). Anything beyond this extreme point seems to constitute a denial of the solidarity inherent in rebellion.

The rebel is motivated by the desire "to serve justice so as not to add to the injustice of the human condition". Accordingly, rebellion must "refuse to legitimise murder because rebellion, in principle, is a protest against death". However, rebellion only exists because injustice and violence "are part of the rebel's condition" (R: 285; E: 688–9). As a consequence of this, according to Camus, the rebel faces what appears to be his greatest dilemma:

> He cannot, therefore, absolutely claim not to kill or lie, without renouncing his rebellion and accepting, once and for all, evil and murder. But no more can he agree to kill and lie, since the inverse reasoning which would justify murder and violence would also destroy the reasons for his insurrection. Thus the rebel can never find peace. He knows what is good and, despite himself, does evil. The value that supports him is never given to him once and for all; he must fight to uphold it, unceasingly. . . . In any case, if he is not always able not to kill, either directly or indirectly, he can put his conviction and passion to work at diminishing the chances of murder around him.[2]

What then should be the attitude of the rebel? He cannot turn away from history and seek solace in an extemporal fantasy, and neither can he immerse himself in the tide of history, in pursuit of its supposed "true" direction. Further, if the rebel refuses to make a choice, he effectively chooses "silence and the suffering of others" (R: 287*; E: 691). In *The Rebel* Camus identifies two conventional ways of interpreting political violence, the "bourgeois" and the "revolutionary", both of which he considers fatally problematic. He defines the "bourgeois" account of political violence as simply the refusal to recognize one of the terms of the dilemma highlighted by political violence. This response judges all forms of direct violence morally impermissible, but finds it acceptable to sanction the varied forms of violence that are enacted daily on the stage of world history. The second interpretation, the "revolutionary" interpretation of political violence, is premised for Camus on the belief that violence is necessary, necessary to the point of making history nothing but "a continuous violation of everything in man which protests against injustice".[3] Camus had in mind here arguments such as that advanced by Merleau-Ponty in his *Humanism and Terror*, which sought to justify revolutionary violence on the basis that, since the world is pervaded by violence, "we ought to prefer revolutionary violence because it has a future of humanism" (Merleau-Ponty 1969: 107).

These observations from Camus deserve our close attention, not because they are especially complex or innovative, but because they indicate to us quite clearly that the ideas regarding the relative legitimacy of particular acts of political violence developed in *The Rebel*, the play *The Just Assassins* and elsewhere constitute neither a philosophy of necessary, humanizing or cathartic violence, nor, more importantly, a defence of the political status quo, on the grounds that political violence could potentially precipitate a deterioration, rather than an amelioration, in the general welfare of society. This latter charge, as we shall see, is more often than not brought against Camus when his writing on political violence is given any attention at all.

In contrast to these two conventional views of political violence, Camus proposes an alternative limited defence of political violence, which he illustrates by reference to the "military wing"[4] of the Russian Socialist Revolutionary Party, one-time political rivals, and ultimately political victims, of the Bolsheviks. We shall see that the Socialist Revolutionary Ivan Kaliayev, who appears in *The Rebel* and features in *The Just Assassins*, is at the heart of Camus's ideas about legitimate political violence. For Camus, Kaliayev "proves", no less, "that though the revolution is a necessary means, it is not a sufficient end". The revolutionary tradition exemplified by Kaliayev recognizes human solidarity ("universal recognition") as a "necessary" condition of legitimate revolution, although, crucially, it also recognizes this solidarity as "insufficient" (*R*: 172–3; *E*: 578–9). The twentieth century has, according to Camus, been marked by the suppression of this paradoxical conception of political revolt and the success of what he calls "state terrorism", "rebellion, cut off from its real roots, unfaithful to man in having surrendered to history", a messianic conception of revolution that, as he argued in *The Rebel*, has given birth "to the totalitarian revolution of the twentieth century" (*R*: 174; *E*: 579–80). But Kaliayev was only one of a number of such "scrupulous assassins", whose distinctive spirit is perhaps best summed up by another Socialist Revolutionary, Maria Spiridonova, who in 1906 assassinated General Luzhenovsky for his brutal treatment of the peasants in the Tambov province of Russia, and who, during the 1917 revolution, was "the most loved and the most powerful woman in all Russia".[5] By September 1918, however, Spiridonova was imprisoned in Moscow, from where, refusing to answer the charges brought against her or to recognize the jurisdiction of the court, she published an open letter addressed to the Central Committee of the Bolshevik Party. Protesting against the grotesquely violent regime that the Bolsheviks had initiated in order to consolidate their position, she wrote:

> You call this terror. But in the history of the Russian Revolution this word has never meant to signify revenge or intimidation. . . . The most important element in the terror was *protest* against the oppression of despotism, an attempt to arouse indignation in the souls of humiliated men and women, to fire the conscience of those who stood silent in face of this humiliation. That is how the terrorist advanced on the enemy. And almost always did the terrorist combine his deed with the voluntary sacrifice of his own life and freedom. I believe that only thus was it possible to justify the terrorist act of the revolutionary.   (Quoted in Steinberg 1955: 132)

The terrorists (as they called themselves) no doubt desired the destruction of the absolutist regime of tsarist Russia, and sought it through direct and violent action. Yet we see from this declaration of Spiridonova that central to the terrorism prac-tised by the Socialist Revolutionaries was the assassin's willingness to sacrifice his or her own life. It is here that we begin to see that which constitutes, for Camus, the particular importance of the terrorism of the Socialist Revolutionaries: they forgot nothing of what he considered the origins of revolt and the paradoxical premise on which it was based, human solidarity.

The hero of *The Just Assassins*, Kaliayev, waits on a Moscow street for the car-riage of the Grand Duke Sergius Alexandrovitch Romanov, the Tsar's uncle and Governor of Moscow, into which he is to throw a bomb.[6] However, when the carriage appears, Kaliayev notices that it carries not just the Grand Duke, but also his wife and his young nephew and niece. Kaliayev abandons his task, unwilling to sacrifice the lives of children. This refusal to throw the bomb is understood by all his associates but one, Stepan, who believes that the lives of two children would be a small price for the liberation of the serfs. Kaliayev finds such reasoning repugnant: the ends, he believes, cannot justify the means. Thus far, Camus has pitched a "scrupulous assassin", Kaliayev, against the totalitarian revolutionary (in the guise of Stepan) and, of course, in this regard, there is no surprise regarding where Camus's sympathies lie. Two days after the aborted assassination attempt, Kaliayev tries again. This time the carriage carries the Grand Duke alone. The bomb is thrown, and the Grand Duke is killed. Kaliayev makes no effort to escape, refuses all deals with the police and even an offer of pardon from the Grand Duke's widow. It is in these respects, and not simply in his ultimate self-sacrifice, that Kaliayev is differ-entiated from Stepan. The latter clearly resembles the archetypal revolutionary as described in Nechayev's *Revolutionary Catechism*: "The revolutionary is a marked individual. He has no interests, no business, no personal feelings, no bonds, nothing that is his alone, not even his name. Everything in him is swallowed up by a single exclusive interest, a single thought, a single passion: Revolution" (quoted in *NB2*: 177–8; *C2*: 226). And although Kaliayev defended revolutionary action "for the sake of life – to give life a chance", and his comrade Annenkov insists that "you must not say that everything is justifiable . . . thousands of us have died to prove that everything is *not* justifiable!", Stepan insists: "Not until the day comes when we stop being sentimental about children, will the revolution triumph and we be masters of the world. . . . Nothing that can serve our cause should be ruled out. . . . There are no limits."[7]

As we have seen, in *The Rebel* Camus asserts that rebellion is based upon the recognition of a common human condition, and finds its justification only in solidarity: "I rebel – therefore we exist" constitutes the rebel's *cogito* (R: 22; E: 432). Accordingly, the values of rebellion and solidarity are presented to us as the basis for an ethical understanding of legitimate political action:

> We have, then, the right to say that any rebellion which claims the right to deny or destroy this solidarity loses simultaneously its right to be called rebellion and becomes in reality an acquiescence in murder. In the same way this solidarity, except in so far as religion in concerned, comes to light only on the level of rebellion. And so the real drama of revolutionary thought is announced. In order to exist, man must rebel, but rebellion must respect the limit it discovers in itself – a limit where minds meet and, in meeting, begin to exist. Rebellious thought cannot therefore dispense with memory: it is a perpetual state of tension. In studying its actions and its results, we shall have to say, each time, whether it remains faithful to its first noble promise or if, through indolence or folly, it forgets its original purpose and plunges into a mire of tyranny or servitude.   (R: 22; E: 431)

The Socialist Revolutionaries never denied or ignored the paradoxical position in which they found themselves: "necessary and inexcusable – that is how killing appeared to them".[8] Rather than seeking repose in a theory that offered them resolution at the price of hypocrisy, they conceived the idea of offering their own lives as a justification for their acts. The principle of paying for a life with a life here appears to form the basis for a radically different theory of legitimate violence.

There seem, however, to be clear inconsistencies in such a conception of legitimate violence. First, it appears that certain acts of killing may not require that a perpetrator voluntarily offer up his or her own life in exchange: in cases of self-defence, for example, or in cases of resistance against murderous oppression (Camus would hardly have suggested that French *résistants* ought to have given themselves up to Nazi justice). Secondly, it would seem that a life taken has not the same moral value as a life offered. Kaliayev may have been prepared to sacrifice his own life, but obviously his victim, Grand Duke Sergi, did not in any way "offer" his.[9] Specifically, this willingness to die on the part of the perpetrator compromises the idea that there is a moral equivalence between the two deaths. Being willing to *die* for what one believes is perhaps admirable, but it doesn't itself justify *killing* for what one believes. Clearly, then, there is something flawed in the idea that some kind of moral equilibrium is restored with the self-immolation of the assassin.

Nevertheless, the example of Socialist Revolutionaries is undoubtedly fundamental to Camus's conception of legitimate violence, and we shall see that the ideas regarding morally permissible killing developed in *The Rebel* and elsewhere appear to take full account of both of the objections outlined above. What the rebels of 1905 illustrate, says Camus, is that rebellion cannot lead to "the consolation and comfort of dogma". In fact, the characteristic that seems to best define Kaliayev in Camus's mind is not his self-sacrifice, but his doubt. He states explicitly that it is the fact of this doubt, combined with the fact that this doubt does not prevent him from acting, that makes of Kaliayev "the purest image of rebellion".[10]

For Camus, the history of twentieth-century political violence has been the history of the travesty of these ideas. The revolutionary groups that spread throughout Russia through the late nineteenth and early twentieth centuries culminated in the revolution of 1917. But from the revolution of 1917 emerged not a realization of the dream shared by these early rebels, but the era of what Camus calls "caesarean socialism" and "state terrorism", in which the Bolsheviks set out to consolidate their position by systematically liquidating their ideological opponents. "Caesarean socialism", says Camus, "undoubtedly condemns individual terrorism to the extent that it revives values incompatible with the domination of historical reason. But it will restore terror on the level of the State"; state terrorism is "rebellion, cut off from its real roots, unfaithful to man in having surrendered to history".[11] The paradox of revolt, exemplified in Kaliayev, is suppressed in the name of historical expediency and historical reason.[12]

In contrast, as we have seen in the previous chapter, Camus insists that the rebel conscious of the origins of his revolt will recognize that the values that motivate his actions, and that his actions are designed to defend, are never absolute: the rebel, as we have already noted, is not concerned with either absolute justice or absolute freedom, because they are deemed to be incompatible (*R*: 287–8; *E*: 691). All individuals can aspire to is a more or less accurate approximation to these values. But more radically, he was also suggesting that rebellion is not itself a demand for these absolute values. A legitimate revolutionary act – "a revolutionary action which wishes to be coherent in terms of its origins" – must be uncompromising as to its means, but will accept an approximation as far as its ends are concerned (*R*: 290; *E*: 694). However, this constructive attitude cannot be the full solution, and Camus has already recognized that there are instances when violence is a legitimate response to oppression. Nevertheless, he suggests, even in instances of legitimate violent revolt certain limits must be observed if just revolt is not to become unjust. In fact, if we examine the acts of justified killing in the works of Camus, specifically the assassination of Grand Duke Sergi in *The Just Assassins* and that of Caligula in the eponymous play (the latter surprisingly neglected in respect of Camus's ideas on political violence), we can identify a number of characteristics that appear to distinguish an act of justified killing.[13] These characteristics may, of course, be interpreted in terms of their dramatic effect or the exigencies of theatrical production, but it seems that they also offer substantial insight into Camus's thoughts on legitimate political violence. A consideration of *Caligula* in this regard seems especially fecund, not least because there is no suggestion that the assassination of Caligula ought to be followed by the deaths of his assassins. Indeed, the subtle yet significant ways in which Camus's Caligula differs from Suetonius's make it difficult, in my view, to exaggerate the importance of the play with respect to the present discussion. I would suggest that a consideration of the acts of assassination at the heart of *The Just Assassins* and *Caligula* indicates that for Camus the following conditions, at least, must be met for an act of killing to be deemed legitimate:

- The victim is a tyrant. The character of Caligula, of course, is synonymous with tyranny, and in *The Just Assassins*, Kaliayev repeatedly insists that the target of his bomb is the "despotism" and "tyranny" represented by, or manifested in, the Grand Duke.[14]
- The act must be discriminate. Although it is otherwise similar, in detail Camus's *Caligula* differs from his source, Suetonius, in two highly significant ways. First, in Suetonius, Caligula's assassins also kill his mistress, Caesonia, and his young daughter. In Camus's version the daughter is written out of the play and, as if to underline his monstrous nature, Caligula himself kills Caesonia. Similarly, we remember that in *The Just Assassins* Kaliayev aborts his first assassination attempt on Grand Duke Sergi because the carriage carrying the Grand Duke also carries his nephew and niece. The innocence of civilians is central to Camus's thinking on political violence, as is highlighted by one of his most important (not to say effective) interventions in the Algerian war, his "Call for a Civil Truce" in January 1956.
- The assassination is committed by a rebel in close proximity to his victim, and the assassin must accept full responsibility for his individual action. This brings us to the second way in which Camus's *Caligula* differs from Suetonius. In Suetonius the facts of the assassination of Caligula are uncertain, but in Camus's play, it is stated clearly that the play's hero, Cherea, actually stabs Caligula in the face, a peculiarly brutal detail, meaningful only in so far as it is of precise symbolic value.[15] In *The Just Assassins*, Kaliayev throws the bomb into the Grand Duke's carriage from a distance of a few feet; he makes no attempt to escape and immediately accepts responsibility for his action.[16] This point regarding the proximity of the assassin needs much refinement, but its contemporary relevance should not be underestimated at a time when wars, especially those fought by wealthy countries, are so often fought, in large part, from safe distances.
- There is no less violent alternative to assassination. This is effectively implied in the first condition above, relating to the tyrannical nature of the victim (Caligula wished his horse to be consul, the Romanovs had their Bloody Sunday), but it should be stated explicitly nevertheless.

Camus is clearly acutely aware of the ambiguities surrounding talk of permissible killing. His primary intention is to show not that in certain instances killing is morally unproblematic, but that the killing of a human being must remain the greatest exception to ordinary human experience, that while it might be sometimes morally justifiable, it can never be habitual. He writes approvingly of the moral dilemma upon which the Socialist Revolutionaries continually reflected, a dilemma that, nevertheless, did not prevent them from acting (*R*: 169; *E*: 575). It is for this reason, perhaps, that his discussion of permissible killing in *The Rebel, The Just Assassins* and elsewhere is so frequently ambiguous. An act of permissible killing must achieve the status in society not just of an exception, but of the greatest of all exceptions. Although certain acts of killing may be morally justified, it is imperative for Camus that such acts are never represented as being morally transparent or unambiguous. He is adamant that an act of justifiable killing should never be con- sidered as anything less than an act of killing. Hence the paradoxical name by which he refers to Kaliayev and his comrades, "the scrupulous assassins" (*R*: 164*; *E*: 571).

If we assume that Camus was generally sympathetic to the "scrupulous" violence of the Socialist Revolutionaries, we still cannot be sure precisely what conditions he would insist upon in order to make Kaliayev's actions justifiable.[17] I have identified several factors I believe Camus thought necessary for an act of killing to be just. However, there remains a further, and crucial, point of ambiguity: must the just assassin sacrifice his own life in order to excuse his act of killing? This point is cru- cial because, as we shall see, the coherence of Camus's ideas on political violence appears to rest on our interpretation of it.

According to some critics, Camus insists that the rebel must sacrifice his own life to atone for the life he has taken. This may take the form of suicide, or as in the case of Kaliayev, it may involve surrendering oneself to the police after the act has been committed, with the certainty that one faces execution. For the sake of clarity I will refer to this reading of Camus's thought on violence as the "life for a life" theory. This is the view of Herbert Hochberg, for example, who argues that under scrutiny Camus's "life for a life" thesis collapses into incoherence, an incoherence exem- plified by the fact that "on the basis of the absolute value of life Camus has rejected suicide, capital punishment and murder. He ends by acquiescing in certain cases to all three, for the suicide of the just assassin is suicide in the form of self-imposed capital punishment."[18]

Of course, even if Camus was advocating the "life for a life" thesis, this would still in no way constitute self-contradiction.[19] First, *The Myth of Sisyphus* does not pre- sent a moral argument against suicide, but argues that the absurd does not dictate suicide. Secondly, Camus's concern in *The Rebel* is not with "murder" as such, but with ideological rationalizations of "murder". And thirdly, Kaliayev's acceptance of his death cannot be reasonably interpreted as an acceptance of the legitimacy of capital punishment, for such an interpretation would require that Kaliayev be pre- pared to die in order to aid the destruction of an autocratic regime whose system of justice he nevertheless defers to. The justice that Kaliayev may believe he is satisfy- ing by sacrificing his own life is not the justice of the Romanovs, but his own care- fully wrought sense of justice and expiation.[20] The fact that the execution is carried out in the name of the Romanovs is of no consequence to Kaliayev: something made clear when he refuses their offer of clemency.

Nevertheless, there is considerable agreement among his critics that Camus's abhorrence of killing had indeed led him to adopt the "life for a life" theory, a theory that, they argue, is fundamentally untenable. According to this view Camus believed that in order for killing to be justified, the assassin's life must also be taken, as if in an act of primordial reparation. For example, Philip Thody writes that "to recommend that all conscientious rebels commit suicide after they have been obliged to kill in the service of the revolution is rather an impractical suggestion. No political organisation fighting against a tyranny could possibly succeed if its leaders follow Kaliayev's example" (Thody 1961: 127). Similarly, George Kateb asserts that Camus's alleged claim that the assassin, in order to be just, must sacrifice his own life actually inaugurates and defends a peculiar new doctrine: "the stain of blood can be wiped clean by more blood". The crux of these arguments is that Camus's alleged principle of "a life for a life" renders political violence untenable. For Kateb the application of Camus's doctrine would mean that the revolutionary forces "would be constantly losing their numbers" through their duty to self-sacrifice, and concludes that "the perpetuation of the established order would seem to be guaranteed: rebellion . . . is to take its moral superiority as compensation enough for its inevitable failure" (Kateb 1963: 39, 40).

This is harsh criticism indeed. However, it is in no way certain that Camus is arguing in *The Rebel* that the assassin, like Kaliayev, must actually die in order to justify his action. What is important, one can argue, is not that the assassin dies, but that he is *willing* to die in order to carry out his task, or that he accepts his own death as a likely or possible outcome of his carrying out the attack. In *The Rebel* Camus argues that violence, if it cannot be avoided, must always be accompanied not by the death of the perpetrator, but by "a personal responsibility" and "an immediate risk".[21] Further, in "In Defence of *The Rebel*", he explicitly rejects the idea that *The Rebel* had defended a "life for a life" thesis, claiming "I wanted nothing more than to refute legitimate killing and to ascribe to its demented venture a precise limit" (*SCHC*: 217*; *E*: 1713). In the same short essay, and again in his preface to Alfred Rosmer's *Moscou sous Lénine* (1953), although he continues to insist on the fundamental importance of their example to his understanding of legitimate political violence, Camus criticizes the Socialist Revolutionaries for their complete lack of political realism:

> It's fair for Lenin to give lessons in realism to the solitary terrorists. But it was, and is, indispensable that the rebels of 1905 call to order the revolutionaries who were marching towards state terrorism. Today, now that this state terrorism is in place, the example of 1905 must be incessantly held up before twentieth-century revolution not in order to negate it, but in order to make it once again revolutionary.   (*SCHC*: 210; *E*: 1707; cf. *E*: 789)

However, I think Camus was far from comfortable defending political realism, whatever the circumstances. He offers a far more ingenious criticism of the terrorism of the Socialist Revolutionaries in his *Carnets*, where he identifies what seems to him a flaw in the *moral* character of their violence:

> The great purity of the terrorist of the Kaliayev type is that for him murder coincides with suicide (cf. Savinkov: *Memoirs of a terrorist*). A life is paid for by a life. The reasoning is false, but respectable. (A life taken is not worth a life given.) Today, murder by proxy. No one pays.   (*NB2*: 156; *C2*: 199)

This claim is first, in fact, a stronger criticism of the "life for a life" theory than any presented by Camus's critics: the "life for a life" argument is flawed, according to Camus, because although in general terms one life can be said to be of equal value to another, a life willingly offered or sacrificed cannot be said to be equal to, or to atone for, a life taken without the individual's consent. Therefore, even if Kaliayev himself believed that his death would expiate his action, this does not seem to have been Camus's own view. Secondly, and crucially, despite its rejection of the so-called "life for a life" thesis, we can see that this *Carnet* note is not an argument against all forms of political violence, a position one might call "absolute pacifism by default". Kaliayev's reasoning may be "false" in Camus's estimation, but it is also "respectable", and the character of his violence is seen to contrast starkly with that of the contemporary era, from which Kaliayev's scrupulousness is conspicuously absent ("Today, murder by proxy. No one pays"). Camus was here referring to the expanding gulf between contemporary advocates of revolutionary violence – given the date of the *Notebooks* entry, 1947, he almost certainly had in mind Merleau-Ponty's *Humanism and Terror* – and the victims of the political violence they recommended.[22]

If Camus finds Kaliayev's reasoning to be "false", what could permit him to nevertheless insist on a fundamental distinction between his terrorism and the innumerable instances of "murder by proxy" that so distinguished the twentieth century? In this reading it is precisely his willingness to die, his personal commitment to the violence he himself commends, rather than his actual death that differentiates Kaliayev from Camus's contemporaries.[23] The point, then, is not that Kaliayev must die in order "to atone" for his action, but that he is willing to die as a consequence of it: if the just assassin is prepared to kill in the name of justice or freedom, he must also be willing to die in the name of justice or freedom. To be willing to kill, but to be unwilling to die, suggests a failure to appreciate what for Camus remains the exceptional nature of the act. Simone Weil expresses a strikingly similar view of legitimate killing:

> To keep the love of life intact within us; never to inflict death without accepting it for ourselves. Supposing the life of X . . . were linked with our own so that the two deaths had to be simultaneous, should we still wish him to die? If with our whole body and soul we desire life and if nevertheless without lying, we can reply "yes", then we have the right to kill.   (Weil 2002: 86)

However, this alone is not sufficient to differentiate the just assassin from the rest. I have shown by reference to his *Carnets* that Camus is of the view that the sacrifice of one's own life does not itself accord legitimacy to acts of killing (on the grounds that a life freely given does not equate to a life taken). By the same reasoning, neither could the willingness to die itself justify killing (for neither could the life willingly offered equate to a life taken). In this view, those factors listed earlier (the victim must be a tyrant; the assassin must accept responsibility for his act; the act must be discriminate; there can be no democratic alternative) must also be present for an act of killing to be legitimate.

Camus's primary claim is that political violence must not be granted institutionalized legitimacy: hence his rejection of both "bourgeois" and "revolutionary" interpretations of violence, mentioned earlier in this chapter. Furthermore, Camus's theoretical defence of certain acts of violence (illustrated, in particular, by reference to the assassination of Grand Duke Sergi) must, I think, be understood primarily in the context of a general prohibition of killing and, indeed, he often appears less concerned with describing or defining justifiable political violence than with countering the generalized rationalizations of violence in vogue at that time. Although he explicitly rejects pacifism, calling "absolute non-violence . . . the negative basis of slavery and its acts of violence", Camus's moral sensibility is scandalized by the ease with which his contemporaries feel capable of endorsing violence for political ends in general terms (and from safe distances), while exhibiting nothing of the profoundly personal commitment to violence we see in Kaliayev (*R*: 291; *E*: 695). As we have already noted, this is clearly expressed by Camus in 1948, in a letter responding to criticism of "Neither Victims nor Executioners" levelled by D'Astier de la Vigerie:

> I believe that violence in inevitable; the years of Occupation taught me as much. To tell the truth, there were, at that time, terrible acts of violence which posed no problems for me . . . I have a horror of comfortable violence; I have a horror of those whose words exceed their actions. It is in this respect that I distance myself from certain of our great minds, for whose appeals to murder I will cease feeling contempt only when they themselves take up the executioner's gun. (*E*: 355–6)

I have argued that Camus was neither a reluctant pacifist nor an advocate of self-immolating scrupulous assassins who, in the words of Kateb, would take their moral superiority as sufficient compensation for their inevitable political failure. Too often, Camus's distrust of all totalizing narratives is reduced by critics to culpable political naiveté or over-earnest anti-communism. Norman Podhoretz, for example, argues that "the truths of *The Rebel* were on the whole the truths of the 'Right' ", before going on to criticize Camus for not having the powerful political insights of his own book (Podhoretz 1986: 47). On the contrary, I believe that Camus's ideas on violence lead us in quite a different direction.

The main discussion above, dealing with acts of terrorism perpetrated by individuals, inevitably leads one to question the contemporary relevance of Camus's thought with regard to terrorism, particularly suicide bombing. It seems clear that what makes suicide bombing morally reprehensible is the habitual deliberate targeting of civilians, and I have argued that this concern for innocent victims, for civilians, is central to Camus's discussion of legitimate political violence, in his insistence that the act of legitimate violence be discriminate. Indeed we note that it is this concern for civilians, and not, as many have claimed, simply the risk to his own family, that constitutes the basis of Camus's controversial rejection of the FLN's tactics in the Algerian war: "I must also condemn the use of terrorism which is *exercised blindly*, in the streets of Algiers for example, and which could one day strike my mother or my family."[24] More generally, it seems that when we consider the series of factors that I have argued Camus considered necessary to acts of legitimate violence, the fundamental distinction between terrorist and soldier, necessary to so much contemporary discussion of political violence, becomes difficult to maintain. What this points to, I contend, is not the obsolescence of Camus's argument in the present era of technically advanced violence, but, on the contrary, its particular importance.

Camus distinguished himself from so many of his contemporaries in immediately condemning the bombing of Hiroshima in August 1945, seeing in it the inauguration of a new level of barbarity in human relations. Quite alone among his peers, Camus condemned the bombing, identified with palpable dread the increasing role that technology was to play in warfare – "the civilisation of the machine has just achieved its ultimate degree of savagery" – and must have recognized in this milestone in the history of total war, and in the enthusiasm with which it was greeted in much of the world's media, the refutation of his carefully wrought principles of discriminating, legitimate political violence:

> One has the right to think that there is something indecent about celebrating in this way a discovery that has been put to its first use by the most formidable destructive rage that man has exhibited for centuries. In a world that has torn itself apart with every conceivable instrument of violence and shown itself incapable of exerting any control while remaining indifferent to justice or even mere human happiness, the fact that science has dedicated itself to organised murder will surprise no one, except perhaps an unrepentant idealist.
>
> These discoveries must be reported and commented on for what they are and announced to the world so that man has a proper idea of his destiny. It is intolerable for these terrible revelations to be wrapped in picturesque or humorous essays.   (*CC*: 236; *CAC8*: 569–70)

Furthermore, he suggests that whereas it is intolerable that such destruction "be wrapped in picturesque or humorous essays", there are other, political rather than moral, reasons for reflecting carefully on the bombing of Hiroshima. Considered as a forceful assertion of political power, the attack underlines the need for "a genuine international organisation in which the rights of the great powers will not outweigh the rights of small and medium-sized nations, and in which war, a scourge now made definitive by the fruits of the human mind alone, will no longer be decided by the appetites or doctrines of any one state" (*CC*: 236–7; *CAC8*: 569–71).

It seems that when applied to contemporary political events, Camus's reflections on political violence would lead us to conclude that for the same principal reason that we find suicide bombing morally impermissible (that is, because of its cost in civilian lives), the kind of warfare generally practised with self-declared moral impunity by the West must also be considered morally impermissible. But this is surely no reason to dismiss those reflections as obsolete. The twentieth century – termed by Camus the "Century of Fear" – saw a rapid rise in the number of civilian casualties of war: from 5 per cent in the First World War, to 50 per cent in the Second World War, to 90 per cent in Vietnam.[25] Juxtaposed with these statistics, military and media talk of "targeted attacks" and "precision bombing" can be seen as serving to disguise the fact that advances in military technology have invariably served to reduce the number of casualties among those who possess the technology, while causing a concomitant and disproportionate rise in the number of innocent victims.

Finally, let me say that from my perspective it is certain that Camus would have found the current so-called "war on terrorism" morally and politically dubious.[26] The attitude of the current American administration to international law and global political consensus, exhibited, for instance, by its invasion and occupation of Iraq (the illegal nature of which was affirmed by the then UN Secretary General, Kofi Annan[27]), should immediately remind us of Camus's anxious defence of international democracy in "Neither Victims nor Executioners" in 1946. Here he identifies international democracy as the only viable means of ensuring global stability, and saving the world from mass destruction on a hitherto unknown scale. He insists that international democracy, like national democracy, exists when the law is above those who govern, and identifies as the gravest flaw in the burgeoning international democracy represented by the UN the fact that "[international] law is made and unmade by governments, that is, by the executive. We are therefore in a regime of international dictatorship." Here Camus is taking clear aim at the so-called "Big Five", the permanent members of the UN Security Council (the USSR, the USA, the UK, France and China), and most especially at the veto these countries enjoyed, and continue to enjoy. He goes on to insist:

> The only way out is to place international law above governments, which means that the law must be made, that there must be a parliament for making it, and that parliament must be constituted by means of worldwide elections in which all nations will take part. And since we do not have such a parliament, the only option open to us it to resist this international dictatorship on an international level using means not in contradiction with the ends we seek.[28]

There may seem to us something awkwardly naive in this, but one can surely find sufficient evidence here to argue that to take Camus's thought seriously in the present time is not to feel a warm consolatory nostalgia for youthful political idealism;

instead it compels one to actively oppose the moral and political recklessness of those who are certain that they are right and who are in possession of the political and military means to articulate this conviction: as Camus wrote in "Neither Victims nor Executioners", "we suffocate among people who think they are absolutely right" (*CC*: 259*; *CAC8*: 611).

"Reflections on the Guillotine"

> After the liberation of Paris, I went to see one of the purge trials. The accused was, to my mind, guilty. However, I left the trial before the end because I ended up on the side of the prisoner; I've never been back to a trial of that kind. In every guilty person, there is some innocence. It is that which makes all absolute condemnation repulsive.[29]

One of Camus's most interesting contributions to the question of political violence is his essay on capital punishment, "Reflections on the Guillotine", first published in 1957 (a time when France was actively executing Algerian militants). Whereas, as we have seen, several of Camus's works recognize the legitimacy of political violence in certain circumstances, in this essay he rejects the use of capital punishment, which he considered to be state-sanctioned murder, under any and all circumstances. He begins the essay with a memory of a story relating to an execution that his father had witnessed. The prisoner who was to be executed had committed an especially heinous crime, murdering an entire family before robbing them. The crime disgusted his father to such an extent that he decided he wanted to witness the execution himself. However, his anger at the injustice of the killings committed by this man quickly turned to revulsion when he witnessed what was committed by the state in the name of justice:

> What he saw that morning he never told anyone. My mother relates merely that he came rushing home, his face distorted, refused to talk, lay down for a moment on the bed, and suddenly began to vomit. He had just discovered the reality hidden under the noble phrases with which it was masked. Instead of thinking of the slaughtered children, he could think of nothing but that quivering body that had just been dropped onto a board to have its head cut off.[30]

Although Camus begins his essay with a personal memory, its purpose is not to elicit from the reader an emotional state conducive to his argument. It is instead designed to confront the reader with what he suggests the institution of capital punishment seeks to hide from him: the actuality of execution. "Reflections on the Guillotine" constitutes not an emotional appeal for abolition, but a reasoned argument against capital punishment based on the view that capital punishment is itself irrational. Camus states his position baldly from the beginning: speaking of the execution witnessed by his father, he asserts that the execution "is no less repulsive than the crime, and this new murder, far from making amends for the harm done to the social body, adds a new blot to the first one". He argues that the true awfulness of executions is kept from the general public through the complicity of officials and reporters: "hence we read at breakfast time in a corner of the newspaper that the condemned 'has paid his debt to society' or that he has 'atoned' or that 'at 5 a.m. justice was done'. The officials call the condemned man 'the interested party' or 'the patient' or refer to him by a number." Camus declares that his intention, in contrast, will be "to talk about it crudely". When obscene acts are committed in silence, "then there is no other solution but to speak out and to show the obscenity hidden under the verbal cloak" (*RRD*: 176–7; *E*: 1021–2). Such an exposé of the facts of execution is especially warranted because responsibility for the continued practice of this "primitive rite" belongs to the public in general (it is, after all, in the name of the people that these acts are committed). He asserts that the public responds to news of executions only with "the ceremonial phrases that have been drilled into it. When the imagination sleeps, words are emptied of their meaning: a deaf population absent-mindedly registers the condemnation of a man." Nevertheless, he asserts that if this cloak is pulled away, and the brutal mechanism of state-sponsored murder is revealed, "then public imagination, suddenly awakened, will repudiate both the vocabulary and the penalty" (*RRD*: 177; *E*: 1022–3).

Camus's argument against capital punishment is based on an analysis of the two arguments habitually deployed by its proponents: the deterrence argument and retributivism. The deterrence argument, which Camus refers to throughout as the argument from "the exemplary value of the punishment", is based upon the assumption that people "refrain from crime because they fear punishment", and "since people fear death more than anything else, the death penalty is the most effective deterrent" (*RRD*: 179; *E*: 1024; Schuessler 1971: 182). Camus suggests that the most obvious problem with this argument is that, as he has already suggested, when executions are discussed in the media, they are discussed euphemistically. If the purpose of the death penalty is to deter people, he asks, wouldn't it be made more effective if the media at least reported it accurately? He surmises that society itself proves that it does not believe the deterrence argument, and suggests that were the purpose of the death penalty really to deter, society "would exhibit the heads", that if society really did believe in the deterring power of executions, it would "give executions the benefit of the publicity it generally uses for national bond issues or new brands of drinks". Instead, the execution is described in euphemism: "whom do they hope to intimidate . . . by that example forever hidden, by the threat of a punishment described as easy and swift?"[31]

The second objection Camus has against the deterrence argument is that it cannot be verified empirically, as it is not possible to show with any certainty that a particular act of murder would have been committed were it not for the existence of capital punishment. Indeed, he suggests that what circumstantial evidence does exist tends to prove the very opposite: as is reflected, he says, in the fascination "thousands of criminals" exhibit for the death penalty (*RRD*: 181; *E*: 1024). In order, he says, to defend the deterrence argument against statistical evidence, which appears to prove that there is no correlation between levels of serious crimes and the presence or absence of the death penalty, one is forced to present an argument like the following: "Nothing proves . . . that the death penalty is exemplary; as a matter of fact, it is certain that thousands of murderers have not been intimidated by it. But there is no way of knowing those it has intimidated; consequently, nothing proves that it is not exemplary." In this way, says Camus, "the greatest of punishments . . . rests on nothing but an unverifiable possibility", and he asks, "should there not be a certainty to authorise the most certain of deaths?"[32] As Camus reads this argument, the execution is defended "not so much for the crime he committed but by virtue of all the crimes that might have been and were not committed, that can be and will not be committed". Accordingly, "the most sweeping uncertainty . . . authorises the most implacable certainty".[33] Whereas there is no statistical evidence to support the deterrence argument, there is, Camus suggests, a good deal of anecdotal evidence suggesting that the death penalty serves as no deterrent whatever. This is the case for two related reasons. First, he suggests that although the deterrence argument assumes a certain degree of premeditation on the part of the serious criminal or murderer, there is a great deal of anecdotal evidence suggesting that the vast majority of serious crimes (especially murders) are committed without premeditation.[34] Secondly, the deterrence argument fails to deal adequately with those criminals such as "the man who doesn't know that he is going to kill, who makes up his mind to it in a flash and commits his crime in a state of frenzy or obsession". Neither does it deal with the so-called hardened criminal, for whom the threat of execution instils no fear (*RRD*: 188; *E*: 1031).

In this light, Camus suggests that, far from deterring potential criminals, the death penalty may serve to brutalize society: "[it] is already possible to follow the exemplary effects of such ceremonies on public opinion, the manifestations of sadism they arouse, the hideous vainglory they excite in certain criminals. No nobility in the vicinity of the gallows, but disgust, contempt, or the vilest indulgence of the senses." He cites in evidence the testimony of executioners, wardens and chaplains, who speak of the "keen sense of personal shame", the "horror, shame and humiliation", of "[the] slang of the administrators of justice[,] quite as cynical and vulgar as that of the criminals".[35] Camus concludes that although it hardly seems to exist for those not connected to it, the death penalty has at least one incontrovertible effect: "to depreciate or destroy all humanity and reason in those who take part in it directly" (*RRD*: 196; *E*: 1037). He finds evidence for such brutalization in the macabre satisfaction some executioners evidently derive from the administration of their duties, but also in the following "hallucinatory" account of an execution provided by Père Devoyod, the chaplain of the Santé prison in Paris, quoted at length:

> The morning of the execution, the condemned man was in a very bad mood and refused the consolations of religion. Knowing his heart of hearts and the affection he had for his wife, who was very devout, we said to him: "Come now, out of love for your wife, commune with yourself a moment before dying", and the condemned man accepted. He communed at length before the crucifix,

then he seemed to pay no further attention to our presence. When he was executed, we were a short distance from him. His head fell into the trough in front of the guillotine and the body was immediately put into the basket; but by some mistake the basket was closed before the head was put in. The assistant who was carrying the head had to wait for a moment until the basket was opened again; now, during the brief space of time we could see the condemned man's eyes fixed on me with a look of supplication, as if to ask for forgiveness. Instinctively, we made the sign of the cross to bless the head, and then the lids blinked, the expression of the eyes softened, and finally the look, that had remained full of expression, became vague.

(Devoyod 1955, quoted RRD: 184–5; E: 1028)

Using such eye-witness accounts as evidence, Camus argues that the real reason people support the death penalty has nothing whatever to do with deterrence and is, in fact, much simpler: "[let] us call it by the name which, for lack of any other nobility, will at least give the nobility of truth, and let us recognise it for what it is essentially: a revenge". This defence of the death penalty, the retributivist defence, is, says Camus, "as old as man", and he characterizes it as "the law of retaliation [*le talion*]. Whoever has done me harm must suffer harm; whoever has put out my eye must lose an eye; and whoever has killed must die." He rejects this retributivist defence of capital punishment because, he argues, it is based not on reasoned principles but on a "particularly violent" emotion: retaliation, he says, "is related to nature and instinct, not to law", and law is "not intended to reproduce that nature", but, specifically, to "correct it". Camus also claims that whereas the retributivist argument is based upon the crude arithmetic of an eye for an eye, there is in fact no equivalence between the two acts, the murder and the execution, because execution "adds to death a rule, a public premeditation known to the future victim, an organisation, in short, which is in itself a source of moral suffering more terrible than death. Hence there is no equivalence" (*RRD*: 197–9; *E*: 1037–9). Premeditated acts of murder are usually thought of as morally more reprehensible than murders committed without premeditation, and capital punishment, he says, is clearly "the most premeditated of all crimes". In fact capital punishment is such that it inflicts two deaths on the victim, thereby exceeding the *lex talonis* itself:

> what man experiences at such times is beyond all morality. Not virtue, nor courage, nor intelligence, nor even innocence has anything to do with it. . . . All equity and all dignity have disappeared. . . . Two deaths are inflicted on him, the first being worse than the second, whereas he killed but once.
>
> (RRD: 204–5; E: 1042–3)

I have already noted that Camus's opposition to the death penalty was confirmed in the context of the post-war purge, and first publicly articulated when he added his signature to a petition requesting clemency for Robert Brasillach in 1945. I also noted that both Sartre and Simone de Beauvoir supported the decision to execute collaborators and refused to sign the petition for Brasillach. In fact this trial and execution prompted de Beauvoir to formulate her own version of the retributivist argument, in an essay entitled "An Eye for an Eye".[36] De Beauvoir identifies the thirst for vengeance, such as that exhibited during the purge, as "a response to one of the metaphysical demands of man". She suggests that what makes certain crimes exemplary is that they involve the refusal to identify the very personhood of the victim: a crime becomes "a scandal from the moment that one human being treats other human beings as objects, when by means of torture, humiliation, servitude or murder, he denies their status as human beings". The respect we demand for ourselves, by virtue of our humanity we extend to all others: this, says de Beauvoir, "is the metaphysical basis of the idea of justice". De Beauvoir contends that while no punishment, however severe, can undo the harm already inflicted by the perpetrator, an opposite and equal action also satisfies "a deep human need". Vengeance thus is an attempt to secure a balance destroyed by violence, and if it were to renounce vengeance, society would "give up on concretely linking the crime to the punishment". Although she insists that "social justice" cannot be achieved through violence alone, and suggests that "the verdict counts more than the execution; it is the will to kill the criminal that matters, more even than his death", she is nonetheless persuaded that "if a wrong weighs heavily enough, only one penalty is heavy enough to counterbalance it: death . . . death is the only penalty that can express the violence with which society refuses certain crimes" (de Beauvoir 2004: 247–9*, 254, 252; de Beauvoir 1948a: 113–16, 129, 124). Indeed, the main purpose of the essay is to defend her decision to *refuse* to sign the petition requesting clemency for Brasillach:

> when a man deliberately tries to degrade man by reducing him to a thing, nothing can compensate for the abomination he causes to erupt on earth. There resides the sole sin against man. When it is accomplished no indulgences are permitted and it belongs to man to punish it . . . for the life of a man to have a meaning, he must be held responsible for evil as well as for good, and, by definition, evil is that which one refuses in the name of the good, with no compromise possible. It is for these reasons that I did not sign the pardon petition for Robert Brasillach when I was asked to.
>
> (De Beauvoir 2004: 257; de Beauvoir 1948a: 135–6)

Although de Beauvoir's argument may appear more rational than the general retributivist argument characterized by Camus, it seems that it does not answer his chief objection, that the *lex talionis* (which is explicitly evoked by de Beauvoir) disguises the fact that in cases of capital punishment there is no equivalence between the original crime and the execution.[37]

There is for Camus a further problem with the retributivist argument, one not entirely unrelated to the conduct of the purge.[38] If vengeance is ever justifiable, he suggests, it could only be in cases where the avenger is innocent. The suggestion that capital punishment might succeed in restoring a putative harmony or balance presupposes the innocence of the executioner. And, declares Camus, society is far from being completely innocent of the crimes committed by some of its members; every society, he goes so far as to say, "has the criminals it deserves".[39] Recognizing that certain acts of especial barbarity, such as infanticide, can hardly be explained solely on the basis of social deprivation, noting that "there is no question of reducing the culpability of certain monsters", he continues:

> But those monsters, in decent dwellings, would perhaps have had no occasion to go so far. The least that can be said is that they are not alone guilty, and it seems strange that the right to punish them should be granted to the very people who subsidise, not housing, but the growing of beet for the production of alcohol.[40]

A combination of state apathy, in relation to social housing, and state subsidy, in relation to alcohol production, is seen by Camus to be at least in part responsible for some serious crime.[41] "The State that sows alcohol", he says, "cannot be surprised to reap crime. Yet instead of showing surprise, it simply goes on cutting off heads into which it has poured so much alcohol. It metes out justice imperturbably and poses as a creditor: its good conscience does not suffer at all."[42] At the same time, however, it must be recognized that Camus is not making "a reductive correlation between social conditions and crime". His claim, as Donald Lazere (1996: 374) points out, "is that *any* society that fosters, and allows profiteering from, poverty and vice bears a minimal share of responsibility for the criminal consequences". Recognizing that there are certain criminals who are likely to remain dangerous in any social environment, he still insists that the death penalty does not "solve" the problem posed by these individuals, but merely serves to "suppress" it (*RRD*: 211*; *E*: 1047).

Camus is more immediately concerned with the use of the death penalty in those cases where the convicted individual is, or may be, "remediable", and more particularly still, where the convicted individual may be innocent. The possibility of what has become known as a "miscarriage of justice" seems to Camus to be the most compelling justification for the abolition of the death penalty, and he notes approvingly that the recognition of the possibility of error has caused both Belgium and England to consider the abolition of the death penalty, but notes that in France "consciences are apparently untroubled". He continues:

> If justice admits that it is fallible, would it not be better for justice to be modest and to allow its judgements sufficient latitude so that a mistake can be corrected? Could not justice concede to the criminal the same weakness in which society finds a sort of permanent extenuating circumstance for itself? Can the jury decently say: "If I kill you by mistake, you will forgive me when you consider the weakness of our common nature. But I am condemning you to death without considering those weaknesses or that nature"? There is a solidarity of all men in error and aberration. Must that solidarity operate for the tribunal and be denied the accused?   (*RRD*: 213, 216–17*; *E*: 1049, 1051–2)

For Camus justice has no other meaning than the recognition of this solidarity. Furthermore, this solidarity cannot divorce itself from compassion, a compassion that, he notes, "does not exclude punishment, but . . . suspends the final condemnation".[43] According to Camus, society has no right to condemn individuals to death unless it can fulfil each of the following criteria. First, it must show that it has the metaphysical or religious authority to do so.[44] Secondly, it must show the accused, and the accused alone, to be guilty of the crimes committed. Thirdly, it must show that there is no possible doubt over the guilt of the accused. The satisfaction of these criteria is impossible, given the essentially limited nature of human knowledge, and accordingly, in no instance can the death penalty be justified.

Furthermore, capital punishment denies the criminal the opportunity to make amends, and Camus insists that no man should be denied the opportunity to add to the sum of his actions "a little of the good that will make up in part for the evil we have added to the world. Such a right to live, which allows a chance to make amends, is the natural right of every man, even the worst man." However, Camus further insists that he is far from advocating "that there is no responsibility in this world and that we must give way to that modern tendency to absolve everything, victim and murderer, in the same confusion". Instead he asserts that the criminal should be given every opportunity to reform himself. "We know enough to say that this or that hardened criminal deserves hard labour for life. But we don't know enough to decree that he be shorn of his future – in other words, of the chance we all have of making amends" (*RRD*: 221, 230–31; *E*: 1055, 1061–2).

Camus's view, he stresses, is not consequent on a particularly optimistic view of human nature, nor on an especially optimistic vision of the future: "On the contrary, its abolition seems to me necessary on the grounds of reasoned pessimism, of logic, and of realism." That reasoned pessimism, logic and realism are founded on the absurd, on Camus's recognition of the strict limitations of human understanding and of human fallibility. Echoing themes present in *The Plague* and the absurd works, Camus asserts: "Capital punishment upsets the only indisputable human solidarity – our solidarity against death – and it can be legitimised only by a truth or principle that is superior to man."[45] It is here, in relation to Camus's insistence on the limits imposed by experience, that "Reflections on the Guillotine" most closely reflects the ideas of the absurd and rebellion that inform his most important works. Camusian rebellion, as we have seen, is consequent on the recognition of the principle of the absurd and the experience of solidarity, as well as the awareness of "limits" that emerge from that identification. Essential to the concept of revolt, here and especially in relation to *The Rebel*, and central to the modest yet determined humanism that he relates to it, is the acceptance of "limits" and the recognition of fallibility. If we renounce any claim to absolute certainty, capital punishment becomes unjustifiable. This fallibility does not render all serious action impermissible (for instance, in the case of a convicted murderer, Camus suggests life imprisonment as an alternative to capital punishment), but the idea of limits is supposed to inculcate in us a suspicion of the tendency of individuals or states to proclaim for themselves absolute objectivity.

Camus's reassertion of his belief that the individual is the only possible source of value, combined with his general criticism of the death penalty, leads him to conclude that "our society must now defend herself not so much against the individual as against the State". Society, he claims, ought to revoke the state's authority to execute on its behalf. He asserts that "forbidding a man's execution would amount to proclaiming publicly that society and the State are not absolute values, and that nothing authorises them to legislate definitively or to bring about the irreparable".[46] The state has taken the right of a "natural and human society" to defend itself, and replaced it with "a dominant ideology that requires human sacrifices". Hence it falls to the people to "call a spectacular halt and proclaim, in our principals and institutions, that the individual is above the State". Concluding this essay in 1957, Camus declares, as he had in "Neither Victims nor Executioners" in 1946, his hope that the abolition of the death penalty might manifest itself in a future unified Europe, asserting that the "solemn abolition of the death penalty ought to the first article of the European Code we all hope for".[47]

5 | CAMUS AND SARTRE

Sartre or nostalgia for the universal idyll[1]

The "revolted soul"

By the time Camus and Sartre were formally introduced in 1943, they were already familiar with, and had publicly expressed measured admiration for, each other's works. In 1938 and 1939 Camus had quite favourably reviewed Sartre's *Nausea* and *The Wall* (*SEN*: 167–72; *E*: 1417–22). In 1943 Sartre wrote favourably of *The Outsider* (Sartre 1962a: 108–21; Sartre 1993: 92–112). They first met in Paris in June 1943, at the opening of Sartre's play *The Flies*, and shortly thereafter Sartre became involved with *Combat* (where Camus was now editor), although he did not write for it until after the Liberation. In an interview in 1944, Camus declared himself to "have three friends in the literary world, André Malraux, even if I no longer see him because of his political positions, René Char, who is like a brother to me, and Jean-Paul Sartre".[2] In the same year Sartre asked Camus to direct and act in his play *No Exit*. In 1945 Camus offered Sartre the opportunity to travel to America to write a series of reports for *Combat*. While there he wrote of his friend in *Vogue* magazine:

> In Camus's sombre, pure works one can already detect the main traits of the French literature of the future. It offers us the promise of a classical literature, without illusions, but full of confidence in the grandeur of humanity; hard but without useless violence; passionate, without restraint. . . . A literature that tries to portray the metaphysical condition of man while fully participating in the movements of society.
>
> (Quoted in Cohen-Solal 1987: 233–4; Sartre 1981: 1917–21)

However, their apparent mutual respect and admiration was certain out considerable qualification. Camus's reviews of *Nausea* and *The W* Sartre for "thinking that life is tragic because it is wretched". "Life car ficent and overwhelming", Camus writes, "that is the whole tragedy." C to have had serious reservations about the implications of Sartre's depiction of solipsistic, absurd freedom, noting that "the realisation that life is absurd cannot be an end in itself but only a beginning. It is a truth which nearly all great minds have taken as their starting point. It is not the discovery which is interesting but the consequences and rules for actions which can be drawn from it" (*SEN*: 168–9, 191; *E*: 1418–19, 1421). Reservations are also apparent in Sartre's review of *The Outsider*, which while complimenting Camus's talents as a novelist, expresses reservations about *The Myth of Sisyphus* (which he suggests reflected a limited understanding of existentialist philosophy).[3] He also places Camus in the tradition of the French *moralistes*, a tradition for which it is unlikely Sartre himself felt much sympathy. In a letter written to Jean Grenier discussing Sartre's review, Camus agreed that "most of his criticisms are fair", but complained of the "acid tone". A few months later, in July 1943, shortly after meeting Sartre for the first time, Camus wrote, again to Grenier, "In spite of appearances I don't feel much in common with the work or the man. But seeing those who are against him, we must be with him" (Camus & Grenier 2003: 66, 75; Camus & Grenier 1981: 88, 99).

In fact, despite their undoubted, if limited, friendship, their political and philo-sophical differences were fundamental. These differences, which initially concerned their respective ontologies (illustrated by their differing accounts of the absurd), later focused on the distinctly different character of their political commitments. We have noted already that, for example, unlike Camus, Sartre did not sign the peti-tion requesting clemency for Robert Brasillach in January 1945. Whereas Camus had decided that he could no longer add his voice to those calling for the execution of collaborators, Sartre and de Beauvoir were of the view that although "vengeance is useless", "there were certain men who could have no place in the world we were trying to build" (de Beauvoir 1968: 28). Although there was certainly a great deal that brought the two writers together, it is clear that neither Sartre nor Camus felt entirely comfortable with the image generated in the media of them as close intel-lectual allies (Camus seems to have been especially sensitive to being characterized as a Sartrean acolyte). Indeed, in at least five interviews and articles between 1944 and 1946, Camus publicly and explicitly distanced himself from existentialism and Sartre.[4] In the same period, on at least two occasions, Sartre also insisted on the pro-found political and philosophical difference separating himself from Camus, declar-ing that their association in the popular imagination "rests on a serious confusion".[5] Besides the straightforward point that Camus was "not an existentialist", we also see in these articles the genesis of arguments that were to prove central to their ultim-ate disagreement in the pages of *Les Temps modernes* in 1952. In December 1945, Sartre explained that Camus's true masters were not the existentialists, but rather the seventeenth-century French moralists; in the same month Camus explained that he found the existentialists' conclusions false, most especially those existentialists, such as Sartre, whose philosophy concludes, Camus said, with a "divinisation of history, history considered as the sole absolute value" (Sartre 1981: 1912–17; Camus *E*: 1427–9).

We have seen that Camus's series of articles "Neither Victims nor Executioners" was indirectly criticized by Sartre in 1946 and 1947. However, the clearest indication of the significance of their political and philosophical differences had already come to pass by this time, with Sartre's founding of *Les Temps modernes* in 1945. Camus's refusal of the offer of a place on the editorial board has been explained by the fact that by this time he was editor-in-chief of *Combat* (see, for example, de Beauvoir 1968: 22; Burnier 1968: 20; Aronson 2004: 57). However, it is abundantly clear that Camus did not share the values that *Les Temps modernes* sought to promote, and in January 1946 he publicly stated his fundamental disagreement with the ideas expressed in Sartre's "manifesto" in the inaugural issue of the journal, calling it "unacceptable" [*inacceptable*].[6]

Differing opinions on legitimate political violence were at the heart of Sartre's disagreement with "Neither Victims nor Executioners", but what Camus objected to in Sartre's *Les Temps modernes* manifesto is perhaps less certain, although it was most probably the idea of "committed literature", which the manifesto sought to define and defend. About a year after the manifesto was published, Camus observed in his notebooks: "I prefer committed men to literatures of commitment . . . I should like to see them less committed in their works and a little more so in their daily lives" (*NB2*: 140–41; *C2*: 180). He would probably also have disagreed with the primacy given by Sartre's manifesto to class consciousness in the amelioration of social conditions. Having already asserted in 1944 that the "class struggle is a fact to which I subscribe completely", in this editorial Sartre defines the politics of *Les Temps modernes* in contrast with what he calls "the official doctrine of bourgeois democracies", which he characterizes primarily as a blindness to the fundamental reality of the class structure, in place of which a spurious unifying "human nature" is posited: "it persists in seeing no more than men, in proclaiming the identity of human nature in every diverse situation, but it is against the proletariat that it makes that decision" (Sartre 1974b: 159; Sartre 1988: 258). Although he does not in any way limit the significance of social and economic inequality, we have seen that in *The Rebel* and elsewhere Camus attempts to justify a form of solidarity that is not class-based, that is based on human nature (or at least on a human condition), and that is therefore in fundamental conflict with the primacy given to class by Sartre.

Given that Sartre had insisted upon both the legitimacy of revolutionary violence and the centrality of class conflict, it is hardly surprising that both he and the *Les Temps modernes* group generally would disagree with the arguments of *The Rebel*, or indeed that they would consider those ideas to be politically reactionary. Although after the disagreement over Merleau-Ponty's "Le Yogi et le Prolétaire" in 1946 they effected a certain rapprochement in 1947, there remained a discernible distance between Camus and Sartre. In 1948, Jean Daniel drew attention to their diverging views on morality and politics by publishing in consecutive issues of his magazine *Caliban* Sartre's "To Be Hungry Already Means that You Want to Be Free" and Camus's starkly contrasting "Democracy Is an Exercise in Modesty".[7] The extent of these differences can also be seen in their responses to Merleau-Ponty's *Humanism and Terror* (1947) (of which the 1946 essay was part), a book that could be said to have had an equal and opposite effect on Camus and Sartre. Whereas, as we have seen in Chapter 2, the essay was for Camus an expression of the worst kind of intellectual "fellow travelling", Sartre compliments it with giving "me the push I needed to release me from my immobility" (Sartre 1965: 253). The extent of the political and philosophical differences now separating Camus and Sartre was further highlighted by the publication of *The Plague* in mid-1947, a novel that seemed to confirm the suspicion of Sartre and de Beauvoir that Camus had "rejected history": "to treat the Occupation as the equivalent of a natural calamity was", according to de Beauvoir, "merely another means of escaping from History [*sic*] and the real problems" (de Beauvoir 1968: 138). It is hardly surprising given the radically different political positions adopted by Sartre and Camus by this time, as well as their complete awareness of these political differences, that when the time came, *Les Temps modernes* would review *The Rebel* negatively, and indeed Camus could not have been unaware of their likely reaction.[8]

The editorial board of *Les Temps modernes*, with Sartre at the head, met every two weeks, and at each meeting since its publication in October 1951 the need to review *The Rebel* was discussed. According to de Beauvoir, although nobody on the board liked the book, neither did anyone want to review it (the reason she gives for this, that Sartre "wouldn't let any one say anything bad about it because of their friendship", is somewhat contradicted by subsequent events).[9] Finally, Sartre decided that Francis Jeanson should write it: "He will be the harshest", he said, "but at least he will be polite."[10] Ultimately, however, Jeanson was far from polite. Indeed, by the time he first met Sartre in 1947, Jeanson had already developed a sophisticated and highly critical account of Camus's thought, so it seems plausible to suggest that Sartre chose him to write the review not because of a putative politeness, but because Jeanson had already developed a complex criticism of Camus, and, crucially, because, as became apparent when he addressed Camus directly, Sartre was in complete agreement with Jeanson's analysis. In an interview in 1945, Sartre had insisted that his conception of the absurd and Camus's were "completely different", that Camus's conception of the absurd involved a sense of "scandal and disappointment", and was born from "the themes of classical pessimism" (Sartre 1981: 1916). In an article published in1947 Jeanson sought to identify the implications of Camus's conception of the absurd, and argued that his insistence on "maintaining the absurd" did not imply consenting to the facts of experience but, instead, meant abandoning philosophical thought altogether. To him, Camus "subscribed to a form of defeatism that led to 'absurdism' by converting the fact of absurdity into a value" (Aronson 2004: 138–9; see Jeanson 1947b, c). For Jeanson, then, the absurd as construed by Camus could only result in political quietism. This perspective on Camus's intellectual trajectory was confirmed for Jeanson by his reading of *The Rebel* itself – as is indicated in the title of his 21-page review – "Albert Camus – or the Revolted

Soul".[11] The review began with an ironic overview of the critical praise the book had received: "a turning point in Western thought", "one of the greatest books in recent years", "no comparable oeuvre has appeared in France since the war". Jeanson said that were he in Camus's position, receiving such lavish praise from the political right wing, he would be worried, and indeed he understood that Camus was worried (*SCHC*: 79–80*; Jeanson 1952a: 2070).

Fundamentally, Jeanson's argument is based on the claim that Camus had rejected or denied history, and that he represented "that Manichaeism which situates evil within history and good outside of it", which requires "that we choose against history whenever possible" (*SCHC*: 97; Jeanson 1952a: 2086). Having accomplished this supremely reactionary task, Jeanson surmises, Camus has adopted the position of the Hegelian "beautiful soul" (*belle âme*), who prefers to remain pure, uncontaminated by contact with reality, and who is "satisfied with the reiteration of an abstract Idea void of all dialectical energy".[12] He further criticizes Camus for what he judged to be his superficial reading of Hegel and Marx, and his readiness to reject revolution without being able to offer any feasible alternative.[13] In so doing, Camus achieves "the 'objectively' reactionary task" of condemning the Marxist experiment, without having anything positive to offer in exchange. He asserts that "if Camus's revolt chooses to be deliberately static, it can only concern Camus himself", and suggests that although intellectual disquisitions are fine *hors contexte*, in history they can be used for reactionary purposes (he claims, for example, that in practice Camus's rebellion is directed solely against revolutions). Thus, he surmises: "In our view incorrigibly bourgeois, it is quite possible that the face of capitalism is less 'convulsed' than that of Stalinism. But what face does it offer to the miners, to the state workers sanctioned for striking, to the Madagascan tortured by the police, to the Vietnamese 'cleansed' by napalm, to the Tunisian *ratissé* by the Legion?" In a world weighed down with such social injustice, the choice facing the intellectual is either to side with the oppressed, which can only be done effectively by supporting the Communist Party, or to "deny" history in the name of a transcendent metaphysics. It is precisely that latter choice that Jeanson accuses Camus of having made. Although he admires Camus's voice – "so human and charged with such genuine torment" – Jeanson ultimately condemns the essay, "this pseudo-philosophy of a pseudo-history of 'revolutions'". *The Rebel*, he concludes, "is above all a failed great book: hence, precisely, the myth to which it has given birth. We beg Camus not to yield to fascination, and to rediscover in himself that personal voice – by which his work remains for us, despite everything, irreplaceable."[14]

Camus was greatly exercised by Jeanson's implication that he was at least indirectly condoning the murderous repression by capitalist regimes of oppressed peoples who would "undertake to struggle against those responsible for their hunger", and that in doing so, was serving to ease the consciences of the bourgeoisie while giving political ammunition to the Right. Yet it is important to point out that although there was certainly a degree of wounded vanity reflected in Camus's response, his primary objection to the review was Jeanson's failure to address the main question posed by the book: the question of whether or not Marxist historical determinism perpetuated tyranny and legitimized police and state terrorism. And indeed Jeanson had failed to address this question (neither, as Aronson acknowledges, was it addressed by Sartre in his letter responding to Camus). Camus did not read the review simply as an expression of the views of Jeanson (whom his response effectively ignored, referring to him only as "your colleague"), but as the view of the entire *Les Temps modernes* board and, in particular, the view of Sartre. Accordingly, it was to Sartre (addressed formally as "Monsieur le Directeur") that he sent his letter. The August 1952 issue published Camus's response to Jeanson's review (seventeen pages), along with further replies from Sartre (twenty pages) and Jeanson (thirty pages). Camus began: "I shall take as a pretext the article which, under an ironical title, your magazine has devoted to me to submit to your readers some remarks concerning the intellectual method and the attitude demonstrated by this article."[15] His letter, which argued that Jeanson's article was more a symptom of the malaise that he had tried to describe in *The Rebel* than a valuable criticism of it, centres on three related points.

First, Camus insists that Jeanson's article not only misrepresents the arguments of *The Rebel*, it in fact attributes to Camus a view that he had explicitly criticized at length in his book. He accuses Jeanson of reducing the entire book to a defence of the view that "all evil is found in history and all good outside of it" (*SCHC*: 97; Jeanson 1952a: 2086). Camus responds:

> Here, I really must protest and tell you calmly that such tactics are disgraceful. . . . In fact, *The Rebel* seeks to demonstrate – nearly a hundred quotations could prove it, if necessary – that pure anti-historicism, at least in today's world, is as harmful as pure historicism.[16] It is written there, for those who wish to read, that he who believes only in history marches towards terror and that he who does not believe in it at all authorises terror . . . above all, it demonstrates that "the denial of history is equivalent to the denial of reality" in the same way, neither more nor less, that "one separates oneself from reality by wanting to consider history as a self-sufficient totality". But what's the use of texts! Your colleague pays no attention to them.[17]

Camus argues that far from his essay being a renunciation of history in the name of transcendent values, "anyone who has seriously read" it knows that for him "nihilism coincides with disincarnated and formal values", that *The Rebel* criticized both "the formal and bourgeois revolution of 1789" and "the cynical revolution of the twentieth century". In both cases, "nihilism and terror are justified, although by contrary excesses – either because values are placed above history or because they are absolutely identified with it". By "systematically suppressing one of the aspects of this double critique", says Camus, Jeanson "sanctifies his thesis but shamelessly sacrifices the truth", the truth that *The Rebel* "does not deny history (a denial that would make no sense) but only criticises the attitude that aims to make history into an absolute". Rather than ridiculing a false version of his thesis, "a judicious and honest critic would have dealt with my true thesis: namely, that whoever seeks to serve history for its own sake ends in nihilism". However, Jeanson "replaces historicism with history, which, in effect, is enough to transform the book into its opposite and its author into an unrepentant idealist".[18] Jeanson had similarly claimed that *The Plague* provides evidence of Camus's exit "from history" (*SCHC*: 82–3; Jeanson 1952a: 2072–3). Camus notes in his reply that the intellectual trajectory from *The Outsider* to *The Plague* is precisely the opposite of that which Jeanson claims; that is, *The Plague* marks a move from solitary revolt towards collective action: "After all, nobody, except in your journal, would have thought to dispute the fact that if there is an evolution from *The Outsider* to *The Plague*, it is towards solidarity and participation. To claim otherwise is either to lie or to dream" (*SCHC*: 112; Camus 1952: 321).[19]

Secondly, Camus argues that Jeanson's wilful misreading of *The Rebel* allowed him to ignore the central arguments of the book. He ignores, for example, the question of whether or not there is a dimension of Marxist philosophy that Camus calls "a Marxist prophecy", and whether or not such a prophecy, if it exists, is not "contradicted today by numerous facts". In particular, Jeanson is accused of ignoring "everything in my book that deals with the misfortunes and specifically political implications of authoritarian socialism". According to Camus, Jeanson's avoidance of what he considered to be the main arguments of his book reveals "a more profound antinomy" – an antinomy that, as we shall see, Camus had already hinted at in *The Rebel* itself. Camus interprets Jeanson's refusal to respond directly to the discussion of Marxist historicism in *The Rebel* as not only an implicit admission of faith in that doctrine, but also an admission that such a faith was incompatible with the prevailing existentialism of *Les Temps modernes*. This is an important point, and one that has been little noted in the scholarship. As I have noted above, Camus had observed in 1945 an emerging tendency towards what he called the "divinisation of history" in Sartre's philosophical and political thinking. He returns to this point again, arguing that had Jeanson directly confronted the arguments in his book, he would have been obliged to defend the Marxian idea that history had both a necessary meaning and an end. Furthermore, Camus observes that Jeanson would also have had to demonstrate why this view was not in contradiction with the existentialist principles that, in Camus's view, remain the basis of editorial policy at *Les Temps modernes* (Camus may have been in the wrong in assuming Sartrean existentialism as editorial policy, but certainly the criticism was relevant to Sartre himself):

> Only the principles of prophetic Marxism (along with those of a philosophy of eternity) can justify the complete rejection of my thesis. But can one, without contradiction, clearly affirm them in your journal? Because, after all, if man does not have an end that can be chosen as a principle of value, how could history have a meaning that could be perceived right now? And if it has one, why would man not make it his end? And if he does so, how could he find himself with this terrible and incessant freedom of which you speak? These objections, which could be developed further, are, to my mind, considerable. No

doubt, they are no less so in the eyes of your critic, since he totally avoids the only discussion that would have interested *Les temps modernes*: that concerning the end of history.   (*SCHC*: 123; Camus 1952: 329–30)

Camus argues in *The Rebel* that the sacrifices demanded by Marxist revolution "can only be justified in the context of a happy end to history", and now writes that Jeanson's "professed existentialism would be threatened in its very foundations if he accepted a foreseeable end to history". In order to reconcile his existentialism with Marxism, at the very least Jeanson would need "to demonstrate this difficult proposition: history has no end but it has a meaning that, however, does not transcend it. Perhaps this perilous reconciliation is possible, and I would love to read it." But, Camus concludes, as long as this contradiction between the fundamental freedom of the individual and the inexorable progression of history towards its end remains, the political and philosophical perspective of *Les Temps modernes* will remain contradictory, something that is both terribly cruel (because of the reality of those regimes founded on the ideology in question) and terribly trivial (because the contradiction is fundamental to *Les Temps modernes*' political agenda).[20]

Thirdly, Jeanson's article completely ignores Camus's lengthy discussions of revolutionary violence, and the possibility of legitimate political violence. The importance of this can hardly be overestimated when we consider that it is precisely Camus's consideration of the legitimization of violence that leads him to critique historical materialism. Jeanson ignores his analysis of non-Marxist left-wing thought; and in particular, he makes no comment on Camus's discussion of revolutionary syndicalism and anarchism (except to pour scorn upon it, writing "Ah! Revolutionary Syndicalism is so fine, when it has no need to be revolutionary [cf. the Scandinavian countries]"[21]). Camus responds:

> The First International and the Bakuninist movement, still alive in the masses of the C.N.T. in both France and Spain, are ignored. The revolutionaries of 1905, whose experiences are at the centre of my book, are completely ignored. Revolutionary syndicalism is mocked, while my arguments in its favour, resting on its achievements and on the properly reactionary nature of caesarean socialism, are ignored. Your colleague writes as if he were ignorant of the fact that Marxism no more inaugurated the revolutionary tradition than *The German Ideology* inaugurated philosophy. Although, while exalting the tradition of non-Marxist revolution, [*The Rebel*] does not deny the importance of Marxism, your article, curiously, develops as if there were no other revolutionary tradition than that inherited from Marx.
>   (*SCHC*: 118–19*; Camus 1952: 326)

"Hostile to history"

Unsurprisingly, Sartre was infuriated by the assumption implicit in Camus's letter that the views of Jeanson were also his own (as justifiably annoyed as Sartre was, nothing in his letter suggests that he was not in complete accord with Jeanson's arguments).[22] It is unsurprising, then, that the issue of *Les Temps modernes* that contained Camus's letter also contained replies from Sartre and Jeanson. Jeanson's was taken up mainly with defending his original criticisms, but Sartre, whose association with Camus in the popular mind was becoming a political liability, had a vastly more significant task. His letter, which began "Our friendship was never easy, but I shall miss it", accused Camus of having become "the victim of a bleak immoderation which masks your internal difficulties and which you call, I believe, Mediterranean *mesure*", adding, "Sooner or later someone would have told you; let it be me" (Sartre 1952: 334; *SCHC*: 131–2*; trans. Lottman 1979: 504). Like Jeanson, Sartre appears initially to reproach Camus for having turned his back on his former heroes:

> Where is Meursault, Camus? Where is Sisyphus? Where are those Trotskyists of the heart today, who preached permanent revolution? Without doubt, murdered or in exile. A violent and ceremonial dictatorship has taken possession of you, supported by an abstract bureaucracy, and pretends to rule according to moral law.[23]

He seems to assert here that what had interested him and others about Camus was the paradox of his absurdist philosophy combined with his political commitment, and that in *The Rebel* Camus has replaced this dynamic with a profoundly reactionary conservatism. Crucially, Sartre is arguing *at this point* in his letter that the position Camus outlines in *The Rebel* marks a distinct break from his thought in the past, the thought of the Camus they had so much admired:[24]

> You had been for us – and you could be again tomorrow – the admirable conjunction of a person, an action, and a work. This was in 1945. We discovered Camus, the Resistant, as we discovered Camus, the author of [*The Outsider*]. And when the editor of the clandestine *Combat* was joined with Meursault, who carried honesty to the point of refusing to say that he loved his mother and his mistress, and who our society condemned to death, when we knew, above all, that you had ceased neither to be the one nor the other, when this apparent contradiction made us progress in the knowledge of ourselves and of the world, then you were not far from being exemplary. . . . You were a real *person*, the most complex and the richest, the last and the most gifted heir of Chateaubriand and the scrupulous defender of the social cause.[25]

However, examined in the light of the article as a whole, it becomes abundantly apparent that this is *not* Sartre's view. In fact, in his letter Sartre deploys a series of arguments designed precisely to demolish the perception of Camus as a political writer and to show not only that *The Rebel* is ahistorical and politically reactionary, but that precisely in its political irrelevance it is the culmination of Camus's entire *oeuvre*. We have noted already the centrality of history and historicism to both the intellectual relationship between Camus and Sartre and the argument of *The Rebel*. We have seen too that in his letter responding to Jeanson's criticism, Camus asked Sartre to explain how *Les Temps modernes'* implicit faith in Marxist historical determinism did not contradict its founding existentialist principle of radical freedom. This particular point, made more elaborately some years later by Raymond Aron, is ignored by Sartre.[26] Instead, Sartre returns to Jeanson's earlier argument regarding Camus's own relation to history, and he attempts to show conclusively that Camus proves himself "completely hostile to history".[27] In other words, whereas Camus's letter questioned Sartre's relationship with Marxist historical materialism and the implications that might have for his existentialism, Sartre responded by questioning Camus's relationship to his own historicity.

He alleges that Camus, once a powerful voice on the Left, was fast becoming a tool of the bourgeoisie, no longer simply a member of that class, like Sartre or Jeanson, but a representative of their interests. His writing, exemplified in his letter to *Les Temps modernes*, had become, says Sartre, terroristic.[28] It was not possible to disagree with Camus: to do so was to be on the side of totalitarianism, was to deny the existence of concentration camps in the USSR. Like the bourgeois who, in spite of their horror, rejoiced in the discovery of the camps because it proved the communist experiment to be a failure, Camus too "exploits the Turkestani and the Kurd to more effectively demolish a critic who did not happen to praise [him]".[29] Sartre further insists that one must earn the right to critique the communists: "To merit the right to influence men who are struggling, one must first participate in their struggle, and this first means accepting many things if you hope to change a few of them. . . . But when a man can only see in present struggles the idiotic duel of two equally abject monsters, I hold that this man has already abandoned us. He has gone into a corner all by himself to sulk" (*SCHC*: 147*; Sartre 1952: 345). That is to say, with the critique of Soviet communism in *The Rebel*, and most especially with his determination to replace class conflict with human nature as the unifying principle behind political action, and his insistence that the obscurely defined concept of "rebellion" was as the heart of legitimate revolution, Camus had proclaimed a "false solidarity" between the classes and made himself completely irrelevant politically: "You decided against history; and rather than interpret its course, you preferred to see it only as one more absurdity . . . Your personality, which was real and vital as long as it was nourished by events, became a mirage. In 1944, it was the future. In 1952, it is the past."[30] We have already observed, in discussing his response to Jeanson, Camus's insistence that in *The Rebel* "the denial of history is equivalent to the denial of reality", and that Jeanson's article "replaces historicism with history, which, in effect, is enough to transform the book into its opposite and its author into an unrepentant idealist" (*SCHC*: 114–16*; Sartre 1952: 322–4). Irrespective of the legitimacy of this distinction, Sartre ignores it completely, something that may be explained by his evident desire not to be drawn into the subject that remained at the heart of the debate, that of political violence and its theoretical legitimacy. As Ronald Santoni points out, "the criticism that Camus levelled against Jeanson could just as aptly be applied to Sartre: specifically, that he had been reluctant to discuss some of the crucial issues of *The Rebel* – for example, 'a limit [regarding violence] revealed by the . . . movement of rebellion itself' " (Santoni 2003: 129).

However, Sartre's letter is not only concerned with exposing the "hostility to history" he finds embodied in *The Rebel* and, in fact, he uses the immediate task of critiquing the essay, and Camus's defence of it, to launch a scathing attack on Camus's entire *oeuvre*. Although Sartre begins his review by asking the question "How could an author so central to French life after the war become so irrelevant so quickly?", the conclusion he comes to questions the worth of Camus's entire *oeuvre*. The remarkable conclusion at which Sartre arrives is not simply that *The Rebel* marks an abdication from the great act of affirmation of human value present in the early "absurd" works, but that the irrelevance of Camus was inevitable because of his persistence in seeing the causes of human misery in strictly metaphysical terms. Accordingly, what began as a critique of a book and its author's precious defence against its detractors becomes a profound and scathing critique of a writer's entire *oeuvre*. What Sartre sets out to prove is that, given Camus's absurd premise, his work inevitably evolved towards a kind of critical entropy that culminated in the profoundly ahistorical and reactionary work that was *The Rebel*. In this context, it will become apparent that, despite his appeal to Camus's reason – "You had been for us – you could again be tomorrow – the admirable conjunction of a person, an action, and a work" – Sartre was, at least by 1952, entirely convinced of Camus's political irrelevance.[31] For Sartre *The Rebel* was, precisely in its insignificance, the culmination of its author's life work, and like Jeanson, he perceived the source of Camus's political insignificance precisely in his conception of the absurd. Hence, although Sartre claims to have been immediately attracted by Camus's remarkable courage in seeking only temporal truths ("you only wanted to be concerned with truths 'which must rot'"), it transpired that this actually masked a far more significant fact, that Camus identified injustice as eternal, as transcendent of history. Sartre, therefore, characterizes Camus's conception of the absurd in the following terms:

> You rejected the fraud of the Soul and of the Idea. But since, in your own terms, injustice is *eternal* – that is since the absence of God is a constant throughout the changes of history – the immediate and continually re-affirmed relation of man who insists on *having* a meaning (that is to say, who demands that one be given him) to this God who maintains an eternal silence, is itself transcendent to History [*sic*]. The tension by which man realises himself . . . is thus a veritable conversion that wrenches him from his daily "agitation" and from "historicity" in order to make him finally coincide with his condition. One can go no further: there is no place for progress in this instantaneous tragedy.   (*SCHC*: 148–9*; Sartre 1952: 346)

There are at least two problems with Sartre's argument here. First, we should note that man's insistence on meaning in no way implies, as Sartre has it, that "[man] demands that he be given one". Instead it suggests that man has the capacity to create meaning. This is suggested by the very lines from *Letters to a German Friend* quoted by Sartre in the same paragraph: "man must exalt justice in order to fight against eternal injustice, create happiness in order to fight against eternal injustice" (*RRD*: 28; *E*: 240; quoted in *SCHC*: 148; Sartre 1952: 346). The verbs here denote action or creation on the part of the individual. Further, we should note that this act of creating meaning is necessarily done *in history*. Secondly, Sartre claims to identify in Camus's idea of metaphysical injustice the assertion that all forms of injustice have metaphysical origins. There is no doubt that Camus continues to see, in the context of the absurd, the human condition characterized by an absence of justice (as opposed to the presence of injustice), and there is no doubt that he also sees rebellion as emerging out of this context. We have seen in Chapter 1 that this may appear vulnerable to the "pointless lament" argument advanced by A. J. Ayer. However, Camus also clearly understands rebellion in a political context, as *The Rebel* makes clear. Whatever eternal "metaphysical injustice" Camus may have identified, it does not itself diminish the political critique he was also engaged upon. Crucially, at no point does Camus assume that the immediate cause of political injustice is anything other than political. Although he identifies a correlation between metaphysical revolt, which is exemplified by both Sisyphus in *The Myth of Sisyphus* and Prometheus in *The Rebel*, and political revolt, which is exemplified by the Socialist Revolutionaries, and although both acts of rebellion are based on a sense of limit, it is in no way clear, as Sartre assumes, that these equivalences themselves make one form of rebellion (i.e. political) dependent upon the other (i.e. metaphysical). In any event, Sartre now claims that, despite appearances, Camus's philosophy is profoundly conservative, and firmly situated

> within our great classical tradition which, since Descartes, and with the exception of Pascal, has been completely hostile to history . . . you didn't reject History through having suffered from it and because you discovered its face with horror. You rejected it, previous to all experience, because our culture rejects it, and because you located human values in the struggle of man "against heaven".   (*SCHC*: 149–50*; Sartre 1952: 347)

Sartre's interpretation of Camus's intellectual trajectory makes Camus's involvement with *Combat* difficult to understand, or at least leads one to suspect that his motivation for being involved was different from that of most other *résistants*. Absorbed by the perpetual bitter fight of man against the injustice of his fate, what could interest Camus in the struggle against the Nazis? Sartre does acknowledge the extent of Camus's involvement in the Resistance but argues that Camus fought against the Nazis only because he was able to imagine them as having taken sides with that universal injustice, as, "accomplices of the blind forces of the universe, they sought to destroy man" (*SCHC*: 151; Sartre 1952: 348). Hence, for Sartre, Camus identified the struggle against the Nazis in strictly ahistorical terms, and only then did the fight become worthwhile. Not only is this premised on a faulty conception of the absurd; it ignores Camus's explicit commitment to history in both the early and late works: in *The Myth of Sisyphus*, for example, he declared, "Conscious that I cannot stand aloof from my time, I have decided to be an integral part of it. . . . Between history and the eternal I have chosen history because I like certainties", and in *The Rebel* he insists that the rebel "cannot turn away from the world and from history without denying the very principle of his rebellion" (*MS*: 80–81; *E*: 165; *R*: 287; *E*: 690). Similarly, he noted at the outbreak of war in 1939 that "the dilettante's dream of being free to hover above his time is the most ridiculous form of liberty" (*NB1*: 143; *C1*: 172). Nevertheless, Sartre purports to find evidence in *Letters to a German Friend* to support his view of Camus's "hostility" to history, so we should look carefully at the details of his argument: "You accused the Germans of taking you away from your struggle against heaven, of forcing you to take part in the temporal combats of men. 'For so many years now, you have tried *to make me enter into History*', and further on, 'you did what you had to do, *we entered History*'" (*SCHC*: 150*; Sartre 1952: 348).

These quotations, thinks Sartre, constitute clear evidence of Camus's "hostility to history", and they constitute the only direct evidence Sartre provides as evidence of Camus's "refusal" of history.[32] In fact in his letter (a letter in which he berates Camus for a "mania for not going to the source") Sartre quotes from *Nuptials* (1939), *Letters to a German Friend* (1945) and the "Neither Victims nor Executioners" articles (1946), but not once from either Camus's letter to *Les Temps modernes* or, crucially, from *The Rebel* itself.[33] Moreover, closer inspection leads us to question the accuracy of Sartre's interpretation of his second quotation from Camus ("you did what you had to do, *we entered History*"), because of the use of the first person plural. Whatever Camus was describing, by attributing it to people other than himself (as indicated by the "we"), he is clearly not referring to the solipsistic exile that Sartre claims Camus enjoyed. Further, it is clear that Camus was talking about a specific act precipitated by a specific cause, rather than presence or absence of a general "commitment" to history. What becomes evident from a careful reading of this specific passage is that Camus is talking about his own involvement with the Resistance, with the violent struggle against Nazi domination, rather than a generalized affirmation of the importance of political action. Camus believed in justice, but refused the affirmation of justice at the expense of happiness. Yet his experience of Nazi occupation caused him to conclude that there were instances when immediate happiness could be sacrified in the cause of justice:

> We thought that happiness was the greatest of conquests, a victory over the fate imposed upon us. Even in defeat this longing did not leave us. But you did what you had to do, and we entered History. And for five years it was no longer possible to enjoy the call of the birds in the cool of the evening. . . . For five years the earth has not seen a single morning without death agonies, a single evening without prisons, a single noon without slaughters. Yes, we had to follow you. *But our difficult achievement consisted in following you into war without forgetting happiness.*[34]

Moreover, and crucially, the first quotation provided (twice) by Sartre ("For so many years now, you have tried *to make me enter History*") is in fact a fabrication. Camus actually wrote the following (I include the previous two sentences, as the context shows Camus to have meant something almost exactly the opposite of what Sartre alleges): "For a long time we both thought that this world had no ultimate meaning and that consequently we were cheated. I still think so in a way. But I came to different conclusions to the ones you used to talk about, which for so many years now, you have been trying to introduce into history."[35] Although it is peculiar, to say the least, that Sartre's letter makes no direct reference to the text that was supposed to have been at the heart of the dispute, *The Rebel*, it seems difficult to exaggerate the significance of this misquotation.

Sartre continues with the claim that after Camus had "served [his] five years with History, [he] thought [he] could return (and all men with [him]) to the despair from which man must derive his happiness". Camus was prepared to struggle against the Nazis because he identified in them an accord with the metaphysical forces that thwart the human pursuit of happiness. Unless he was capable of making this association between metaphysical cause and political effect, Sartre seems to allege, social injustices were ignored: "You revolted against death, but in the iron belts that surrounded cities, other men revolted against social conditions which raised the toll of mortality. When a child died, you blamed the absurdity of the world and this deaf and blind God which you had created in order to spit in his face. But the child's father, if he were an unemployed worker or an unskilled labourer, blamed men."[36]

Having ignored Camus's question regarding the implications of Marxist historicism, and having established to his own satisfaction Camus's abdication from historical responsibility, Sartre can accuse Camus of never having dreamt, in Marx's phrase, of "making history": "The proof", he says, alluding perhaps to the modest proposal of "Neither Victims nor Executioners", is that "after the war, you envisaged only the return of the *status quo*".[37] As I hope the previous chapters have indicated, this is, to say the least, a peculiar assessment of Camus's political trajectory. Indeed, there is contrary evidence in the very texts cited by Sartre. In *Letters to a German Friend* Camus declares: "I belong to a nation which for the past four years has begun to relive the course of her entire history and which is calmly and surely preparing out of the ruins to remake another history", and in "Neither Victims nor Executioners" he explicitly rejects the idea of maintaining the status quo, calling it "a completely utopian position insofar as it assumes that history is immobile" and "the impossible dream of bringing history to an abrupt halt" (*RRD*: 10; *CC*: 266; *E*: 225, 341–2). Therefore the allegation that Camus welcomed the return to the status quo after the war seems utterly disingenuous. Even a cursory look at Camus's *Combat* writings shows this to be the case (indeed even a look at the newspaper's masthead, bearing the slogan "From Resistance to Revolution", would be adequate).

It is groundless, then, for Sartre to claim that "even when, for us, you still incarnated the man of the immediate past, perhaps even the man of the near future, you had already become, for ten million Frenchmen, one of the privileged. They didn't recognise their only too real anger in your ideal revolt. This death, this life, this earth, this rebellion, this God, this no and yes, this love, were, they said to you, the games of a prince. Others went as far as to call them circus acts." Despite the fact that "for a few years, you were what could be called the symbol and the proof of class solidarity", Sartre now accuses Camus of locating the cause of human misery outside history, or human control (*SCHC*: 153, 152; Sartre 1952: 350, 349). To Sartre's mind Camus had effectively ignored the class struggle. He accuses the author of "indulging and displaying his moral sensibilities while leaving the world to its own resources" (Judt 1998: 95). Far from being working class, Camus was, like Jeanson and Sartre himself, bourgeois. But Camus, unlike either Sartre or Jeanson, now represented the interests of the bourgeoisie. Sartre continues:

> Today, it is different. It is no longer a matter of *defending* the *status quo*, but of changing it. This is what you will not accept, unless accompanied by the most formal guarantees. And I suppose that if I believed that history is a pool of filth and blood, I would act just like you and look twice before diving in. But suppose that I am in it already, suppose that, from my point of view, even your sulking is proof of your historicity.   (*SCHC*: 156*; Sartre 1952: 352)

"Freedom without brakes"

So far, the main purpose of Sartre's letter has been to highlight what he considers to be Camus's hostility to history, hostility more or less latent in his earlier writings and given full expression in *The Rebel*. However, there is a separate point: Camus's letter is clearly addressed to Sartre directly, and this leads him to comment on what he considers to be Camus's misinterpretation of his writings, saying "I have at least this in common with Hegel: you have not read either of us." Specifically, according to Sartre, Camus has radically misunderstood his conception of absolute freedom, as articulated in *Being and Nothingness* (1943), misinterpreting it as an assertion of absolute political freedom, rather than absolute ontological freedom. He supports this view by purporting to quote Camus attributing to him (Sartre) the idea of "freedom without brakes", an accusation that originates, says Sartre, not in his own writings, but in those of the Jesuit critic Roger Troisfontaines. Sartre goes on to say that when it is understood as an ontological concept, "you cannot put a brake on freedom", and that with his talk of "freedom without brakes" Camus has confused "politics and philosophy" (*SCHC*: 145–6; Sartre 1952: 343–4). The implication of this alleged confusion is significant, for it permits Camus to attribute to Sartre a view of freedom that licenses the nightmare of contemporary totalitarianism. Ronald Santoni endorses this reading of Camus, pointing to his claim in *The Rebel* that absolute freedom "is the freedom to kill". According to Santoni, Camus misunderstood Sartre's concept of freedom, and confused "ontological freedom and practical/political freedom" (Santoni 2003: 129–30). However, this argument does not stand up to a great deal of scrutiny. First, we note that, as Sprintzen points out, the phrase "freedom without brakes" [*liberté sans frein*] appears neither in Camus's letter nor in *The Rebel* itself. Furthermore, the view Camus actually attributes to Sartre in his letter, "this terrible and incessant freedom of which you speak", is to be found in *Being and Nothingness*: "this terrible necessity of being free".[38] Secondly, it is clear from a careful study of the material in question that Camus did not confuse ontological freedom with political freedom; instead (as I have argued above) he questioned whether a philosophy of teleological socialism could be reconciled with absolute ontological freedom. He claims that such a "perilous reconciliation" is necessary to the coherence of the philosophical and political agenda of *Les Temps modernes*, and he considers Jeanson's failure to address this question directly as an endorsement of his suspicion that such a reconciliation is impossible.[39] Curiously, although Ronald Santoni fails to recognize the argument as it appears in Camus's letter, he later makes the same argument himself, suggesting that interpreted through the optic of *Being and Nothingness* certain of Sartre's later writings would seem to be in bad faith because they impose "an unsurpassable limit on the unlimited freedom of every individual in the group . . . freedom has now placed chains on itself". Later, referring to the discussion of "necessary" violence in Sartre's "Rome Lecture" (which I discuss below), Santoni asks, "what is the sense of the word 'necessary' in this context? It is surely not a 'necessary' that precludes freedom to do otherwise in this situation. That would violate Sartre's ontology", and concludes with an observation that echoes Camus's complaint: "it is the inexactness of his words as well as the duplicity in his position that moves the reader to seek more *moral* definition or closure with regard to his revolutionary 'contradiction' (his word)" (Santoni 2003: 48, 160).

The strength of Camus's argument seems to be further endorsed by Sartre's more conspicuous failure to address it directly in his open letter, and it could be said that it is precisely this question, that of the compatibility of his existentialism with his Marxism, that Sartre eventually addresses in his *Critique of Dialectical Reason* (1960). Strikingly, when Sartre goes on to discuss political freedom directly in his response to Camus, he asserts that "The limit of a right (i.e. a freedom) is another right (that is to say, still another freedom) and not some human nature" (*SCHC*: 146; Sartre 1952: 344). Santoni is probably correct to interpret this reference to "human nature" as a "swipe" at Camus, although on the surface there seems to be nothing in Sartre's assertion with which Camus would disagree, except to note that the recognition of another's freedom might itself presuppose a common human nature (Santoni 2003: 130). It is perhaps worth noting that in his 1946 essay "Materialism and Revolution", Sartre expressed a view strikingly similar to Camus in this regard ("The declaration that 'We too are men' is at the bottom of any revolution" (Sartre 1955a: 217)), but it is clear that by 1952 for Sartre the dilemma created by the fact of incompatible freedoms is not resolved by resort to talk of human nature, but only through conflict: freedom today, he says in his letter to Camus, "is nothing but *the free choice to fight in order to become free*" (*SCHC*: 146; Sartre 1952: 345, original italics). The implicit denial of this reality, the reality of oppression, in *The Rebel*, says Sartre, is proof of Camus's irrelevance. Here we find ourselves back on familiar territory: Camus is seen as "hostile to history", has "gone into a corner all by himself to sulk", belongs in "the Galapagos islands" and so on (*SCHC*: 149, 147, 144; Sartre 1952: 347, 345, 343). But Camus's question, regarding the putative incompatibility of Sartre's existentialism with his Marxism, remained unanswered.

Until now Sartre has interpreted Camus's critique of historicism as a rejection of his own historicity, his own historical "situatedness", the implication of which was his locating the source of all social or political injustice outside history, beyond human agency. However, in the letter's penultimate paragraph he appears to acknowledge that what Camus was really questioning was the assertion that history had a necessary end or objective. Sartre responds to this argument by claiming that "Marx never said that History would have an end. How could he? One might as well say that one day man would be without goals. He spoke only of an end to prehistory, that is, of a goal that would be reached within History itself and then surpassed like all goals" (*SCHC*: 157; Sartre 1952: 353). Of course, from the point of view of a critique of historicism, whether it was the end of prehistory or history that Marx had predicted was irrelevant, for the principle of historical determinism would still apply, and it was against precisely this principle that *The Rebel* was substantially addressed. Indeed, Camus explicitly addresses this Marxist distinction between history and prehistory in the essay – "Capitalism is the last of these stages of production [the Marxist 'objective stages of historical development'] because it produces the conditions in which every antagonism will be resolved and where there will be no more economy. On that day our history will become prehistory" – and finds it spurious, noting that "we come no nearer to solving the problem by declaring that it is not a question of the end of history, but of a leap into the midst of a different history. We can only imagine this other history in terms of our own history; for man they are both one and the same thing. Moreover, this other history poses the same dilemma. Either it is not the solution of all contradictions and we suffer, die, and kill for almost nothing, or it is the solution of contradictions and therefore, to all intents and purposes, terminates our history" (*R*: 197, 223; *E*: 602, 627).

Concluding his letter, Sartre rephrases the essence of his response thus: "Does History have a meaning, you ask? Has it an end? For me this question has no meaning. Because History, apart from the men who make it, is only an abstract and static concept, of which it can neither be said that it has an end, nor that it doesn't have one. And the problem is not to *know* its end, but to give one to it" (*SCHC*: 157; Sartre 1952: 352). This is interesting for two reasons. First, one could suggest on the basis of it that whereas Camus sought to give history a meaning ("I continue to believe that this world has no ultimate meaning. But I know something in it has meaning, and that is man, because he is the only creature to insist on having one" (*RRD*: 28; *E*: 241)), Sartre seems to have sought to give history an objective or end ("the problem is not to *know* its end, but to *give* it one" (*SCHC*: 157; Sartre 1952: 352)). It is precisely this that Camus finds objectionable in Marx – whether one seeks to create history's end by giving history an end one desires, or one claims to have determined the nature of that end in advance of its coming into being, Camus asserts that when we live towards ends, the bodies pile up (of course, giving human existence "meaning" is not at all the same as "giving history an end"). In the course of another, not entirely unrelated, polemical exchange in 1955, Camus asserted:

> When I criticize twentieth century Communism for judging everything in terms of the future, it is because that future is represented as definitive, and that that happy end of history then authorizes all excesses. The future in history, when one calculates it, is simply the gathering of different possibilities, and in order to decide upon an attitude toward history it is necessary to consider each of these options. The future of history, then, can justify no dogmatism, but demands that a risk be taken. It is utterly unreal to consider history as so determined in advance as to not bother trying to give it, through risk and commitment, a meaning by which we can live.   (*E*: 1755)

Raymond Aron similarly notes that Sartre's point here "lacks something of the rules of honest discussion. There is no doubt that we give an objective to History by our actions. But how are we to choose that objective, without recourse to universal values or a unified understanding?"[40]

The second reason why the conclusion to Sartre's letter is interesting is because it is based upon an entirely spurious premise. Camus nowhere asks whether "history [or, for that matter, 'History'] has a meaning". What he does ask, in his reply to Jeanson, is whether history has "a *necessary* meaning and an end". Camus clearly believes that although no such necessary meaning can be known to exist, a limited meaning can be *created* by man.[41] There is perhaps not a great deal that is philosophically complex about Camus's argument here, but there is something distinctly unsubtle about Sartre's wilful misreading of it. Although Sartre criticizes Camus for being "no longer anything but an abstraction of a rebel", it is precisely such abstraction (including Sartre's) that Camus is writing against in *The Rebel* (*SCHC*: 158; Sartre 1952: 353). In fact, Camus's is precisely a revolt *not* based upon abstraction.

Since there are few moments in Sartre's letter when he is not, in one way or another, underlining for his readers the extent of his political and philosophical differences with Camus, it is ironic that when he turns to explain his ideas in contrast to Camus's alleged "rejection of history", he actually articulates a view that in certain respects is remarkably similar to that of Camus:

> Whether or not there are values transcendent to history will not be discussed. It will simply be noted that, if there are any, they are manifested through human actions which are, by definition, historical. And this contradiction is essential to man. He makes himself historical in order to pursue the eternal, and discovers universal values in the concrete action that he undertakes in view of a specific result. If you say that this world is unjust, you have already lost the game. You are already outside, busily comparing a world without justice to a Justice without content. But you will discover Justice in each effort that you make to organise your efforts; in each effort to reapportion the burdens among your comrades; in each effort to subject yourself to discipline

or to apply it. . . . It is not a question of knowing whether History has a meaning and whether we should deign to participate in it, but to try, from the
moment we are up to our noses in it, to *give* to it the meaning that seems best
to us, by not refusing our support, however weak it may be, to any concrete
action that may require it.   (*SCHC*: 157–8; Sartre 1952: 352–3)

Although there does seem to be a great deal here with which Camus would concur,
there are at least two crucial points with which I think he would disagree: first,
Camus's modesty would prevent him from claiming to "pursue the eternal" in any
context; secondly, as we have seen, Camus was not of the view that the world was
unjust, but instead claimed in *The Rebel* that life must be lived with an effort to
create justice where it is found to be absent. On the other hand, in general terms, it
seems that Sartre's claim that we ought to try to give history a meaning seems close
to Camus's own thinking.

Camus and Sartre on violence

Notwithstanding this disconcerting affinity, it remains clear, as I have tried to show
throughout this chapter, that there were marked differences in the political evolution of Camus and Sartre. Chief among these differences, as the exchange of letters
in *Les Temps modernes* shows, was their conflicting attitudes to political violence and
its theoretical legitimization. I have discussed Camus's ideas on violence in detail
elsewhere, and although it is beyond the scope of this book to give a detailed account
of the trajectory of Sartre's thought on violence, it is perhaps worth attempting a
summary here, if only in order to illustrate the depth of the philosophical differences that existed between him and Camus. Ronald Santoni (2003) has provided an
exhaustive study of Sartre's ideas on violence, analysing them from their initial
ontological context in *Being and Nothingness* (1943) to their latest, and most surprising, formulation in the controversial *Hope Now* interviews, which took place
shortly before Sartre's death in 1980. Although he suggests a number of curious
similarities between Camus's writings on violence and Sartre's (notably in Sartre's
posthumously published *Notebooks for an Ethics*, written in 1947–8), for present
purposes it is reasonable to focus on those works where his ideas on violence
achieve their fullest expression: in the two volumes of the *Critique of Dialectical
Reason* (1960, 1985; trans. 1991; hereafter *CDRI* and *CDRII*) and the unpublished
"Rome Lecture" (1964), which Sartre scholars have interpreted as an "ethical sequel"
to *CDR*.[42]

In *Being and Nothingness* Sartre identified conflict as "the essence of the relations
between consciousnesses". It defines the nature of the relation between the self and
the other: "it is necessary above all that I be the one who is not the Other, and it is in
this very negation . . . that I make myself be and that the Other arises as the Other"
(Sartre 1956: 429, 283). However, the *Critique of Dialectical Reason* marks the
philosophical culmination of Sartre's post-war focus on the socio-historical context

of human existence, so rather than a phenomenological account of the origins of conflict, Sartre here emphasizes "how the economic, political, and social structures that humans create 'make' human beings" (Anderson 1993: 88). In this context, Sartre now interprets violence "in terms of purposive human activity aroused by conditions of material scarcity", noting, furthermore, that "scarcity makes the passive totality of individuals within a collectivity into an impossibility of co-existence".[43] This impossibility serves as the background to *CDR*'s description of the dialectical movement of social organization from individual praxis (the individual working on nature to satisfy his or her needs) to the common or group praxis (the group working on nature to satisfy their common needs), what Sartre calls the "group-in-fusion". Through this dialectic what Sartre calls "seriality" is "dissolved and human freedom is resurrected" (Santoni 2003: 42). Raymond Aron has observed that although the constitution of the "group-in-fusion" may represent what he calls a "perfect moment", "perfect moments do not last" (Aron 1975: 59, quoted in Santoni 2003: 43). Sartre himself acknowledges that "alienation exists as a constant danger within the practical group. . . . The most lively and united group is always in danger of relapsing into the series from which it came". To combat this danger, Sartre proposes as a "practical device" what he calls the oath or pledge, which he believes will "bind the group in unity and permanence". It is through this pledge that "the potential for violence and its justification – presumably within the framework of a new humanity – emerges in full force".[44] Indeed Sartre declares the oath to be "a statute of violence", a statute that "finds its origin in fear and its strength and élan through violence and the threat of *Terror*. The pledge purports to guarantee the freedom of everyone against necessity . . . even at the cost of one's life. 'To swear is to say, as a common individual, I demand that you kill me if I secede [or betray the group]. And this demand has no other goal but to establish Terror in me against the fear of the enemy'."[45] Terror becomes what Sartre calls the "fundamental statute" of the "pledged group", "the reciprocal 'right' of everyone in the group over the life and death of every other member" (*CDRI*: 430, 433; Santoni 2003: 44). Furthermore, in Sartre's analysis, far from destroying, terror unites, indeed it constitutes the "primary unity" of the pledged group. Through the combination of the "creative act of the pledge" and the statute of terror, what Sartre calls "fraternity-terror" is born (*CDRI*: 437).

Based on the synopsis so far, one might be inclined to agree with Raymond Aron's assessment of *CDR*, and view it simply as articulating "a philosophy of violence" (Aron 1975: 160, 214, quoted in Santoni 2003: 45). And the ethical anxieties that might be aroused in the reader by Sartre's talk of "fraternity-terror" are nowhere addressed in *CDR* itself, indeed are not addressed directly and substantively until the 1964 "Rome Lecture". In *CDR* violence is interpreted more or less unambigu-ously as the recuperation (or creation) of a right, and as counterviolence (violence against the violation of freedom), and therefore presents itself as justified, even as "cleansing" and regenerative (*CDRI*: 720; Santoni 2003: 46). Perhaps the clearest expression of this legitimate revolutionary violence, for Sartre, was to be found in anti-colonial violence. The violence of the Algerian insurrection, for example, in the midst of which *CDR* was published, was according to Sartre "simply an adoption of the despair in which the colonialist maintained the natives; its violence was simply a negation of the impossible [i.e. the impossible condition of the colonized subject] . . . The violence of the rebel *was* the violence of the colonialist; there was never any other."[46]

The second volume of *CDR*, drafted in 1958, left unfinished and published posthumously in 1985, should be read as an effort to apply the discoveries of the first volume to the question of "History". Specifically, Sartre says in the first volume, "it will attempt to establish that there is one human history, with *one* truth and *one* intelligibility" (*CDRI*: 69). Sartre's method of positing a single history is to interpret history as a "totalization". According to this interpretation, although actions and events follow one another sequentially, "the relations between them are not like those of links in a chain".

> The dialectical claim [i.e. Sartre's claim in *CDR*] is that while action A is fol-
> lowed by action B and then B by C, the relations between them are such that
> action B *contains* action A, and action C contains both A and B. In Sartre's
> terminology, action B *totalises* action A, and action C totalises action B. Again,
> using Sartre's terminology, the relations between actions A, B and C from a
> dialectical point of view are relations of interiority, and this, according to
> Sartre, is the point of view required to understand the historical process.
>
> (Dobson 1993: 64–5)

Further, since "the totalising nature of individual actions makes for dialectical intelligibility", "the bonds of interiority which make dialectical reason the right reason to 'read' history ensure that nothing is left 'outside' the 'totalisation without a totaliser', which is History".[47] Consequently, *CDRII* can be read as "an attempt to substitute unity for plurality at the level of history, not – as in volume one – through the formal demonstration of the dialectical intelligibility of 'practical structures' (groups, organisations and institutions), but by revealing the dialectical intelligibility of *struggles*". In order to do this Sartre seeks to show "the totalising movement" present "at the heart of even the most apparently disunited society – one riven by class struggle, for example: 'if the class struggle is to be intelligible to the historian's dialectical reason, one must be able to totalise classes in struggle – and this comes down to discovering the synthetic unity of a society riven through and through'" (Dobson 1993: 98, quoting *CDRII*: 15–16). Although he continues to see the "deep source" of conflict as "scarcity", Sartre now suggests that each particular case of disunity or conflict actually constitutes "an incarnation and singularisation of class struggle as it unfolds in contemporary forms of capitalism. *All* violence is 'gathered in, clarified and made explicit' in the single conflict or act of violence. . . . In this way, Sartre believes, violence and conflict – and, of course, History, the main focus of *Critique II* – can be rendered dialectically intelligible" (*CDRII*: 23; Santoni 2003: 64, quoting *CDRII*: 50).

This lengthy digression should serve as a sketch of the philosophical context in which the ideas regarding violence and its justification expressed in the "Rome Lecture" can be understood. According to Santoni, on whose summary of the unpublished lecture I largely rely, the "justificatory question" at the heart of the lecture can be put thus: "If there is but one way to humanity and it involves *means* incompatible with a human world, isn't action with humanity as its *end* impossible?" Sartre's response to this question, says Santoni, "is in the negative: humanity as end can continually look back at, scrutinise, alter, and moderate the means. Even terror – in which 'subhumans become the means of humanity' – introduces sanctions to accompany its orders." In order to better understand Sartre here it is important to take into account what he has to say about the relationship between means and ends. Contrary to the accepted view, but perhaps unsurprisingly given the philosophy of history he has developed in *CDRII*, Sartre does not think that the means can be considered separately from the ends in a given scenario. Accordingly, the so-called "scale metaphor", whereby means and ends are weighed against one another in determining the moral justness of a given action, is rejected by Sartre in favour of a conception of ends and means in which both are considered as constitutive parts of human action, where "the end synthesises or totalises the means [and where] the end does not come after the means", but "pervades their use, keeps them together as means and even guides them". Accordingly, "justificatory questions", of the type "If there is but one way to humanity and it involves *means* incompatible with a human world, isn't action with humanity as its *end* impossible?", which separate ends from means when determining moral legitimacy, "appear to be misdirected and/or to betray a radical misunderstanding of the structure of human action and the means–end 'unity' on which Sartre here insists" (Santoni 2003: 145–7).

All this forces a radical reinterpretation of the possibility of legitimate political violence because revolutionary means, forming a "synthetic unity" with revolutionary ends, can no longer be weighed independently of those ends. Looked at in this way, it becomes obvious that for Sartre "revolutionary praxis requires no external justification". Given the baldness of this assertion, Santoni wonders "whether the end of revolutionary praxis would preclude any means as part of its synthetic unity", or whether "all means [are] dialectically synthesisable with the 'end' of revolutionary praxis". Sartre provides a "quick answer" to this question, by asserting that "all means are good except those that denature the end" (Santoni 2003: 147).

Santoni finds an illustration of the meaning of this denaturing of ends in Sartre's early essay *What Is Literature?*, in which, he says, "Sartre had expressed serious reservations about systematically lying to a party's militants for the sake of abolishing oppression. . . . The lie itself, [Sartre] contended, is a form of oppression, and lying would, unfortunately, contribute to the creation of a '*lied-to* and *lying* mankind'" (Santoni 2003: 148). However, in the passage in question, Sartre does not in fact assert that lying is impermissible *because* it creates "a *lied-to* and *lying* mankind", but only *if* it creates "a *lied-to* and *lying* mankind". Although he claims that "the politics of the Communist Party, which consist of lying to its own troops, of calumniating, of hiding its defeats and its faults, compromises the goal which it pursues", he also notes that "on the other hand, it is easy to reply that in war – and every revolutionary party is at war – one cannot tell soldiers the whole truth".[48] In other words, Sartre here does not object to lying because it might denature the revolutionary end, but he will object to lying if it denatures the revolutionary end. This point is highlighted when Sartre goes on to discuss the "permissibility of terror". Whereas the legitimate use of terror is assumed in both *CDR* and his "Preface" to Fanon's *The Wretched of the Earth*, in the "Rome Lecture" Sartre attempts to *explain* its moral legitimacy. He does so by characterizing it not as a revolutionary means with the potential to denature the revolutionary end, but instead, within the context of the means–end synthetic unity, as "one of the 'night time moments' [*moments de nuit*] of 'making the human'"; terror "is a necessary action of counterviolence" against oppressive and dehumanizing systems (Santoni 2003: 148, quoting the "Rome Lecture"). As I have suggested earlier, probably the clearest instance of such terror, for Sartre, is to be found in anti-colonial violence, such as was practised by the Front de Libération Nationale in Algeria.

Notwithstanding the paradoxical relation between the assertion that "all means are good except those that denature the end" and the assertion of the legitimacy of terror as "necessary counterviolence", Santoni suggests that at this point in the lecture "Sartre proceeds to answer the kind of challenge regarding terror that Camus put to him [in the *Temps modernes* exchange]", by placing the following four "'enabling' or 'limiting' conditions" on its permissibility (Santoni 2003: 149):

- Terror is permissible only as a "provisional expedient" and only when it can be prevented from becoming "an alienating system like that of the oppressing adversary". In short, "if Terror is to be used only as a means to produce yet another exploitative system or to keep human beings in a state of subhumanity, it must *not* be permitted".
- Terror is permissible only "if those who employ Terror can preclude and therefore avoid all ideologies of Terror . . . Stalin's 'socialism in one country' is an example of what would not be permissible".
- Terror is permissible "only if no justification of Terror is offered other than its *necessity*", meaning that if a less violent and equally effective option is available then no grounds (such as, that it is "easier") can justify resorting to it.
- Terror is permissible "only if Terror has its 'origins in the masses'". Further, it must be considered "a deviation of humanity due to urgency", and, more, "a technique totally unjustifiable outside its effectiveness".[49]

Sartre believed that on meeting these conditions, "terror becomes revolutionary justice", and consequently, "the humanization of terror" becomes "possible *in principle*". It is clear that the above conditions would sanction the violence of, for example, the Algerian insurrection against French rule, but they would not sanction, says Santoni, "the institutionalised terror of the USSR, which made terror the keystone of an 'ideologically justified' system of government". Although Santoni

suggests that Sartre's argument constitutes "a belated elaboration and refined ration-
ale for what he and Jeanson were militantly contending against Camus in their
1952 confrontation", he acknowledges that it is not "completely without ambiguity"
(Santoni 2003: 151–2). However, I suspect that if we are to treat Sartre's argument
as a *moral* argument its "shortcomings" are evidently far more serious than Santoni
admits.

First, just as Sartre's "denaturing of the end" criterion, mentioned earlier, "does
not easily or unambiguously distinguish what is not permissible", his resort here to
terms such as "necessity" and "effectiveness" (not to mention such heavily weighted
terms as "ideologies", his use of which implies the Marxist commonplace that it
itself was not an ideology) seems to undermine whatever moral sense his arguments
appear at first to possess. After all, legitimizing violence on the grounds of "effectiveness" is surely the opposite of an ethical or moral argument. Secondly, we note
that Sartre's insistence on the synthetic unity of the means and ends ("the end does
not come after the means", he says at one point, but "pervades their use, keeps
them together as means and even guides them") implies not only a certainty that
terror will contribute to the achievement of that end, but that the end itself is
inexorable (Santoni 2003: 152, 146). Thirdly, and finally, as Thomas Anderson has
observed, "none of the conditions Sartre presents involves distinguishing between
violence against innocent people and violence against aggressors seeking to destroy
human beings. Yet such a distinction seems crucial to any moral consideration."
Santoni, too, conceded that this failure on Sartre's part constitutes a "significant
omission".[50]

This might suggest that Sartre's arguments in defence of political violence,
although self-evidently justificatory, are not meant to be *moral* arguments. In this
view, although Sartre evidently seeks to justify political violence, and indeed suggests a number of limiting conditions that can be applied to the use of such violence,
the arguments he deploys to this end are not themselves moral arguments. When
we consider his assertion, for instance, that in the context of revolutionary violence
"all means are good except those that denature the end", we might conclude that
Sartre's arguments are based simply on the expediency of revolutionary means in
achieving revolutionary ends. Similarly, we could explain Sartre's failure to incor-
porate a consideration of innocent victims into his analysis of violence on the basis
that, in the context of revolutionary praxis (a context in which Sartre believed that
humanity "does not yet exist, . . . is incomplete, lacking and alienated"), there are
no grounds on which such a morality could be established (Santoni 2003: 142
n.11). This view seems to be endorsed by Elizabeth Bowman and Robert Stone, who
note that "Sartre's dialectical ethics" contains no "general rules or principles of right
action" because "for Sartre, no such positive norm is required to justify revolutionary praxis". In fact, Bowman and Stone (who are probably the foremost experts on
Sartre's "Rome Lecture") note elsewhere that according to Sartre, "due to class, sex,
race, ethnic and other oppressions that deny freedom, a universal morality is not
now possible", and that "revolt is 'justified' not by a morality (such an end is only in
process of construction) but by the oppression of systemic exploitation to which it

responds" (Bowman & Stone 1986: 209; Bowman & Stone 2004: 8). They illustrate this point with a pertinent contemporary statement from Sartre:

> Sartre held that the mark of the "false intellectual" is to affirm *there is* such a universal morality "here and now", though it can only be that of the small bourgeois class. By denying society is "an arena of struggle between particular groups . . . for the statute of universality" such intellectuals act as watchdogs for that class. By contrast "true intellectuals" insist "man does not exist" but is rather "the distant goal of a practical and daily enterprise" consisting of [the] "liquidation of particularisms" in a movement of "universalization" on the part of "the immense majority, particularized by the oppression and exploitation which make of them the products of their products".
>
> (Bowman & Stone 2004: 24 n.22, quoting "A Plea for Intellectuals",
> in Sartre 1974c: 249–58)

However, Bowman and Stone also make it clear that, paradoxically, Sartre *did* consider his justification of violence in the "Rome Lecture" to be a moral justification, calling it a "socialist morality", which asserts both "the present impossibility of being moral" and "the moral primacy of revolution". Evidently the morality proposed here is a revolutionary morality, which he pits against the various oppressive moralities (sexist, racist, classist etc.) of the status quo. Sartre's "socialist morality", they explain, "is a set of guidelines for securing conditions of concrete freedom that will make moral conduct on such a universal standard possible" at some point in the future (Bowman & Stone 2004: 6–8, 16). It may well be that, as Linda Bell argues, Sartre believed that violence could never be legitimated according to what he himself calls "a universal morality", but that question seems of little significance, given that Sartre succeeded in granting political violence legitimacy according to a revolutionary morality of his own devising (termed an "*interim* morality of universalization" by Bowman and Stone), and given that he appears to have accorded such violence unique authority in making such a future "universal morality" possible.[51]

It is probably this absence of a moral sense not subsumed under the revolutionary agenda of the *CDR* that leads Benny Lévy to suggest in *Hope Now* that there is in Sartre's work "a profound tendency toward an ethic of violence" (Sartre 1996: 93). It is also probably the basis of that "combination of moral neutrality and necessitarianism" that Ronald Aronson identified in *CDRII* (Aronson 1987: 179, quoted in Dobson 1993: 104). Furthermore, although critics may disagree about the legitimacy of interjecting "extraneous moral judgements into [the] properly historical and theoretical account" of *CDRII*, no such objection can be made regarding the "Rome Lecture" because it presents itself precisely as a moral defence of political violence (Aronson 1987: 179; Dobson 1993: 104). Although Sartre continued to reflect on the possibility of legitimate violence, most notably in *Hope Now* (where, *contra CDR*, he declares violence to be "the very opposite of fraternity" (Sartre 1996: 93)), it seems that the "ethical" argument contained in the "Rome Lecture" leaves a great deal to be desired.

Although the lecture was written more than a decade after the dispute with Camus, we must remember that its approach to morality is distinctive only in its articulation of the so-called limiting conditions on terror, and its general thesis on morality and violence, which is so obviously at odds with the philosophy of *la mesure* in *The Rebel*, had been worked out much earlier. In fact, we see an early expression of Sartre's posited philosophy of "unfolding totalization" (Bowman & Stone 1991: 68) in his *Saint Genet: Actor and Martyr*, which was published shortly before his response to Camus's letter in 1952:

> Either morality is stuff and nonsense or it is a concrete totality which achieves a synthesis of Good and Evil. . . . The abstract separation of these two concepts expresses simply the alienation of man. The fact remains that, in the historical situation, this synthesis cannot be achieved. Thus, any Ethic which does not explicitly profess that it is *impossible today* contributes to the bamboozling and alienation of men. The ethical "problem" arises from the fact that Ethics is *for us* inevitable and at the same time impossible. Action must give itself ethical norms in this climate of nontranscendable impossibility. It is from this outlook that, for example, we must view the problem of violence or that of the relationship between ends and means. To a mind that experienced this agony and was at the same time forced to will and to decide, *all high-minded rebellion, all outcries of refusal, all virtuous indignation, would seem a kind of outworn rhetoric.*   (Sartre 1964a: 186n., emphasis added)

I have already noted that Camus's quarrel with Sartre over *The Rebel* was preceded by a conceptually related dispute over Merleau-Ponty's "Le Yogi et le Prolétaire" in 1946. I have also noted that in his editorials in *Les Temps modernes* and in works such as *Baudelaire* and *What is Literature?* (both 1947) Sartre had begun to articulate a political position plainly at odds with that of Camus, particularly with regard to political violence.[52] It could be said, however, that the extent and nature of the differences between Sartre's and Camus's ideas on political violence only really became explicit with the appearance of their respective plays, *Dirty Hands* (1948) and *The Just Assassins* (1949).[53] Although the submerged dialogue we can discern between the two plays can be seen to presage the very public disagreement that followed a few years later, it is important that it be seen in this broader context as well.

Immediately on comparing the two plays one is struck by the clear thematic similarities, the most important of which is their common preoccupation with the question of the legitimacy of political violence. Both plays are concerned with individual acts of political assassination (one based on the assassination of Grand Duke Sergi, the other, much more loosely, on the assassination of Trotsky) and both generate a good deal of their dramatic momentum by pitting the arguments of a revolutionary "realist" (Stepan in the case of *The Just Assassins*, Hoederer in the case of *Dirty Hands*) against those of a revolutionary "idealist" (Kaliayev in the case of *The Just Assassins*, Hugo in the case of *Dirty Hands*). Although in the context of his play

Sartre declared that "a good play ought to present problems, not solve them", there is abundant evidence that, as Simone de Beauvoir states, Sartre's "sympathy went to Hoederer", the revolutionary realist, rather than Hugo the idealist (Sartre 1974a: 188; de Beauvoir 1968: 160). It is Hoederer who insists that revolution "is not a question of virtue but of effectiveness", who articulates and defends the concept of "dirty hands":

> How you cling to your purity, young man! How afraid you are to soil your hands! All right, stay pure! What good will it do? Why did you join us? Purity is an idea for a yogi or a monk. You intellectuals and bourgeois anarchists use it as a pretext for doing nothing. To do nothing, to remain motionless, arms at your sides, wearing kid gloves. Well, I have dirty hands. Right up to the elbows. I've plunged them in filth and blood. But what do you hope? Do you think you can govern innocently?   (Sartre 1989: 229, 218)

Sartre himself repeatedly asserts in contemporary interviews that "politics requires us to 'get our hands dirty' " and insists that in rejecting Hoederer's "politics of compromise", Hugo "is still acting from the bourgeois idealism which was precisely what had made him rebel against his class and which he did not succeed in overcoming".[54] An illustrative example of Hoederer's willingness to dirty his hands can be seen in his attitude to lying. In contrast to Hugo, who says that on joining the (Communist) Proletarian Party "for the first time I saw men who didn't lie to other men", Hoederer insists, "we have always told lies, just like any other party . . . I'll lie when I must . . . I wasn't the one who invented lying. It grew out of a society divided into classes, and each one of us has inherited it from birth. We shall not abolish lying by refusing to tell lies, but by using every means at hand to abolish classes."[55] Ironically, given Sartre's insistence that Hoederer's was also *his* view, it seems that the public (and the communists) continued to interpret the play as being anti-communist, something to which Sartre objected and that ultimately led him, in December 1952, to prohibit production of the play anywhere without the imprimatur of the local Communist Party.[56]

This interpretation of *Dirty Hands*, and its contrast with Camus's evolving ideas on the legitimacy of political violence (to which I will turn shortly), is given further endorsement by Sartre in an interview with his Italian translator, Paolo Caruso, in 1964. Although he admits to having "great understanding for Hugo's attitude", Sartre says that Hoederer "is the man I'd like to be if I were a revolutionary". He further relates that, after attending one of the play's final rehearsals, Camus told him there was a detail in the play he did not "approve of", and asked "Why does Hugo say, 'I don't love men for what they are but for what they ought to be' . . . and why does Hoederer answer, 'And I love them for what they are'? The way I see it [says Camus], it should have been just the opposite." Sartre insists that Camus's interpretation was based on a fundamental confusion: "He really though that Hugo loved men for what they are since he didn't want to lie to them, whereas Hoederer, on the contrary, became in his eyes a dogmatic Communist who weighed men in terms of what they ought to be and who deceived them in the name of an ideal. This is just the opposite of what I meant to say."[57] Ronald Aronson's gloss on this statement is instructive: "For Camus, sticking to principle and refusing to lie for the sake of politics was inseparable from respecting people and loving them. For Sartre, acting on principle dictated being true to long-term ends" (Aronson 2004: 106). Sartre himself goes on in the same interview to explain in some detail what he *did* mean to say in *Dirty Hands*:

> I think there should be as little lying as possible *within the limits imposed by the imperatives of praxis*. Lying should not be condemned nor, of course, approved *a priori* (by making a Machiavellian technique of it, for instance) but there is nothing abnormal about its happening, when circumstances require it. When Hoederer says, "It is not I who invented the lie and I shall use it if it is necessary", I think he is quite right. There has never been a political situation in which lying, by omission at any rate, does not become absolutely essential . . . Hoederer tries to speak the truth as far as possible; lying is not in his nature, except that he does not recoil either from lying or from political murder when they are the necessities of praxis.[58]

Where Sartre articulates and defends a view of history in which, as de Beauvoir puts it, "the vanity of morality" confronts "the efficacy of *praxis*",[59] it is hardly surprising to find that Camus favoured the idealist's approach to the use of revolutionary violence. Although Camus was far from considering the Socialist Revolutionaries to be perfect models of legitimate political violence (we remember that in "Defence of *The Rebel*" he criticized them for what he perceived to be their *complete* lack of realism), he unambiguously favoured the revolutionary idealism of Kaliayev over the realism of Stepan, and sought to construct his ethic of legitimate violence precisely *against* such realism as was by then being advocated by Sartre. For example, Kaliayev's decision not to throw the bomb into the Grand Duke's carriage because it contained his nephew and niece provokes Stepan's "realist" declaration that "nothing that can serve our cause should be ruled out". Stepan also makes explicit what for Camus is the implication of such "realism" in his assertion: "Not until the day comes when we stop being sentimental about children, will the revolution triumph and we be masters of the world" (*COP*: 186, 185; *TRN*: 337, 336). Camus's favouring of idealism over realism was, naturally, interpreted by Sartre and others as representing an ideology of "clean hands", or the *de facto* pacifism of a "beautiful soul"; indeed, it was seen to involve the same "rejection of history" that he and Jeanson identified in *The Rebel*.[60] None of this, though, should lead us to suspect that Camus was, perhaps despite himself, a pacifist. If not entirely won over to the view of Camus as pacifist, Ronald Santoni, for example, repeatedly exhibits a tendency to articulate it: for example, he asserts near the end of his discussion of *The Just Assassins* that "it is evident that [Camus] is mobilizing all the arguments he can against revolutionary violence and murder and putting before the reader the human consequences of so-called justified murder" (Santoni 2003: 115). As I have shown elsewhere, violence remained for Camus inevitable and, under certain circumstances, legitimate. His main concern was to address the enthusiasm with which some of his contemporaries embraced violence, and the arguments they offered in its defence. Ronald Aronson, too, is ambiguous on Camus's attitude to political violence. Although he recognizes that Camus was not a "pacifist", he nonetheless highlights what he calls Camus's preoccupation "with keeping his hands clean".[61] What "clean hands" means for Aronson is not always very clear, for at one point he characterizes it (justly, I believe) as Camus's insistence "on the use of violence only when absolutely necessary, within limits, [and] in response to a vital threat", yet elsewhere he characterizes Camus as "the man who so decried violence and sought clean hands", and suggests that having "only reluctantly accepted violence" in *Letters to a German Friend*, after the Second World War Camus became "more and more visible as an opponent of political violence", an opposition that, according to Aronson, culminates in *The Rebel* (Aronson 2004: 90, 219, 34). Whereas Camus deliberately maintained a paradoxical attitude to political violence, declaring it, for example, "at the same time unavoidable and unjustifiable", both Santoni and Aronson display a tendency to read Camus as insisting that violence was simply "unjustifiable", while understating (though not necessarily discounting) the properly paradoxical nature of his interpretation of political violence. Aronson also seems to see in *The Just Assassins* an articulation of what I have called elsewhere the "life for a life" thesis, whereby the revolutionary's violent action is granted legitimacy only at the cost of the revolutionary's own life (*E*: 355–6; Aronson 2004: 117, 123, 124; Santoni 2003: 164).

In any event, what *Camus* meant by "clean hands" can be readily discerned by a cursory examination of his use of this phrase. He suggests, for example, that because the French were not responsible for starting the Second World War, they entered it with "clean hands": "Time will tell", he wrote as Paris was being liberated in August 1944, "that the men of France did not want to kill and that they went with clean hands into a war that was not of their own choosing."[62] "The choice to kill was not ours", he says in an editorial from the previous day. "We were placed in a position where we had either to kill or to bend our knees" (*CC*: 15; *CAC8*: 148). What this suggests is that "clean hands" for Camus did not necessitate the rejection of all violence, but only that violence be accepted under specific circumstances (in this case, under the circumstances of an unwanted, unprovoked war). This is what Camus means when he says in *Letters to a German Friend* that not only did the Resistance go into war with clean hands, but that they will also emerge from the war with clean hands.[63] Therefore, Camus's supposed preference for clean hands, such as it is (expressed in print on three occasions between 1943 and 1944), does not in any way preclude the possibility of legitimate violence.[64]

A final observation that should be made here regarding Camus's "clean hands" versus Sartre's *Dirty Hands* is that the examples of legitimate political violence in Camus's works – the assassinations of Caligula and Sergi – quite literally involve the protagonists dirtying their hands. As I have argued elsewhere, the direct involvement of the perpetrator in his or her violence seems to have been central to Camus's conception of its legitimacy.[65] A commitment to "dirty hands", a willingness, according to Sartre, to "compromise between the ideal and the real", was for Camus no assurance of revolutionary commitment. For him, genuine fidelity to the revolution necessitated a willingness not only to take an active part in it, but also, perhaps, to be willing to sacrifice one's own life in its defence. Perhaps with Sartre's play in mind, Camus's Kaliayev, angered by Stepan's denigration of his revolutionary commitment, shouts "Look! Do you think that hand will tremble? No, it won't tremble. Do you think that I shall hesitate when the Grand Duke is there in front of me? Surely you cannot think that!", and crucially, Kaliayev concludes: "And even if my arm did begin to tremble . . . I know a sure way of killing him . . . I'd throw myself under the horses' feet" (*COP*: 171; *TRN*: 318). The question of dirty hands, then, is a pseudo-question, one which implies that there are only two possible approaches to the issue of political violence: the view that it is necessary and legitimate ("dirty hands") and the view that it is never necessary and never legitimate (what Aronson seems to mean by "clean hands"). Such talk of dirty and clean hands seems to permit little more than a fine display of bombast regarding the depths of one's revolutionary commitment, while side-stepping all of those issues that it might be said *should* be at the heart of a discussion of political violence, such as the possible criteria for ascribing to it a degree of moral legitimacy. Camus would certainly have found something rather grotesque in the implication that the refusal to have innocent blood on one's hands was to refuse to get one's hands dirty, and indeed he objected most strenuously to the conspicuous cleanness of the hands of precisely those defending a philosophy of dirty hands.

In the more general context of Sartre's political evolution, it is important to point out that at the time of Jeanson's review of *The Rebel* and the subsequent exchange of letters, Sartre was in fact attempting to align himself publicly with the communists. This stage of his political development culminated in the writing of *The Communists and Peace*, which coincided exactly with his split with Camus in 1952: indeed, Camus's letter and Sartre's response literally interrupt the serial publication of the essay in *Les Temps modernes*.[66] According to Ronald Aronson, this lengthy essay presented "the theoretical argument for his identification of the PCF with the proletariat", as well as the "social and historical basis for this identification". What this identification meant in practice, however, according to another critic, was that "the Party's politics must, therefore, be accepted", since "the future of democracy is in the hands of the working man and the Communist Party is the party of the working class" (Aronson 1980: 219; Burnier 1968: 83). Examining this essay now, we can see clearly that the arguments in his letter to Camus are entirely consistent with those in *The Communists and Peace*, and in a certain respect the letter and the serialized essay form a coherent whole. Further, given the extent of what Sartre called his "conversion", it seems plausible to suggest that although he may not have sought such a dramatic public split with Camus, it was unlikely to have caused him much upset when it occurred. He had, after all, decided at this time that "an anti-Communist was a rat", and Camus was for Sartre precisely such an anti-communist.[67] As Ronald Aronson illustrates, the "political evolution" evinced in

Sartre's attack on Camus did not go unnoticed in the communist press, and "the break earned [him] points with the Party" (Aronson 2004: 166). Speaking of *The Communists and Peace* and Sartre's letter to Camus, de Beauvoir asserts that the two pieces of writing

> had the same meaning: the postwar period was over. No more postponements, no more conciliations were possible. We had been forced into making clear-cut choices. Despite the difficulty of his position, Sartre still knew he had been right to adopt it. [Quoting from Sartre's unpublished notes, she continues] "I had to take some step that would make me 'other'. I had to accept the point of view of the USSR in its totality."   (De Beauvoir 1968: 274)

Although Sartre's attitude to the communists was to change (notably after the Soviet invasion of Hungary in 1956), his view of Camus did not, and the position taken by the latter on Algerian independence, which is discussed in the next chapter, was seen as conclusive proof of his fundamental "hostility to history". After Camus's death in 1960 Sartre wrote little about their relationship, and what he did write was often contradictory. For example, his frequently cited and anthologized obituary associates Camus with the French *moralistes*, and admires his "stubborn humanism, strict and pure, austere and sensual, [which] delivered uncertain combat against the massive and deformed events of the day". He also observes that "by the unexpectedness of his refusals, he reaffirmed, at the heart of our era, against the Machiavellians, against the golden calf of realism, the existence of the moral act".[68] As profound and generous as these words seem, they are somewhat complicated by Sartre's own disdain for the *moralistes*, and by subsequent comments made to his friend John Gerassi:

> There is a little falsehood in the obituary I wrote about Camus, when I say that even when he disagreed with us, we wanted to know what he thought. . . . He wasn't a boy who was made for all that he tried to do, he should have been a little crook from Algiers, a very funny one, who might have managed to write a few books, but mostly remain a crook. Instead of which you had the impression that civilisation had been stuck on top of him and he did what he could with it, which is to say, he did nothing.[69]

However, as personally antagonistic as they may have remained, Sartre's reference in his obituary to the "golden calf of realism" does seem to suggest a certain self-criticism and a softening of his views of the historical imperatives of revolutionary violence. In this light it is perhaps useful to follow Ronald Aronson in considering the Sartre and Camus dispute in the context of the competing values of politics and morality. For Aronson, Camus locates morality "outside history", and suggests that his morality, untethered from the weighty demands of the political, too easily turned to moralizing.[70] This, of course, was also the view of Sartre: "You became violent and terrorist when History – which you rejected – rejected you in turn. . . . Your morality first changed into moralism. Today it is only literature. Tomorrow perhaps it will be immorality."[71] Although there is no evidence that Camus located the morality "outside history", it is certainly the case that for him the prerogatives of morality always outweighed those of politics (in so far as they could be separated from the political). Sartre, as we have seen, developed a markedly different approach to the relationship between politics and morality. For him "ethics became indistinguishable from history and politics", and "being moral involved acknowledging that we and our world are inescapably violent". Sartre "finally articulated the framework for an ethics that would satisfy him, namely, that radical political change is the only path for creating a world in which moral human relations are possible" (Aronson 2004: 112). Clearly then, if Camus subordinated politics to morality, Sartre subordinated morality to politics. Although Camus's attempt at a resolution of politics and morality may be seen to have failed, it was surely a far less egregious failure than that committed by Sartre. Indeed Sartre seemed to recognize that his attempt to forge a politically efficacious morality had been a failure when, in the mid-1970s, he spoke frankly of his reasons for rejecting "moralism" in favour of political realism: "you do it because it works, and . . . you evaluate it according to its efficacity rather than some vague notions having to do with morality, which would only slow things up". However, he also insists that "that whole idea didn't sit too well with me, it upset me no end, despite the fact that – ignoring my own better judgement – I carried it through and finally arrived at a pure realism: what's real is true, and what's true is real. And when I had reached that point, what it meant was that I had blocked out all ideas of morality."[72]

This does appear to suggest a greater sympathy with Camus's "stubborn humanism", his principled stand "against the Machiavellians, against the golden calf of realism" (Aronson (2004: 229) goes as far as to suggest that the unfinished second volume of Sartre's *CDR* "poses precisely the same questions" as *The Rebel*: "how did a revolution aiming at human emancipation create hell on earth?"). However, while I have suggested when discussing *The Rebel* that there are good reasons to consider Camus as an advocate of "anti-political politics", and while it is helpful to consider his reconciliation of politics and morality by resort to this idea, there appears to be a very different kind of ambivalence in Sartre's attempt at the same reconciliation. In the same interview in which he admits to a period of commitment to political realism, he identifies as the moment when he reintroduced morality into politics his encounter in the late 1960s with the Maoists, saying that although Marxism had always presupposed a morality, "it's Mao who clarified it and gave it flesh" (Sartre 1978a: 80). Accordingly, we can say that Sartre's reconciliation of politics and morality is neatly described in his defence of what he identifies as the distinct "morality" of Maoist violence:

> For the Maoists . . . everywhere that revolutionary violence is born among the masses, it is immediately and profoundly moral. This is because the workers, who have up to that point been the objects of capitalist authoritarianism, become the subjects of their own history, even if only for a moment. . . . Yet

even though the economic and political motives of the explosions of popular violence are obvious, the explosions cannot be explained except by the fact that these motives were *morally* appreciated by the masses. That is, the economic and political motives helped the masses to understand what is the highest immorality – the exploitation of man by man. So when the bourgeois claims that his conduct is guided by a "humanistic" morality – work, family, nation – he is only disguising his deep-seated immorality and trying to alienate the workers: he will never be moral. Whereas the workers and the country people, when they revolt, are completely moral because they are not exploiting anyone.[73]

Although the general idea of a reconciliation of morality and politics might indeed be discernible in the works of both Camus and Sartre, we can only conclude that the respective reconciliations they sought (let alone whatever reconciliation they might be said to have achieved) were of markedly different varieties.

6 | CAMUS AND ALGERIA

> Today Algeria is a territory inhabited by two peoples ... Yet the two peoples of Algeria have an equal right to justice and an equal right to preserve their nation.[1]

> I should like to be able to love my country and still love justice. I don't want just any greatness for it, particularly a greatness born of blood and falsehood. I want to keep it alive by keeping justice alive. You retorted: "Well you don't love your country".[2]

A new Mediterranean culture

Camus's attitude to Algerian independence remains highly controversial, but his position can be stated simply: although he believed that Algeria was culturally and historically inextricable from France, he loathed the injustice of its system of government, which served the interests of the tiny minority of wealthy European *colons*. Any attempt at understanding Camus's paradoxical attitude to Algeria must begin by avoiding the easy assumption that the conflict that broke out in Algeria in 1954 was simply between the demands of French imperialism and those of Algerian independence. Although the conflict *can* be reduced to this, it is not always helpful to do so, because it obscures some factors that are necessary to a reasonably clear understanding of the conflict itself, as well as Camus's response to it. Perhaps the most important of these factors are the circumstances of Camus's Algerian background. Camus was not in Algeria, as Conor Cruise O'Brien puts it, by right of conquest (the same right, Cruise O'Brien notes, by which the Nazis were in France). Like virtually all the *pieds noirs* in Algeria in the mid-twentieth century, Camus lived in Algeria by virtue of having been born there. Indeed, both his parents and two of his grandparents were born in Algeria (his other grandparents were born in Minorca and Marseilles). Of course, notwithstanding this genealogy, one might insist that Camus was at least culturally French (he was, after all, the beneficiary of the French colonial educational system, and was a French citizen). But this too only accounts for part of Camus's background. His father was fatally wounded fighting at the First Battle of the Marne in 1914, and Camus was brought up in the home of his maternal grandmother (who was born in Minorca), and it would probably be more accurate to

assert that he was culturally *pied-noir*, meaning of the distinctive melange of Mediterranean European cultures present in Algeria at that time. Of the million or so
pieds-noirs living in Algeria at this time, the majority were of French descent, and
many of those were descendants of the refugees who came to Algeria in the wake
of the loss of Alsace and Lorraine after the disastrous Franco-Prussian war in 1871
(it is significant that Camus believed that his French ancestors belonged to this
group of refugees). Although the institutional racism of French rule in Algeria is
undoubted, it is also clearly not the case that Algeria was divided simply into a dis-
enfranchised Arab and Berber majority and a parasitic wealthy French minority.
Germaine Tillion points out that of 1.2 million non-Muslims in Algeria in 1958, only
about 45,000 constituted "settlers" in the sense that they or their families were landowners (of whom, by her calculations, a little over 1,000 were rich). The remaining
European population of Algeria, "well over a million men, women and children",
were "skilled workers, government officials, office employees, taxi-drivers, garage
proprietors, station-masters, nurses, telephone girls, labourers, tradesmen and
heads of businesses" (Tillion 1958a: 4–5). The young Camus, as the son of a cellar-
man who was killed in the Great War in 1914, and an illiterate cleaning woman,
would have found himself at the bottom end of this economic scale. Although the
poverty among the worst off of the Arabs and Berbers was still worse that that
endured by the working-class European Algerians, it is doubtful that Camus, in
refusing Algerian demands for independence, was concerned to defend the economic and political rights of a parasitic class of wealthy landowners.[3]

What Camus did wish to defend in the face of the demands for Algerian independence was what he called in a youthful lecture from 1937 a "new Mediterranean
culture", and more controversially, an "indigenous culture". Writing in the context
of the rise of fascism and anti-Semitism across Europe, and indeed in Algeria, in the
context of the Spanish Civil War and the Italian invasion of Ethiopia, Camus insists
upon the reality of a Mediterranean culture and, crucially, upon its difference from
the pro-fascist and often anti-Semitic doctrine of "Latinity", an ideology then popular with the *pied-noir* political elite in Algeria, most notably with the then Mayor of
Algiers, Augustin Rozis (who, a year earlier, had banned the performance of *Révolte
dans les Asturies*, a play about the 1934 workers' revolt in Asturias co-authored by
Camus). Camus argued that the real heart of Mediterranean culture was Hellenic
rather than Roman, and furthermore, he asserted that it is this mistaken identification with Rome that converts humanist Hellenic Mediterranean culture into
chauvinistic regionalism:

> It may indeed seem that serving the cause of Mediterranean regionalism is
> tantamount to restoring empty traditionalism with no future, celebrating the
> superiority of one culture over another, or again, adopting an inverted form of
> Fascism and inciting the Latin against the Nordic peoples. This is a perpetual
> source of misunderstandings. The aim of this lecture is to try to dispel them.
> The whole error lies in the confusion between Mediterranean and Latin, and
> in attributing to Rome what began in Athens. . . . What we seek is not the lie

that triumphed in Ethiopia but the truth that is being murdered in Spain. . . .
We are, here, on the side of the Mediterranean against Rome.

He identifies the claims of "Latinity" with nationalism, which, in turn, he dismisses
as a sign of cultural decadence. In contrast, his conception of Mediterranean culture
is one of internationalism, an internationalism inspired by the humanist "principle"
of "man" (*LACE*: 189–96; *E*: 1320–27).

However, although Camus was clearly convinced that the ideologies of Franco,
Mussolini and the *pied-noir* proponents of Latinity were anathema to true Mediterranean humanism, he seems less sure himself what such a culture actually stands
for. Contrasting Francis of Assisi (who "transformed Christianity from an inward-
looking, tormented religion into a hymn to nature and simple joy") with Martin
Luther ("Protestantism is, actually, Catholicism wrenched from the Mediterranean,
and from the simultaneously pernicious [*néfaste*] and inspiring influence of the
sea"), he stresses the ability of the Mediterranean to "humanize rigid religious and
political doctrines" (*LACE*: 192; *E*: 1323; Foxlee 2006: 79). Beyond this, and a clear
sense that the battle between authentic Mediterranean culture and its Latinist rival
was then being fought in Spain, there is little explanation of what he considers
Mediterranean culture to be. Furthermore, although he condemns Mussolini's
colonialist intentions in Africa, he fails to consider this Mediterranean humanism in
the context of the French colonial presence in Algeria. Indeed, although the lecture
cannot be said to justify the French possession of Algeria, it does appear to take it for
granted. Nevertheless, if we consider this argument for Mediterranean humanism
as an early version of the defence of *la pensée de midi* articulated in *The Rebel*, we
can perhaps more clearly see the visceral importance for Camus of the success of his
aspirations for Algeria, for failure would imply the failure of his entire philosophical
oeuvre, to the extent to which it can be said to rest on the idea of "Mediterranean
humanism", moderation, "limits" etc.

Postcolonial criticism rejects this humanist conception of Mediterranean culture
as an obfuscating fantasy. It reads the lecture exclusively within the context of
French colonial domination of Algeria, and tends to ignore all other circumstances
(such as the rise of fascism in Europe and Algeria). It reads the lecture not only as
a naive paean to internationalism, but as an intervention that served to obscure
the realities of the French imperial presence in Algeria (the degree to which Camus
was consciously complicit in this deception varies from critic to critic). Conor
Cruise O'Brien, for example, in his *Camus* (perhaps *the* foundational text in the
postcolonial study of Camus), quotes the following excerpt from the lecture:

North Africa is one of the few countries where East and West live together
and at this confluence there is no difference between the manner of life of a
Spaniard or an Italian on the quays of Algiers and the Arabs who are around
them. The most essential element in the Mediterranean genius springs from
this encounter unique in history and geography born between East and West.
. . . This truth of a Mediterranean culture exists and manifests itself on every

point: one, linguistic unity, facility of learning one Latin language when one knows another; two, unity of origin, prodigious collectivism of the Middle Ages, order of knights, order of religious feudalities, etc.

(Cruise O'Brien 1970: 12. See *LACE*: 194–5; *E*: 1325)

Undoubtedly Cruise O'Brien is justified in criticizing Camus here for his assertion of a Latin-based linguistic unity in a region "where the majority of inhabitants were Arabic-speaking", as well as his affirmation of a cultural unity based, Cruise O'Brien says, on an appeal to the Crusades (*ibid.*). However, this cannot legitimately be said to be the whole story of the lecture, although Cruise O'Brien and subsequent post-colonial critics treat it as if it is.

Edward Said's influential critique of Camus is partly occupied with criticizing Cruise O'Brien's book, which though an "agile demystification", which "shrewdly and even mercilessly exposed the connections between Camus's most famous novels and the colonial situation in Algeria", ultimately "lets [Camus] off the hook" (Said 1993: 209). According to Said, O'Brien sees Camus as a representative of "so relatively a weightless thing as 'Western consciousness'", and characterizes "the colonial tie as one between Europe and its frontier". Clearly dissatisfied, Said sets about constructing what he believes to be a more rigorous account of Camus's relation to Algeria, in which Camus is seen as a representative of "Western *dominance* in the non-European world".[4] He does so, however, by almost completely ignoring everything Camus wrote on the subject, focusing instead on the Algerian settings of some of Camus's fiction, arguing that these works can be seen to "very precisely distil the traditions, idioms, and discursive strategies of France's appropriation of Algeria", while neglecting to explain why the large body of Camus's Algerian journalism does not contradict this view.[5]

Cruise O'Brien asserts that "it is quite clear, though never explicitly stated, that [Camus's] Mediterranean culture is a European one and in Algeria, a French one, and that the Arabs who have a part in this culture will have become French Arabs", but, as David Carroll points out, "whatever the naiveté and political limitations of Camus's vision, it is not European culture (or the French language) *per se* that Camus defends in his speech but, throughout history, Europe's encounter with the non-European 'East'" (Cruise O'Brien 1970: 12; Carroll 1997: 522). For Carroll, Camus's lecture must be understood not as a defence of a Eurocentric Mediterranean culture that erases the reality of African Algeria, but as a defence of an internationalist, collectivist European Mediterranean culture that should be accepted by "all men of the left" (Camus's phrase), because "it would guarantee justice for both European and Arab Algerians". As Carroll argues elsewhere, however generous and beautiful it may be, the Algeria described by Camus "is anything but a *political* paradise" (Carroll 1997: 522; Carroll 2007a: 155).

Nevertheless, even if Neil Foxlee is correct to suggest that it was possible in 1937 for Camus to be both a humanist and an example of what Albert Memmi called the "well-meaning coloniser", it is less than clear that such a reconciliation was possible at the height of the Algerian war, when Camus continued, in the face of massive popular support in Algeria (and significant support in France), to reject the idea of Algerian independence (Foxlee 2006: 77). On the other hand, it seems that the post-colonial reading of Camus depends to a very large extent on concentrating exclusively on certain passages of certain texts, and on either ignoring or categorizing as of secondary importance all other texts and all other contexts (see, for example, Cruise O'Brien's relegation to an endnote of Camus's remarkable comparison in 1947 of French policy in Algeria to the Nazis in France). The extent of the general textual selectivity of postcolonial critics is highlighted when we consider a contemporary political intervention by Camus, which relates specifically to the relationship between France and Algeria, but which is ignored by postcolonial critics (including Cruise O'Brien).

In December 1936, the French Popular Front government published the *Projet Blum-Viollette*, a bill that proposed giving full French citizenship, including voting rights, to approximately 20,000 Algerian Muslims (about 0.35 per cent of the Muslim population at that time). In the face of the threat of mass resignation by the *pieds-noirs* members of the French parliament and the expressed hostility of the then President of the Republic, Albert Lebrun (who declared that were the plan to succeed the French National Assembly "would become the Tower of Babel and France would be governed by her former subjects"), the project was abandoned even before reaching the Chamber of Deputies (Ferhi 2004). In May 1937 Camus published a manifesto explicitly defending the plan against these attacks, arguing that when French intellectuals reject it in the name of a French ideal, it is the ideal itself that they have abandoned.[6] It suggests that although intellectuals may only have the right to speak on behalf of culture, the current situation in Algeria was such that its cultural life was being suffocated: "culture could not live where dignity was dying, and a civilisation could not flourish under laws which crush it. . . . One cannot speak of culture in a country where 900,000 inhabitants are denied schools, or of civilisation, when it is a question of a people weakened by unprecedented poverty and destitution and bullied by emergency legislation and inhuman regulations" (*E*: 1328). Clearly, as Foxlee suggests, even if Camus can be accused of naiveté in his claim in his lecture on Mediterranean humanism that the lives of the Arabs and Europeans in Algiers were fundamentally the same, "he shows here that he was under no illusion as to the inferior economic, legal, and political status" that native Algerians (or Algerian Arabs and Berbers) were forced to endure (Foxlee 2006: 89). As "the only means to restore the dignity to the Muslim masses was to allow them to express themselves", Camus asserts in the manifesto, the Viollette plan must be defended as "a step toward the attainment of their right to life, which is the most elementary of rights . . . a stage in the complete parliamentary emancipation of Muslims . . . a minimum in the work of civilisation and humanity which ought to be that of the new France" (*E*: 1328–9).

The postcolonial account of Camus's relationship with Algeria offers no discussion of this manifesto, and doubtless would justify this omission on the grounds that the Viollette plan was an effort at colonial assimilation, designed primarily to permit an elite 20,000 Algerian Muslims to be treated as if they were Frenchmen

(Frenchwomen did not have the right to vote until 1944). Although the Viollette plan was undoubtedly assimilationist, this does not justify completely ignoring Camus's manifesto in support of it, not least because of the radical egalitarianism the manifesto also defends. The persuasiveness of the postcolonial critique seems also to be mitigated by the context in which these two interventions – the lecture and the manifesto – take place. For, as Herbert Lottman's monumental biography has shown, at this time Camus was deeply involved, perhaps as much as any other European Algerian, in the campaign for civil rights for Algerian Arabs and Berbers.[7] This political commitment saw Camus, through the 1930s, politically aligned with reformist and moderate nationalists such as Sheik Ben Badis, Sheik El Okbi (both of the Association of Algerian Ulema) and Ferhat Abbas. It is even suggested that Camus may have done some editing and proofreading for the newspaper of Messali Hadj, the only Algerian nationalist to have rejected the Viollette plan. Furthermore, postcolonial criticism not only tends to disregard Camus's relationship with Algerian nationalists; it also habitually ignores perhaps one of the most spectacular moments in Camus's early career as a political activist: his expulsion from the Algerian Communist Party (PCA). Camus joined the party in 1935, claiming that his adherence was necessary "in order to remain close to people with whom he identified, the working class of Algiers, whose cause the Communists had annexed".[8] Camus, as an activist, said that his role was that of "recruiting Arab militants and having them join a nationalist organisation", specifically Messali Hadj's Etoile Nord Africain (ENA). He accepted this role and became friends with many of the Arabs he met. However, about this time the Communist Party in Algeria was instructed by Moscow to abandon its pro-Arab militancy. In January 1937 the ENA was proscribed by the French government, and Camus found former comrades being imprisoned, and their organization being forcibly dissolved, "in the name of a policy approved and encouraged by the [Communist Party]" (Camus & Grenier 2003: 152–3; Camus & Grenier 1981: 180). Camus made his objections to the new policy well known and was soon summoned to party headquarters, where he was asked to amend his position. Instead he reiterated it, "observing that the Party had been right to support Muslim nationalists earlier and it did not have the right to discredit them now, thereby playing into the hands of the colonialists".[9] Camus was advised by friends to resign, but refused, so the party was left with no choice but to expel him.[10]

The coherence of the postcolonial critique of Camus, at least in its best-known and radical form (that of Cruise O'Brien and Edward Said), depends to a very great extent on the exclusion of examples not conducive to its own edifying interpretation. This selectiveness usually takes the form of a simple reductiveness, whereby all contexts other than the colonial are ignored. The implications of this tendency are clear, for the postcolonial account tends not only to highlight its own interpretative preoccupations, but also to reduce all other interpretations to it. Hence, according to this account, Camus's lecture on Mediterranean humanism is concerned with internationalist Mediterranean humanism or with the rise of fascism and anti-Semitism in Europe and Algeria only to the extent that these concerns permit Camus to obscure the reality of colonial Algeria. More significantly, this same reductivism can also manifest itself in the tendency to either ignore or undermine the significance of something one might have thought would have been of interest from a postcolonial point of view (such as Camus's manifesto in defence of the Viollette plan). This technique seems especially egregious when, as in the case of both Cruise O'Brien and Said, the critic accuses Camus of being deaf to historical realities.[11]

There is another methodological problem with the postcolonial criticism of the kind presented by Edward Said and Conor Cruise O'Brien. As Neil Foxlee suggests, the postcolonial critique of Camus is anachronistic, in so far as it judges Camus "from a retrospective rather than contemporary perspective" (Foxlee 2006: 78). This anachronistic perspective is problematic because its criticism of Camus's failure to support Algerian independence is derived, in part, from the fact of Algerian independence after 1962. For example, the postcolonial critic Azzedine Haddour claims that Camus "espoused and never relinquished the outdated assimilationist ideals of *jeunes algériens*", an early indigenous political movement that sought reforms in the ways Algerian was governed. However, as Foxlee points out, not only does Haddour ignore the "radical egalitarianism" of Camus's political pronouncements on Algeria; his claim that Camus's position was "outdated" relies on the "retrospective viewpoint of Algerian independence".[12] A further problem with this sort of critique is highlighted when we look at Edward Said's related assertion that Camus was "simply wrong historically", by which he means that Camus was wrong because the federalized future he envisioned for Algeria did not transpire (Said 1993: 211). As Foxlee points out, by this reasoning Messali Hadj's militant MNA would also have to be dismissed as "wrong historically", because they were ultimately liquidated by the Front de Libération Nationale (FLN) after a protracted internecine conflict. Buried in Said's assertion seems to be a sort of semantic slippage that allows the critic to use the term "wrong" to mean both "incorrect" and "unjustified". Hence, Camus was "historically wrong" (incorrect) because the future he envisaged for Algeria never materialized, but he was therefore "historically wrong" (unjustified) to envisage such a future. From this reasoning might also be derived the apparent corollary that whatever did happen, being "historically right", is also justified.

In contrast to the highly critical accounts of Said and Cruise O'Brien, it is worth noting the views of two of Camus's contemporaries, both of whom played significant roles in the history of Algerian independence: Amar Ouzegane and Albert Memmi. According to Ouzegane, who was Secretary General of the PCA at the time of Camus's expulsion, and a senior member of the FLN during the war with France, in political terms Camus was "in the avant-garde in 1935".[13] He believed Camus to be "like the Arabised Europeans who had accepted and identified themselves with Arabs, with Algerians", even that Camus thought that "the struggle for Algerian independence took precedence over the struggle against Fascism in Europe". Furthermore, far from suffering from "western ethnocentrism" (as Cruise O'Brien and Said might suggest), according to Ouzegane, Camus contributed to the popularity of the nationalist movement in Algeria, and was far more clear-sighted (even "more revolutionary") than those of his liberal peers who were at that time advocating assimilation.[14]

Similarly, although Albert Memmi's canonical text in postcolonial criticism, *The Colonizer and the Colonized* (1957), is frequently cited as ascribing to Camus the dubious accolades of "the colonizer who refuses" and the "colonizer of good will" (*colonisateur de bonne volonté*), it is not always made clear what is meant by this. According to Conor Cruise O'Brien, whose book is in many ways an elaboration on the same theme, "Memmi's central point" (which Cruise O'Brien clearly believed applied to Camus) was "that left-wing intellectuals, even communists, unconsciously shared the assumptions of a colonialism which they consciously rejected" (Cruise O'Brien 1970: 13). Although Cruise O'Brien's interpretation of "the colonizer who refuses" may be disputed (see, for example, Carroll 1997: 520–21n.), it is possible to glean considerable insight into Memmi's thoughts on Camus's attitude to Algerian independence by examining a brief article he published a few months after *The Colonizer and the Colonized*, entitled "Albert Camus ou le colonisateur de bonne volonté" ("Albert Camus, or the Colonizer of Good Will"). In November 1957 the magazine *La Nef* published an article that was deeply critical of Camus's attitude to Algeria:

> For fifteen years he has been known to us, and for fifteen years he has remained silent. . . . The pacification in Algeria did not disrupt his habits [*bouscula ses habitudes*]. He was tormented, but things were more complicated than you might have thought: one either kept one's distance or one trapped [*emprisonnait*] the liberal Europeans who, alone, would have known how to *really* help resolve the problem. It's a shame, and it's distressing, but what is one to do when every time one writes, every time one speaks out, everything is distorted? And then there was the *admirable* example of Faulkner, who loved the blacks, who felt himself wholeheartedly on their side, who would have wished that all whites were like him, but who, based on a few news wires (more often than not unbelievable) no longer felt he had the right to condemn his own race. Let us be clear: for Camus, another great *écrivain charnel*, Algeria was his Deep South.   (Frank 1957: 61–3)

This, however, was written not by Memmi, but by the French journalist Bernard Frank, to whose criticism Memmi's article, published in the following issue of *La Nef*, constitutes a partial rebuttal. Curiously then, what is sometimes thought to be the first postcolonial criticism of Camus is actually a partial defence of Camus against the sort of criticism that would later be advanced by Cruise O'Brien and Said. Memmi's response begins with what he considers the necessary inversion of the perspective offered by Frank: "far from being able to speak about North Africa because it is from there that he comes, Camus was led into silence because everything which concerns North Africa paralyses him" (Memmi 1957: 95–6). Camus, says Memmi, as a French Algerian "belongs to a minority which finds itself historically in the wrong".[15] Although "there are few points regarding North Africa" on which Memmi says he could agree with Camus, he also notes:

it must be understood that his position is hardly easy: it is difficult, both emotionally and intellectually, to have one's entire family on the side being morally condemned. One might regret, perhaps, that Camus was unable to really go beyond the clan, to place himself from the outset on the level of the universal. But I should add immediately that had he done so, it would not have ended there: he would have been even more hated by his own community. In fact Camus's situation is such that it was guaranteed to reap the suspicions of the colonized, the indignation of the left-wing metropolitan French and the anger of his own community. From this springs his silence, or semi-silence, for one is dealing here with a false impression: Camus has spoken [on Algeria], and more frequently than many others. But his situation is such that he can only succeed in angering everybody. Camus embodies, quite accurately, what I have called the colonizer of good-will. It is an ambiguous role, but I must stress that it is neither comic nor contemptible.[16]

Clearly, then, for Memmi the term "good will" was meant to be understood not as a purely ironic assertion, but as being at the heart of the paradoxical position in which Camus found himself. Although Memmi's book may constitute the starting point for Cruise O'Brien's critique, it is clear that this critique far exceeds Memmi's, at least in so far as the latter applied to Camus. Although Memmi clearly and consistently disagreed with Camus about the justice of Algerian independence, his sympathy for the position of Camus was also clearly and consistently evident: in 1985, for example, Memmi declared that whereas he doubted that Sartre (who wrote the preface for his *The Colonizer and the Colonized*) "had really understood, or rather felt, our problems", "with Camus, I had the sense of being immediately on the same emotional and sentimental register".[17] With this in mind, it seems that an alternative account of Camus's relationship with Algeria, one not in conformity with those of Cruise O'Brien or Said, is both worthwhile and defensible, and I will spend the remainder of this chapter presenting a version of this argument.[18]

Camus's political activism continued after his expulsion from the Communist Party in 1937. By 1938 he had joined the socialist newspaper *Algér republicain*, for which he began writing book reviews (such as those on Sartre's early works mentioned in Chapter 5). In this period Camus was also writing his "absurd" works, and crucially it was also at this time that he began writing political journalism. In June 1939 he wrote a series of articles covering the trial of Sheikh El Okbi, whom Camus met while working with the PCA, and who was facing allegations relating to the assassination in 1936 of the then Mufti of Algiers, the city's main religious leader. It was generally understood that the charges were politically motivated (El Okbi, unlike his alleged victim, was unpopular with the colonial administration). In his articles Camus championed the cause of El Okbi, although he did so primarily by highlighting the evident weakness of the prosecutor's case. The sheikh was eventually acquitted. Amar Ouzegane considered Camus's articles to amount to participation "in a just anti-colonialist combat", which proved that the journalist "was therefore not a dupe".[19]

However, the most significant of Camus's political interventions at this time was his series of articles on the destitution he witnessed among the Berbers of the Kabylie region of Algeria, "Misère de la Kabylie".[20] Prompted by reports in the bourgeois press extolling "the delights of Kabylie", Camus was sent to the region to report accurately on the conditions there. Perhaps with these reports in mind, he wrote shortly after his arrival in Kabylie: "One morning in Tizi-Ouzou, I saw children in rags fighting Kabylie dogs for the contents of a dustbin. . . . The poverty of this village is like a denial [*interdit*] of the world's beauty."[21] His reports (eleven in all, each illustrated by at least one photograph) went on to describe the "horrifying" destitution of the inhabitants of the region, how they were dependent on charity for their very survival, otherwise having to forage for herbs, nettles, roots and thistle stalks. While the obvious cause for this misery was overpopulation (the population of Kabylie, says Camus, was 247 persons per square kilometre, as opposed to an average of 71 in France), this was aggravated by the fact that although the price of wheat (which the population consumes) had increased, the price of olives and figs (which they produce) had not. The consequent economic hardship, Camus shows in meticulous detail, was massively exacerbated by the total indifference of Algeria's political elite.[22] Articles such as these prompted the authorities to shut down the newspaper at the outbreak of the Second World War in 1939. Indeed, Camus was by this time so unpopular with the colonial administration that they made it impossible for him to secure work in Algeria, effectively exiling him to France, where his former editor-in-chief, Pascal Pia, had found him a job as editorial assistant at the popular daily *Paris-Soir*.[23]

Although the focus of Camus's political concern during the war, as articulated in his articles in *Combat*, was with the struggle against Nazism, his concern for the rights of Algerian Muslims became prominent again very soon after the liberation of France. Coinciding with celebrations in France of VE Day in May 1945, Algerian nationalists paraded, celebrating the European victory over Nazism but also protesting against the recent French decision to exile Messali Hadj, and waving the green and white *Messaliste* flag (now the national flag). Across Algeria, but in the towns of Sétif and Guelma especially, many of the marches turned to violent protests. Although the details remain obscure, it is clear that the marches in these two towns turned to rioting, resulting in the deaths of about one hundred Europeans. The French army responded with merciless repression: thousands of Muslims (some estimate that as many as seventy-five thousand) were killed.[24] Many consider this mass murder at Sétif and Guelma to constitute the real beginning of the Algerian insurrection against France. Certainly it served to radicalize many Algerians. The Berber poet Kateb Yacine, for example, observed: "I was sixteen years old and I have never forgotten the shock of that merciless butchery which took thousands of Muslim lives. There at Sétif the iron of nationalism entered my soul" (quoted in Humbaraci 1966: 45). Ferhat Abbas even suggested that Messali Hadj conspired with the colonial police to try to provoke the massacres, as a means of destroying his more moderate political party, Amis du Manifeste et de la Liberté (AML) (quoted in Quandt 1969: 52). On the other hand, thanks to a largely quiescent media, the metropolitan French seemed to remain generally oblivious to the bloodbath carried out, in some measure, in their name. (Sartre, for example, doesn't seem to have mentioned it in print until his Preface to Fanon's *The Wretched of the Earth* in 1961, whereas de Beauvoir claimed that "we heard very little about what had happened at Sétif" (quoted in Horne 1977: 27)). Although his peers may have failed to notice what had happened at Sétif, Camus himself had just returned from Algeria, where he had spent more than two weeks travelling 1,500 miles around the country. The information he gathered on this journey, formulated in the context of the still unclear reports of the massacre and bloody reprisals, was then published as a series of articles in *Combat*, beginning on 13 May.[25]

In these articles we see much of the same language that we saw in the articles on the famine in the Kabylie. He begins by noting that although France might be satisfied with pretending that Algeria does not "exist", no such ignorance is to be found among the Algerians: he notes how in one village 500 miles from the coast he met people angered by an article recently published in *Le Figaro*, deemed to have been "ill-informed and insulting" to Algerians. He speaks of economic, humanitarian and political crisis in Algeria, of the continued failure of the French to realize that "most Algerians are experiencing a famine". He argues that France has fallen so low in the estimations of most Algerians that it will have to be "conquered" again, and that this can only be done by realizing that "people are suffering from hunger and demanding justice. We cannot remain indifferent to their suffering", says Camus, alluding to the Nazi occupation, "because we have experienced it ourselves." Hence, says Camus, rather than respond "with condemnations, let us try to understand the reasons for their demands and invoke on their behalf the same democratic principles that we claim for ourselves". He speaks of the inherent injustice of a society that allocates more grain to the settler population than to the Arab population, and further that neglects to ensure that the Arab population even gets its allocated share. "To quell the cruellest of hungers and heal inflamed hearts: that is the task we face today. Hundreds of freighters filled with grain and two or three measures of strict equality: this is what millions of people are asking of us, and perhaps this will help to make it clear why we must try to understand them before we judge them." This economic and humanitarian crisis is exacerbated by the underlying political problem of an Algerian policy "distorted by prejudice and ignorance" (*CC*: 201, 205, 207; *CAC8*: 501, 509, 510, 514). He suggests that French colonial policy has been from the outset marked by incoherence. Although in theory twentieth-century colonial policy in Algeria favoured assimilation, all attempts at realizing this policy had ended in failure. He describes how the "by no means revolutionary" 1937 Blum-Viollette Bill, though approved by the Algerian Muslim Congress (an extension of Ben Badis's Association of Algerian Ulema), was effectively scuttled by political inaction and aggressive lobbying on the part of groups representing the wealthiest among the *grands colons*,[26] and, furthermore, how although it would have been "welcomed enthusiastically" by Arabs in 1936, such an offer, were it to be made now, would be met "only with wariness". He suggests that having been offered only a "caricature" of it, Algerian Arabs (and Berbers) "seem to have lost their faith in democracy. . . . They hope to achieve by other means a goal that has never changed: an improvement in their condition." What this means, according to Camus, is the "unfortunate" fact that majority Arab opinion now rejects assimilation. He goes on to speak very favourably of Ferhat Abbas, Aziz Kessous and their moderate-nationalist political party, Amis du Manifeste, which rejects the policy of assimilation (declaring it an "inaccessible reality"), and calls for a federal solution to Franco-Algerian relations.[27] Although Camus does not here declare himself a proponent of a federal solution, he does argue that the response of the French administration to the Amis du Manifeste, "imprisonment and repression[,] . . . was stupidity, pure and simple". In the concluding article in the series, Camus laments the evanescence of French media interest in Algeria, a fact compounded by efforts to limit retrospect-ively the significance of the recent events at Sétif, with suggestions that they had been exaggerated or that they could be blamed on a few "professional agitators". He insisted upon the need to recognize the fact of a political crisis in Algeria "to which it would be pointless and dangerous to close one's eyes", and repeated the same call he had made in his "Misère de la Kabylie" articles for *Alger Républicain*: an appeal for the application of French justice in Algeria.[28]

Although Camus continued to think of justice as something France should grant Algeria, as opposed to something Algerians should take for themselves, this never-theless flatly contradicts the view of Cruise O'Brien and others, who accuse Camus of being unconsciously complicit in the creation of a fictionalized French Algeria; that is, an Algeria where French justice already existed (Cruise O'Brien 1970: 23). The clearest refutation of this assumption is to be found in Camus's unprecedented attack in 1947 on French policing and military tactics in Algeria and Madagascar. He reminds his readers of the use of "collective repression" in the wake of the riots at Sétif and Guelma, and the recent revelation regarding the existence of a "spon-taneous confession chamber" in Fianarantsoa in Madagascar, and compares this to the Nazis' use of torture as a weapon against the French: "the facts are there, the clear and hideous truth: we are doing what we reproached the Germans for doing". He suggests that if the French react to this news with indifference it can only mean that they, like the Nazis, were "unconsciously certain" of their superiority to those victims of torture. Furthermore, he suggests that only when the French have "van-quished" that "racism" will they have earned the right "to denounce the spirit of tyranny and violence wherever it arises".[29]

Repeatedly, in this post-Sétif period, Camus intervened in defence of North African nationalists, including members of Messali Hadj's more radical Mouvement pour la Triomphe des Libertés Démocratiques (MTLD). In 1951, he submitted an affidavit in defence of fifty-six Algerians being tried in connection with their MTLD activism. In 1952, responding to the criticism that he was not concerned about the "victims of colonialism", Camus insisted that for twenty years he had "never really pursued any other political struggle".[30] In July 1953, in a letter to the editor of *Le Monde*, Camus protested against the killing by police of seven *Messalistes* at a protest march in Paris, demanding an inquiry into who authorized the use of lethal force, and attributing the police violence "to a racism that dare not say its name" (quoted in Lottman 1979: 526. See *E*: 1839–47). In April 1954 he personally appealed to President Coty on behalf of seven Tunisian nationalists who had been condemned to death (and whose testimonies were understood to have been extracted by torture). Shortly thereafter, he condemned outright "the profound infirmity of French colonialism", which "presents itself with the Declaration of the Rights of Man in one hand and the truncheon of repression in the other". In July 1954, less than four months before the beginning of the Algerian insurrection, he warned that "the time for talk of fraternity is over, now we must act positively" in order to prevent Franco-Algerian relations from further deteriorating (*E*: 1862, 1865).

In November 1954 the FLN insurrection against French rule in Algeria began. In May 1955, eight years after retiring from full-time journalism and *Combat*, Camus began writing occasional editorials in the liberal *L'Express*. The newspaper supported the socialist politician Pierre Mendès-France, who, while continuing to see Algeria as "irrevocably French", had succeeded during a brief tenure as head of government between 1954 and 1955 in withdrawing France from Indochina and instigating a policy that would eventually result in the independence of both Morocco and Tunisia (quoted in Horne 1977: 98). Camus contributed two articles to the newspaper in July, in which he argued for round table negotiations involving all sides in the conflict. He argued that necessary to the future of Algeria would be dialogue between European and Arabs in the political sphere, and that in order for this to happen, the current Algerian Assembly (which was, he pointed out, the product of a rigged election) should be dissolved, and a fresh election held. A fair election could result, he suggested, in legitimate representatives of both Europeans and Muslims engaging in the creation of a new Algeria, no longer a colonial possession but part of a French federation, with internal autonomy (*CAC6*: 38–53).

Although officially the revolution against French rule in Algeria began in November 1954, the initially period of the war has been retrospectively characterized as a "phoney war", which came to a sudden and spectacular end in August 1955, when the FLN massacred more than one hundred European Algerians and moderate Algerian nationalists (including Ferhat Abbas's nephew, Allouah Abbas) in and around the town of Philippeville (Stora 2001: 33–41). As with the events in Sétif in 1945, these attacks were followed by widespread, indiscriminate and disproportionate repression by the French military. This reflected a significant change in tactic for the FLN (which had not hitherto generally targeted civilians), and it also marked a significant change in France's attitude to the war, where voices demanding repression were fast drowning out calls for liberal reform and compromise.

The events at Philippeville, and the rapidly polarizing rhetoric consequent upon these events, also prompted Camus's decision to intensify his journalistic efforts on behalf of a peaceful solution. He was anxious that the polarization of positions should not force all other voices into silence. In an open letter published in the first issue of *Communauté algérienne*, a newspaper set up by his friend Aziz Kessous, a former colleague of Ferhat Abbas, Camus declares that since the news of Philippeville he has been "on the verge of despair", that he suffers from Algeria "the way that some suffer from their lungs". He expresses solidarity with Kessous's sentiment that European and Muslim Algerians "are condemned to live together", affirms his common cultural identity with Kessous, as an Algerian "brother", and asserts that although the existence of one million European Algerians cannot be ignored, neither is there any reason why "nine million Arabs should live on their land like forgotten men; the dream that the Arab masses can be cancelled out, silenced and subjugated is just as mad". Camus recognizes that maintaining such a position, in the context of the Philippeville massacre and its wake, "amounts to taking one's stand in the no man's land between two armies and preaching amid the bullets that war is a deception". However, the "essential thing", he maintains in the context of rising tensions after the massacre, "is to leave room, however limited it may be, for the exchange of views that is still possible . . . I shall be told, as you will be told, that it is too late for reconciliation, that the only thing to do is to wage war and win. But you and I know that this war will not have any real victors and that, once it is over, we shall still have to go on living together forever on the same soil" (*RRD*: 126–30*; *E*: 963–5).

Although Camus sought to create a space between warring factions where dialogue might take hold, it is not the case that he sought to keep this space unsullied by the presence of either of the warring factions. Given their targeting of civilians, Camus's abhorrence for the FLN hardly needs explanation, but the tendency to assume that he refused to have anything to do with them because they were "terrorists" is untenable.[31] It is just such a view that Cruise O'Brien expresses:

> In 1955 [Camus] had proposed an Algerian round table without the FLN and in 1958 in the foreword to his *Chroniques algériennes* (Actuelles III), he points out that negotiation with the FLN would lead to: "the independence of Algeria controlled by the most implacable military leaders of the insurrection; that is to say, the eviction of 1,200,000 Europeans of Algeria and the humiliation of millions of Frenchmen, with the risk involved in that humiliation". He makes it clear that he rejects this independence and therefore the negotiation. The rejection of negotiation is basic and necessarily implies support for the substance, if not the detail of the methods, of the French government's policy of pacification.[32]

There are at least three problems with this assertion. First, on both occasions when Camus proposes round table negotiations in his 1955 *L'Express* articles, he *does* include the FLN. In July 1955 he calls for a round table discussion involving representatives from government, from the colonial administration, from Ferhat Abbas's UDMA, the Algerian Ulémas, "and the two factions [*deux tendances*] of the MTLD" (*CAC6*: 46). The two factions of the MTLD refer to the group that eventually became Messali's new party, the MNA, and its chief rival, the FLN (see, for example, Julien 2002: 453). Camus's writing displays a curious reluctance to name the FLN as the group executing the war against French rule, but in this instance the reasoning behind his not referring to them by name was, probably, to inform his readership that the FLN did not appear *ex nihilo*, but was the product of a long history of Algerian nationalism (a history with which Camus was intimately familiar, but of which many of his peers were culpably ignorant).[33] Similarly, in October 1955 he again calls for round table negotiations involving "all factions [*toutes les tendances*]" (*CAC6*: 70). Secondly, Cruise O'Brien's quotation is gently selective, subtly, though substantially, distorting the intended meaning of the passage quoted. Camus states: "Those who, in purposely vague terms, advocate negotiation with the FLN cannot fail to be aware, after the precise statements of the FLN, that this means the independence of Algeria under the direction of the most relentless military leaders of the insurrection – in other words, the eviction of 1,200,000 Europeans from Algeria and the humiliation of millions of Frenchmen, with all the risks that such a humiliation involves. That is a policy to be sure, but we must see it for what it is and stop cloaking it in euphemisms."[34] When we compare the passage from Camus in its context with Cruise O'Brien's reconstruction and extrapolation, we see that Camus's point in the 1958 preface is that those who call for negotiations with the FLN are really advocating Algerian independence, since the FLN had by this time made its acceptance a prerequisite of any negotiations.[35] Cruise O'Brien subtly reworks this so that Camus is presented as having "rejected independence and therefore the negotiation", whereas he has rejected only that independence be accepted as a condition of negotiations. Thirdly, Cruise O'Brien infers from this alleged refusal to negotiate with the FLN Camus's support "for the substance if not the detail" of the French policy of pacification (read "collective repression") in Algeria. This argument constitutes an instance of the kind of retrospective argument on which much postcolonial criticism is based. Because the FLN eventually won the war in 1962, Camus is criticized for his refusal to support them. Moreover, his refusal to support the FLN is also retrospectively weighted with responsibility for failing to support the only party that *should* have "won", or at least (since the morality of some of the FLN's tactics both during and after the war was questionable) the only party that *could* have "won" the war. Again, buried in this retrospectivism, we see assumed without argument the dubious claim that whatever happened was "right".

A civilian truce

While Camus continued to press for round table negotiations involving all parties to the conflict, in the wake of Philippeville he also developed what was to be his most significant intervention in the conflict, the "*trêve civile*" or civilian truce. In an article in *L'Express* on the first anniversary of the FLN uprising, Camus suggested that all sides in the conflict agree, simultaneously, not to harm the civilian population, irrespective of the circumstances (*CAC6*: 83–5; see Lottman 1979: 568). This measure, were it to be adopted, would preclude both the FLN's targeted attacks on civilians and the French use of collective repression. This idea, developed in subsequent *L'Express* articles, culminated in a piece entitled "Trêve pour les civils", published on 10 January 1956. Here Camus calls for both communities to recognize what is legitimate in the other's demands. Ultimately, the consequence of such a recognition, he says, would be a civilian truce, a "truce until a solution is finally arrived at, a truce to the massacre of civilians, on both sides! As long as the accuser does not show an example, the accusations are vain . . . there is no other solution but that of which we speak. Beyond it, there is only death and destruction" (*E*: 983–5). At the same time that Camus was calling for reconciliation in Algeria, he was in regular contact with associates and friends in Algiers, in the hope of contributing to a more direct effort to the same end. Some of these friends were members of a group, the Association des Amis du Théâtre d'Expression Arabe, which was made up of both Europeans and Muslims, such as his old friend Charles Poncet and his former comrade in the PCA, Amar Ouzegane (Ouzegane, Camus later discovered, was by this time a member of the FLN, as were several of the other Muslim members of the group). Concerned by the escalating violence in Algeria, the group agreed that an effort needed to be made to attempt some degree of compromise between the two communities. They decided that they would ask Camus to take a prominent role in the group "and to write its manifesto" (Lottman 1979: 566–7). As a result of their efforts the Comité pour une Trêve civile was formed, which comprised leading intellectuals from both the European and Muslim communities. This organization sought to forge an agreement between the two sides in the conflict whereby civilians on either side of the cultural and political divide would not be seen as legitimate targets. The group's efforts culminated in the "Call for a Civil Truce", a meeting in Algiers on 22 January 1956 at which Camus was the keynote speaker.

Camus's speech echoes much of what he had been writing in *L'Express* in the previous six months. He dismisses the naive view that the conflict in Algeria is a question simply of a homogeneous Arab majority subjugated by a small but powerful alien French colonial minority. In Algeria, he says, "there are a million Frenchmen who have been here for a century, millions of Muslims, either Arabs or Berbers, who have been here for centuries, and several rigorous religious communities".[36] He asserts that as bleak as things look in Algeria, there is still hope of recovery from the seemingly endless cycle of reprisals: if each individual, "Arab or French, made an effort to think over his adversary's motives, at least the basis of a fruitful discussion would be clear". All Algerians, Arab, Berber and European, "must live together at the crossroads where history has put them". It is in this context that Camus situates his call for a civil truce. Although not sufficiently optimistic to believe that a general cessation of hostilities can be achieved in the midst of such a bloody conflict, Camus does suggest that it is at least possible "to have some impact on the most hateful aspect of the conflict: we can propose, without making any change in the present situation, that we refrain from what makes it unforgivable – the murder of the innocent". The "civilian truce" would serve the dual function of reducing the number of non-combatants being killed in the war, and of creating a climate "for a healthy discussion that would not be spoiled by ridiculously uncompromising attitudes". If a civil truce were to hold, it would prepare "the ground for a fairer, subtler understanding of the Algerian problem" (*RRD*: 135–8*; *E*: 994–6).

It is precisely because the appeal for a civilian truce in many ways constituted the culmination of Camus's activism in favour of what he considered a just solution to the Algerian problem that postcolonial criticism tends to be so dismissive of the effort. As *The Rebel* was for Sartre, postcolonial critics tend to see the civilian truce as a clear register of how politically irrelevant Camus's ideas about the future of Algeria had become. For example, Conor Cruise O'Brien, who calls the truce Camus's "one concrete idea", quickly dismisses it with the claim that when Camus came to Algiers to promote it he was "barracked by the Europeans" and "largely ignored by the Muslims".[37] However, the civilian truce was not as absurdly fanciful as Cruise O'Brien suggests. Rather than jeering at him, right-wing *pieds-noirs* issued death threats against Camus, and attempted to hijack the meeting at which the idea of the truce was launched (by producing forged invitations), such was their implacable hostility to any policy even resembling negotiation with the FLN. In the end an angry crowd of about one thousand *pieds-noirs* did congregate outside the hall where the meeting was held, some shouting slogans such as "Camus to the wall", "Mendès to the wall", "Down with the Jews", and making fascist salutes. This group was met by an even larger group of Muslims, "thousands . . . who had descended from the Kasbah to contain the opposition demonstrators".[38] Furthermore, far from being "largely ignored by Muslims", Camus was joined on the podium by Ferhat Abbas, who was to become independent Algeria's first president (Abbas, though a moderate nationalist, aligned himself with the FLN shortly after the failure of the civilian truce and in 1963 resigned his presidency when the FLN declared Algeria a one-party state).[39] Sheik El Okbi, who knew Camus in the 1930s, also made an appearance, frail and stretcher-bound. And although the FLN publicly disavowed the appeal, they secretly infiltrated the committee set up to oversee it, and made certain that the conference was protected by FLN militants. Mohamed Lebjaoui, a member of the truce committee, informed Camus on the evening before the truce was presented to the public that he was also a member of the FLN. He insisted "that the FLN was ready to respect the rules of the civil truce if the French government would". However, Lebjaoui warned Camus, the FLN was sure that the French would never accept the plan. Camus replied that if the FLN agreed to a civil truce, but the French did not, he would "proclaim the fact everywhere in France".[40] Although Lebjaoui's claims regarding the serious commitment of the FLN to the truce appeal may have been exaggerated, he was entirely correct in his assessment of the likely reaction of the French to the proposal for a civilian truce.[41] Neither Jacques Soustelle, the then Governor General in Algeria, nor Robert Lacoste, Soustelle's replacement in February 1956, nor indeed Guy Mollet, the French premier, showed any serious interest in the proposal. Camus's failure to "proclaim the fact everywhere in France", on the other hand, may be explained by the FLN's apparent loss of interest in the plan in the weeks following the appeal.[42]

From a practical point of view, there may have been difficulties with such a proposal (for example, in a popular guerrilla war, how easy would it have been to differentiate between civilians and combatants?), and it was also likely that there was little popular appetite for such a proposal, either in Algeria or in France. Simone de

Beauvoir, for example, thought that "Camus's language had never sounded hollower than when he demanded pity for the civilians" (de Beauvoir 1968: 354). On the other hand, it is surely worth noting that Germaine Tillion, an ethnologist who began working in Algeria in the 1930s, continued to believe, even in 1958 (two years after Camus's appeal) that such a civilian truce was possible. In July and August 1957 she met the FLN leader Saadi Yacef, who promised her that if the French ceased executing imprisoned Algerian "patriots", the FLN would stop targeting civilians. Although the French initially showed interest, they continued to execute Algerian militants. The FLN, on the other hand, appear to have stopped their attacks on civilians, and did not resume until Yacef himself was arrested that September.[43] In any event, the failure of Camus's truce appeal quickly resulted in his decision to withdraw from public discourse on Algeria: after making one final appeal in favour of the truce, he resigned from *L'Express*. The polarization of opinion, which had shocked him when he visited Algeria, and which he evidently blamed for the complete failure of the truce proposal, convinced Camus that he could no longer have any influence regarding the future of Algeria. As Yves Courrière asserts, Camus went to Algeria hoping for an exchange between communities, and all he encountered were death threats (Courrière 1969: 257). He did not refuse dialogue, as has been alleged, but instead found himself in a political context where dialogue was no longer possible, and it was for this reason that he chose silence.[44] He told friends Jean Daniel and Mouloud Feraoun:

> The repression by the French is without justification, without excuse . . . it is necessary to say the same thing, if we are fighting for justice, about the methods of the FLN who see in every French individual living in Algeria a representative of French colonial oppression. . . . It is necessary to fight for the truce, for the end to the massacre of innocent individuals, in order to establish the political and moral conditions which will finally permit dialogue. And if we no longer have influence over either side, perhaps it is necessary to remain silent for a while.[45]

> When two of our brothers engage in a fight without mercy, it is criminal madness to excite one or the other of them. Between wisdom reduced to silence and madness which shouts itself hoarse, I prefer the virtues of silence. Yes, when speech manages to dispose without remorse of the existence of others, to remain silent is not a negative attitude.[46]

However, for some, Camus's silence was not only further proof of his political irrelevance, it amounted to an act of political and even moral irresponsibility. Steven Bronner, for example, finds in Camus's response to the Algerian crisis the consequence of his complete lack of "political realism", claiming that Camus's own Algerian heritage "does not justify his completely impractical politics".

Indeed, just because he was disgusted with the fanaticism of *both* Algerian national self-determination and French imperialism, his *primary ethical aim* should have led him to embrace the side with the best chance of ending the bloodshed. There was only one concrete position for a humanist ethically opposed to terror to take ... the only practical hope for ending the conflict lay with the FLN ... Camus obviously sought to balance his experience of two cultures and two continents, but in fact he transposed the liberal presumption concerning the rational resolution of grievances into a situation in which the institutions for securing such a process were not present. His choice was a refusal to choose between the only serious alternatives available.[47]

Of course Bronner isn't criticizing Camus for refusing "to choose between the only serious alternatives available", because the "alternative" he suggests to the French surrender of Algeria to the FLN is for the French army to maintain French rule in Algeria by whatever means necessary, which is clearly not a "serious alternative" at all, least of all for Camus. In this light, we see that Bronner is really criticizing Camus not for his silence, but for his refusal to support the FLN.[48] Similarly, when the future Minister for Education in independent Algeria, Ahmed Taleb Ibrahimi, met Camus in 1956 he objected not to any supposed silence about French atrocities in Algeria, but to Camus's refusal to distinguish between the violence of the FLN and the violence of the French: Camus insisted "that he could not condemn [the violence] of the paratroopers without at the same time condemning that of the terrorists. All of our arguments left him cold and indifferent" (Taleb Ibrahimi 1973: 182). And the reason Camus refused to support the FLN was quite simple: they saw French and Algerian civilians as legitimate targets in their war of independence, they were less a liberation organization than a nationalist organization, and the nationalism they espoused was essentialist and anti-humanist. After all, whereas Camus had constructed an idea of legitimate political violence around the fragile image of the scrupulous assassins, the FLN had launched their "open war" with France in August 1955 with the brutal, spectacular massacre of civilians at Philippeville (Stora 2001: 43–8).

Furthermore, although such complaints about Camus's lack of political realism with regard to Algeria are commonplace, they are not as persuasive as they might at first seem. First, we can see that they exhibit that same "retrospectivism" commonly found in postcolonial critiques of Camus. The claim that the FLN should have been supported relies on the knowledge of their successes (not least, their success in liquidating other nationalist groups, including Messali Hadj's MNA).[49] As David Schalk points out, recent scholarship suggests that even at the time of Camus's death in 1960 "France was still winning militarily", so from a strictly "realist" point of view it might appear that Camus ought to have supported the French policy of collective punishment (Schalk 2004: 345–6). Similarly, the claim that the truce appeal was unrealistic relies to a considerable extent on the retrospective knowledge of its failure. Although the collapse of the truce plan may have surprised neither Bronner nor Cruise O'Brien, it seems that at the time a considerable number of people either hoped or feared that it would succeed (including, on the one hand, Ferhat Abbas and, on the other, hundreds, even thousands, of *pieds-noirs*). Secondly, such criticism fails to address Camus's own distinct aversion to such realist arguments, especially when deployed in defence of political violence. Bronner correctly compares Camus's attitude to that of Václav Havel's "anti-political politics", but he suggests that when applied to Algeria such ideas "nearly" became "platitudes", and he fails to notice that at the heart of Camus's attitude to the FLN was the view, very far from being a platitude, that their ideology was informed by precisely the same Manichaeism it had itself identified in colonialism (Bronner 1999: 115).

Camus's objection to this perceived Manichaeism was strengthened by what he considered to be the legitimate right of the *pieds-noirs* to live in equitable peace in Algeria. This is usefully highlighted by criticism he drew for defending the right of the Hungarian insurrection against Soviet domination in 1956. Susan Dunn and James Le Sueur both perceive a contradiction between Camus's support for the Hungarian insurrection and his continued rejection of the FLN (Dunn 1994: 161; Dunn 1998: 353; Dunn 1999; Le Sueur 2001: 103). However, for Camus the differences between the situation in Algeria and that in Hungary were not ideological, but were factual and historical. In a letter to *Encounter* in 1957, addressing the same criticism, Camus claimed that "any effort to assimilate the Algerian question to the Hungarian comes up against a historical fact – a fact one may regret but which is a fact nevertheless":

> There was not in Hungary, installed for more than a century, more than a million Russians . . . whose lives, whose rights (and not merely privileges) the Hungarian revolution menaced. The Hungarian problem is simple: the Hungarians must be given back their liberty. The Algerian problem is different: there, it is necessary to assure the liberties of the two peoples of the country. There is also another difference . . . not a single Russian voice has been raised to demand justice for the Hungarian people. Many French voices have for a long time now been raised in support of the Algerian Muslims. These are the advantages of freedom.[50]

Unsurprisingly, one of Camus's strongest critics on the subject of Algeria was Sartre, who considered his political differences with Camus to have been at their most significant during the Algerian war (de Beauvoir 1984: 269). In two consecutive articles in *L'Express* in October 1955 Camus had made ironic use of the claims of Mendès-France and Mitterrand that "Algeria was France", as well as counter-claims that it was not. Camus insisted that such simplifications served only to exacerbate the problem, and argued that in Algeria the French and the Arabs were destined either to live together or to die together (*CAC6*: 65–71). In the November 1955 editorial in *Les Temps modernes*, titled "Algeria is not France", Sartre argued that indeed Algeria is not France and that only violence will succeed in achieving its liberation. He observed that as soon as the Algerians' right to struggle against colonial domination was defended, "morality enters the scene, horrified, deploring extremism, and its impure consequences, glimpsing the depths of injustice, only to be frightened by this 'infernal cycle of terror and repression'". "Who do they think they're kidding?" he asked, "What accord, in Algeria, did the rebellion jeopardise? What reform was hindered? What sudden gesture of love did it interrupt?" (Sartre 1955b: 578). It seems quite likely that Sartre had Camus in mind here, as he appears to allude to one of Camus's *L'Express* articles, "Terrorism and Repression", in which Camus argues that both FLN terrorism and French repression were "purely negative, doomed to pure destruction, with no future but an intensification of both fury and folly" (*CAC6*: 43). Although Sartre nowhere mentioned him by name, the extent to which he was opposed to Camus on the subject of Algeria became clearly evident in the immediate wake of the truce appeal. Five days after Camus's speech in Algiers calling for a civilian truce, Sartre gave a speech in Paris at a rally "for peace in Algeria" (which began with the announcement of the FLN's benediction). Sartre's speech, published under the title "Colonialism is a System", begins with a warning: "I would like to put you on your guard against what might be called 'neocolonialist mystification'. Neocolonialists think that there are some good *colons* and some very wicked ones, and that it is the fault of the latter that the situation of the colonies has deteriorated" (Sartre 2006: 36*). In contrast, Sartre speaks of the "infernal cycle of colonialism", and insists that "it is not true that there are some good *colons*, and others who are wicked. There are *colons* and that is it", each of whom embodies "the very principles of the colonial system".[51] Whereas Camus had insisted that the task that faced Muslim and European Algerians was to find a way to live together, and had called for immediate economic and political reforms, Sartre criticizes the "tender-hearted realist who suggested massive reforms to us, saying 'The economy first!'", and argues that, rather than radically overhauling the colonialism of French Algeria, the role of the French must be "to help it to die", concluding that the "neocolonialist is a fool who still believes that the colonial system can be overhauled – or a clever cynic who proposes reforms because he know that they are ineffective".[52]

Doubt about the feasibility of a peaceful resolution to the Algerian conflict may have been at the source of Camus's public silence, but this silence did not mean that he had abandoned Franco-Algerian politics. We have already observed that the question of the legitimacy of political violence had been central to Camus's political thinking since the 1940s, and we have seen how his attempt to apply this thinking to the war in Algeria, through the civilian truce, had ended in failure. We have also noted the growing significance of capital punishment in Camus's evolving sense of justice, particularly since its widespread abuse during the post-Second World War purge. Unsurprisingly, it was in relation to the execution of Algerian militants that Camus hoped he could still effect some amelioration in the deteriorating situation in Algeria. As James Le Sueur observes, Camus perceived a "direct correlation between the escalation of terrorism against European civilians and the uncompromising use of the death penalty – the ultimate abuse of state power – against Algerian nationalists" (Le Sueur 2001: 107). Throughout this period he was actively involved in petitioning on behalf of Algerian militants condemned to death: according to Jean Daniel and Germaine Tillion, Camus intervened in more than 150 such cases.[53] Furthermore, beyond these direct political interventions, in 1957 Camus also published "Reflections on the Guillotine", which, as we have seen, called for the abolition of the death penalty, condemning the practice as "obviously no less repulsive than the crime" that it is designed to punish, and declaring that "this new murder, far from making amends for the harm done to the social body, adds a new blot to the first one" (*RRD*: 176; *E*: 1021). Nevertheless, Camus's support for clemency for condemned militants was not given unconditionally, and he insisted that his petitions not be used as part of a public appeal. For example, in December 1957 Camus agreed to petition the court on behalf of Mohamed Ben Saddok, who was facing a death sentence for his assassination in Paris of Ali Chekkal, a former vice-president of the Algerian National Assembly who favoured assimilation. Camus agreed to do so on condition that Ben Saddok's lawyer, Pierre Stibbe, keep his involvement out of the public domain. He told Stibbe that for two years he had "refused all public demonstrations likely to be exploited politically, thereby adding to the misfortune of my country. In particular, I wish in no way to lend good conscience, by declarations which cause no risk to myself, to a stupid fanatic who may shoot on a crowd in Algiers which could contain my mother or family [*les miens*]. This reason, which might seem naive in Paris, has for me the strength of a passion endorsed by reason" (Camus & Koestler 2002: 263; see *E*: 1845). Before Camus sent the letter, however, news of his appeal on behalf of Ben Saddok and, in particular, the conditions on which it was offered, were reported in the French press. Consequently, Camus angrily withdrew his offer of support.

According to de Beauvoir, who attended the Ben Saddok trial, several witnesses "quoted [Camus] in their pleas to the judge for clemency, though with a slight touch of sarcasm in some cases" (de Beauvoir 1968: 394). In his testimony, Sartre explicitly compared Ben Saddok to the protagonists of Camus's *The Just Assassins*.[54] This suggests that for de Beauvoir and Sartre, Ben Saddok's act mirrored Kaliayev's, and that Camus's failure to support the Algerian militant was ultimately proof of his bad faith. In de Beauvoir's mind, the war in Algeria began to imitate the Nazi occupation of France: on seeing French paratroopers on the streets of Paris she reports experiencing "the old impotent, raging disgust: exactly the same symptoms the sight of an SS man had always produced. French uniforms were having the same effect on me that swastikas once did. . . . Yes, I was living in an occupied city, and I loathed the occupiers even more fiercely than I had those others in the forties, because of all the ties that bound me to them." Accordingly, she imagines Ben Saddok as a heroic member of the *maquis*, saying "acts analogous to the one he had committed had been acclaimed during the Resistance as heroic deeds", and calls the assassinated Chekkal "one of the most notable Muslim collaborators". Sartre, on the other hand, was more direct in his defence of political violence: "To think that I stood there and eulogised Chekkal! And spoke against terrorism: as if I was against terrorism! All to please the Poujadists on the jury!" In any event, both de Beauvoir and Sartre shared a belief in the same essential Manichaean truth: "In Algeria, there was only one choice: fascism or the FLN."[55]

For many, final and conclusive proof of his political obsolescence seemed to be provided by Camus himself on the occasion of his Nobel Prize for Literature, awarded in 1957. At an informal question and answer session with a group of students at Stockholm University, an Algerian student asked Camus why he intervened so readily in Eastern Europe but never in Algeria. Before Camus could respond, the student began a long monologue comprising accusations and insults. Camus waited for silence and then began by asserting that he had never spoken to an Arab or FLN militant as he had just been spoken to. He continued: "You are for democracy in Algeria, so be democratic right now and let me speak." Visibly upset, Camus told his audience that he had been the only French journalist obliged to leave Algeria (his country of birth) because of his militancy in favour of rights for the Muslim majority and that his support for a democratic Algeria was well known. He assured the Algerian questioner "that some of his comrades were alive today thanks to actions of which the young man was not aware, and Camus was sorry to have to speak about that".[56] He continued:

> I have been silent for a year and eight months now, though that does not mean that I have ceased to struggle. I have always been a partisan of a just Algeria, where the two peoples can live in peace and in equality. I have repeatedly called for justice to be done for the Algerian people, that they be granted a fully democratic regime . . . I have always condemned the use of terror. And I must also condemn the use of terrorism which is exercised blindly, in the streets of Algiers for example, and which could one day strike my mother or my family. I believe in justice, but I will defend my mother before justice.[57]

For de Beauvoir, and one imagines for a great many of her contemporaries, this statement was proof that although he pretended to be "above the battle", Camus was in reality "on the side of the *pieds-noirs*". In fact, for de Beauvoir, the "humanist" in Camus had in any case "given way to the *pied-noir*" years before.[58] Conor Cruise O'Brien suggested that the statement amounted to a confession that "the defence of his mother required support for the French army's pacification of Algeria" (Cruise O'Brien 1970: 75; see also Taleb Ibrahimi 1966: 78). Susan Dunn agrees, claiming that the presence of Camus's mother in Algeria "was sufficient to counterbalance for him the entire colonial situation" (Dunn 1998: 353). Even sympathetic critics, such as Camus's biographer Olivier Todd, consider the claim to be regrettable and grounded on "poor logic" (Todd 1996: 700; Todd 1998: 378). In fact, Camus made the same point on several occasions, and consequently we should avoid treating it as an unguarded comment, let alone as "a kind of Freudian slip".[59] Indeed, the reference to his mother – far from unfortunate – pithily expressed the key philosophical concept of *limites* as it pertains to the legitimatization of political violence. The year 1957 had seen an escalation in the number of FLN attacks on civilians in Algeria (in June and July they bombed several tram stops and a casino). Such violence was only part of the endless cycle of bombings, tortures and executions, but it was nevertheless being committed in the name of justice. Camus certainly did not believe there was any justice to the French policy of brutal retaliation and *ratissage*, but the justice of the FLN's fight was frequently taken for granted (not least by his Algerian questioner), and it was this assumption that he sought to address. Responding to the question implicit in the student's intervention – why didn't Camus support the FLN? – Camus's point was that an idea of justice that, in his estimation, licenses the indiscriminate killing of innocent civilians ("terrorism practised blindly in the streets") is an idea of justice that he would never defend. The targeting of civilians is morally repugnant not because such attacks could conceivably kill Camus's mother, but because the victims of such an attack were inevitably like Camus's mother; that is, innocent civilians. This identification of civilians as legitimate targets was a practice Camus had addressed directly in his analysis of political violence in *The Just Assassins* and *The Rebel* and, of course, in his call for a civil truce. Accordingly, when the *pied-noir* poet, and one-time protégé of Camus, Jean Sénac complained to Camus that he would "try to defend my mother and justice together", he displayed only a failure to understand the point begin made.[60]

Furthermore, Camus's discussion of Algeria while in Stockholm was not restricted to this infamous comment. He also argued that a Franco-Muslim community was not only possible; it was necessary. He defended the idea of a federalized Algeria, where each ethnic community, Arab, French and Berber, "would be represented on the basis of equality in a legislative assembly which remained to be defined" (quoted in Lottman 1979: 614). Six months earlier, in the English magazine *Encounter*, Camus summarized his position on Algeria as follows. First, there ought to be a "proclamation of the end of colonial status for Algeria". Secondly, there must be a "round-table conference, without any preconditions, that would include all the representatives of Algerian parties and groups (an idea approved by numerous trade unions and – more important – by the National Algerian Movement [i.e. the MNA])". Thirdly, this conference would include in its agenda the "discussion of the possibility of an autonomous, federated . . . Algeria, which would preserve the liberties of the two peoples who inhabit the country" (Camus 1957: 68; *E*: 1877–81).

In June 1958, Camus published an anthology of his writings on Algeria, *Chronique algérienne 1939–1958*, a volume that sought to delimit and explain his silence over events in Algeria, firmly attributing it to the polarization of opinion:

> it seemed to me both indecent and harmful to protest against tortures in the company of those who readily accepted Melouza or the mutilation of European children. Just as it seemed to me harmful and indecent to condemn terrorism in the company of those who are not bothered by torture. The truth, alas, is that a part of French opinion vaguely holds that the Arabs have in a way earned the right to slaughter and mutilate while another part is willing to justify in a way all excesses. To justify himself, each relies on the other's crime. But that is a casuistry of blood, and it strikes me that an intellectual cannot become involved in it, unless he takes up arms himself. When violence answers violence in a growing frenzy that makes the simple language of reason impossible, the role of the intellectual cannot be, as we read every day, to excuse from a distance one of the violences and condemn the other. . . . If they do not join the combatants themselves, their role . . . must be merely to strive to calm the situation so that reason will again have a chance. . . . We could

have used moralists less joyfully resigned to their country's misfortune and patriots less ready to allow torturers to claim that they were acting in the name of France. It seems that metropolitan France was unable to think of any policies other than those which consisted in saying to the French in Algeria: "Go ahead and die; that's what you deserve" or else "kill them; that's what they deserve". That makes two different policies and a single abdication, for the question is not how to die separately but how to live together.

(RRD: 116–17*; E: 894–6)

In other words, Camus attributes his silence to the polarization of discourse in relation to Algeria. He explains his silence in the context of others' silence: on the one hand, the silence of the *pieds-noirs* in the face of the use of torture by the French, even after the publication of Henri Alleg's infamous *exposé, La Question* (1958), and, on the other hand, the silence of the pro-FLN French in the wake of FLN massacres of *pieds-noirs* in Philippeville (1955) and of Arab MNA supporters in Melouza (1957).[61] He especially objected to the "lethal frivolity" with which the French Left adopted the FLN's cause, beating their *mea culpa* "on someone else's breast" (as Sartre would in 1961, in his Preface to Fanon's *The Wretched of the Earth*).[62] As he had in his exchange with d'Astier de la Vigerie in 1948, Camus condemns those intellectuals willing to "excuse" violence without themselves taking up arms.

Camus also includes in this volume a statement of what he believes to be legitimate and illegitimate in the demands of Algerian nationalists (*RRD*: 143–53; *E*: 1009–18). He argues that they are right to denounce and reject "colonialism and its endemic abuses", "the perennial lie of constantly proposed but never realised assimilation" and "the obvious injustice of the agrarian [land] allocation and of the distribution of income". "Arab demands on all these points", Camus states, are "beyond doubt . . . thoroughly legitimate". However, he rejects the demand for complete Algerian independence, asserting that "as far as Algeria is concerned, national independence is an entirely emotive expression [*est une formule purement passionnelle*]. There has never yet been an Algerian nation. The Jews, the Turks, the Greeks, the Italians, the Berbers would have equal right to claim the direction of that virtual nation."[63] This is not only a statement of historical fact; it is also the reiteration of an assertion made twenty years earlier by Ferhat Abbas (as his Algerian audience would probably have recognized).[64] Furthermore, far from being a general dismissal of Algerian demands as illegitimate, as Edward Said and others suggest, it is a direct riposte to the FLN's stated aim, the "*restoration* of the sovereign Algerian state".[65] One may, of course, argue that even if there has never been, historically, an Algerian nation, and the territory had been ruled or occupied successively by Berbers, Phoenicians, Romans, Vandals, Arabs, Turks and Europeans, and settled in by peoples from every country in the Mediterranean region (in fact it is estimated that by 1917, only 20 per cent of European Algerians were of true French descent, and these included Alsatians and Corsicans (Horne 1977: 51)), it was nevertheless the case that the vast majority of the people living in Algeria were Arabs and Berbers, and they no longer wanted to live under French rule. However, this takes no account of the 1.2 million European "natives", who in contrast to the popular image of "a million colons with riding crops and cigars, driving around in Cadillacs", were actually significantly less well-off than their metropolitan co-citizens.[66] Neither does it make the FLN's aim to "restore" the sovereign Algerian state any less spurious. And it was precisely this claim that Camus was addressing.

This point leads us to Camus's second objection to Algerian independence: the nature of Algerian nationalism. Democracy, Camus wrote in his *Carnets*, "is not the rule of the majority, but the protection of the minority" (*C3*: 260). It is not possible, Camus appears to think, for France to countenance surrendering territory on which over one million of its citizens live to an authority deemed implacably hostile to it and its people. (In 1957, Frantz Fanon declared in the FLN's newspaper *El Moudjahid* that "every Frenchman currently in Algeria is an enemy combatant".[67]) Camus, perhaps mistakenly, attributes this aspect of the FLN's demands to Nasser-inspired "Arab imperialism", and he sees as its chief consequence "the systematic murder of French civilians and Arab civilians killed without discrimination and solely because they were French or friends of the French".[68] He also warns that the USSR has used this rise in Arab nationalism to its own advantage, a claim that might now seem like scaremongering, although at the time there was a genuine anxiety in Europe about the possibility of Soviet encirclement. Certainly, Camus was right to note that Soviet support for independence among colonies of the western powers contrasted starkly with its own imperialist acquisitions in Eastern Europe, not to mention its vicious repression of Muslim cultures in the Caucasus region of the USSR, in Dagestan, Chechnya and Azerbaijan, for example.

This analysis leads Camus to conclude that he is left in a paradoxical position. Although he can approve of the "basic causes" of Algerian aspirations for independence, indeed, from the beginning of his career he had been calling on France to address Algerian grievances, he cannot accept the demand for independence itself. As Camus sees it, the aspects of the problem in Algeria can be summarized as follows:

- the amends that must be made to eight million Arabs who have lived until now under a particular form of oppression;
- the right of 1,200,000 autochthonous French people to exist, and to exist in their native land without ever again being subjected to the discretion of fanatical military leaders;
- the strategic interests that determine the freedom of the West (*RRD*: 147; *E*: 1014).

According to Camus, if it is agreed that these are the fundamental problems contained in the Algerian question as it is being posed in France, then as a matter of urgency, the French government must make it clearly known "that it is ready to grant complete justice to the Arabs of Algeria and to liberate them from the colonial system", that it will "give up none of the rights of the Algerian French" and that it will fight to protect France, and Europe, against the encroachment of Soviet influence (what Camus calls, after the Soviet-appointed leader of Hungary who deposed Imre Nagy, "the Kadarization of Europe"). In this light he suggests that France make a direct appeal to the Algerian Arabs (he notes that "since the beginning of hostilities no French Chief of State or any Governor has spoken directly to the Arab population"), proclaiming again that the era of colonialism is over, admitting to past and present mistakes and, while refusing to "yield to violence", offering "to make amends".[69] Camus further proposes that France offer to the Algerian Arab population "a regime of free association in which every Arab, on the basis of the Lauriol Plan, will truly find the privileges of a free citizen".[70] The Lauriol Plan envisaged a new French parliament made up of Metropolitan French, Muslim Algerian and *pied-noir* representatives, constituted strictly on the basis of proportionality, and therefore comprising approximately 600 Metropolitan, 100 Muslim Algerian and 15 French Algerian deputies. The parliament in full session, with all representatives, would have authority over everything concerning both France and Algeria (such as taxation and the budget) but, crucially, the Muslim deputies would have the right to legislate independently on all affairs concerning them alone. This arrangement would ultimately be the basis for a French Commonwealth (incorporating, for example, an Algerian Assembly and a Federal Senate in which Algeria would be represented).[71]

Although he freely admits that with such an offer of a federalized Algeria the difficulties only begin, Camus is quite convinced that the only equitable solution to the Algerian question, which "would do justice to all parts of the population", is some sort of federalism. The Lauriol Plan seemed to Camus "particularly adapted to Algerian realities and likely to satisfy the need for justice and freedom felt by all the communities". It respects what is particular about both communities yet brings them together "in the administration of their common interest". France, says Camus, has no choice but to accept such a federal plan and, further, if it fails to introduce it, "Algeria will be lost and the consequences will be dreadful for the Arabs and for the French. This is the last warning that a writer who for twenty years has been devoted to the service of Algeria feels he can voice before resuming his silence."[72]

Camus's support for the Lauriol Plan is easy to criticize, but that criticism frequently overlooks the fact that, as Jeffrey Isaac notes, "it was not just the Arab that Camus expected to settle for less than absolute sovereignty". The internationalist perspective he defended in "Neither Victims nor Executioners" (and elsewhere) suggests that he hoped for a similar federal system operating in Europe, and beyond, as well (Isaac 1992: 206). Furthermore, although it is not difficult to criticize Camus's endorsement of the Lauriol Plan – and his rejection of the FLN in general – for being politically unrealistic, there are a number of reasons why this realist argument may not be as persuasive as it might at first seem.[73] First, as we have already seen, the realist argument for supporting the FLN is "retrospectivist", in that it is informed by a retrospective viewpoint from which Algeria has achieved independence (an achievement that we have noted was, even as late as 1960, far from being a forgone conclusion). Secondly, it fails to address Camus's own objections to the realism on which it is firmly grounded. For example, in his speech in favour of a civilian truce, Camus claimed:

> People are too readily resigned to fatality. They are too ready to believe that, after all, nothing but bloodshed makes history progress and that the stronger always progresses at the expense of the weaker. Such fatality exists perhaps. But man's task is not to accept it or to bow to its laws. . . . The task of men of culture and faith, in any case, is not to desert historical struggles nor to serve the cruel and inhuman elements in those struggles. It is rather to remain what they are, to help man against what is oppressing him, to favour freedom against the fatalities that close in upon it.   (*RRD*: 141; *E*: 998–9)

"That", says Camus, "is the condition under which history really progresses, innovates – in a word, creates. In everything else it repeats itself, like a bleeding mouth that merely vomits forth a wild stammering."[74] James Le Sueur alleges that Camus "remained opposed to Algerian independence because he simply refused to acknowledge the existence of two irreconcilable 'personalities' in Algeria and he believed that France (and the French) belonged there" (Le Sueur 2001: 87). Camus, of course, did not refuse to recognize the existence of two "personalities" in Algeria; he rejected only the assumption that they were "irreconcilable". Thirdly, it is not clear that Camus's position *vis-à-vis* Algerian independence was any less realistic than those that envisaged a pluralist FLN-led Algeria (as did Jean Sénac).[75] Nor is it clear that his position was any less realistic than that adopted by those who either ignored the existence of the million *pieds-noirs* who found themselves facing the wrong direction in the tide of history, or indulged in the sort of morbid adolescent fantasy we find in Sartre's Preface to Fanon's *The Wretched of the Earth*: "to shoot down a European is to kill two birds with one stone, to destroy the oppressor and the man he oppresses at the same time; there remains a dead man and a free man . . . The child of violence, at every moment he draws from it his humanity. We were men at his expense, he makes himself a man at ours: a different man, of higher quality."[76] What Sartre does here is inadvertently suggest that what Fanon considered the "Manichaean" character of colonialism, with "the settler paint[ing] the native as a sort of quintessence of evil", is mirrored exactly in the mortal antipathy the FLN and its sympathizers appear to have felt for the European Algerians, two Manichaean visions that, as we have already noted, were described by Camus thus: " 'Go ahead and die; that's what you deserve' or else 'kill them; that's what they deserve'. That makes two different policies and a single abdication, for the question is not how to die separately but how to live together."[77]

The policy of Arabization and Islamization introduced by the FLN on taking power in 1962 (to say nothing of the exodus of almost 1.5 million European and other refugees, and the FLN's thirty-year suspension of elections) constituted the conclusive destruction of Camus's long-dreamt-of pluralist, communal "Mediterranean humanism" in Algeria and a powerful endorsement of his antipathy for the ideology and actions of the FLN.[78] In the euphoria following independence in 1962, the Berber poet Kateb Yacine, who had joined the FLN during the war, proclaimed a vision of independent Algeria not unlike that imagined by Camus: "Algeria is above all Algeria! There is no Berber Algeria, no Arab Algeria, no French Algeria: there is one Algeria, which must not be mutilated. Algeria is 'multinational', it is very rich to the extent to which it is 'multinational'."[79] However, the reality of independent Algeria was to be quite different: one form of cultural and political hegemony (Arab) replaced another (French). Under Minister for Education Ahmed Taleb Ibrahimi, who also happened to be one of Camus's most vociferous and celebrated anti-colonial critics in this period, a strict policy of Arabization and Islamization was introduced into the Algerian educational system.[80] Whereas Camus has been accused of being ignorant of the cultural complexity of Algeria,[81] it was Taleb Ibrahimi, then Minister for Information and Culture, who wrote in 1973 that "In reading everything this has been written on the Arabs and the Berbers in Algeria, we realise that a real effort was made to undermine and divide the Algerian people. To advance, for example, that the Algerian population is composed of Arabs and Berbers is historically false."[82] Accordingly, the 1976 Algerian National Charter not only omitted all mention of Berber culture and language (the culture and language of about 20 per cent of the Algerian population); it specified that "the generalised use of the Arabic language and its mastery as a creative functional instrument is one of the primordial tasks of Algerian society" (quoted in Stora 2001: 181). The FLN also rewrote the history of Algerian nationalism, denying its pluralist character prior to the rise of the FLN, and negating the significance of nationalist leaders such as Messali Hadj and Ferhat Abbas.[83] Ultimately, the Algerian society envisaged by the FLN was not one characterized by the cultural pluralism imagined by Camus or Kateb Yacine but one that "rested on the conception of the organic solidarity of the community", a conception that underlies "the necessity felt by the new leaders to achieve social cohesion through authoritarian means".[84] Noting this level of cultural imperialism in post-independence Algeria is intended only to highlight the extent to which the ideology and actions of the FLN were anathema to Camus's conception of Mediterranean humanism. Although Camus's proposed federal solution may not have been viable, it needs to be understood in the context of his rejection of political realism as well as the political disaster fomented by thirty years of FLN anti-democratic rule. Ultimately, if Camus was "wrong historically" about Algeria, he was surely to some extent also "right historically".

CONCLUSION

La mesure is not therefore the casual resolution of contraries. It is nothing other than the affirmation of contradiction, and the firm decision to hold on to it in order to out-live it. That which I call *la démesure* is that movement of the soul which passes blindly across the frontier where contrary facts balance one another to finally come to rest in an act of drunken consent, of which our world abounds in cowardly and cruel examples.[1]

I began this study with the claim that it was singularly unhelpful to read Camus as an existentialist (at least in the technical sense), and that it was more fruitful to examine his writings in the context of the relationship between the ontological con-cept of the absurd, as articulated in *The Myth of Sisyphus*, and the moral–political concept of revolt, as articulated in *The Rebel*. This perspective, I have argued, indi-cates a profound coherence between these two concepts. This coherence is perhaps especially striking when we note the distinct similarities between Camus's rejection of existentialism in the context of the absurd, and his rejection of Marxism in the context of revolt. His rejection of teleological and messianic Marxism (its "deifica-tion of history"), in favour of a conception of revolt that places the precariously bal-anced values of relative justice and relative freedom at its heart, has, it seems, a great deal in common with his rejection of the "religious" "forced hope" he identified in existentialism in favour of a more modest hope or optimism. For Camus, it seems, Marxists no less than existentialists "deify what crushes them and find reason to hope in what impoverishes them".[2] The common theme here appears to be Camus's idea of the "proper use" or the limits of human reason (Henry 1975: 106–107). As we have seen, he describes the absurd as "lucid reason noting its limits", and claims that for Husserl, "reason eventually has no limits at all" (*MS*: 29; *E*: 134). Similarly, although he rejects the title of philosopher on the basis that he did not have "sufficient faith in reason", his rejection of Marxism in *The Rebel* is premised on the "historical reason" deployed by Marxists, a reasoning that concludes in the justifica-tion of "rational crimes".[3] The absurd, then, no less than revolt, implies a rejection of all forms of rational absolutism, all forms of totalization.

Far from revealing a failure of political nerve, or from being a belated admission of rather conventional and chauvinistic prejudices hitherto disguised behind a disarmingly charismatic moralist exterior, Camus's words and actions in respect of Algeria accurately reflect these same conceptual preoccupations.[4] As Maurice Robin suggests, the philosophy of revolt expounded in *The Rebel* amply illustrates why Camus "could not but accept the necessity of an Algerian revolution" and at the same time "why he could not accept the method in which it was conceived and executed by the FLN", because in Camus's eyes the goal of the FLN revolution "was the creation of a new man, the Algerian, who was exclusively Arab and Muslim by denying the diversity of the [existing] Algerian community".[5] Camus was resistant to the FLN, not because it sought to redress the glaring economic and political inequalities between Muslims and Europeans, but because it posited as the basis of its argument the same violently sectarian Manichaeism that he found among the *colons* and had criticized throughout his writing career.[6] The FLN gathered much of its strength from the reality of the social and economic oppression of the Muslim population of Algeria, but by asserting itself in antithetical relationship to the culture of the European settlers, it was for Camus no less closed and absolutist.[7] In a letter to his Catholic Berber friend Jean Amrouche – who acted as envoy between the FLN and the French government – Camus wrote: "you have the right to choose the position of the FLN. Personally, I believe it to be murderous for the present, blind and dangerous for the future."[8] According to Mouloud Feraoun, Camus considered the FLN to be "fascist" and that it would be "unthinkable" to place the future of Algeria in its hands (Feraoun 2000: 184–5). In his letter requesting clemency for Ben Saddok, the assassin of Ali Chekkal, Camus declared himself an opponent of "both the ideology [*des thèses*] and the actions of the FLN" (Camus & Koestler 2002: 264). Chief among the FLN's actions that Camus found objectionable was undoubtedly their targeting of civilians (the majority of whom, he noted, were Arabs, *RRD*: 115; *E*: 894). Although this policy may have been an exasperated response to the French use of collective repression, it was nevertheless anathema to Camus's conception of legitimate political violence. In terms of FLN ideology, as we have seen, Camus objected to their avowed aim, the "*restoration* of the sovereign Algerian state", claiming it, with some justification, to be spurious. He objected, too, to the FLN's treatment of Muslim Algerians who refused to support it, issuing an appeal in 1957, for example, calling for action to be taken in defence of the pro-MNA Union of Algerian Workers (*Union Syndicale des Travailleurs Algériens*), senior members of which were at that time being assassinated by the FLN, which sought to assert itself as the only legitimate representative of Algerian interests. Indeed, the range of targets considered legitimate by the FLN was such that it was clearly at odds with Camus's assertion in *The Rebel* that "man's solidarity is founded upon rebellion, and rebellion, in its turn, can only find its justification in this solidarity. Any rebellion that claims the right to deny or destroy this solidarity loses simultaneously the right to be called rebellion and becomes in reality an acquiescence in murder."[9] "The Algerian revolution, in this light," says Robin, "is not a rebellion but is the murder of a community" (Robin 1986: 188).

If we can characterize Camus's Mediterranean humanism as a rejection of both colonialism and integral nationalism (in particular, their resort to violence), as a defence of pluralism grounded in non-sectarian political solidarity, then it would

seem that we are justified in interpreting it as a version of "*la pensée de midi*" articulated and defended in *The Rebel*.[10] As I have already suggested, in this light we can
perhaps more clearly see the visceral importance for Camus of the success of his
aspirations for Algeria, for failure would appear to critically undermine a central
theme of his philosophical *oeuvre*, grouped around the idea of *la mesure* (or
sophrosyne), most clearly manifested in the argument that absolute freedom denies
justice and that absolute justice denies freedom, and the suggestion that "to be fruitful, the two ideas must find their limits in each other" (*R*: 291; *E*: 694). To have
accepted the legitimacy, let alone the inevitability, of an FLN-led Algeria would have
meant admitting to the illegitimacy, or impossibility, of Mediterranean humanism
and, indeed, the civilization of *mesure* imagined in *The Rebel*. He clearly believed the
FLN represented the ideological antithesis of his Mediterranean humanism, seeing
in its ideas and actions the mirror image of the *démesuré* Manichaeism of the colonial regime, and that the democratic foundations necessary to such a humanistic
society were more likely to be established through federation with France (such as
that proposed in the Lauriol Plan) than through independence under the FLN.
Certainly the FLN's subsequent effort to create an exclusively Arab and Muslim
Algeria constituted the definitive refutation of Camus's Mediterranean humanism,
as well as his subversive *cogito*, "I rebel – therefore we exist" (*R*: 22; *E*: 432). Nevertheless, it is this prioritization of solidarity, and the demands of relative freedom and
relative justice that stem from it, that are at the heart of Camus's contemporary
relevance.

NOTES

Introduction

1 *E*: 312–13; *CC*: 100*; *RRD*: 58–9*. "I can only tell you this – I have too much taste for life and a feeling for the world to believe that all is nothingness . . . I do not believe that negation encompasses everything, I only believe that it is at the beginning of everything" (quoted in Todd 1998: 215; Todd 1996: 397).

2 *LACE*: 205*, 201–2; *E*: 1421, 1419. The perceived solipsism of Sartre's characters is significant with regard to both Camus's depiction of the solipsistic Sisyphus (he was obviously acutely sensitive to the dangers of solipsism) and Sartre's depiction of Camus as solipsistic in his reaction to *The Rebel*.

3 *L'Arbalète*, Summer 1943, reprinted in *E*: 1415, trans. Sprintzen 1988: 43.

4 "Le Pessimisme et le Courage", *Combat*, 3 November 1944, reprinted in *CC*: 100; *E*: 312; J.-P. Sartre, "A More Precise Characterization of Existentialism", *Action*, 29 December 1944; reprinted in Sartre 1970: 653–8, 654; Sartre 1974a: 155–60, 156.

5 "Non, je ne suis pas existentialiste", *Les Nouvelles littéraires*, 15 November 1945, reprinted in *E*: 1424–7; *LACE*: 345–8*.

6 Arban 1945: 2 (this interview is not reprinted in *E* or *TRN*).

7 Interview with Sartre in *Paru*, December 1945, reprinted in Sartre 1981: 1912–17, 1916. In an interview with de Beauvoir in 1974, Sartre notes "People thought they would please us by calling all three of us existentialists and that enraged Camus. In fact he had nothing in common with existentialism" (de Beauvoir 1984: 166).

8 Interview in *Servir*, 20 December 1945, reprinted in *E*: 1427–9. The question of whether Camus was a philosopher in the technical sense of the word has received some attention (see especially the essays collected in Amiot & Mattéi 1997). If Camus did reject systems of philosophical thought, he did not reject methodical thought: "It is not logic that I refute but rather ideology, which substitutes for living reality a logical succession of arguments" (interview with Pierre Berger in 1952, *E*: 741–2).

9 Interview in *Servir*, 20 December 1945, reprinted in *E*: 1427–9.

10 "It is an open philosophy, and in that sense, I am a Marxist" (interview with Sartre in *Paru*, December 1945, reprinted in Sartre 1981: 1912–17, 1916. Although Sartre's relationship with Marxism is infinitely more complex than this discussion might suggest, the beginning of his *rapprochement* certainly began at this time (see Birchall 2004: 71).

11 "Existentialism kept Hegelianism's basic error, which consists in reducing man to history. But it did not keep the consequence, which is to refuse in fact any freedom to man" (*NB2*: 141*; *C2*: 180).

12 Letter to editor of *La Nef*, January 1946, reprinted in *TRN*: 1743–4.

13 *R*: 249; *E*: 650–51. See Aronson 2004: 113, 126, 136, 139–40, 142. For other related references by Camus to existentialism and Sartre see *NB2*: 88–9, 91, 120, 124, 141, 145–6, 171; *C2*: 116, 119, 155, 160, 180, 185–6, 218; *C3*: 113, 147; Letter to Hazel Barnes from October 1959 (quoted in Barnes 1997: 160–61); interview for *Venture* magazine in December 1959 (*Venture*, Spring/Summer, 1960, reprinted in *E*: 1926–7).

14 "I understand that you could see in me what I should prefer to call an existential writer rather than an existentialist writer. I simply insist on being precise. For many years now I have not believed in either the premises or the conclusions of existentialist philosophy, or of what has been called that in intending to refer to Sartre's philosophy. In fact, Pascal, Kierkegaard and Nietzsche are existentialist thinkers and Sartre is not one. But since we must use the terminology and the vocabulary of our time, even when they are false or unintelligent, it is better to say that if Sartre is an existentialist, Pascal, Nietzsche and Kierkegaard are not. These nuances will explain to you that I understand very well your point of view, that I am not offended by it and that I am simply and sincerely grateful for the interest and sympathy that you wish to show me" (Barnes 1997: 160–61). On Camus as a *moraliste* see Henry 1975: 109–13; Bronner 1999: ix; Judt 1998: 121–2; Peyre 1958, 1962; Roth 1955; and Pierce 1966: 144–7.

15 There are two biographical details that are of particular significance in a philosophical interpretation of Camus's works. First, we should be conscious of his tuberculosis (he had his first attack in 1930, and subsequent attacks in 1936, 1942 and 1949). His experience of this disease, as we shall see, had a major influence on his concept of the absurd. The second detail that should be borne in mind relates to Camus's experience of resistance during the Occupation. His work with *Combat* was not his first foray into the world of political commitment, but it did underline the need for solidarity and specifically personal commitment in the struggle against tyranny. Perhaps more importantly, the experience of the purge in the immediate post-war period convinced Camus that even retribution could not be absolute.

16 Sprintzen 1988: 120–21, 133; Busch 1999: 9; Sagi 2002: 107, 111, 113; Kamber 2002: 79–80.

17 Avi Sagi, for example, disagrees with those who see a continuity, claiming that in later works Camus "revealed a profound dismay with the results of *The Myth of Sisyphus*" and concluded that the absurd "leads to immorality", that "the absurd is evil and injustice" (Sagi 2002: 113, 107, 111).

18 See especially Aronson 2004; Birchall 1994; Forsdick 2007; Santoni 2003; Sprintzen & van den Hoven 2004.

Chapter 1 The absurd

1 *SEN*: 168–9; *E*: 1418–19. As we shall see, Camus also claims that, far from being the defining characteristic of existentialism, the "realisation that life is absurd", combined with the sense that this realization "cannot be an end but only a beginning", "is a truth nearly all great minds have taken as their starting point" (*ibid.*).

2 This point can be illustrated by the famous lines from Tolstoy's story "The Death of Ivan Ilyich": "The syllogism he had learned from Kiesewetter's logic: 'Caius is a man, men are mortal, therefore Caius is mortal', had always semed to him correct as applied to Caius, but certainly not as applied to Ivan Ilych" (Guerney 1943: 621).

3   "What does eternity matter to me? You can lie in bed one day and hear someone tell you: '... you are going to die'; lie there with the whole of your life clasped in your hands, and all your fear in your bowels and a look of stupidity in your eyes. What does the rest matter? Waves of blood come throbbing to my temples and I feel I could crush everything around me" (*SEN*: 79; *E*: 65). Discussing this period in 1958, Camus noted "Yes, I feared that I might die. And after numerous treatments, I could read it on the faces of the doctors too" (Viggiani 1968: 209). On the significance of the respiratory trope in Camus's works see the following from Germaine Brée: "The access to air is a brusque, spasmodic one in the case of Meursault and accompanies his first conscious contact with life; in *La Peste* it comes after a protracted struggle against death. In *L'Etat de siège*, the respiratory rhythm sustains the play as it moves into the suffocating realm of the plague and out of it again. Camus' universe is therefore closely bound to an essential physiological rhythm and anguish, a personal one, no doubt.... The breath of air from the sea, the sea itself, are what free Camus' world from the oppression of death and always open it, in the end, to the normal rhythms of life from which it is temporarily cut off. It is within this atmospheric drama that the events in the two novels take place. It is in relation to the threat of death by suffocation that they take on their tense and dramatic colour. They develop concretely the theme of an approach to an arbitrary death, imposed from outside, which the atmospheric theme suggests" (Brée 1951: 96).

4   Ayer 1946: 159. Furthermore, as Thomas Busch notes, as brief and unsophisticated as Camus's comments on science may be, "they have the ring of the accepted Kuhnian assessment of science prevalent today" (Busch 1999: 4; see Kuhn 1996). Ayer professed an even lower opinion of Sartrean existentialism, suggesting on the basis of his reading of *Being and Nothingness* that it "was principally an exercise in the art of misusing the verb 'to be'" (Ayer 1977: 284). See Ayer 1945, 1950.

5   Camus interviewed in 1951, *LACE*: 349–57: 356; *E*: 1337–43, 1342–3. In the published text the word "absurd" is printed as "Absurd". I have changed the text because Camus himself always referred to "l'absurde", never "l'Absurde". In fact, in a page from a proof copy of *Le Mythe de Sisyphe* corrected by Camus, which is reprinted in Abdelkader Djemaï's *Camus à Oran*, we see that Camus deliberately corrected the printed "l'Absurde" to be reprinted as "l'absurde" (Djemaï 1995: 69). See also the following comment on the indiscriminate use of the term "absurd": "Thus one becomes a prophet of the absurd. Yet what did I do except reason about an idea which I found in the streets of my time? It goes without saying that both I and my whole generation have nourished this idea (and that a part of myself still does so). What I did, however, was to set it far enough from me to analyse it and decide on its logic. Everything that I have been able to write since then is sufficient proof of this. But it is more convenient to exploit a cliché than a nuance. They choose the cliché: so I am absurd as before" ("L'Énigme", in *Nuptials*; *SEN*: 144; *E*: 864).

6   *MS*: 21; *E*: 109. Thomas Nagel also argues that in several respects "philosophical perceptions of the absurd [resemble] epistemological skepticism" and suggests that "a situation is absurd when it includes a conspicuous discrepancy between pretension or aspiration and reality" (Nagel 1979: 18, 13). In relation to the commonality between philosophical perceptions of the absurd and epistemological scepticism, Nagel asserts, "In both cases the final, philosophical doubt is not contrasted with any unchallenged certainties, though it is arrived at by extrapolation from examples of doubt within the system of evidence or justification, where a contrast with other certainties *is* implied. In both cases our limitedness joins with a capacity to transcend those limitations in thought (thus seeing them as limitations, and as inescapable)" (*ibid.*: 18). Mitchell Gabhart associates Camus's absurd with David Hume's concept of "mitigated" scepticism, in which "undistinguished doubts are, in some measure, corrected by common sense and reflection" (quoting Hume's *Enquiry concerning Human Understanding* (Ch. XII, Pt 3), Gabhart 1994: 76).

7   Busch 1999: 4. Camus makes similar criticisms of Chestov and Jaspers (see Henry 1975: 97–9).

8   *MS*: 44–5, 47; *E*: 129–31, 132. Camus's editors trace the passage quoted to Husserl's *Logical Investigations Vol. 1* (*E*: 1439). I have used here the translation in Husserl 2001: 97.

9   Placing Camus's essay within the tradition of "French anti-rationalism", Patrick Henry observes: "Many anti-rationalists, Pascal, Rousseau, and Bergson for example, stressed the limits of reason but substituted another means of knowledge, like faith, sentiment or intuition, in its place. Camus, as well as Voltaire, stressed the limitations of reason, without substituting an alternative. Indeed . . . Voltaire repudiated both Pascal and Rousseau for having done so, just as Camus reproached the Existentialists for the same reason" (Henry 1975: 96; see also Cruickshank 1960: 50–58).

10   *MS*: 43; *E*: 128. This section of *MS* is generally considered to be its weakest. In his review Sartre suggested that Camus "shows off a bit by quoting passages from Jaspers, Heidegger and Kierkegaard, whom, by the way, he does not always seem to have quite understood" (Sartre 1962a: 109).

11   *MS*: 35; *E*: 122. "To Chestov reason is useless but there is something beyond reason. To an absurd mind reason is useless and there is nothing beyond reason" (*MS*: 38; *E*: 124). Jaspers, the "apostle of humiliated thought, will find at the very end of humiliation the means of regenerating being to its very depth" (*MS*: 36; *E*: 122–3). Philosophical suicide occurs when "starting from a philosophy of the world's lack of meaning, [the mind] ends up by finding a meaning and depth in it" (*MS*: 44; *E*: 129). "Now to limit myself to existential philosophies, I see that all of them without exception suggest escape. Through an odd reasoning, starting out from the absurd over the ruins of reason, in a closed universe limited to the human, they deify what crushes them and find reason to hope in what impoverishes them. That forced hope is religious in all of them" (*MS*: 35; *E*: 122).

12   "Camus defines the proper sphere of reason between Husserl, for whom ['reason eventually has no limits at all'], and Kierkegaard, who not only abandons reason but ends by exalting the non-rational. . . . Camus marks out with great precision the legitimate boundaries of human reason and then stoically adheres to these limits" (Henry 1975: 105, quoting *MS*: 49; *E*: 134).

13   We will be reminded of this phrase when we read Sartre's letter to Camus in 1952: "Where is Sisyphus? Where, today, are these Trotskyites of the heart, who preached permanent revolution?" (Sartre 1952: 334; *SCHC*: 132).

14   *MS*: 55; *E*: 139. Cf. "The absurd has meaning only insofar as it is not agreed to" (*MS*: 35; *E*: 121).

15   As Avi Sagi perceptively notes, "The decision to embrace the absurd is not reached through a process of logical inference; rather, it becomes a test for human beings asking whether they really wish to live a life of conscious clarity" (Sagi 1994: 279).

16   Busch 1999: 6. "*Doxa*", for Busch, refers to "the realm of appearance, relativity, antinomy, the very stuff traditional Western philosophers and theologians have set about to straighten out, rationalise, and remove for us in order to relieve us from our existential perplexity, doubt, fear and terror" (1999: 2). The validity of this interpretation of Camus is substantially endorsed by the assessment of *MS* offered by the arch logical-positivist A. J. Ayer (Ayer 1946).

17   *MS*: 34–5; *E*: 121, partly quoted in Carroll (2007b: 59).

18   *MS*: 107, 109; *E*: 195, 196. Thomas Nagel, whose ideas regarding the absurd appear remarkably similar to those of Camus, suggests that this aspect of Camus's thought is "romantic and slightly self-pitying. Our absurdity warrants neither that much distress nor that much defiance" (Nagel 1979: 22). Certainly, the fact that *The Myth of Sisyphus* was written and published during the Nazi Occupation of France had an influence on its tone. However, such a "romantic" philosophy is certainly no less controversial than the view of Nagel, who views such writings as betraying "a failure to appreciate the cosmic unimportance of the situation" (*ibid.*: 23).

19   "I understand then why the doctrines that explain everything to me also debilitate me at the same time. They relieve me of the weight of my own life and yet I must carry it alone. . . . The absurd man can only drain everything to the bitter end, and deplete himself. The absurd is his extreme tension which he maintains constantly by solitary effort, for he knows that in that

consciousness and in that day-to-day revolt he gives proof of his only truth which is defiance" (*MS*: 54–5; *E*: 139).

20   It is not the case that Camus believed that "quantity is always more important than quality" (Kamber 2002: 60). One of the immediate consequences of the recognition of the absurd, for Camus, is that it seemed to render talk of qualitative differences impossible.

21   Indeed, Camus warns us against reading these images as models: "Do I need to develop the idea that an example is not necessarily an example to be followed (even less so if possible in the absurd world) and that these illustrations are not, therefore, models? Besides the fact that a certain vocation is required for this, one becomes ridiculous, with all due allowance, when drawing from Rousseau the conclusion that one must walk on all fours and from Nietzsche that one must maltreat one's mother. 'It is essential to be absurd . . . It is not essential to be a dupe'. . . . A sub-clerk in the post-office is the equal of a conqueror if consciousness is common to them" (*MS*: 66; *E*: 150). And again: "Let me repeat that these images do not propose moral codes and involve no judgements: they are sketches. They merely represent a style of life" (*MS*: 84; *E*: 169). Hence it is erroneous of Ayer to assert that the purpose of these characters is "to illustrate, and incidentally to recommend, a certain attitude to life" (Ayer 1946: 163).

22   *MS*: 73, 78, 82; *E*: 157, 162, 166. McCarthy also notes that ambiguities surround these characters: "Don Juan is not a passionate lover, the actor juxtaposes his energy with the awareness that he is playing a part, while the conqueror knows that he can win no political victories. All three are conscious of limits. . . . Moreover, other values emerge from the free acceptance of limits. Don Juan demonstrates courage and lucidity. . . . Refusing to believe in the false mystique of love he seduces his last woman and waits to die, aware that he is old and ridiculous. The actor shows lucidity when he emphasises the edge of nothingness that is present in all his roles. . . . Don Juan is generous rather than kind, virile rather than tender, stoical rather than sensitive. . . . When he writes that the conqueror can never win Camus is attacking the mystique of revolution which is another form of false oneness like religion or cartesianism" (McCarthy 1982: 151–2).

23   *E*: 173. The English translation, which follows the first and second editions of *Le Mythe de Sisyphe*, has "metaphysical honour" in place of "metaphysical joy" (*MS*: 86). See *E*: 1447 for details of the textual revision. (I owe this observation to David Carroll's excellent essay on *The Myth of Sisyphus*: Carroll 2007b.)

24   Carroll 2007b: 60. The artist plays a similarly exalted role in *The Rebel*.

25   *MS*: 86–7, 111, 108; *E*: 173–4, 198, 196. "Perhaps even", Carroll continues, "the 'something' of a politics of revolt" (2007b: 64).

26   *MS*: 66; *E*: 150, see note 21.

27   *E*: 1430. See *MS*: 10; *E*: 97. The note originally appeared preliminary to the rest of the essay, but in both the Pléiade edition and the English translation the brief text is erroneously placed under the heading of the first chapter, "An Absurd Reasoning". This minor error has been corrected in the latest Pléiade edition.

28   From an interview in 1951, *LACE*: 356; *E*: 1342–3. Similarly, in 1950 he wrote, "What is the point of saying yet again that in the experience which interested me, and on which I happened to write, the absurd can be considered only as a point of departure – even though the memory and the feeling of it still accompany the later steps in the argument? Similarly, with all due sense of proportion, Cartesian doubt, which is systematic, is not enough to make Descartes into a sceptic. In any case how could one restrict oneself to saying that everything is meaningless, and that we should plunge into absolute despair? . . . You choose to stay alive the moment you do not allow yourself to die of hunger, and you consequently recognise that life at least has a relative value. What in fact does a literature of despair mean? Despair is silent. Moreover, even silence is meaningful if your eyes speak. True despair is the agony of death, the grave or the abyss. If it speaks, if it reasons, above all if it writes, immediately a brother reaches out his hand, the tree is justified, love is born. A literature of despair is a contradiction in terms" (*SEN*: 144–5; *E*: 864–5).

29 *R*: 9; *E*: 418. David Carroll, among others, believes that in his writings after *The Myth of Sisyphus* Camus "abandoned the concept of absurd" (2007b: 54, 66).

30 We should, however, not overlook the fact that Camus's career as a politically and socially active journalist precedes both the writing of *The Myth of Sisyphus* and his joining *Combat*, a fact that serves to support his claim that the absurd was always for him "a method and not a doctrine" (see especially his anti-colonial journalism for *Alger républicain* in the late 1930s, briefly discussed in Chapter 6).

31 When Camus originally offered the three "absurds" to his friend and publisher Edmond Charlot, he requested that they be published together in one volume, thus wrapping up the "absurd question" (Lottman 1979: 248–9; cf. Camus & Pia 2000: 61).

32 *TO*: 118–19; *TRN*: 1920–21 (from the 1955 "avant-propos" to the American college edition). In what seems to be an earlier version of this text, Camus writes: "One had wanted to see [in *The Outsider*] a new kind of immoralist, which was completely incorrect. The main issue in question here is not morality, but the universe of the trial which is as much bourgeois as Nazi or Communist. . . . With respect to Meursault, there is something positive in him, and that is his refusal, to the point of death, to lie. To lie is not only to say what isn't true, but to say more than one feels, usually in order to conform socially. Meursault is not on the side of the judges, of social rules, of conventional sentiments. . . . If you consider the book from this perspective, you will find a moral of sincerity, and an exaltation, simultaneously ironic and tragic, of terrestrial joys" (*E*: 1611).

33 Cruise O'Brien 1970: 23. There were earlier postcolonial critiques, but Cruise O'Brien's was perhaps the most systematic and least forgiving. For Cruise O'Brien even Camus's journalistic writing on Algeria evinces nothing more than "a painful and protracted failure" to come to terms with "the situation in question" (*ibid.*: 26).

34 Kréa 1961; Nora 1961. Quoted in Cruise O'Brien 1970: 25. Whereas for Cruise O'Brien the trial at which a *pied-noir* is convicted for murdering an Arab is a "historical fiction", for Nora, the condemnation of Meursault is "a disturbing admission of historical guilt".

35 *TO*: 93; *TRN*: 1194. It is worthy of note that not long after beginning his journalistic career with *Alger républicain*, Camus reported on several major criminal trials, including that of Sheikh El Okbi (discussed in Ch. 6). As Susan Tarrow notes, in each of these cases Camus drew attention to the political motivations behind the proceedings. The title Camus gave one of his articles, "The Story of a Crime; or, How a Crime is Thought Up for the Purposes of a Criminal Charge", Tarrow drily notes, could have been a subtitle for *The Outsider* (Tarrow 1985: 53, 203n.2; see *CAC3*: 512).

36 Cruise O'Brien 1970: 20–21. Cruise O'Brien also claims that Meursault "lies to the police" in order to get Raymond, who was prone to what he considered "affectionate" domestic violence, discharged (*ibid.*). This is not quite true: Meursault did tell the police that "the girl had 'cheated' on Raymond", but he did so because, "as far as he could see", this was true (*TO*: 50, 34–5; *TRN*: 1158, 1145).

37 Cruise O'Brien notes this as well. However, and as we will see, the critic fails to recognize *why* this is the case.

38 *TO*: 36; *TRN*: 1148, italics added. The same reasoning that takes place when he "lies" for Raymond is expressed in the following passage: "I then wanted a cigarette. But I hesitated because I didn't know if I could smoke in front of mother. I thought it over, it really didn't matter. I offered the caretaker a cigarette and we smoked" (*TO*: 14; *TRN*: 1129).

39 Reprinted as an "Afterword" in *TO*: 118; *TRN*: 1920. In this brief text, in which Camus insists on Meursault's honesty, he makes no reference whatever to the absurd.

40 Meursault continues: "But a few minutes later it began to get dark. They told me how to lay out the mat I had to sleep on. . . . A few days later I was confined to a cell by myself" (*TO*: 71; *TRN*: 1175).

41 *TO*: 78; *TRN*: 1180. This event constitutes the essence of Camus's play, *Le Malentendu* (translated as *The Misunderstanding* or *Cross Purpose*). Summarizing the meaning of that play, Camus wrote: "It amounts to saying that in an unjust or indifferent world man can save

himself, and save others, by practicing the most basic sincerity and pronouncing the most appropriate word" (Camus 1958: vii).

42   At least the Meursault we see after the killing of the Arab, the Meursault who becomes conscious of the absurd, and stays courageously true to its consequences.

43   In the 1955 "avant-propos" to the American "College" edition of *L'Etranger*, printed as an "Afterword" in the Penguin edition of *The Outsider* (*TO*: 118–19; *TRN*: 1920–21). Similarly, although Meursault was an office employee, Camus asserts in *The Myth of Sisyphus* that "a sub-clerk in the post-office is the equal of a conqueror if consciousness is common to them" (*MS*: 66; *E*: 150).

44   It is significant that one of the most powerful of these peddlers of false positivism, the magistrate, should refer to Meursault as "Mr Antichrist" (*TO*: 70; *TRN*: 1174), when, for Camus, he is "the only Christ that we deserve" (*TO*: 119; *TRN*: 1921).

45   A minor instance of this: at first, Meursault did not know to whom the court was referring when they mentioned "his mistress" (*TO*: 96; *TRN*: 1194). For Meursault, Marie was Marie.

46   "And I fired four more times at a lifeless body and the bullets sank in without leaving a mark. And it was like giving four sharp knocks at the door of unhappiness" (*TO*: 60; *TRN*: 1166).

47   *TO*: 68, 70, 119; *TRN*: 1173, 1174, 1921. The magistrate and, later on, the chaplain are bewildered by Meursault's lack of religiously inspired remorse, and both complain that all previous prisoners in Meursault's position "turned towards Him" (*TO*: 112, 69; *TRN*: 1205–206, 1173).

48   *TO*: 98; *TRN*: 1195. Earlier in the trial, when asked whether Meursault is being accused of burying his mother or killing a man, the prosecution replies that the two cannot be dissociated: "Yes . . . I accuse this man of burying his mother like a heartless criminal" (*TO*: 93; *TRN*: 1194).

49   *TO*: 97–8, 99; *TRN*: 1195, 1196. David Carroll suggests that after his arrest "Meursault loses his privileged place as a French citizen in colonial Algeria and over the course of the second half of the novel is increasingly identified with and put in the place of the colonised Arab, the anonymous, indigenous Other" (Carroll 2007a: 31–2).

50   *TO*: 98–9; *TRN*: 1195. Indeed, through the whole trial proceedings (as reported by Meursault) there are only two references to Meursault's "victim" (*TO*: 91, 92; *TRN*: 1191), and three references to the "Arab" (*TO*: 85, 96, 99; *TRN*: 1186, 1194, 1196), the last of which is made by Meursault himself. In contrast, there are eighteen references to Meursault's mother in the course of the trial (*TO*: 85, 86, 87, 88, 90, 91, 92, 93, 96, 98, 100; *TRN*: 1186, 1187, 1188, 1190, 1191, 1192, 1194, 1195, 1197).

51   "He told me almost spitefully that whatever happened the warden and staff of the home would be called as witnesses and that 'this could make things very unpleasant for me'. I pointed out to him that none of this had anything to do with my case, but he merely replied that I had obviously never had anything to do with the law" (*TO*: 65; *TRN*: 1170–71).

52   *TO*: 86; *TRN*: 1188–9. The warden's testimony can be usefully contrasted with the honest, though ineffectual, testimony of his girlfriend Marie and his friend Céleste, the two witnesses who best knew Meursault, and whom Camus claimed to be those of his characters (along with Dora from *Les Justes*) who were especially dear to him (in an interview in 1952; Brisville 1970: 188). It is worthy of note that the choice of witnesses at the trial makes it abundantly clear that it is Meursault's behaviour after his mother's funeral, rather than his killing of the Arab, that constitutes the court's concern.

53   *TO*: 10; *TRN*: 1126. The context in which Meursault later declines the offer to see his mother needs to be read in context. At the end of his brief interview the warden says "I expect you'd like to see your mother?" Meursault "stood up without saying anything and [the warden] led the way to the door", and they walked together to the mortuary. When he arrives in the mortuary he meets the caretaker, who tells Meursault: " 'We covered her up. But I was to unscrew the coffin to let you see her.' He was just going up to the coffin when I stopped him. He said, 'Don't you want to?' I answered, 'No.' He didn't say anything and I was embarrassed because I felt I shouldn't have said that. After a moment he looked at me and said, 'Why not?' but not

reproachfully, just as if he wanted to know. I said, 'I don't know.' He began twiddling his white moustache and then, without looking at me, he announced, 'I understand'" (*TO*: 11–12; *TRN*: 1126–7).

54   It is certainly an act of vengeance, not justice. Meursault at one point states: "In a way they seemed to be conducting the case independent of me" (*TO*: 95; *TRN*: 1195). Also: "I stupidly felt like crying because I could tell how much all these people *hated* me" (*TO*: 87; *TRN*: 1187, italics added). This also, perhaps, suggests that the world of the absurd is perhaps no less murderous than that of the bourgeois state.

55   "[T]his reasonless killing which everything seems to require that we excuse" (Brisville 1970: 58). Similarly Carol Petersen asserts that the Arab "in truth, was murdered by the sun and not by Meursault" (Petersen 1969: 48). Louis Hudon alleges "The muscular contraction which causes the revolver to fire is an involuntary act, most carefully presented as such, an accident. At worst, it is involuntary manslaughter, not murder. The four other shots, those which condemn him, are simply an act of immense exasperation, exercised on what must be presumed at that point, to be an inanimate object" (Hudon 1960: 61). "A long time ago I summed up *The Outsider* in a sentence which I realise is extremely paradoxical: 'Any man who doesn't cry at his mother's funeral is liable to be condemned to death'" (*TO*: 118; *TRN*: 1920). The logical confusions that have led some critics to read Camus's claim that Meursault was executed for failing to exhibit the correct emotional responses as in fact meaning that Camus believed Meursault was not responsible for the killing of the Arab is clearly evident in René Girard's "Camus's Stranger Retried" (Girard 2001).

56   *MS*: 65; *E*: 150. Years later, when his wife appeared to have attempted suicide, Camus told his friend and editor Roger Quilliot that he felt responsible but not guilty (Quilliot, interviewed in the television documentary "Albert Camus: The Madness of Sincerity", BBC2, 11 October 1997). For a brief commentary on various discussions of guilt in *The Outsider* see Henry 1975: 131–2.

57   *TO*: 87; *TRN*: 1187. Close to the end of the novel, thinking of his mother, Meursault declares, "So close to death, mother must have felt liberated and ready to live her life again. No one, no one at all had any right to cry over her" (*TO*: 117; *TRN*: 1209).

58   *TO*: 97; *TRN*: 1194. Camus seems to associate the sense of guilt (as opposed to the sense of responsibility or fault) with the idea of sin. Near the end of the novel Meursault is visited by the prison chaplain, who told Meursault that although he was certain his appeal against his execution would be granted, Meursault was "still burdened with a sin from which [he] must free [himself]". Meursault replies that he "didn't know what a sin was", that he'd "simply been told that [he] was guilty": "I was guilty and I was paying for it and there was nothing more that could be asked of me" (*TO*: 113; *TRN*: 1206–7).

59   *TO*: 101; *TRN*: 1199. We see here that all of Meursault's nostalgia is directed towards the natural world; it is especially noteworthy that whereas Maria's dresses and smile feature in Meursault's store of fond memories, Maria herself does not. This is a point that will be developed later in relation to "absurd solipsism".

60   "*The Plague* has a social meaning *and* a metaphysical meaning. They amount to the very same thing. It's exactly the same. Such ambiguity is in [*The Outsider*] too" (*NB2*: 36; *C2*: 50).

61   We note here a comment made by Camus to Elsa Triolet in 1943: "you're absolutely right, there can be absurd myths, but absurd thought is not possible" (Letter quoted by Roger Grenier in *Album Camus* (1982): 115–16, quoted in Todd 1996: 328; Todd 1998: 165). Similarly, in "The Enigma" Camus claims that "A literature of despair is a contradiction in terms" (*SEN*: 144–5; *E*: 864–5).

62   Camus began working on *Caligula* as early as 1936 or 1937 and completed a "first version" in 1941. Between 1941 and 1944, when the play was first published, substantial changes were made to the text. Further, much less significant, changes were made in 1947 and 1958. The version of the play published in *TRN* is that from 1958; the version published in translation by Penguin is that from 1947 (the translation was first published in 1948). The extent to which Camus's Caligula can be considered a historical character is reflected by the degree to which

Camus's emperor mirrors that in Suetonius, the chief historical source for information on the tyrannical emperor.

63   We can read the following entry from the *Carnets* as an early character sketch of Caligula: "The only liberty possible is a liberty as regards death. The really free man is the one who, accepting death as it is, at the same time accepts its consequences – that is to say the abolition of all life's traditional values. Ivan Karamazov's 'Everything is permitted' is the only expression there is of a coherent liberty. And we must follow out all the consequences of his remark" (August 1938. *NB1*: 95; *C1*: 118–19).

64   Camus's interest in the relation between the absurd and tyrannical power has an obvious historical motivation. We find the following entry in the *Carnets*: "The Absurd and Power – develop (cf. Hitler)" (*C1*: 225; *NB1*: 190).

65   "My plan of life may not be logical", says Cherea, "but at least it's sound" (*COP*: 82). It is worth noting that throughout the play the honesty and courage of Caligula are repeatedly contrasted with the sycophancy, hypocrisy, greed and dishonesty of the patricians.

66   *COP*: 83*; *TRN*: 78–9. Although *Caligula* was substantially revised between 1941 and 1944, it is worth noting that this exchange does appear in the 1941 version (*CAC4*: 88).

67   "[B]elief in the absurd is tantamount to substituting the quantity of experience for the quality. If I convince myself that this life has no other aspect than that of the absurd, if I feel that its whole equilibrium depends on that perpetual opposition between my conscious revolt and the darkness in which it struggles, if I admit that my freedom has no meaning except in relation to its limited fate, then I must say that what counts is not the best living but the most living. It is not up to me to wonder if this is vulgar or revolting, elegant or deplorable. Once and for all, value judgements are discarded here in favour of factual judgements" (*MS*: 59; *E*: 143).

68   *COP*: 43, 54; *TRN*: 21, 35. Caligula also admits at one point to Scipio: "you are single-minded for good, and I am single-minded . . . for evil" (*COP*: 68; *TRN*: 58)

69   Davis 2007: 106, 115. Seemingly central to Davis's thesis is the claim that "for all its intellectual seriousness, the theoretical and ethical discussion of murder in Camus's essays can be understood as an anxious, defensive neutralisation of the fascination with gratuitous violence which emerges, sometimes, in his fictional texts" (Davis 2007: 109).

70   Caligula, too, seems to share Sisyphus's solipsistic exile: see his final monologue performed in front of a mirror (which he later breaks): "I stretch out my hands, but it's always you I find, you only, confronting me, and I've come to hate you. I've chosen a wrong path, a path that leads to nothing. My freedom isn't the right one" (*COP*: 103; *TRN*: 107–8).

71   See the letter from Camus to his friend René Leynaud (18 March 1944): "For me, Caligula is right in his undertaking, but he is mistaken in the means he adopts. . . . When I write my next play my hero will choose not to be alone – it is through men that he will seek the impossible – and my idea is that he can find it" (Letter reprinted in Comte-Sponville 2001: 45–7). Colin Davis identifies in Camus's assertion of solidarity a form of what he calls "altericide", or a radical denial of "alterity", where the otherness of the other is effectively denied. I believe, in contrast, that such solidarity as Camus posits in *The Rebel* is a prerequisite to a recognition of the "other".

72   From Kierkegaard's *Purity of Heart*, quoted in *MS*: 120; *E*: 208. For an alternative translation see Kierkegaard 1956: 169. The "Hope and the Absurd in the Work of Franz Kafka" section of *MS*, originally intended as a chapter, was removed from the first edition because of Kafka's Jewish heritage (*MS* was published in Paris during the Nazi Occupation). It appeared as an appendix in all editions after 1948.

73   *MS*: 34; *E*: 121. "The idea that a pessimistic philosophy is necessarily one of discouragement is a puerile idea. . . . The writers who are the butt of the articles have proved, as best they could, that though they lacked philosophical optimism, man's duty at least was not alien to them. Hence an objective mind would be willing to say that a negative philosophy was not incompatible . . . with an ethics of freedom and courage . . . it is essential for us to know whether man, without the help either of the eternal or of rationalistic thought, can unaided

create his own values" ("Pessimisme et Courage", *Combat*, 3 November 1944, reprinted in *E*: 311–13; *RRD*: 57–60). In both *E* and *RRD*, the article is misdated "September 1945"; the article was written more specifically in response to an article alleging that "pessimistic" philosophy, such as that of Camus and Sartre, leads to Nazism.

74   This is central to the argument that there is a clear line of intellectual development rather that a paradigm shift between Camus's early and late works.

75   Camus in a letter to Guy Dumur in 1943: "We must be pessimistic in relation to the human condition, but optimistic in relation to man. We have not done enough for man, or more precisely, he has not done enough for himself. It's true, he who has hope in the human condition is mad, but he who despairs of events is a coward" (*E*: 1669; cf. *NB2*: 124; *C2*: 160, *RRD*: 73; *E*: 374, and the passage on pessimism in Camus's interview with Dominique Arban quoted in the introduction).

76   From a certain perspective, there seems to be a striking similarity between Camus's defence of a certain kind of hope, and Richard Rorty's concept of "social hope". Like Camus's, Rorty's concept of hope is developed in explicit contrast to Christian eschatology and Marxist theory of history (the relevance of this last point to Camus will become clearer in later chapters). Rorty imagines that such a form of "social hope", exemplified for him in the antipolitical politics of Václav Havel, "can exist, and can sometimes even be fulfilled, without the backup of a philosophy of history and without being placed in the context of an epic or tragedy whose hero is Humanity" (Rorty 1998a: 243).

77   We should remember here that Cherea, for one, asserts a value in the face of the absurd, despite being aware of it. He says of Caligula that "he is converting his philosophy into corpses and – unfortunately for us – it's a philosophy that's logical from start to finish" (*COP*: 53; *TRN*: 35).

78   Cf. "Essay on revolt. . . . The theme of the relative – but the *relative with passion*. Ex.: Torn between the world that does not suffice and God who is lacking, the absurd mind passionately chooses the world. Id.: Divided between the relative and the absolute it leaps eagerly into the relative" (*NB2*: 45–6; *C2*: 62–3, *c*.December 1942). This, written in 1942, prefigures some of the themes developed in *The Rebel*.

79   There are a number of entries in the *Carnets* that illustrate this point well: "Raising the question of the absurd world amounts to asking: 'Are we going to accept despair, without doing anything?' I suppose that no one honest can answer yes" (*NB2*: 89; *C2*: 116, *c*.February 1944); "Absurd. Restore ethics by the personal form of address. I do not believe that there is another world in which we will have to 'render account'. But we already have our account to render in this world" (*NB2*: 72; *C2*: 95, *c*.May 1943).

Chapter 2   Camus and *Combat*

1   *R*: 22; *E*: 432. For Camus, life does not begin to acquire meaning in the logical axiom: "I think, therefore I am", but in a moral commitment, and one that is based fundamentally on solidarity: "I revolt – therefore we exist."

2   This is not to say "necessarily consequent", for we have seen that Caligula's nihilism is also consequent on the absurd. In *The Rebel* Camus suggests that there may indeed be a human nature (*R*: 16; *E*: 425).

3   The first letter was published in *Revue Libre*, No. 2, 1944 (dated July 1943); the second, under the pseudonym Louis Neuville, in *Cahiers de la Libération*, No. 3, 1944 (dated December 1943); the third in *Libertés*, 1945 (dated April 1944). The fourth letter is dated July 1944. They were published together for the first time by Gallimard in 1945, and republished with an important preface (written for the Italian edition) in 1948. This later edition also carried a dedication to René Leynaud, Camus's *Résistance* friend who was killed by the Nazis in 1944.

4   In fact, even before *The Myth of Sisyphus* was published, Camus was recommending active

resistance rather than sterile despair in the face of Nazism. See 'Comme un feu d'étoupes', *La Tunisie française*, 24 May 1941 (in *E*: 1465–6).

5   The German in question is obviously a fictional construction, and there is no doubt that the author of the letters is Camus himself.

6   *RRD*: 27–8*, 32; *E*: 240, 241, 243. We can perhaps see here the positing of a "finite hope" in the face of nihilistic despair.

7   Busch 1999: 9. Bizarrely, Ronald Aronson (2004: 33) claims that *Letters to a German Friend* constitutes an affirmation of "French national superiority", betraying behind an apparent rejection of nationalism a degree of "nationalist fantasy and self-righteousness". In contrast, Jeanyves Guérin finds in *Letters to a German Friend* evidence of internationalist humanism: "[Camus] opposes Nazi nationalist dogma [*mystique*] not with another nationalist dogma, laden with xenophobia, but with a humanist ethic of justice and freedom" (Guérin 1994: 108–9).

8   *RRD*: 26; *E*: 239. See Senancour 1909: 390.

9   *CC*: 89*; *E*: 1536. As Judt (1998: 107) notes, "Simone de Beauvoir, or the head-hunting purgers of the Communist press, could not have expressed it better."

10 The dates of these articles are listed in *E*: 1508. See Lottman 1986: 143–4; Weyembergh 1998: 104–9.

11 Quoted in Winock 1997: 383. Two days before Mauriac's article Camus had already signalled that his confidence in the success of the purge was collapsing, and asserts, with a certain degree of irony, that "Obviously M. Mauriac was right: we are going to need charity" (*CC*: 165n.395; *CAC8*: 433n.1).

12 *CC*: 168–9; *CAC8*: 439–41. See also Camus's letter of condolence to Mme Leynaud in Comte-Sponville 2001: 44–7.

13 In fact, Camus had already resigned from the CNE in late 1944, explaining, "I am far too uncomfortable to express myself in a climate where the spirit of objectivity is treated as self-evidently malevolent criticism and where simple moral independence is so poorly tolerated" (Grenier 1991: 228–9; quoted in Todd 1996: 371; Todd 1998: 198). Peter Novick attributes Camus's resignation specifically to what was essentially a "takeover" of the CNE by communist writers (Novick 1968: 128).

14 See Kushnir 1972; Kaplan 2000; Lottman 1986; Novick 1968.

15 Quoted in Todd 1996: 374; Todd 1998: 200. With many others, Sartre and de Beauvoir both refused to sign the petition. According to de Beauvoir, Camus had in public expressed the same views as herself in relation to Brasillach. However, a few days after the conviction of the collaborator, Camus confessed "with some embarrassment" to de Beauvoir that "as a result of certain pressures and for reasons he explained badly" he had signed the petition appealing for clemency (de Beauvoir 1968: 29*). Patrick McCarthy warns that "Simone de Beauvoir's memoirs are, of course, a dubious source for Camus because by the time she wrote them she cordially detested him" (McCarthy 1982: 183). As evidence of the degree to which she disliked Camus, Deirdre Bair quotes her as follows: "'Camus couldn't stand intelligent women' she said in 1982. 'They made him uncomfortable, so he either mocked or ignored them, depending on how much they irritated him'" (Bair 1990: 290). See also de Beauvoir's interview with Sartre (Sartre 1976a: 116–32, esp. 119–20; Sartre 1977: 93–108, esp. 96–7).

16 *CC*: 249–50*; *CAC8*: 594, 595. Tony Judt notes that "75 per cent of the judges who had presided over [the purge trials] had held office under Vichy" (Judt 1992: 72–3).

17 Leynaud, although a member of the *Combat* Resistance group in Lyon, did not write for the *Combat* newspaper. For Camus's introduction to Leynaud's *Poésies posthumes* see *E*: 1471–82; *RRD*: 46–54. Several of Camus's letters to Leynaud are reprinted in Comte-Sponville 2001: 36–57. *Combat* also published an editorial on Leynaud (*CC*: 90–92; *CAC8*: 290–94).

18 *RRD*: 53; *E*: 1478–9. Quilliot notes, in his commentary on Camus's "Introduction", that this introduction seems to date from the summer of 1945, although *Poésies posthumes* was not published until 1947 (*E*: 1472).

19 This lecture was given in 1946, and first published in 1948 (*RRD*: 70; *E*: 371–2. See Todd 1996: 375–7; Todd 1998: 198–202). Camus's ability to admit personal fallibility was strikingly absent from many of his contemporaries, especially Sartre, to whom has been attributed the assertion that he "had been right to be wrong" (Mimouni 1994: 8; Le Sueur 2001: 127). More accurately, the assertion was suggested to Sartre by Michel Contat, and rejected by Sartre (Sartre 1976a: 183; Sartre 1977: 51). Others suggest that the phrase nevertheless does accurately represent Sartre's reasoning (Castoriadis 1977a: 103). See also Lévy 2003: 313, 373.

20 *CC*: 19; *CAC8*: 155. A few days later Camus also claimed that political realism was behind the failure of France to support the Spanish republicans, a cause to which he remained ardently attached (*CC*: 29–30; *CAC8*: 174–6). He might have said the same about the communists' change of policy regarding Algerian rights in 1937.

21 *CC*: 122; *CAC8*: 351–2. Cf. Rorty 1998a: 229; Willhoite 1968: 184.

22 *CC*: 62–3; *CAC8*: 238–40. Writing shortly thereafter in *Resistance ouvrière* (*Workers' Resistance*), Camus wrote "we have no desire for politics without morality, because we know that such morality alone justifies politics. We also know that it is a moral instinct . . . that leads the working class to politics" ("Au service de l'homme", *Resistance ouvrière*, 14 December 1944; quoted in *E*: 1544–6). The final assertion here finds a fuller expression in the opening pages of *The Rebel*.

23 These final two articles, from 1 September and 15 November 1945, have only recently been attributed to Camus. Lévi-Valensi included them in the comprehensive edition of Camus's *Combat* writings, *Camus à Combat*, considering them to be "very likely by Camus" (*CC*: 251–4; *CAC8*: 597–603).

24 Camus & Pia 2000: 143–5; *CAC8*: 90–91. Herbert Lottman notes that although Camus might have disagreed with some of *Combat*'s "policies" at this time, he also would have enjoyed complete editorial freedom (Lottman 1979: 363).

25 *CC*: 63; *CAC8*: 240. Asked in December 1945 why he had "abandoned" journalistic activity, he responded by saying only that he had "good reasons" for doing so ("Interview à *Servir*", *E*: 1429). Although the conduct of the purge and the mutual contempt of the various political factions most clearly refuted Camus's hope that there would be a moral dimension to post-war French politics and, I would suggest, were largely responsible for his withdrawal from journalism in 1945, as we shall see in a later chapter his hopes and aspirations for a post-war consensus were also clearly damaged by the US attacks on Hiroshima and Nagasaki earlier in the same month. Writing the day after the attack on Hiroshima, Camus was almost alone among his contemporaries in condemning it. See *CC*: 236n.570; *CAC8*: 569n.3. On Camus's article on Hiroshima see Santoni 1988 and Debout 1998.

26 Cohen-Solal 1987: 332; Hayman 1986: 240; Lottman 1979: 405; de Beauvoir 1968: 120; Aronson 2004: 66.

27 Merleau-Ponty 1969: 107. "Le Yogi et le Prolétaire" was published in instalments in *Les Temps modernes* in October 1946, November 1946 and January 1947. In July 1947 *Les Temps modernes* printed a related editorial, "Apprendre à lire" ["Learn to Read"]. Although it was signed by Merleau-Ponty, both he and Sartre have attributed it to the other (see Sartre 1974a: 182). A slightly revised version of the three parts of "Le Yogi et le Prolétaire" and "Apprendre à lire" were published in book form as *Humanism and Terror* (1947). On reading "Apprendre à lire" Camus committed the following to his *Notebooks*: "[Merleau-Ponty] complains of having been read carelessly – and misunderstood. I should have been inclined to this kind of complaint at one time. Now I know that it is not justified. There is no misunderstanding." Alluding to a passage in which Merleau-Ponty complains of "the scoundrel who defends 'rigid ethics' ", Camus observes that he would prefer such a scoundrel to "a puritan who kills everyone", let alone a scoundrel "who wants to kill everyone" (*C2*: 212; *NB2*: 166–7; the passage alluded to appears in Merleau-Ponty 1969: xliii).

28 Merleau-Ponty 1969: 141. When necessary, I use Merleau-Ponty's original "History" instead of the translator's "history". See Roth 1988: 47–57 for a succinct account of Merleau-Ponty's

essay that concentrates on the idea of the "logic of history". For a detailed comparison of the essay with Camus's "Neither Victims nor Executioners", see Weyembergh 1998: 101–36.

29 Merleau-Ponty 1969: 175, 109. Much like Sartre's ideas on violence, which we will consider later on, Merleau-Ponty's account of the genesis of violence begins with Hegel's assertion that "each self-consciousness aims at the destruction and death of the other" (Merleau-Ponty 1969: 102; see Hegel 1977: 113).

30 Roth 1988: 50–51. Roth also notes that Raymond Aron criticizes this point (Aron 1955: 155–277).

31 Roth 1988: 51, quoting Merleau-Ponty 1969: 121, 113*.

32 Merleau-Ponty 1969: 107. Indeed, he acknowledges in the introduction to the essay that his perspective on communist violence is nothing other than the perspective of communism itself (Merleau-Ponty 1947: xxn.; mistranslated in Merleau-Ponty 1969: xxvn.).

33 Merleau-Ponty 1969: 126. We will see in a later chapter that Sartre too considers the opposition of "means" and "ends" a bourgeois fallacy.

34 Appeared originally as a series in *Combat*, 19–30 November 1946, reprinted in *Caliban* (November 1947). I have used Arthur Goldhammer's translation in *Camus at Combat* (2006). I have also made use of Dwight Macdonald's translation (Camus 1964). The source for Camus's title is almost certainly Baudelaire: either "I am the wound and the knife! / I am the slap and the face! / I am the rack and the stretched, the victim and hangman!" ("Heautontimoroumenos" in Baudelaire 2006: 105) or "Not only would I be happy to be the victim, neither would hate being the executioner, in order to experience the Revolution both ways" (Baudelaire 1976: 961).

35 Besides the *Combat* articles already discussed there are a number of other articles in which we can see the ideas in "Neither Victims nor Executioners" germinating: "Remarque sur la revolte", in J. Grenier (ed.) *L'Existence* (Gallimard, 1945); "Nous autres meurtriers", *Franchise*, no. 3, 1946, reprinted in *OCII*: 686–7, translated as "We too are Murderers" (trans. L. Abel), *Art and Action: Twice a Year 1938–1948 (10th Anniversary Issue)*, 1948: 74–5; "La Crise de l'Homme", *OCII*: 737–48, translated as "The Human Crisis" (trans. L. Abel), *Twice a Year* Fall/Winter, 1946/7: 19–33, reprinted in *Albert Camus 5*, 1972: 156–76.

36 *CC*: 262*; *CAC8*: 617. The 38th Congress of the SFIO (the French Socialist party) took place in August and September 1946. "In a still-famous speech Blum attacked the 'totalitarian vestiges' in the 'slogans rather than convictions' championed by Mollet, and in very Camusian terms called for 'Democracy and justice', but was not backed by the majority. Mollet succeeded Daniel Mayer as the party's secretary general" (*CC*: 262n.44).

37 *CC*: 263 (see also *ibid.*: 274–5); *CAC8*: 619. As we have already noted, in *Humanism and Terror* Merleau-Ponty ascribes precisely this logic to history (see Merleau-Ponty 1969: 15, 69, 120, 123n., 127, 140, 141, 153).

38 *CC*: 266*; *CAC8*: 624–5. Camus's talk of a modest politics and a relative utopia is of course motivated by the absurd to a far greater extent than by the failure of the French Left to realize their vision of an egalitarian France rising from the ashes of collaboration.

39 *CC*: 271–3*; *CAC8*: 635–9. The towns La Brigue and Tende were ceded to France as part of Italy's war reparations. Camus described the members of the Paris Peace Conference as "21 deaf men . . . discussing peace", and as "future war criminals" (*CC*: 267; *CAC8*: 627).

40 *CC*: 274–5*; *CAC8*: 640–43. These arguments also feature in *The Rebel*. Sartre also uses the phrase "escape from history" in his essay *What Is Literature?* (Sartre 1967: 51, 116, originally published February–July 1947 and therefore post-dating "Neither Victims nor Executioners"). Aronson suggests that the latter part of Camus's argument implied a "misreading" of Sartre (Aronson 2004: 92–3).

41 Quoted in Walusinski 1979: 22–3. In the USA, Groupes de Liaison Internationale was known as the Europe American Groups (see Camus's correspondence with Dwight Macdonald in Macdonald 2001).

42 *E*: 1576–9, 1577. What is perhaps most significant about this text is that it forms the basis for "A First Call to International Opinion", a declaration published in *Esprit* in November 1947,

signed by Camus and Sartre among others. The authorship of this text is usually attributed to Sartre (Sartre 1974a: 205–7; Sartre 1970: 194–7). Ronald Aronson notes that "the first political intervention credited to Sartre was a collective redraft of a statement written by Camus" (Aronson 2004: 101). Furthermore, both versions appear in the new edition of Camus's collected works (*OCII*: 701–4, 758–60).

43   On Camus's anarchist sympathies and related subjects, see Aubery 1968; Boulouque 2001; Dunwoodie 1993; Fauré 2000; Isaac 1992: 182–3; Lottman 1979: 458–63; Martinet 1960; Walusinski 1979. After Camus was awarded the Nobel Prize in 1957, *La Révolution Prolétarienne* wrote "what we do know of Camus is his solidarity, a thousand times manifested, with militants from Spain, Bulgaria and Hungary" (quoted in Brisville 1970: 202).

44   For Camus's defence of Gary Davis see "What Is the UN Accomplishing?" and "Responses to an Unbeliever" (*CC*: 301–8; *CAC8*: 689–702). Davis's campaign continues on the web: http://www.garrydavis.org/

45   Sartre 1974a: 230; Sartre 1970: 217, quoting "Jean-Paul Sartre ouvre un dialogue", *Peuple du monde*, 18–19 June 1949 (*Peuple du monde* was a supplement to *Combat*). Much of this criticism, it seems, could have been directed at Camus.

46   Sartre 1946b. The publication of "Neither Victims nor Executioners" actually coincided with the outbreak of hostilities in Indochina, with the French shelling of Haiphong in November 1946 killing several thousand people.

47   Camus *had* written about Indochina in 1945 and again in 1947 – although not to any great extent (*CC*: 173, 182–3, 239–40: 281; *CAC8*: 449, 466–7, 575–6, 652). See also David Carroll's comments on Camus's statements on Indochina as they relate to his position on Algeria (*CC*: xvii–xix).

48   Sartre 1947a: 109; Sartre 1967: 214. Years later, Sartre was more pointed, if still indirect, in his criticism of "Neither Victims nor Executioners": "A fine sight they are too, the believers in non-violence, saying that they are neither victims nor executioners" (Sartre's "Preface" to Fanon 1967: 21). It hardly needs to be pointed out that in "Neither Victims nor Executioners" Camus did not claim that *he* was neither victim nor executioner, but that humankind should strive to be neither.

49   Sartre 1950: 51–2; Sartre 1946a: 1345; Sartre 1947b: 58–9. Of course, as will be seen in the next chapter, Camus did not see rebellion and revolution as mutually exclusive. Sartre, on this evidence, clearly did. This criticism of Camus by Sartre, if that is what it is, is hugely significant, in that it, in 1946, contains the crux of his 1952 criticism of *The Rebel*, which would end their association in the public mind. The essay of Camus's in question is "Remarque sur la révolte", which although published in 1945 dates from 1943–4, perhaps as early as 1942 (*Existence*, 1945: 9–23, quoted in *E*: 1682–97. See *E*: 1618; Camus & Grenier 2003: 56, 220).

50   Emmanuel d'Astier de la Vigerie, "Arrachez la victime aux bourreaux", *Caliban*, April 1948: 12–17; Camus, "Où est la mystification?", *Caliban*, June 1948, reprinted in *E*: 355–63.

51   The passage quoted concludes with the following: "And, to be precise, I recall the day when the waves of revolt within me reached their climax. It was a morning, in Lyon, and I had just read in the newspaper of the execution of Gabriel Péri" (first reply to d'Astier, "Où est la mystification?", June 1948, *E*: 355–6). Gabriel Péri was a leader of the French Communist Party, executed by the Nazis in December 1941. Cf. Tarrou's account of the death penalty in *TP*.

52   Camus's response prompted an *ad hominem* from d'Astier, entitled "Pontius Pilate among the Executioners", in the Communist newspaper *Action*. Camus replied again, with an article entitled "We Will Never Support Concentration-Camp Socialism" (*La Gauche*, October 1948, reprinted in *E*: 364–8).

53   *E*: 357, 1516; Weyembergh 1998: 102n.7. It is noteworthy too that Camus felt the polemic of sufficient importance to reprint it in *Actuelles I* (1950).

54   See, for example, Merleau-Ponty 1969: xiii, xv, xxiii, 21, 93, 104, 125, 155, 177; Sartre 1967: 90, 211; Sartre 2001: 8, 9. A version of this last essay, "To Be Hungry Already Means that You Want to Be Free", was in fact published in *La Gauche R.D.R.* in May 1948, immediately after d'Astier's essay and immediately before Camus's reply (see Sartre 1974a: 211). I suggest in a

later chapter that Sartre considered Camus's writings on Algeria to constitute a "neocolonialist mystification".

55   *E*: 360. He makes a similar comment on bourgeois and revolutionary mystifications in *The Rebel* (*R*: 200–201; *E*: 605).

56   Aronson 2004: 91. According to Aronson, by the time of the writing of "Neither Victims nor Executioners", Camus's thought was focused on "connecting Marxism with murder . . . and rejecting Sartre and existentialism's stress on history and commitment" (Aronson 2004: 85). Neither of these claims appears to stand up to much scrutiny.

57   "February 21, 1941. Finished *Sisyphus*. The three absurds are now complete. Beginnings of liberty" (*NB1*: 189; *C1*: 224). It is interesting to note that this entry is followed by two blank pages in the original *cahier*, one assumes in order to emphasize the "beginning of liberty". It should be noted that the next entry is a conversation later included in *The Plague*. We should also note the following, much earlier, entry in Camus's *Carnets*: "The tragic struggle of the suffering world. Pointlessness of the problem of immortality. We are interested in our destiny admittedly, but before, not after" (*NB1*: 36; *C1*: 51, June 1937).

58   *LACE*: 253; *E*: 1120–21. "The universal flail is not the work of God, but of man. Man will at last equal God, but in his cruelty" (*C3*: 116).

59   In *The Rebel* Camus asserts that "in the Western World the history of rebellion is inseparable from the history of Christianity" (*R*: 28; *E*: 440). His reference to *The Plague* as his most anti-Christian work is quoted in Peyre 1962: 15 (cf. *TRN*: 1978).

60   Although the plague is normally seen as a symbol of Nazism, it is fruitful to think of it as a symbol of all totalitarian or genocidal regimes based upon abstract ideologies – indeed, the plague itself is often referred to in the novel as "l'abstraction".

61   Sartre 1967: 231; Sartre 1947a: 114; Etiemble 1947; Pouillon 1947. Writing in *Vogue* in 1945, Sartre had been more enthusiastic about the novel, apparently admiring the modest revolt it exemplified (Sartre 1981: 1920).

62   Jeanson 1952a: 2072–3; Jeanson in *SCHC*: 82–3; Camus 1952: 320–21; Camus in *SCHC*: 111–12; Sartre 1952: 349; Sartre in *SCHC*: 152.

63   Gerassi 1989: 183–4. It is interesting to note that in 1944 Sartre wrote a screenplay that, like *The Plague*, tells the story of a quarantined plague-infested colonial city and the commitment of the medical staff determined to fight it (Sartre 2007).

64   Quoted in Lottman 1979: 543*. See *TRN*: 1973–5; *SEN*: 220–22.

65   Lottman (1979: 543) identifies this collection as *Domaine Français*, edited by Jean Lescure.

66   In this article he goes on to contrast the behaviour of his Christian comrades in the Resistance with the "odious" support the Spanish church gave Franco: "And the entire Church would have been mixed up in the unbelievable scandal that saw Spanish bishops bestowing their benedictions on the rifles of the firing squads if two great Christians had not spoken out immediately: one of them, Bernanos, is now dead, while the other, José Bergamin, lives in exile" (*CC*: 300; *E*: 394).

67   Comment attributed to Camus by Julien Green (1975: 950–51, reprinted in Todd 1996: 419; Todd 1998: 230). The context was a talk given by Camus to a group of Dominicans in Paris in December 1946. An audience member addressed the following comment to Camus: "I have found grace, and you, M. Camus, I'm telling you in all modesty that you have not" (*ibid.*). *The Plague*, in which Rieux admits to not having found "grace", was published in May 1947 (*TP*: 178; *TRN*: 1395). His ambivalent attitude to Christianity is reflected in the following comments: "Secret of my universe: imagining God without human immortality" (*NB2*: 12; *C2*: 21; *c.*March 1942). Asked to explain what he meant by this, Camus said: "Yes, I have a sense of the sacred, and I don't believe in eternal life, that's all" (Brisville 1970: 190, reprinted in *E*: 1923). In an interview in *Le Monde* (31 August 1956) Camus asserted: "It's true that I don't believe in God. But, nevertheless, I am not an atheist. I would agree with Benjamin Constant in finding in irreligion something vulgar, and even hackneyed" (Todd 1996: 662; Todd 1998: 356*; see *C3*: 73). "I often read that I am an atheist, and hear talk of my atheism. However, these words mean nothing to me, have no meaning for me. I do not believe in God, but neither am I an atheist" (*C3*: 128, 1 November 1954).

68   *TP*: 178; *TRN*: 1395. It is nevertheless clear that the child's death affects Paneloux deeply: "But, from the day on which he saw a child die, something seemed to change in him. And his face bore traces of the rising tension of his thoughts" (*TP*: 180; *TRN*: 1397).

69   *TP*: 107–8; *TRN*: 1323. Camus notes in *The Rebel* that although the rebel is not necessarily an atheist, he is inevitably a blasphemer (*R*: 24; *E*: 436). In *MS* Camus wrote: "The absurd, which is the metaphysical state of the conscious man, does not lead to God." He then added as a footnote: "I did not say 'excludes God' which still amounts to asserting" (*MS*: 42; *E*: 128).

70   *C2*: 240; *NB2*: 188. "Profound complicity of Marxism and Christianity . . . That is why I am against them both" (August 1957, *C3*: 209).

Chapter 3   *The Rebel*

1   There are of course several very good, though less detailed, examinations in English, most recently Sprintzen 1988, Isaac 1992 and *SCHC*. Besides the negative accounts of Sartre and his colleagues, which I discuss in Chapter 5, Camus's essay has been negatively judged by Tony Judt, who concludes that *The Rebel*, in "its effort to bring together artistic, philosophical, and political revolt in a single story is a messy failure", and Conor Cruise O'Brien, who dismisses the book as "tedious and pretentious" (Judt 1998: 96; Cruise O'Brien 1988: 250). Curiously, in a little-known article from 1955, Cruise O'Brien offers an insightful and far more sympathetic interpretation of the essay (Cruise O'Brien 1955).

2   "For me *Le Mythe de Sisyphe* marks the beginning of an idea which I was to pursue in *L'Homme révolté*" (1955 preface to the English and American editions of *The Myth of Sisyphus*; *MS*: 7). It is worth noting that Camus had considered publishing both essays together in a single volume, which suggests that he saw *The Rebel* as a continuation, rather than a refutation, of the intellectual investigation begun in *The Myth of Sisyphus*. His American publishers, Alfred A. Knopf, had initially intended publishing the two essays in a single volume, and in fact in 1953 Losada, his publisher in Argentina, did publish both essays in a single volume: Albert Camus (1953) *El Mito de Sísifo; El Hombre Rebelde*, L. Echávarri (trans.), Buenos Aires: Losada. Donald Lazere (1973: 141) and David Sprintzen (1988: 133) are among those who see continuity between *The Myth of Sisyphus* and *The Rebel*. Sagi (1994: 279; 2002: 111), Duff & Marshall (1982: 124–5) and Carroll (2007b: 54) share the view that Camus's later work reflects a rejection of the absurd (see Sagi 2002: 107–13).

3   Camus notes, "But on the day of his death, he cries out to his sister: 'I shall lie beneath the ground, but you, you will walk in the sun!'" (*R*: 9; *E*: 418). See "Notes d'Isabelle Rimbaud" (4 October 1891) in Rimbaud 1972: 704.

4   Interview with *Servir*, December 1945 (*E*: 1427), an opinion repeated in a letter to the journal *La Nef* in January 1946: "While I see the historical importance of [existentialism], I do not have sufficient confidence in reason to subscribe to a system – to the extent that Sartre's manifesto, in the first number of *Les Temps modernes*, seems to me unacceptable" (*TRN*: 1743). "Reason does not preach, or if it does, it is no longer reason. That is why historical reason is an irrational and romantic form of reason, which sometimes recalls the false logic of the insane and at other times the mystic affirmation of the word" (*R*: 221; *E*: 625). For a detailed account of Camus's "anti-rationalism" see Henry 1975.

5   In 1942, in *The Myth of Sisyphus*, Camus famously declared that "there is but one truly serious philosophical problem and that is suicide"; already by 1946 he was of the view that "there is only one problem today, and it is the problem of murder" (*MS*: 11; *E*: 99; "We too Are Murderers", p. 75; *OCII*: 686–7).

6   Curiously, a similar view was expressed by Simone de Beauvoir in her post-war essay "An Eye for an Eye", where she argues that the respect we demand for ourselves, by virtue of our humanity, we extend to all others: this, says de Beauvoir, "is the metaphysical basis of the idea of justice" (de Beauvoir 1948a: 116; de Beauvoir 2004: 249).

7   *R*: 22; *E*: 431. The differences between solidarity based on class and that based on the common bonds of humanity are partly illustrated in Camus's short story "Les Muets" ("The Silent Men").

8   *R*: 22; *E*: 431–2 (cf. *E*: 1685). "But it is already worth noting that this concept of values as pre-existent to any kind of action contradicts the purely historical philosophies, in which values are acquired (if they are ever acquired) after the action has been completed. Analysis of rebellion leads at least to the suspicion that, contrary to the postulates of contemporary thought, a human nature does exist, as the Greeks believed. Why rebel if there is nothing in the world worth preserving?" (*R*: 16; *E*: 425). Herbert Hochberg alleges that by proclaiming the existence of human nature while denying the possibility of "transcendence", Camus is led into contradiction. According to Hochberg, Camus's confusion rests on the different meanings that one can attribute to "universals". He alleges that Camus introduces human nature as a universal of the "common property" type, but from that point proceeds to interpret human nature as a universal of the "transcendent" type. However, it seems clear that everything Camus says about human nature is consistent with human nature as a "common property". The possible existence of a human nature exclusive of individual human beings is clearly not of interest to Camus (Hochberg 1972: 323–47).

9   "For what can be the justification of revolution if not its bringing into being a social order rooted in personal and communal liberty that institutionalises human dignity and mutual self-respect? Thus, the essential unity of rebellion and revolution" (*SCHC*: 18). As we shall see in detail in a later chapter, a clear instance of this unity is to be found in the fact that Kaliayev's uncompromising opposition to the realist Stepan does not lead him to abandon his radicalism, although "it does lead him to a chastened and self-critical understanding of what this radicalism involves and what limits it should not overstep" (Isaac in *SCHC*: 260).

10   *R*: 32; *E*: 443. In a speech given by Camus at a conference of international writers in 1948, he also spoke of Cain and Abel: "And today, Cain does not simply kill Abel, he kills Abel in the name of logic and then claims *la Légion d'honneur*" (*E*: 400).

11   *R*: 100; *E*: 508. *The Rebel* also contains discussion of rebellion and surrealism, most notable for the angry response it provoked from André Breton as well as for its introduction of the terms "totality" and "unity", which are discussed later. The section on surrealism is generally not thought to add anything of significance to the general argument, so much so that the entire section is omitted from the standard UK edition of *The Rebel*, published by Penguin.

12   *R*: 105; *E*: 515. An appeal to these values is implicit in metaphysical rebellion as well: Sade is a philosopher of absolute freedom, Ivan the prophet of absolute justice.

13   *R*: 117; *E*: 525–6, quoting the revolutionaries Vergniaud and Anarchasis Cloots respectively.

14   Despite recognizing that "Camus was never a monarchist", Susan Dunn persists in reading Camus as a sort of crypto-monarchist, who viewed the execution of Louis XVI as "the most significant and tragic event in French history" (Dunn 1994: 143, 140).

15   I have already noted that according to the revolutionary "Declaration of the Rights of Man" "the law is the expression of the general will". An assertion of Rousseau's "General Will" also appears in the First Article of Saint-Just's draft constitution (Saint-Just 1946: 110; see also 105).

16   *R*: 124; *E*: 532, quoting Saint-Just, *L'Esprit de la Révolution et de la Constitution de France* (1791) (Pt 4, Ch. 12 : "De la procédure criminelle") http://classiques.uqac.ca/classiques/saint_just/esprit_revolution/saint_just_esprit_revol.pdf

17   *R*: 124; *E*: 533. Contrasting starkly with Camus's *The Rebel*, see Saint-Just's brief "Portrait d'un homme révolutionnaire" (in his "Rapport sur la police générale, la justice, le commerce, la législation et les crimes des factions" (1794) in Saint-Just 1946: 178–9).

18   *R*: 125; *E*: 533. These correspond to the "two contemporary forms of nihilism: individual nihilism and State nihilism" (*R*: 131; *E*: 539). Camus notes that "If Sade's formula were 'Open your prisons or prove your virtue', then Saint-Just's would be: 'Prove your virtue or go to prison'" (*R*: 125; *E*: 533).

19   Camus's use of the term "unity" here is slightly confusing because later, when he introduces contrasting concepts of "unity" and "totality", it is clear that Saint-Just's goal would belong to the second category.

20   *R*: 126; *E*: 534. Saint-Just's assertion appears in his "Sur les factions de l'étranger" (1794), quoted in Saint-Just 1957: 173.

21   Rousseau 1968: 64. As an illustration of this point consider Camus's comment on Marat: " 'They question my right to the title of philanthropist', Marat exclaims . . . 'Ah, what injustice! Who cannot see that I want to cut off a few heads to save a great number?' A few – a faction? Naturally – and all historic actions are performed at this price. But Marat, making his final calculations, claimed two hundred and seventy three thousand heads [and] he compromised the therapeutic aspect of the operation by screaming during the massacre: 'Brand them with hot irons, cut off their thumbs, tear out their tongues' " (*R*: 126; *E*: 534–5).

22   Nietzsche, *Untimely Meditations* [VIII], quoted by Isaac (*SCHC*: 255), cf. Nietzsche 1997: 104–5.

23   *R*: 133–4; *E*: 541–2. By 1946 Camus was already of the view that "when one believes, like Hegel . . . that man is made for history and not history for man, one cannot believe in dialogue: one believes in efficacity and the will to power. Ultimately, one believes in murder" (*Terre des Hommes*, 26 January 1946; quoted in Thody 1961: 105).

24   Camus's discussion appears to mirror much of Kojève's text (*R*: 138; *E*: 545). In a footnote (missing from the English translation) he acknowledges that he has placed deliberate emphasis on the consequences of Master–Slave dialectic. He also notes that this critical analysis "takes nothing from the value of certain admirable analyses of Hegel" (*E*: 545; missing from *R*: 138). See Kojève 1980; M. Roth 1988: 83–146; Judt 1992: 76–9.

25   Kojève 1980: 7, 12. Much of the following summary of Kojève's account of Hegel's "Master–Slave" analysis comes from Ronald Santoni, who uses it to illustrate the phenomenological ontology of Sartre's *Being and Nothingness* (Santoni 2003: 7–10). Kojève's influence can also be seen in Fukuyama 1992.

26   Kojève 1980: 16, 227, 231. In a footnote written in 1968, Kojève explains that in 1948 he realized that Hegel had been correct to see the end of History in Napoleon's triumph over Prussia at the Battle of Jena in 1806. What has happened since then – including "the democratisation of Imperial Germany (by way of Hitlerism)" – "was but an extension in space of the universal revolutionary force actualised in France by Robespierre–Napoleon" (Kojève 1980: 160n.).

27   *R*: 139, 146, 147; *E*: 547, 554. An interesting account of a conversation between Hegel and Goethe provided by Eckermann is worth quoting here: "Thurs. Oct 18 [1827] Hegel is here, whom Goethe personally esteems very highly, though he does not much relish some of the fruits produced by his philosophy. . . . The discourse then turned upon the nature of dialectics. 'They are in fact', said Hegel, 'nothing more than the regulated, methodically-cultivated spirit of contradiction which is innate in all men, and which shows itself great as a talent in the distinction between the true and the false'. 'Let us only hope', interposed Goethe, 'that these intellectual arts and dexterities are not frequently misused, and employed to make the false true, and the true false'. 'That certainly happens', returned Hegel; 'but only with people who are mentally diseased' " (Eckermann 1883: 302).

28   *R*: 4; *E*: 414. We are reminded of Thody's complaint that Camus's argument in *Letters to a German Friend* was purely emotive. Concerning Camus's position as a defence of innocence, consider the following: "In the face of the Hungarian tragedy we were, and are, somehow powerless. But not completely. The refusal to accept a *fait accompli*, a vigilance of heart and mind, the denial of public space to lies and liars, the desire not to abandon innocence even after it has been done to death; these are the rules of a possible action. Inadequate, undoubtedly, but needed – in order to face down that other necessity, the so-called 'historical' one, to respond to it, to stand up to it, occasionally to counter it, and in the long run to overcome it and thereby advance, however little, the true history of humankind" (*E*: 1788–9; Judt 1998: 128*).

29   McBride in *SCHC*: 240. *R*: 136. McBride does not accuse Camus of *misunderstanding* Hegel; he "find[s] Camus guilty" (*SCHC*: 240).

30   McBride, in *SCHC*: 240. Similarly, Ronald Aronson dismisses Camus's account of Hegel as "a caricature" (Aronson 2004: 123).

31   R: 200; E: 604. McBride evidently believes that this critique is motivated by Camus's own belief in transcendent universal values.

32   Hegel's *Phenomenology* "ends with a radical denial of all transcendence. Revealed-infinite-eternal-Being – that is, the absolute Spirit – is the infinite or eternal being of this same Being that existed as universal History. This is to say that the Infinite in question is *Man's* infinite" (Kojève 1980: 167). Similarly, Yirmiyahu Yovel argues that "Hegelian spirit, even at its highest point, remains embodied in empirical persons, societies, books, cults, works of art, and the like. There is no transcendence, even at the end", and that Hegel is "a philosopher of immanence. Philosophy is to give a new meaning and a higher, even more divine, value to this world in all its concreteness. This goes against the transcendent tendency which despises the world and makes it depend upon the 'thread of light linking it with heaven'" (Hegel 2005: 13, 78).

33   R: 177–8; E: 583–4. It is worth noting that although the subject under discussion is Nazism, Camus does add the following in a footnote: "It is striking to note that atrocities reminiscent of these excesses [the Nazi massacre at the Czech town of Lidice, where the entire population was either executed or deported and then the town itself was literally obliterated] were committed in colonies (India, 1857; Algeria, 1945; etc.) by European nations that in reality obeyed the same irrational prejudice of racial superiority" (R: 185; E: 590). We see clearly here that the view that was to become commonplace in years to come, that of Camus as an apologist for French colonialism, is highly dubious.

34   Femia 1993: 14. Much of this summary of Marx's theory of history is taken from Femia.

35   *Ibid.* See also Isaac in *SCHC*: 254.

36   See, for example, Engels's *Socialism: Utopian and Scientific* in Marx 1935: 147.

37   CC: 62–3, 164*; *CAC8*: 237–9, 620–21. This implied rejection of Marxism as an "absolute philosophy" seems to be interpreted by Ronald Aronson as an "absolute rejection" of Marxism as a philosophy, for he characterizes Camus's interpretation of Marxism in the following pithy way: "Marxism = murder" (Aronson 2004: 89).

38   Aronson, 2004: 122–3. He elsewhere claims that by 1946 Camus's thought was focused on "two points": "connecting Marxism with murder, under the influence of *Darkness at Noon*, and rejecting Sartre and existentialism's stress on history and commitment" (*ibid.*: 85).

39   R: 189, 192, 193; E: 594, 597, 598. Camus is careful to point out later on that the rebel opposes technology only to the extent that it diminishes human dignity (R: 295; E: 698).

40   For a succinct account of the different stages of historical development according to Marx, see Melvin Rader 1979: 120–29.

41   Cohen 1978: 23. This seems very similar to the Sartrean idea of "scarcity". See Sartre 1991a, b.

42   R: 200–201; E: 605. He later asserts: "There is undoubtedly in Russia today, even in its Communist doctrines, a truth that denies Stalinist ideology. But this ideology has its logic, which must be isolated and exposed if we wish the revolutionary spirit to escape final disgrace" (R: 234; E: 637–8).

43   R: 209; E: 613. Indeed, Camus attributes the following claim to Marx, somewhat incongruously given what follows: "An end that requires unjust means is not a just end" (R: 209; E: 613). Camus appeared to believe that it was not simply from poverty that the proletariat sought liberation, but from the degrading experience of modern working-class life. In an entry to the third volume of his *Carnets* he makes this point: "MAN OF ARAN. Terrible lives of these fishermen. Yet far from pitying them, one admires and respects them. It is neither poverty nor endless work that causes the decline [*déchéance*] of men, but rather the sordid enslavement of the factories and suburban life" (C3: 34).

44   "The history of all hitherto existing society", say Marx and Engels in the *Communist Manifesto*, "is the history of class struggles" (Marx 1935: 204).

45   R: 202, 204; E: 606–7, 609, quoting from Marx's "Moralising Criticism and Political Morality" (1847).

46   R: 204; E: 609. He continues: "What does it matter that this should be accomplished by dictatorship and violence? In this New Jerusalem, echoing with the roar of miraculous machinery, who will still remember the cry of the victim?" (R: 207, E: 612).

47   Camus observes later in a footnote: "From 1920 to 1930, in a period of intense productivity, the number of metallurgical workers decreased in the United States, while the number of salesmen working in the same industry almost doubled" (R: 214; E: 618).

48   Mitrany 1951: 52. Ian Birchall notes that Sartre "was far less sympathetic to the peasantry than most French Marxists", adding "that Sartre largely resisted the romanticisation of the peasantry widespread on the French left is another indication of how rooted his thought was in the classic traditions of the socialist left" (Birchall 2004: 203).

49   Quoted in R: 215; E: 619. From Simone Weil "Allons-nous vers une révolution prolétarienne?" in *Révolution Prolétarienne*, 25 August 1933. Translated as "Prospects: Are We Heading for the Proletarian Revolution?" in Weil 1958: 1–24. Camus was a very early admirer of Weil, and edited and published several of her works in his *Espoir* series at Gallimard. "It seems to me in any case impossible to imagine for Europe a renaissance which does not take into account the exigencies which Simone Weil defines in *l'Enracinement*" (E: 1701, see E: 1699–702).

50   R: 216; E: 620. Both capitalism and Marxism, for Camus, treat productivity as an end in itself. He adds in a footnote: "It is worth specifying that productivity is only injurious when it is considered as an end, not as a means, in which case it could have a liberating effect" (R: 218; E: 623).

51   R: 220, 221–2; E: 624, 625–6. Cf. Camus's reflections on modern science in *The Myth of Sisyphus*.

52   R: 222, 223; E: 626. Roger Caillios, *Description du marxisme* (NRF, 1950).

53   R: 226; E: 630. In a letter responding to a review of *The Rebel*, Camus claimed that it was as a result of the "deification of Marx that Marxism has perished" ("Révolte et Romantisme", E: 752).

54   R: 226; E: 630. It is important to note that Camus's attitude to Lenin remained ambiguous. Although his criticism of Leninism in *The Rebel* seems unequivocal, he does suggest in "In Defence of *The Rebel*" and in his preface to Alfred Rosmer's *Moscou sous Lénine* a certain sympathy with Lenin, so much so, in fact, that Tony Judt attributes to Camus the "long since dismissed" view that "there had been a 'good' Russian Revolution (that of Lenin) followed by a 'bad' Soviet dictatorship, Stalin's" (Judt 1998: 132). For an example of this ambiguity see R: 232; E: 635–6.

55   R: 226; E, 630. See "Should Revolutionaries Work in Reactionary Trade Unions?", *Left-Wing Communism: An Infantile Disorder*: http://www.marxists.org/archive/lenin/works/1920/lwc/ch06.htm

56   R: 226, 230, 231; E: 629, 634, 634–5. Nestor Makhno was a Ukrainian anarchist, whose party (like the Socialist Revolutionaries) was liquidated by the Bolsheviks. In 1921, dissatisfied with the direction the Bolshevik revolution was taking, sailors at the naval base at Kronstadt began calling for a return of political freedoms. The Bolsheviks brutally suppressed the uprising, accusing the sailors of taking part in a counter-revolutionary conspiracy.

57   R: 101; E: 509. "But can totality claim to be unity? That is the question which this book must answer" (R: 108; E: 517). He concludes that "totality is not unity" (R: 240; E: 643) and that "Rebellion's demand is unity; historical revolution's demand is totality" (R: 251; E: 653).

58   R: 233, 196; E: 636, 601. Camus had earlier asserted that only the Soviet regime, because of its limitless ambition, its determination to erect "after the death of God . . . a city of man finally deified", can properly be called "totalitarian" (R: 186; E: 592).

59   "Generally speaking, the complete and adequate 'revelation' of the dialectical human reality is . . . the discursive or conceptual understanding of the Totality of Being given to Man and created by him" (Kojève 1980: 244–5; see Jay 1984).

60   R: 234; E: 637. Already in 1948, Camus had claimed that "what the conqueror of the Right or Left seeks is not unity – which is above all the harmony of opposites – but totality, which is the stamping out of differences" (Camus 1949: 537; E: 404). Camus's opposition of "totality" and "unity" could usefully be compared with Lévinas's opposition of totality with infinity (see Lévinas 1969). The distinction should also be kept in mind when considering Sartre, whose

Critique of Dialectical Reason presented history as a dialectically intelligible "totalisation without a totaliser" (Sartre 1991a: 805).

61   *R*: 251*; *E*: 653. Similarly, in Hegel, Camus says, "truth, reason, and justice . . . have ceased to be guides in order to become goals" (*R*: 134; *E*: 542).

62   Martin Jay's description of the "beautiful soul" (Jay 1984: 60). Alan Norrie describes the beautiful soul in Hegel's *Phenomenology* as "a form of failed moral being in the world" (Norrie 2004: 48)

63   The phrase "teleological socialism" comes from Christopher Hitchens (2002b: 281).

64   *R*: 249, 251*; *E*: 651, 653. What follows from here is a lengthy discussion of art as an expression of rebellion "in its pure state" (*R*: 252; *E*: 653). According to Camus, the authentic artist exemplifies the attributes of the authentic rebel by his refusal to accept the incoherence of the world and his determination to impose a relative meaning of his own.

65   "In Defence of *The Rebel*", *SCHC*: 217*; *E*: 1713. In *MS*, Camus claims that "the only truth that might even seem instructive to ['a mind imbued with the absurd'] is not formal: it comes to life and unfolds in men" (*MS*: 65; *E*: 150).

66   *R*: 287–8; *E*: 691. In Camus's play *State of Siege*, it is the tyrant, Plague, rather than the hero, Diego, who comes to Cadiz bearing as gifts "silence, order, and absolute justice" (Camus 1958: 173*; *TRN*: 229–30).

67   *R*: 289; *E*: 693. This idea of the competing values of freedom and justice is first expressed by Camus in *Combat* in 1944 (*CC*: 31–2; *E*: 271–2).

68   *R*: 283; *E*: 687. Similarly, Camus argues elsewhere that the rumour that began to gather force "after Marx", that "freedom" was "a bourgeois hoax" [*une balançoire bourgeoise*], was mistaken, for "it should have been said that only bourgeois freedom, and not all freedom, was a hoax, [and] that there were freedoms to be conquered and never again relinquished". "We are still paying", he says, "for that misplaced word in the convulsions of our time" (*E*: 794; *RRD*: 90*). Interestingly, in 1948, Sartre declared that "freedom as it exists in bourgeois democracies is a hoax [*une fumisterie*]" (Sartre 2001: 9; Sartre 1974a: 211; Sartre 1970: 200).

69   Certainly *The Plague* suggests that society is not perfectible. The novel concludes with the reminder that the plague will return and that men will again have to fight against it. In *The Rebel*, Camus claims that "children will still die unjustly even in a perfect society" (*R*: 303; *E*: 706).

70   *R*: 290; *E*: 694. "Approximative thought", says Camus, "is the only creator of reality" (*R*: 295; *E*: 698).

71   *R*: 290, 294; *E*: 693, 697. Ironically echoing the scientific pretensions of Marxism, Camus notes that this philosophy of limits seems to be endorsed by contemporary science, "which only justifies a system of thought based on relative discoveries" (*R*: 295; *E*: 698). Camus's appreciation of the importance of contemporary science has been noted already in relation to *MS*. We should also consider the following very early entry in Camus's *Carnets*: "A reflective man generally spends his time adapting his idea of things to the alterations imposed by new facts. It is in this process of bending and adjusting thought, in this conscious elimination of error, that truth – that is to say, what life can teach us – is to be found" (*NB1*: 139; *C1*: 167).

72   *R*: 290, 298, 299; *E*: 693, 700–701. Camus quotes, in a footnote, the following from a letter from Marx to Engels to support his claim: "The preponderance of the German proletariat over the French proletariat would be at the same time the preponderance of our theory over Proudhon's" (Marx to Engels, 20 July 1871, quoted in *R*: 299; *E*: 701).

73   In 1937, the 24-year-old Camus made much the same point: "Politics are made for men, and not men for politics. We do not want to live on fables. In the world of violence and death around us, there is no place for hope. But perhaps there is room for civilization, for real civilization, which puts truth before fables and life before dreams. And this civilization has nothing to do with hope. In it man lives on *his* truths" (*LACE*: 197; *E*: 1327).

74   *R*: 101–2; *E*: 509. While the similarities between Camus and Karl Popper have been examined elsewhere (see Weyembergh 1998: 137–50), it is worth noting that there is a striking commonality between some of Camus's arguments here and those of Popper in his essay "Utopia

and Violence", where he recommends a "rationalistic attitude" that "presupposes a certain amount of intellectual humility" (Popper 1963: 356).

75   *R*: 3; *E*: 413. In *Combat* in October 1944 Camus suggested that "only the Scandinavian democracies have come close to the necessary reconciliation of [freedom and justice]". He also suggests that "their example is not entirely convincing on account of their relative isolation and of the limited framework within which they have operated" (*CC*: 55; *E*: 1528).

76   "Absolute freedom mocks at justice. Absolute justice denies freedom. To be fruitful, the two ideas must find their limits in each other" (*R*: 291; *E*: 694).

77   The only philosophical or literary tradition with which Camus ever indicated much sympathy was that of the *moralistes*. He noted in an essay on Chamfort that "our greatest *moralistes* are not makers of maxims, but novelists . . . our real *moralistes* have not made phrases, they have observed, and have observed themselves. They have not made laws, they have painted. And in so doing they have done more to explain the conduct of man that if they had patiently polished, for a few wits, a hundred or so set formulas doomed to be material for academic theses. For only a novel is faithful to the particular. Its objective is not to sum up conclusions about life, but to depict its very unfolding. In a word, it is more modest" (Camus 1948*, 12–13; *E*, 1099–100). Incongruous as it may seem, Camus devoted a portion of *The Rebel* to the novel, in which he declares that the genre was "born at the same time as the spirit of rebellion", and that it expresses "on the aesthetic plane, the same ambition" (*R*: 259; *E*: 662. See also *SEN*: 185–91; *TRN*: 1887–94). The importance Camus attached to the novel is, of course, most clearly reflected in his own creative output, especially *The Plague*.

78   See Warren 1992. I think that the translation of "*la mesure*" as "moderation" is in fact adequate, if not ideal, once the weight of meaning accorded to the concept by Camus is also pointed to. For discussion of *sophrosyne* see Plato's "Charmides" (in Plato 2005), Pieper 1966 and, especially, North 1966. On the mistranslation of much else in *The Rebel* see Bieber 1955, 2001.

79   North 1947: 2; North 1966: 33. See also North's essay on *sophrosyne* from *The Dictionary of the History of Ideas* (available online at: http://etext.lib.virginia.edu/cgi-local/DHI/dhi.cgi?id=dv4-49).

80   Regarding the hostile tone of Sartre's letter, Ronald Aronson suggests that it "was nothing less than an attempt to annihilate Camus or, if not destroy him, to silence him" (Aronson 2004: 154).

81   Judt explains, "Not that he was unconcerned with public affairs, or uncaring about political choices. But he was by instinct and temperament an *unaffiliated* person" (Judt 1998: 104).

82   Havel 1987a. For Camus's discussion of "relative utopia" see *CC*: 266, 270, 272n.74. See also *NB2*: 145; *C2*: 186.

83   Isaac 1992: 256, quoting Ellen Meiksins Wood, "The Uses and Abuses of Civil Society", in *The Socialist Register 1990: The Retreat of the Intellectuals* (London: Merlin, 1990): 80, 60.

84   "In Defence of *The Rebel*", in *SCHC*: 205–21; *E*: 1702–16. I disagree with Ronald Aronson, who claims that in this essay Camus "abandons the oppositions that abound in [*The Rebel*] and focuses on interaction and productive tension. He also adjusts his former emphasis on the individual as *opposed to history*, now making each necessary to the other, and observing that their best relationship is one of tension" (Aronson 2004: 162–3). This "productive tension" is in my view at the heart of *The Rebel* as well.

85   Evoking Koestler's famous essay, and more especially, Merleau-Ponty's criticism of that essay in *Humanism and Terror*, Camus writes: "There is, in fact, no conciliation possible between a God who is totally separated from history and a history purged of all transcendence. Their representatives on earth are, indeed, the yogi and the commissar. But the difference between these two types of men is not, as has been stated, the difference between ineffectual purity and expediency. The former chooses only the ineffectiveness of abstention and the second the ineffectiveness of destruction. Because both reject the conciliatory value that rebellion, on the contrary, reveals, they offer us only two kinds of impotence, both equally removed from reality, that of good and that of evil" (*R*: 288; *E*: 691–2).

86   *R*: 186; *E*: 592. In the interview quoted above, Havel makes a similar claim: "As soon as humanity declared itself to be the supreme ruler of the universe – at that moment, the world began to lose its human dimensions" (Havel 1987a).

87   Judt 1998: 94. This was no casual thought for Camus; as we have seen, it was central to much of what he wrote after the war, in particular "Neither Victims nor Executioners". Today the argument is perhaps rather commonplace, but in 1951, as is illustrated by the critical response from Sartre and others, it amounted to political heresy.

Chapter 4   Camus and political violence

1   *R*: 280–81; *E*: 683–5. The "paradigm shift" involved in the move from solitude to solidarity is illustrated by a consideration of the contrasts between the images of Sisyphus and Prometheus. Of course, in the context of the absurd, Sisyphus was necessarily solitary (Sisyphus did not choose his solipsistic exile), but it is a measure of the difference between the absurd and revolt that Prometheus is the new model of human action. Sisyphus defied the gods in his own name; Prometheus does so in the name of humankind.

2   *R*: 285–6; *E*: 689. Camus argues that "only a philosophy of eternity could justify non-violence". But ultimately this "philosophy of eternity" would put "the responsibility for justice in God's hands, thus consecrating injustice" (*R*: 287; *E*: 690).

3   *R*: 169; *E*: 575. In an interview in 1952 Camus explains that one of the essential themes of *The Rebel* "is the critique of formal morality which is at the heart of bourgeois humanism" (*E*: 739–40).

4   *Boevaya Organizatsiya*. For a detailed first-hand account of the group that included Kaliayev see Boris Savinkov (1931). Camus was probably introduced to the Socialist Revolutionaries by Nicolas Lazarévitch, whom he met through the Groupes de Liaison Internationale in the late 1940s, and who co-edited a selection of related writings in Camus's *Espoir* series at Gallimard. See Feuillade & Lazarévitch 1950.

5   Reed 1997: 214. "Scrupulous assassins" is John Cruickshank's translation of Camus's term "*meurtriers délicats*", used in *The Rebel* (where it is translated as "fastidious assassins") to describe Kaliayev and his comrades. See *R*: 164 and Cruickshank's Introduction to *COP*: 26.

6   It is interesting that so many of Camus's plays are based on historical fact. *Révolte dans les Asturias*, a collective effort from 1936 (*TRN*: 395–438), was written to commemorate the revolt of the miners in Oviedo in 1936. *Caligula* is based on the historical account of the life of that Roman emperor by Suetonius. *The Just Assassins* is based upon the memoirs of Boris Savinkov, one of the 1905 Russian revolutionaries.

7   *COP*: 174, 185–7; *TRN*: 322, 336–8. Nechayev, too, was of the opinion that "Everything that serves the revolution is moral" (quoted in *NB2*: 178; *C2*: 226).

8   *R*: 169*; *E*: 575. Similarly, Hannah Arendt argued that "violence can be justifiable, but it will never be legitimate" (Arendt 1970: 52).

9   Although the identity of the Grand Duke is not made explicit in *The Just Assassins* itself, the accompanying *prière d'insérer* does identify him (*TRN*: 1826). Here Camus also states that the play is not to be interpreted as an historical drama, which perhaps explains the relative anonymity of the victim.

10   *R*: 170*, 173; *E*: 576, 579. Jeffrey Isaac notes that Kaliayev's uncompromising opposition to Stepan does not lead him to abandon his radicalism, although "it does lead him to a chastened and self-critical understanding of what this radicalism involves and what limits it should not overstep" (*SCHC*: 260).

11   *R*: 174*; *E*: 580. Roger Quilliot notes that in the manuscript of *The Rebel* given by Camus to his friend René Char the term "bolshevism" appears in place of "caesarean socialism" (*E*: 1645).

12   The significance of historical expediency or efficacy for Camus is pointed to in his notebooks: "Criticism of the idea of efficacy – a chapter" (*NB2*: 157; *C2*: 200).

13   As I see them, those killings perpetrated by Martha, Meursault and Mersault (in *Cross Purpose*, *The Outsider* and *A Happy Death*), unaccompanied by anything like a moral defence, are not relevant to the present discussion.

14   *COP*: 177*, 208; *TRN*: 326, 366. The extent to which the Socialist Revolutionaries considered Grand Duke Sergi a tyrant is made clear in their statement after his assassination: "A bomb has just punished with death the chief author of the Moscow massacre, the murderer of thousands of St Petersburg workers, the hero of Khodynka, the oppressor of Russia, the bitter enemy of liberty and light. This vile debauchee, this unclean hangman who thought he could insult a great people with eternal impunity, is dead" ("Announcement of the Execution", in Postgate 1962: 370–71).

15   *COP*: 104; *TRN*: 108, 1771. The incident would probably be of especial significance from a Lévinasian perspective. Although Lévinas states that it is precisely the face of the Other that prohibits killing, he also states that this interdiction "is to be sure not equivalent to pure and simple impossibility, and even presupposes precisely the possibility which precisely it forbids" (Lévinas 1969: 232). Keeping in mind that Camus considered permissible killing in terms of an exception to a general prohibition of killing, I would suggest that Camus's play complements, rather than contradicts, Lévinas's thought. In his posthumously published essay "In Defence of *The Rebel*", Camus wrote "I would not have written *The Rebel* if I had not found myself, during the forties, faced with men whose way of thinking I couldn't explain to myself and whose acts I didn't understand. To put it briefly, I didn't know men could torture others while looking them straight in the face" (*SCHC*: 205; *E*: 1702).

16   Kaliayev's refusal to attempt escape is here intended to illustrate the extent to which he takes responsibility for his act, and is not itself intended as a characteristic of legitimate killing.

17   Camus writes of "these executioners who risked their own lives completely, made attempts on the lives of others only after the most scrupulous examination of conscience" (*R*: 168; *E*: 574).

18   Hochberg 1972: 345. According to this critic, Camus held life to be an "absolute value", and consequently the assassin, who contradicts this value, must "'remove' the contradiction by killing himself" (*ibid*.: 344). Hochberg's argument rests on the claim that Camus remained unaware of the intellectual conflict lying at the base of the just assassin's act, despite the fact that it is precisely this conflict that is central to *The Rebel* and *The Just Assassins*.

19   Indeed, Hochberg himself admits in a footnote that in reality "no formal contradiction is involved" (*ibid*.: 345n.22).

20   In Kaliayev's declaration from the scaffold, "I consider my death as a supreme protest against a world of blood and tears", we may also find an echo of the original rebellious declaration: "I rebel, therefore we exist" (*R*: 171, 22; *E*: 577, 432). By means of this proclamation, implicit in the acts of these "fastidious assassins", the terrorist simultaneously affirms the world of humanity and demonstrates "for the last time in our history that real rebellion is a creator of values" (*R*: 172; *E*: 578).

21   *R*: 292; *E*: 695. Curiously, Kateb notes parenthetically that "sometimes Camus speaks as if *the mere risk of death* is price enough for him who takes the life of an oppressor; but that does not seem to be the main tendency of his writing" (Kateb 1963: 40).

22   He makes a similar claim in "Neither Victims nor Executioners", where he suggests that the defence of political violence for reasons of political realism requires a lack of imagination when it comes to the lives of others, noting "Just as we now love one another by telephone, and work not on matter but on machines, we kill and are killed nowadays by proxy. What is gained in cleanliness is lost in understanding" (*CC*: 260; *E*: 334).

23   This idea that an act of killing, such as Kaliayev's, would be accompanied by a "willingness to die" should be understood in the sense that one would act in this way even if (*not* only if) one knew with certainty that it would result in one's own death.

24   *E*: 1882, emphasis added. For a forceful reiteration of this point see Camus's correspondence with Jean Sénac in Nacer-Khodja 2004: 155–6, 159.

25   These statistics are quoted from Margalit 2003: 36. For a general discussion of this topic see Glover 1999.

26   The term itself is so lacking in definition that it is used interchangeably by both the adminis-
      tration of George W. Bush and the popular media with "the War on Terror".
27   "I've indicated that [the Iraq war] was not in conformity with the UN Charter. From our point
      of view, from the Charter point of view, it was illegal", "Choice of Words Matters", BBC News
      Online (UK Edition), 16 September 2004, http://news.bbc.co.uk/1/hi/world/middleeast/
      3661976.stm (accessed 10 November 2004).
28   *CC*: 267–8; *CAC8*: 611. The UN Security Council is still routinely referred to in French as
      "*l'exécutif onusien*". In the wake of the Yalta Conference in February 1945, at which this power
      of veto was agreed, an editorial in *Combat* (16 February 1945) attributed to Camus declared
      that if reports of the executive veto turned out to be true, "it would effectively put an end to
      any idea of international democracy. The world would in effect be ruled by a directorate of
      five powers. The decisions they take will still be applicable to all other nations, but any one of
      the five could nullify a decision against its own interests by exercising its veto. The Five would
      thus retain forever the freedom of maneuver that would be forever denied the others" (*CC*:
      172; *CAC8*: 447).
29   Camus & Grenier 1981: 141; Camus & Grenier 2003: 112. See Camus's letters relevant to his
      objection to capital punishment collected in Camus & Koestler 2002: 247–71.
30   *RRD*: 175; *E*: 1021. Meursault recounted the same story in *The Outsider* as he awaited his own
      execution (*TRN*: 1203; *TO*: 106).
31   *RRD*: 180, 185; *E*: 1024, 1029. The last public execution in France took place in 1939. Camus
      comments wryly: "Between the moment when Weidmann was shown to the crowd and the
      moment when he was decapitated, photographs could be taken. A few hours later *Paris-Soir*
      published a page of illustrations of that appetizing event. . . . The administration and the
      government, contrary to all hope, took such excellent publicity very badly and protested that
      the press had tried to satisfy the sadistic instincts of its readers" (*RRD*: 180; *E*: 1025). Camus
      asserts that "Logic, in that affair, was not on the side of the lawmaker . . . the ceremony should
      have been put on television for those who couldn't attend. Either this must be done or else
      there must be no more talk of exemplary value" (*RRD*: 181; *E*: 1025).
32   *RRD*: 193; *E*: 1034–5. This, we should note, relates to a certainty regarding the deterrence
      effect of capital punishment. Camus will address the issue of certainty in relation to the guilt
      of the convicted individual at a later stage.
33   *RRD*: 193–4; *E*: 1035. Camus continues: "The State will keep it then, a little out of the way, not
      without embarrassment, in the blind hope that one man at least, one day at least, will be
      stopped from his murderous gesture by thought of the punishment and, without anyone's
      ever knowing it, will *justify a law that has neither reason nor experience in its favour*" (*RRD*:
      194; *E*: 1035, emphasis added).
34   Camus illustrates the point thus: "According to a magistrate, the vast majority of murderers
      he had known did not know when shaving in the morning that they were going to kill later
      in the day. As an example and for the sake of security, it would be wiser, instead of hiding
      the execution, to hold up the severed head to all who are shaving in the morning" (*RRD*: 186;
      E: 1029).
35   *RRD*: 195; *E*: 1035–6, quoted from the Report of the (English) Select Committee on Capital
      Punishment, 1930; "[the] slang . . ." quoted from the memoirs of Bela Just: *La Potence et la
      Croix* (Fasquelle, 1954).
36   De Beauvoir, "Oeil pour oeil", in *Les Temps modernes* (No. 5, February 1946), reprinted in de
      Beauvoir 1948a: 107–40; "An Eye for an Eye", in de Beauvoir 2004: 245–60. We have noted
      de Beauvoir's dismissive attitude to Camus's position on the conduct of the post-war purge:
      "To me, it seems utterly unjust that economic collaboration should have been passed over,
      but not that Hitler's propagandists in this country should have been so severely dealt with" (de
      Beauvoir 1968: 29).
37   "It strives to satisfy some unknown dark god of symmetry. But above all, it corresponds to a
      profound human need" (de Beauvoir 1948a: 114–15; de Beauvoir 2004: 248).
38   Tony Judt notes that "75 percent of the judges who had presided over [the purge trials] had
      held office under Vichy" (Judt 1992: 72–3).

39   He cites, in evidence, the housing crisis in Paris to illustrate his point, where there are 64,000 overcrowded dwelling places, with three to five persons per room (*RRD*: 206; *E*: 1044).

40   *RRD*: 207*; *E*: 1045. Camus adds in a footnote here: "France ranks first among countries for its consumption of alcohol and fifteenth in building" (*RRD*: 207n.; *E*: 1045n.).

41   He cites the assessment of a lawyer, Maître Guillion, who estimates that alcohol is a dominant factor in 60 per cent of "bloody" crimes (*RRD*: 207; *E*: 1045).

42   *RRD*: 208; *E*: 1045–6. Camus goes as far as to draw a comparison between the state chastizing murderers (particularly alcoholics found guilty of murder) and a pimp chastizing prostitutes "who assure his livelihood" (*RRD*: 209; *E*: 1046).

43   *RRD*: 217; *E*: 1052. Compassion is so important to Camus that he suggests that if the state is to insist on continuing its policy of executions, it could at least follow the Greeks and allow the convict to administer a fatal dose himself, thereby restoring some dignity to an otherwise "sordid and obscene exhibition" (*RRD*: 233; *E*: 1064; cf. *RRD*: 202; *E*: 1041).

44   Consider the following "excerpt" from a "monograph on execution" by Caligula and Helicon as a parody of the supposed authority with which states execute individuals: "Execution relieves and liberates. It is universal, tonic, just in precept and in practice. A man dies because he is guilty. A man is guilty because he is one of Caligula's subjects. Now all men are Caligula's subjects. Ergo, all men are guilty and shall die. It is only a matter of time and patience" (*COP*: 60–61; *TRN*: 46–7).

45   *RRD*: 230, 222; *E*: 1062, 1056. Of course, Camus believed that there were no truths or principles "superior to man".

46   *RRD*: 227–8; *E*: 1059–60. We are reminded of the claim in *The Rebel* that "He who does not know everything cannot kill everything" (*R*: 189; *E*: 693).

47   *RRD*: 229–30; *E*: 1060–61. In "Neither Victims nor Executioners" (1946) Camus suggested that the abolition of the death penalty be the first article in an "International Code of Justice" (*CC*: 273; *CAC8*: 638). Article 2 of the European Convention on Human Rights (1950) had already recognized the right to life. Protocol 6 of the Convention (entered into force 1985) restricted a state's right to exercise capital punishment to time of war or "the immanent threat of war", and Protocol 13 (entered into force 2003) prohibits the death penalty in all circumstances. France, the last western European country to practise capital punishment, abolished the practice in 1981, and in 2007 introduced its prohibition into the French Constitution.

Chapter 5   Camus and Sartre

1   *NB2*: 171; *C2*: 218 (*c.*September 1947). "*Temps Modernes*. They admit sin, but refuse grace. . . . Something in them, ultimately, aspires to servitude" (*C3*: 62, 64 [*c.*August 1952]).

2   *Le Nouvel Observateur*, 9–15 June 1944: 13, quoted in Oxenhandler 1996: 30.

3   "Camus shows off a bit by quoting passages from Jaspers, Heidegger and Kierkegaard, whom, by the way, he does not always seem to have understood" (Sartre 1962a: 109; Sartre 1993: 94). Sartre repeated this assessment of Camus's philosophical competence several times – most notably in relation to *The Rebel*.

4   "Le Pessimisme et le courage", *Combat*, 3 November 1944, reprinted in *CC*: 100; *E*: 312; "Non, je ne suis pas existentialiste", *Les Nouvelles littéraires*, 15 November 1945, reprinted in *LACE*: 345; *E*: 1424–7; Dominique Arban, "Entretien avec Albert Camus", *Opera*, 17 November 1945: 2; Interview in *Servir* 20 December 1945, reprinted in *E*: 1427–9; Letter to editor of *La Nef*, January 1946, reprinted in *TRN*: 1743. Camus's satirical sketch, "L'Impromptu des Philosophes", recently published for the first time, probably dates from 1947 and pokes gentle fun at Sartre, or at least the popular image of Sartre (*OCII*: 769–91, 1376–8).

5   Interview in *Paru*, December 1945, reprinted in Sartre 1981: 1912–17. See also Sartre, "A Propos de l'existentialisme: mise au point", *Action*, 29 December 1944, reprinted in Sartre 1970: 652–8, translated as "A More Precise Characterization of Existentialism", in Sartre 1974b: 155–60.

6   *TRN*: 1743–4. The first issue of *Les Temps modernes* appeared in October 1945 (translated as "Introducing *Les Temps Modernes*", in Sartre 1988: 249–67).

7   Originally published in the October and November 1948 issues of *Caliban*, Camus's article is reprinted in *E*: 1580–83. Ronald Aronson, although overstating the significance of the occasion of their publication in *Caliban*, reprints the texts, in translation, in full (Aronson 2001; see also Aronson 2004: 104–5).

8   In fact, Sartre had warned Camus in advance that the review would not be favourable (Winock 1997: 496).

9   De Beauvoir 1968: 264. Curiously, given the views of the editorial board, in August 1951, two months before the publication of the book, a chapter from it, "Nietzsche et le Nihilisme", appeared in *Les Temps modernes*.

10   Quoted in Lottman 1979: 500. Sartre knew of Jeanson's opinion of Camus, whom he had already criticized in his book *Le Problème moral et la pensée de Sartre*, a book for which Sartre wrote a preface (see Jeanson 1947a).

11   "Albert Camus, ou l'âme révoltée", Jeanson 1952a; "Albert Camus, or the Soul in Revolt", *SCHC*: 79–105.

12   Chiaromonte 1962: 34. Ian Birchall notes that as early as 1947, the communist press had already applied the epithet "belle âme" to Camus and his works, although he neglects to note its appearance in the discussion of Hegel in *The Rebel* itself (Birchall 1994: 137; *R*: 136; *E*: 543).

13   Jeffrey Isaac observes that although Camus's reading of Hegel and Marx in *The Rebel* may be seen as "simplistic", the ostentatious sophistication of the ideas of Jeanson, Merleau-Ponty, and especially Sartre masked certain "deeply essentialist conceptions of human agency and history", with which they defended their "fellow-travelling with the Communists", as well as certain "astonishingly naive readings of current events" (Isaac, in *SCHC*: 257).

14   Jeanson 1952a: 2089–90; *SCHC*: 100–101. In one of the most startling and contradictory passages in Jeanson's review of *The Rebel*, he admits to the importance of revolt: "Kept alive *at the heart of the revolutionary project*, revolt can, no doubt, contribute to the health of the enterprise, by continually expressing this kind of absolute demand and impatient generosity – this love of living men, as Camus puts it so well – that is the very source of his authenticity" (*ibid.*).

15   Jeanson 1952a: 2077; *SCHC*: 87. Aronson 2004: 145, 151. Camus 1952: 317; SCHC: 107*. This translation is from Lottman 1979: 504.

16   Examples include: "Most certainly the rebel does not deny the history that surrounds him; it is on terms of this that he attempts to affirm himself" (*R*: 290; *E*: 693); "To choose history, and history alone, is to choose nihilism, in defiance of the teachings of rebellion itself. Those who rush blindly to history in the name of the irrational, proclaiming that it is meaningless, encounter servitude and terror and finally emerge into the universe of the concentration camps. Those who launch themselves into it preaching its absolute rationality encounter servitude and terror and emerge into the universe of the concentration camps" (*R*: 246; *E*: 648); "What, then, should be the attitude of the rebel? He cannot turn away from the world and from history without denying the very principle of his rebellion" (*R*: 287; *E*: 690).

17   *SCHC*: 114–15*; Camus 1952: 322–3. I have used the term "colleague" here in place of "collaborator". The primary translation of the French term "collaborateur" is "colleague", and there is no reason to suspect that Camus wished to imply anything else. See also McBride in *SCHC*: 231. For contemporary examples of the tendency to confuse history with historicism, see Duvall 2005, McBride in *SCHC* and, to a lesser extent, Aronson 2004.

18   *SCHC*: 115–16*; Camus 1952: 324. I have translated "un critique sagace et loyal" as "a judicious and honest critic", rather than "a loyal and wise critic" (cf. *SCHC*: 116; Aronson 2004: 144, 159, 185, 208, 229). Camus's complaint concerned the absence of honesty and fairness in Jeanson's critique, not the absence of personal loyalty.

19   In 1955 he made the same point in response to criticism from Roland Barthes: "Compared to *The Outsider*, *The Plague* does represent, beyond any possible discussion, the movement from an attitude of solitary revolt to the recognition of a community whose struggles must be shared. If there is an evolution from *The Outsider* to *The Plague*, it is towards solidarity and

participation" (*SEN*: 220; *TRN*: 1965–6). Camus was, he said in his letter to *Les Temps modernes*, "growing tired of seeing myself, and more especially of seeing veteran militants who never walked away from the struggles of their times, being endlessly lectured on efficacy by critics who have never placed anything more than their armchair in the direction of history" (Camus 1952: 332; *SCHC*: 126*). This apparently includes an allusion to Sartre: during the liberation of Paris in August 1944, Camus was said to have found him asleep in the stalls of a theatre he had been sent to secure (Todd 1996: 564; Todd 1998: 308).

20   *SCHC*: 120–23; Camus 1952: 327–30. We will see that Sartre responds to this question with the assertion that "the point is to give [history an end]".

21   Jeanson 1952a: 2083; *SCHC*: 94*. Curiously, in a preface written for Guides Nagel in 1952, Sartre declares Scandinavia to be where "socialist or socialist-like reforms have been advanced the farthest" (Sartre 1974a: 263).

22   Indeed, as Ronald Santoni points out, "Sartre's response gave the appearance of his having a vested interest in Jeanson's initial repudiation of *The Rebel*". Indeed, Santoni himself later refers to the debate as that between "Jeanson/Sartre and Camus" (Santoni 2003: 129, 163).

23   *SCHC*: 131–2*; Sartre 1952: 334. The phrase "Trotskyists of the heart" would most likely have no meaning whatever for Sartre, making his use of it here somewhat telling.

24   This view is repeated by de Beauvoir in her memoirs. Speaking of Camus, she writes: "at one moment forced to yield to History, he attempted as soon as possible to secede from it; sensitive to men's suffering, he imputed it to nature . . . usually, he refused to participate in the particular and detailed political actions to which Sartre had committed himself. While Sartre believed in the truth of socialism, Camus became a more and more resolute champion of bourgeois values; *The Rebel* was a statement of his solidarity with them" (de Beauvoir 1968: 271–2).

25   *SCHC*: 147; Sartre 1952: 345–6. It is interesting that Sartre would compare Camus with Chateaubriand here. De Beauvoir recounts in her memoirs that while she was holidaying with Sartre in Brittany in 1932, Sartre came upon the tomb of the venerable moralist. The pretentiousness of the tomb compelled the philosopher to urinate on it (de Beauvoir 1965: 118).

26   Aron considered Sartre's desired synthesis of existentialism and Marxism to be ultimately "impossible" (Aron 1975: 211).

27   *SCHC*: 149; Sartre 1952: 347. The extent to which Sartre's argument is based on Jeanson's is quite significant.

28   "Terror is an abstract violence. You became violent and terrorist when History, which you rejected, rejected you in turn" (*SCHC*: 158; Sartre 1952: 353).

29   *SCHC*: 144; Sartre 1952: 343. Camus certainly never rejoiced at the news of the camps, and indeed, in 1953, he spoke critically of one of the first witnesses of the Soviet camps to speak in France, Victor Kravchenko (see *E*: 789, 797). We should also note that Sartre here appears to find the existence of concentration camps in the USSR and the use made of the revelation of their existence by the bourgeois press "*equally* unacceptable" (*SCHC*: 142*; Sartre 1952: 342). In January 1950 *Les Temps modernes* published an editorial written by Merleau-Ponty, and co-signed by Sartre, responding to recent revelations made by David Rousset concerning the existence of forced labour camps in the USSR. Although admitting that "there is no socialism when one out of every twenty citizens is in a camp", they also claim that whatever the current state of Soviet society might be, "the USSR is on the whole situated, in the balance of powers, on the side of those who are struggling against the forms of exploitation known to us", and that it therefore deserves their support. Furthermore, they criticize Rousset for the use he has made of the details of the camps, serving as it does in their eyes the anti-Soviet propaganda of those nation states whose record in terms of human rights might be no more admirable than that of the USSR. Thanks to Rousset's supremely reactionary achievement, "the Spanish or Greek governments, the French or English colonial administrations" are freed from all critical scrutiny. "The sacred union against the Russian system", they assert, "solicits all those who detest it for bad reasons as well as good ones; through the concentration camp system it will aim at and hit all parties of socialist inspiration" (Merleau-Ponty & Sartre 1950a: 1155, 1162, 1166–7; Merleau-Ponty 1964: 264, 269, 272). For Rousset, Sartre was "maintaining that

the Soviet camps had no major political or social importance" (quoted in Hayman 1986: 254, see also 262). Although by this time Camus clearly had no sympathy for communism, his position was never simply that of an anti-communist. And whereas Merleau-Ponty and Sartre may have had grounds to criticize Rousset for providing ammunition to those states, such as Spain or Greece, whose own human rights abuses were benefiting from the concentration of moral outrage on the labour camps of the USSR, no such complaint could be made against Camus. As early as November 1948 he had insisted on the indivisibility of moral judgement: repression under Franco, he said, was no different to repression under Stalin (*E*: 389–96; *CC*: 297–301; I note elsewhere that in 1947 Camus compared French colonial policy in Algeria and Madagascar to the Nazi occupation of France). This determination not to distinguish between forms of tyranny on the basis of the quality of its messianic fantasy certainly distinguished Camus from a good number of his contemporaries for whom oppression under a communist regime was somehow qualitatively different from oppression under a non-communist regime. Camus's point was simply that if it was their duty to speak out against the Nazi camps, it was also incumbent upon them as intellectuals to speak out, and with equal vehemence, against Stalin's camps. When *Les Temps modernes* printed Claude Lefort's review of Kravchenko's exposé (*I Chose Freedom* [1947]), it inserted an editorial comment regretting the accusatory tone Lefort had adopted in his treatment of the Soviet Union.

30   *SCHC*: 155; Sartre 1952: 351. It should be pointed out that Camus did not reject the class struggle per se, only the assumption that it was the fundamental principle behind all social rebellion and revolution.

31   *SCHC*: 147; Sartre 1952: 345. Jeanson was similarly lyrical, though no more sincere: "We beg Camus not to yield to fascination, and to rediscover in himself that personal voice – by which his work remains for us, despite everything, irreplaceable" (*SCHC*: 101*; Jeanson 1952a: 2090).

32   Indeed, when he repeats the point in the conclusion to his letter, he repeats the same quotation (albeit with superficial differences, indicating that he was recalling it from memory): " 'For years now, you have tried to make me enter History . . .' 'So that's it', I said to myself, 'since he believes himself outside, it's only normal that he poses conditions before entering it'. Just like the little girl who tests the water with her toe, while asking 'Is it hot?' you view History with distrust. You stick in a finger which you pull out very quickly, and you ask, 'Has it a meaning?' " (Sartre 1952: 352; *SCHC*: 156).

33   *SCHC*: 145; Sartre 1952: 344. In order of appearance, I have sourced the quotations, which appear in the Sprintzen & van den Hoven translation (*SCHC*: 140, 148, 150, 153), to "Neither Victims nor Executioners" (*E*: 332; *CC*: 259); *Nuptials* (*LACE*: 104, 105, 101, 71); *Letters to a German Friend* (*RRD*: 28); *Nuptials* (*LACE*: 95); *Letters to a German Friend* (*RRD*: 29); and *Nuptials* (*LACE*: 91, 100).

34   *RRD*: 29* (italics added); *E*: 241. We are reminded here to some extent of the character of Rambert in *The Plague*, who is initially concerned solely with escaping Oran and its plague and being reunited with his wife. He later concludes, however, that the correct response to the plague is to stay to fight it, saying, "it may be shameful to be happy by oneself", which is itself a significant qualification of his assertion in *Nuptials* (1939) that "there is no shame in being happy" (*TP*: 170; *TRN*: 1387. *SEN*: 72*; *E*: 58, 1348n.9).

35   *RRD*: 27; *E*: 239–40. In his essay "In Defence of *The Rebel*", unpublished at the time of his death, Camus alludes to this falsification (*SCHC*: 207n.; *E*: 1704n.). Ian Birchall notes that Sartre's misquotation was immediately observed in a contemporary review (Jacques Carat, "La Rupture Camus–Sartre", *Preuves*, October 1952), but doesn't himself think the misquotation detracts from Sartre's "fundamentally just" argument (Birchall 1994: 149n.88).

36   *SCHC*: 151–3*; Sartre 1952: 348–9. Responding to Sartre's assertion, Cornelius Castoriadis observed ironically, "On this day the infant mortality rate went down in the working-class neighbourhoods of Paris" (Castoriadis 1988: 238n.9).

37   *SCHC*: 151*; Sartre 1952: 348. Jeanson had made the same point (Jeanson 1952a: 2081; *SCHC*: 92).

38   *SCHC*: 159n.10, 123; Camus 1952: 330; Sartre 1956: 381; Sartre 1943: 422. The syntactically similar phrase, "unbridled freedom" (*liberté frénétique*) does appear in *The Rebel*, but is ex-

plicitly attributed to Sade (*R*: 47; *E*: 457). Curiously, the exact phrase appears in de Beauvoir's essay on Sade, published after *The Rebel* but before Sartre's letter: "[murder] represents the exacerbated demand for unrestrained and relentless freedom [*libérte sans frein et sans peur*]" (de Beauvoir 1951: 1029; de Beauvoir 1962: 41). Furthermore, in his essay on Baudelaire (1947), Sartre accuses the poet of adhering to a strict dandyism "in order to put the brake on his bottomless freedom [*insondable liberté*]" (Sartre 1950: 133; Sartre 1947b: 153). Finally, Sartre would probably have read Mauriac's review of Camus's essay in *La Table Ronde* – not least because Mauriac identifies a "somewhat disdainful [*quelque peu dédaigneuse*]" allusion to Sartre in *The Rebel* (Mauriac, 1951: 103; see Aronson 2004: 113, 126, 136, 139–40, 142). Interestingly, Mauriac (1951: 100) also quotes Camus's claim that Sade "extolled revolutionary societies in the name of unbridled freedom [*la liberté frénétique*]", which, says Camus, "in reality, rebellion does not demand" (*R*: 47; *E*: 457). Perhaps it was from reading this article that Sartre derived the idea that Camus had accused him of extolling "freedom without brakes".

39   Burnier similarly notes the "contradictory" character of some of *Les Temps modernes*' inaugural editorial, noting "it had difficulty in justifying its positions and relating ontological analyses to political positions" (Burnier 1968: 25).

40   Aron 1955: 67. Aron offers a concise analysis of the exchange of letters in his *L'Opium des intellectuels* (1955: 62–9).

41   *SCHC*: 122; Camus 1952: 329. In *The Rebel*, for example, Camus asserts: "History may perhaps have an end; but our task is not to terminate it but to create it, in the image of what we henceforth know to be true" (*R*: 276; *E*: 679).

42   Elizabeth Bowman and Robert Stone quoted in Santoni 2003: 138. In my account of these works I rely heavily on Santoni's own commentary, particularly on his discussion of the "Rome Lecture", which remains unpublished.

43   *CDRI*: 129; Santoni 2003: 55. The Marxist scholar G. A. Cohen has similarly noted that "there is no history when nature is unusually generous", and that "the historical situation of men is one of scarcity" (Cohen 1978: 23, 152).

44   *CDRI*: 67n.29, 420; Santoni 2003: 43. The quotations from *CDR* are taken from Santoni 2003: 42–3.

45   *CDRI*: 431; Santoni 2003: 43, Santoni's own translation. Cf. Rousseau's "common good".

46   *CDRI*: 733. We see a similar account of violence in Sartre's Preface to Fanon's *The Wretched of the Earth*, where he suggests that "their mad 'boomerang' violence" is "the proof of ['the native's'] humanity". And as with the "fused group" of *CDR*, the violent rebellion of the colonized "against counterhumanity constitutes the human being 'recreating himself'. In this way, the native 'cures himself of his colonial neurosis'" (Santoni 2003: 71–2, quoting Sartre's preface in Fanon 1967: 17, 19, 18).

47   Dobson 1993: 65. In stark contrast, according to Camus, "History, as an entirety, could exist only in the eyes of an observer outside it and outside the world. History only exists, in the final analysis, for God. Thus it is impossible to act according to plans embracing the totality of universal history" (*R*: 289; *E*: 692–3).

48   Sartre 1967: 213–14. Sartre repeats this point in an interview with his Italian translator, Paolo Caruso, in 1965 (Sartre 1976b: 222–3).

49   As the lecture is unpublished, my reconstruction of the four limiting conditions is based on the following three summaries: Santoni 2003: 149–50; R. Stone in Aronson *et al.* 2003: 17; Anderson 1993: 127–8.

50   Anderson 1993: 188n.37; Santoni 2003: 152n.42. Furthermore, making much the same observation on reading the manuscript of Santoni's book, Anderson also notes that it is with regard to his failure to consider innocent civilians in his account of legitimate political violence that Sartre differs most from Camus (Santoni 2003: 116n.112; 152n.42). In 1944 Sartre wrote: "'The drama I'd have liked to write was about a terrorist who, by ambushing Germans, becomes the pretext for the execution of fifty hostages. After an ambush, Resistance fighters could save the hostages' lives only by giving themselves up; the play argues that they should neither do this nor feel guilty about causing the deaths of innocent people" (Hayman 1986: 178–9, quoting "Pour un théâtre d'engagement", 1944).

51 Bell 1993: 188, quoted in Santoni 2003: 158. See Bowman & Stone 2004: 7, 8, 16. I have noted elsewhere that Camus would probably have agreed with Hannah Arendt's paradoxical formula that "violence can be justifiable but it will never be legitimate" (Arendt 1970: 52). It is perhaps worth noting, in the context of Bell's thesis, that Arendt's essay was written, to some extent, *against* Sartre.

52 There is one remarkable, if partial, exception to this divergence. Ronald Aronson points out that "the first political intervention credited to Sartre was a collective redraft of a statement written by Camus" (Aronson 2004: 101). The text attributed to Sartre by his bibliographers, entitled "First Call to International Opinion", was first published in *Esprit* in November 1947, and is signed by Camus, Sartre and twenty-one others. Aronson shows it to be a significantly reworked version of an unpublished text written by Camus in September or October 1947 (Camus's text is printed in *E*: 1577–9, the version attributed to Sartre is printed in Sartre 1974a: 205–7; see also de Beauvoir 1968: 148). In a notable twist, the text as published in Sartre 1974a has also been attributed to Camus in the new edition of his *Collected Works* (*OCII*: 701–4, notes: 1354–6). The editor of the text, Philippe Vanney, also offers a slightly different interpretation of the original draft text to that offered by Aronson (*OCII*: 758–60, notes: 1371–3).

53 Sartre's play first appeared in instalments in *Les Temps modernes* in March and April 1948 (Sartre 1974a: 184). The first formulation of Camus's ideas on Kaliayev and his comrades appeared in January 1948, in an article entitled "The Scrupulous Assassins" ("Les meurtriers délicats", *TRN*: 1819–25), although in June 1947 Camus was already writing detailed notes on Kaliayev (*NB2*: 156; *C2*: 199).

54 Interview with Sartre, *L'Aube*, 1 April 1948, reprinted in Sartre 1974a: 189; Interview with Sartre, *Franc-Tireur*, 23 March 1948, reprinted in Sartre 1976b: 207; Interview with Sartre in *Combat*, 31 March 1948, reprinted in Sartre 1974a: 188. See also Sartre's discussion quoted in Jeanson 1955: 48–9.

55 Sartre 1989: 217–18. In the present context it is perhaps worth contrasting Cherea's claim in *Caligula*, "I don't like lying", with that of Stepan in *The Just Assassins*: "Everybody lies. The important thing is to lie well" (*COP*: 83, 168; *TRN*, 79, 313).

56 Sartre made this decision while attending the (communist-backed) Peoples' Congress for Peace in Vienna. In 1954 he justified this act of self-censorship in the name of "the cause of peace" (Sartre 1974a: 191; Aronson 2004: 167; Cohen-Solal 1987: 338). Sartre described the Vienna congress as one of the three moments in his life "which suddenly gave me hope again", comparable with the Liberation of France in 1944 (Sartre 1974a: 274). He ignored the fact that the peace congress took place in the shadow of the execution of Rudolph Slansky, a former Czech Communist Party leader, and ten others, who had admitted to charges of being Zionist agents in the pay of the west. For Camus, "ordinarily, going to Vienna would mean participating in a Cold War act, but going there with the backdrop of eleven hanged men whose names were followed by the word 'Jew' in Czech newspapers is beyond description. . . . Just as our right-wingers were fascinated with Hitler's power, so our leftists are entranced by Communist power, tarted up with the name of 'efficiency'" (Todd 1996: 580; Todd 1998: 314*). Similarly, although Sartre protested the execution of Charles and Ethel Rosenberg in the USA, he failed to protest the near contemporary massacre of more than one hundred workers in East Berlin. Sartre's defence of the Rosenbergs was published not, as Ronald Aronson suggests, on the day of the Berlin massacre, but five days later. The Berlin massacre took place on 17 June 1953, and Sartre's article, entitled "Mad Beasts", appeared in *Libération* on 22 June 1953 (Sartre 1974a: 285; Aronson 2004: 169). For an allusion to Sartre's omission see Camus's "Berlin-Est, 17 juin 1953" (*E*: 1771–5, 1772, noted in Aronson 2004: 169–70).

57 Sartre 1974a: 192–3. Not only the question of legitimate violence, but the question of love becomes a topic in this vicarious debate between Camus and Sartre. In response to the "idealist anti-hero" Hugo's assertion that "As for men, it's not what they are that interest me, but what they can become", Sartre's "realist hero", Hoederer, declares "I love [men] for what they are. With all their filth and all their vices" (Sartre 1989: 220). In Camus's play, to the idealist hero Kaliayev's assertion that "I love life . . . I joined the revolution because I love life",

the realist Stepan responds "I don't love life . . . I love something higher than mere life . . . I love justice" (*COP*: 173; *TRN*, 320).

58 He points out that this will also be the thesis of what is now referred to as the "Rome Lecture", which I discuss above (Sartre 1976b: 222–3). This portion of the interview is not published in Sartre 1974a.

59 A confrontation that, according to de Beauvoir, achieves its ultimate fruition in Sartre's play *The Devil and the Good Lord* (1951): "In 1944, Sartre thought that any situation could be transcended by subjective effort; in 1951, he knew that circumstances can sometimes steal our transcendence from us; in that case, no individual salvation is possible, only collective struggle" (de Beauvoir 1968: 254).

60 Raymond Aron claimed that Sartre "affected" the belief that he (Aron) "was unconditionally opposed to violence" (Aron 1975: 191). Sartre appears to have also affected this belief with respect to Camus (see Santoni 2003: 60n.47, 72, 108).

61 Aronson 2004: 90, 218. In his book, Aronson makes use of the phrase "clean hands" with greater frequency than Camus (2004: 32, 33, 34, 90, 197, 201, 218, 219).

62 *CC*: 16; *CAC8*: 149. I have identified three relevant passages, one in *Letters to a German Friend* (the instance identified by Aronson) and two others among Camus's *Combat* articles. See *RRD*: 8–9; *CC*: 16, 36; *E*: 223, *CAC8*: 149, 186.

63 "It took us all that time to find out if we had the right to kill men, if we were allowed to add to the frightful misery of this world. And because of that time lost and recaptured, our defeat accepted and surmounted, those scruples paid for with blood, we French have the right to think today that we entered this war with clean hands – clean as victims and the condemned are – and that we are going to come out of it with clean hands – but clean this time with a great victory won against injustice and against ourselves" (*RRD*: 8–9*; *E*: 223–4). This "letter" was originally published in 1943. For Francis Jeanson's interpretation of the phrase "clean hands" see his "To Tell You Everything", in *SCHC*: 181–2; Jeanson 1952b: 367–8.

64 There is one subtly different later usage. In response to criticism he received for locating his play *The State of Siege* in Spain rather than Eastern Europe, Camus replies: "Why Spain? Because a few of us refuse to wash that blood from our hands. Whatever reason there may be for anticommunism, and I know some good ones, we will never accept it if it goes so far as to forget the injustice done to Spain, an injustice which, with the complicity of our governments, has been allowed to continue to this day" (*CC*: 298; *CAC8*: 684).

65 A striking photograph of Kaliayev, taken immediately after his assassination of the Grand Duke, was well known to Camus through its reproduction in the Russian journal *Byloie* (*The Past*) (N. N. "Posledniy den' Kaliayeva" [The Last day of Kaliayev], *Byloie* 5, May 1906: 186–90). A copy of the image can be found among Camus's papers at the archive in Aix-en-Provence (CMS2.Ab5-01.01).

66 Serialization of *Les Communistes et la Paix* began in *Les Temps modernes* in July 1952 (the letters were published in the August 1952 issue, as was a note from the editor explaining that the publication of *Les Communistes et la Paix* would continue in September).

67 Speaking of his "conversion" and the writing of *Les Communistes et la Paix* (1952), he wrote, "An Anti-communist is a rat. I couldn't see any way out of that one and I never will" (Sartre 1965: 287; Sartre 1964c: 248). "Your letter amply demonstrates – if one must speak of you the way an anti-Communist speaks of the Soviet Union, alas, as *you* speak of it – that you have become a counter revolutionary" (*SCHC*: 132; Sartre 1952: 334).

68 Sartre 1962b; Sartre 1964c: 126–9. Quoted in Lottman 1979: 673; cf. Judt 1998: 121–5. It should be noted that the French term *moraliste* does not have the strong negative connotations that the term "moralist" has come to have in English (for which the French term is *moralisateur*). Interestingly, this article, referred to by Pierre-Henri Simon as "brief and noble" (Simon 1962: 28), was interpreted as incorporating "the perversity of his dialectic" by Olivier Todd (1996: 755). Todd's translator abbreviates this to "perverse" (Todd 1998: 415).

69 Todd 1996: 827; Todd 1998: 415–16*. See Sartre interviewed by John Gerassi (Interview No. 25, 5 May 1972, GEN MSS 441, box 2 F.24. John Gerassi Collection of Jean-Paul Sartre,

General Collection of Rare Books and Manuscripts, Beinecke Rare Book and Manuscript Library, Yale University). Some years later Sartre told Contat in an interview: "We could not go far on the intellectual level because he grew alarmed quickly. In fact there was a side of him that smacked of the little Algerian tough guy, very much a hooligan, very funny. He was probably the last good friend I had" (Sartre 1977: 64; Sartre 1976a: 196). It is also worth noting that this characterization of Camus corresponds very closely with the stereotype of the *pied-noir* current among the most chauvinistic of the Metropolitan French (see Bocca 1968: 4).

70   Aronson 2004: 93, 33, 91. On the other hand, Aronson also admits that in his letter to Camus, Sartre did not address what he calls "the moral question . . . of means and ends in history . . . Sartre never provided a response to Camus' main challenge, any more that Jeanson did" (Aronson 2004: 151). Of course, more than simply "the moral question", this is precisely the very question at the heart of *The Rebel* and the "main challenge" of Camus's letter to Jeanson.

71   Sartre 1952: 353; *SCHC*: 158. As we have seen, Jeanson claimed that Camus was neither on the left nor the right, but "up in the air" (*SCHC*: 188; Jeanson 1952b: 372).

72   Sartre 1978a: 78 (most of the interviews that make up this text were recorded in 1972); quoted in part in Aronson 2004: 182–3. Curiously, several Sartre scholars seem to be of the view that Sartre's overarching concern was with morality (e.g. Jeanson 1955: 180; Birchall 1994: 138).

73   Sartre 1977: 169–70; Sartre 1976a: 45. It should be noted that Sartre begins this essay with the assertion "I am not a Maoist", although it seems clear from the passage quoted that he considered their violence moral.

Chapter 6   Camus and Algeria

1   Camus in conversation with Jean Daniel (Daniel 1960: 21; reprinted in Daniel 1973: 258).

2   *RRD*: 5; *E*: 221. "I love my country too much to be a nationalist" (*RRD*: 4; *E*: 219; cf. *SEN*: 203; *TRN*: 1711).

3   Further, Camus could with some legitimacy consider himself Algerian. Like his parents, he was born in Algeria. His paternal grandmother and maternal grandfather were also born in Algeria. Although his paternal grandfather was born in Marseilles in 1842, it appears his parents (Camus's paternal great-grandparents) were already residents of Algeria by that time. Finally, his maternal grandmother was born not in France, but in Minorca, from where ultimately all of his maternal ancestors originated. After his father's death in 1914, Camus grew up exclusively in the care of his mother's family. For a concise Camus genealogy, see Lottman 1979: 9–13. Notwithstanding his social and economic background, according to Francis Jeanson, Camus's status as a *pied-noir* meant he was automatically a "privileged member of society" [*un privilégié*] (interview with Jeanson in Starling 1977: 359).

4   Said 1993: 209. Said makes no secret of his antipathy for Cruise O'Brien: "The later O'Brien, with views noticeably . . . different from the gist of his book on Camus, has made no secret of his antipathy for the lesser people of the 'Third World'. See his extended disagreement with Said in *Salmagundi* 70–71 (Spring–Summer 1986), 65–81" (Said 1993: 420n.197).

5   Said 1993: 223, 213. The lack of candour in Said's interpretation is indicated by the following comment added in a footnote in which he cites Lottman's biography: "Camus' actual behaviour during the colonial war itself is best chronicled in Yves Carrière's [*sic*] *La Guerre d'Algérie II: Le Temps des Léopards*" (Said 1993: 420n.198). This suggests a lack of familiarity with both Lottman's biography and Courrière's work, which can hardly be said to chronicle Camus's "actual behaviour during the colonial war". Courrière's discussion of Camus pertains entirely to the appeal for a civilian truce and, furthermore, his sympathetic analysis is substantially the same as that in Lottman (see Courrière 1969: 239–64). In the context of the unwarranted influence of Said's critique of Camus, it is perhaps worth noting that his main "Orientalist" thesis, which constitutes, among many other things, the theoretical basis for his criticism of Camus, has endured frequent and damaging critical scrutiny. See Robert Irwin's

essay "An Enquiry into the Nature of a Certain Twentieth Century Polemic", in Irwin 2006: 277–309, which includes a detailed account of these criticisms; see especially Ernest Gellner's highly critical review of *Culture and Imperialism* (Gellner 1993).

6   "Manifeste des intellectuels d'Algérie en faveur du projet viollette" (*E*: 1328–9). In place of a signature, the manifesto originally appeared with the declaration that it was endorsed by "fifty signatures which will be communicated via the press" (*E*: 1329). Olivier Todd 1996: 150 has attributed it to Camus, and it has appeared in both Pléiade editions of Camus's works (*E*: 1328–9; *OCII*: 572–3).

7   Lottman 1979. Christopher Hitchens's suggestion, in his review of the book, that "further slipshod generalisations about Camus will simply not be tolerable" seems in retrospect optimistic (Hitchens 1990: 95).

8   Lottman 1979: 100, 148. See Lottman 1979: 147–60, 690n.26. Quilliot suggests that Camus joined the party in 1934 (*E*: 1314).

9   Testimony of former Communist Party member Emile Padula, quoted in Lottman 1979: 157. It is important to note that this was not the only reason for the growing conflict between Camus and the leadership of the Communist Party. Although he had never been an ardent member, Camus's disillusionment with communism seems to have mirrored André Gide's, whose critical account of a visit to the Soviet Union, *Retour de l'URSS*, was published in 1936 (Todd 1998: 60–61; Todd 1996: 145–6).

10 Camus claimed in a letter to his friend and editor, Roger Quilliot, to have left the Communist Party in 1935 (*TRN*: xxix). However, most agree (including, seemingly, Quilliot) that he continued to be a member of the party until 1937, when he was expelled. The fact that Camus continued to direct the communist-sponsored "Maison de la Culture" until 1937 would seem to support this interpretation (cf. *C1*: 29; *NB1*: 16; Quilliot 1962).

11 Said claims that "except occasionally, [Camus] usually ignores or overlooks this history" of French Algeria (Said 1993: 211). Cruise O'Brien suggests that Camus's conception of French–Algerian relations contained "unusually strong elements of estrangement, unreality and even hallucination" (Cruise O'Brien 1970: 13).

12 Haddour 2000: 17, 23n.84; Foxlee 2006: 90. Furthermore, as David Carroll points out, Camus's conception of assimilation was, for its time, liberal in the extreme: "His notion [of assimilation] implies that an Algerian would become French *as a Berber, as an Arab, as a Muslim*. Today, this would be considered a multiculturalist position. In Algeria in 1939, it was considered a subversively anticolonialist position" (Carroll 2007a: 136).

13 Amar Ouzegane quoted in Vircondelet 1998: 76. According to Lottman, Ouzegane was a member of the FLN's "national brain trust", and wrote the FLN's "draft war program", the "Plate-forme de la Soummam", which was adopted in August 1956 (Lottman 1979: 695n.9). The "Soummam Platform" is reprinted in Courrière 1969: 575–604. Ouzegane was later arrested for his FLN activities, and in 1959 Camus sent a statement to the tribunal at which his trial was to take place highlighting his involvement in the campaign for a civilian truce (Lottman 1979: 639).

14 Ouzegane quoted in Broyelle 1982: 205 and in Todd 1996: 149. In fact, according to Ouzegane's comrade in the FLN, Mohamed Lebjaoui, Camus believed Algerian independence to be both "logical and inevitable", but that it could be achieved only at the end of a series of lengthy stages, among the first of which would be some form of internal autonomy (Lebjaoui 1970: 41).

15 This point is subtly, though significantly, distinct from Said's assertion that Camus was "simply wrong historically" (Said 1993: 211).

16 Memmi 1957: 95–6, italics in original. Memmi's subsequent comments on Camus essentially concur with this interpretation (Memmi 1972, 1986).

17 Memmi 1986: 194. We note also that in 1954–5 Memmi requested that Camus write a preface for the English translation of his first novel (*Le Statue de sel*, 1953; *Pillar of Salt*, 1955). The preface, which emphasized Memmi's own ambivalent identity, as "French writer from Tunisia who is neither French nor Tunisian", did not appear in print until the second French edition (Gallimard, 1966).

18   For Cruise O'Brien *The Plague*'s fictional reconstruction of the city of Oran without a notice-
     able Arab population is explained by the fact that for many Algerian Arabs "the fiction of a
     'French Algeria' was a fiction quite as repugnant as the fiction of Hitler's new European order
     was for Camus and his friends. For such Arabs, the French were in Algeria in virtue of the
     same right by which the Germans were in France: the right of conquest." From this perspect-
     ive, says Cruise O'Brien, the characters of the novel are not heroes battling the plague; "they
     were the plague itself", and the absence of Arabs constitutes an "artistic final solution to the
     problem of Arabs of Oran" (Cruise O'Brien 1970: 48). However, when the Algerian writer
     Mouloud Feraoun wrote to Camus in 1951 complimenting the novel but expressing regret
     that circumstances did not allow him to know the "indigenous" population, Camus replied
     that to have included Arabs in the book would have required him to write a book different
     to the one he wished to write: had he included Arabs in the book, he would have had to
     write "about a problem which poisons all our lives in Algeria. . . . And, further, I'm not sure I
     have the talent to write that book – perhaps you will write it since you know how to place
     yourself above the stupid hatreds that dishonour our country" (quoted in Nacer-Khodja 2004:
     116–17n.7).

19   Lottman 1979: 198. While Ouzegane maintained that El Okbi was innocent, another FLN
     member, Mohamed Lebjaoui, suggested that he did in fact orchestrate the assassination
     (see Lebjaoui 1970: 247–9; see also *CAC3*: 547–50; Lottman 1979: 197–8; Todd 1996:
     787n.7).

20   The full text of these articles is published in *CAC3*: 278–336. Camus reprinted them in
     abridged form in *Actuelles III* (*E*: 903–38). The reports were so embarrassing to the colonial
     government that Camus quickly became *persona non grata* in Algeria. Indeed, Camus's
     widow, Francine, told Carl Viggiani that the authorities tried to "buy" Camus's silence before
     the articles were published (Viggiani 1968: 215).

21   *E*: 907–8, 909. See Camus's friend Emmanuel Roblès, quoted in Lottman 1979: 198. See also
     Chérifi 2007.

22   Albert Memmi describes these essays as "honest, rigorous, quivering with suppressed anger,
     noble [*beau*] because they are so humane [*très humain*]" (Memmi 1969: 113).

23   Camus lost his job at *Paris-Soir* in December 1941, forcing him to return to Algeria. He left
     Algeria again for France in August 1942. In late 1943 he began work as a reader at the
     Gallimard publishing house. At this time he also began his involvement with *Combat*.

24   For different estimates of numbers killed see Siblot & Planche 1986: 159. For an account of the
     uprising and its consequences, see Halpern 1948: 191–202.

25   *CC*: 198–205, 207–10, 212–17, 225–7; *CAC8*: 497–510, 513–19, 522–34, 549–52. The Sétif
     riots began on 8 May 1945; Camus arrived in Algeria on 18 April, and returned to Paris on
     7 or 8 May (*CC*: 199n.481; *CAC8*: 498n.2).

26   Groups such as the Financial Delegations and the Association of Mayors of Algeria (see
     E: 951). Among Algerian Muslim leaders, it was rejected by Messali Hadj (whose party, *Etoile
     Nord Africain*, was proscribed a few months later).

27   *CC*: 207, 209, 210, 212–14; *CAC8*: 514, 518, 522–7. Cf. Camus's letter to Kessous, printed in
     the first issue of his newspaper, *Communauté algérienne*, in October 1955 (*RRD*: 126–30;
     E: 961–6).

28   *CC*: 214, 225–6; *CAC8*: 527, 549–50. His disdain for the smug complacency of many French
     Algerians is vividly expressed in this *Carnet* entry: "The woman who looked as if she had been
     constipated for three years: 'Oh, these Arabs, they still make their girls cover their faces. Oh,
     they're not civilized yet.' Little by little she lets us see what her idea of civilization is: a husband
     earning 1200 Francs a month, a two-room apartment, kitchen and bath, the movies every
     Sunday, and furniture from the Galeries Barbès for weekdays" (*NB1*: 190; *C1*: 225).

29   *CC*: 291–2; *CAC8*: 671–3. He reiterated the comparison in *The Rebel* (*R*: 185; *E*: 322). The
     communist *L'Humanité*, in rather stark contrast, called the nationalist gatherings "re-
     actionary" riots and "provocations by Hitlerite agents" (Todd 1996: 378). Cruise O'Brien
     notes in his book the comparison made by Camus, but he relegates this to the book's endnotes
     (1970: 89n.10, 90n.4).

30   *E*: 747. In a notebook entry dating from about 1952, Camus describes the consequences of drought and "famine" in southern Algeria: "An entire population scrapes the earth in search of roots. Buchenwald under the sun" (*C3*: 70).

31   Indeed, discussing injustice in Algeria, Camus told Jean Daniel in January 1956 that he was sure he would get along better with a member of the FLN than with a "professor from Paris" (Daniel 1973: 257). In early 1957, Camus had lunch with Mohamed Lebjaoui, a member of the FLN he met while in Algiers promoting a civilian truce (see below). Aware that Lebjaoui was being looked for by the police, Camus offered his apartment as a refuge (Lebjaoui 1970: 48–9, quoted in Courrière 1969: 263).

32   Cruise O'Brien 1970: 74. Cruise O'Brien's view is supported, at least partly, by Ronald Aronson 2004: 187–8.

33   Edgar Morin noted that many prominent French anti-colonialist intellectuals were "profoundly ignorant of all Algerian political realities and incapable of discerning the meaning of the labels CRUA, FLN, MNA" (Morin 1959: 192, quoted in Le Sueur 2001: 43).

34   *RRD*: 122. Moreover, this option is compared with an equally unrealistic "military solution", "a reconquest by means of an all-out war" (*RRD*: 122; *E*: 899). These two unrealistic options, then, can be seen to correspond to the warring sides identified in his open letter to Kessous.

35   The FLN's 1956 manifesto the "Plate-forme Soummam" explicitly asserts as a precondition of any ceasefire or negotiations the recognition of Algeria's right to independence. See Courrière 1969: 589 for the relevant text from the Soummam Platform; see also Connelly 2002: 113 and Quandt 1969: 101.

36   *RRD*: 131–42, 136; *E*: 991–9, 994–5. Indeed, as Camus's own genealogy shows, neither were all the "Frenchmen" in Algeria ethnically French.

37   Cruise O'Brien 1970: 72–3. See also Taleb Ibrahimi 1973: 176. This critical reading of the civilian truce effort is not exclusive to postcolonial critics. Tony Judt, for example, argues that the truce "was a hopeless cause and the audience for such an appeal hardly existed, neither in metropolitan France nor in Algeria, as he discovered when he spoke there" (Judt 1998: 119).

38   The estimate of the correspondent for *Le Monde* (Lottman 1979: 573, 574, 575).

39   André Mandouze, editor of *Consciences maghrébines* and FLN apologist, suggests that Ferhat Abbas's decision to dissolve the UDMA and announce its incorporation into the FLN not long after the call for a civil truce itself indicates that the appeal was destined to fail. Of course, more specifically Abbas dissolved the UDMA and joined the FLN *after* the appeal for a civil truce failed, which indicates not that the appeal was destined to fail as much as that the only alternative to it was the continuation of the violent campaign of the FLN, and this is precisely the point Camus was making (Mandouze 1998: 245).

40   Lottman 1979: 572. Lottman's version of events is based on Lebjaoui's own account: see Lebjaoui 1970: 43. In Olivier Todd's account, Camus did not know that Ouzegane, Lebjaoui and the other Muslim member of the civil truce group were also members of the FLN (Todd 1996: 625–6). On the truce see Ouzegane 1962, Lebjaoui 1970, Lottman 1979, Roblès 1988, Vanney 1994, Rossfelder 2000 and Carroll 2007a. Whether or not Camus knew of the FLN's involvement, I know of no evidence to support Le Sueur's assertion that when he discovered their involvement, Camus "wanted to cancel but was advised not to do so" (Le Sueur 2001: 101). Le Sueur may have been thinking of Lebjaoui's claim that when Camus was told of the risk to both himself and others supporting the civilian truce posed by the extremist *pieds-noirs*, he asked whether it would be best to cancel the meeting, and was strongly advised by his colleagues (including Lebjaoui, who was in the FLN) to proceed (Lebjaoui 1970: 42, 44). According to Yves Courrière, Camus was less concerned for his personal safety, which had apparently been guaranteed by Lebjaoui, than with a possible conflict involving Arabs and *ultras* outside the building (Courrière 1969: 258–9).

41   "The decision was taken by the national leadership [of the FLN] only after a long and serious discussion. In agreeing to support the movement in favour of a civilian truce, the leadership envisaged a gathering of liberal Europeans, in the hope of gradually winning them over to the idea of direct negotiations with the Front. . . . Our acceptance of the principles of the civilian

truce was not a manoeuvre" (Lebjaoui 1970: 47. The same passage is quoted in Carroll 2007a: 224n.20).

42   According to Roblès 1988: 44, 48. For the text of the letter sent by the committee to Mollet see Courrière 1969: 607–9.

43   See Tillion 1958b, d; Tillion 1961: 22–51. Camus knew Tillion and wrote an enthusiastic endorsement for the US edition of her book *Algeria: The Realities* (1958). Elsewhere, he compared her agreement with Yacef to his own effort at arriving at a civilian truce (*C3*: 213–14). For an appreciation of Tillion see Todorov 2003: 291–309.

44   In his lecture in Algeria calling for a civil truce Camus stressed the importance of dialogue (cf. the story "The Silent Men" ["Les Muets"], published in *Exile and the Kingdom*). It was only in a situation where dialogue was impossible that Camus reluctantly chose silence.

45   Camus in conversation with Jean Daniel (Daniel 1973: 259). In his Nobel Prize speech in 1957, Camus declared: "The only really committed artist is he who, without refusing to take part in the combat, at least refuses to join the regular armies and remains a maverick" (*RRD*: 267*; *E*: 1092).

46   Mouloud Feraoun was a Kabylie novelist with whom Camus began to correspond after the publication of Feraoun's first novel *Le Fils de Pauvre* in 1950. Feraoun remembered Camus making the above remark when the two men met in 1958 (quoted in Lottman 1979: 626). Feraoun, who also adopted a policy of "silence" in the face of the war, was executed by the OAS shortly before Algeria won independence in 1962.

47   Bronner 1999: 114, 116, italics in original. Bronner argues that "*realpolitik* is not always incompatible with ethical ends", and contrasts Camus's "completely impractical politics" with the opposition of some American intellectuals to the Vietnam War. Of course, had there been 1.2 million Americans resident in Vietnam, or if Vietnam had been part of the USA for longer than New Mexico or Alaska (indeed, Algeria became "part" of France before either Nice or Savoy), the case would have been different, and so it was in relation to Algeria (see Schalk 2005: 34). A more rewarding comparison of the colonial history of Algeria could perhaps be made with Northern Ireland (see Cruise O'Brien 1971; Lustic 1993; Foley 2007).

48   Bronner's criticism is reiterated by several other critics, although most do not go as far as to attribute the continuation of the war in Algeria to Camus's lack of political efficacy: "his vacillations were less than irrelevant: *they actually hindered bringing the conflict to a close*" (Bronner 1999: 116, italics in original).

49   De Beauvoir's assertion that "the FLN had to a large extent absorbed the MNA and won a spectacular number of adherents to its cause" is, at best, a crude simplification. She goes on: the FLN "was insisting that the conventions of International Law be applied to the ALN [Armée de Libération Nationale, the military wing of the FLN]. When the French government sent two Algerian fighters to the guillotine, three French prisoners were shot" (1968: 399–400). The FLN attempted to assassinate Messali himself in September 1959, and refused him an Algerian passport until 1972 (he died in France in 1974) (Messali Hadj 1982: 318–19).

50   Camus 1957: 68. The reference to the "advantages of freedom" can be understood as a reference to political repression in the USSR, but also as a somewhat prophetic reference to the anti-democratic implications of a FLN-led Algeria. Notwithstanding the evident differences, Camus nonetheless saw certain similarities between the war in Algeria and the insurrection in Hungary, and in a lecture given in defence of the Hungarian Uprising in March 1957 he spoke of "torture, disgraceful torture, as contemptible in Algiers as in Budapest" (*RRD*: 161; *E*: 1783). About the same time, in an interview published in *Encounter*, he observed that "As for Algeria, so far as I know only the MNA of Messali Hadj protested the Soviet intervention in Hungary without relinquishing any of its own protests. I was not aware of any protest on the part of the FLN" (Camus 1957: 3, reprinted in *RRD*: 166). The French version of the interview was published a month before the insurrection (*E*: 1762–5).

51   Sartre 2006: 51, 38. In a footnote, Sartre claims that that he did not consider "minor public officials" and "European workers" in Algeria to be *colons*; they were, instead, both "innocent victims and beneficiaries of the colonial regime" (Sartre 2006: 55n.1*). However, in the essay

itself the distinction is conspicuously absent: "the infernal cycle of colonialism", he says, "is embodied in a million *colons*, children and grandchildren of *colons*, who have been shaped by colonialism and who think, speak and act according to the very principles of the colonial regime" (Sartre 2006: 51*).

52   Sartre 2006: 41, 54. In Camus's *Combat* articles after Sétif, he emphasized the economic problems facing Algeria (e.g. *CC*: 201). In a pointed reference to Camus, in his preface to Fanon, Sartre declared, "Our 'beautiful souls' [*nos belles âmes*] are racists" (Fanon 1967: 18*; see Sartre 2006: 165).

53   Todd 1996: 685; Todd 1998: 369. For details of some of Camus's interventions see Camus & Koestler 2002: 247–71; Le Sueur 2001: 103–9.

54   De Beauvoir 1968: 394; Berne 2005: 222–4. Jean Sénac also compared Ben Saddok to Kaliayev (Nacer-Khodja 2004: 98).

55   De Beauvoir 1968: 362, 397, 393, 392, 394, 382. There is a striking contrast between Sartre's attitude to the conflict in Algeria and the attitude he was to exhibit later in regard to the Arab–Israeli conflict: "I have friends on both sides and I recognise the rights of each. I know my position is purely a moral one, but this is precisely one of those cases which prove that one must reject political realism because it leads to war. I would say that the Arab–Israeli conflict, with the emotional implications it had for me, played a part in abandoning the political realism I went along with to a certain extent before 1968" (Sartre 1977: 87–8). See also Sartre 1996 (*passim*) and Said 2000, in which the author describes what he considered to be Sartre's "fundamental pro-Zionism".

56   *E*: 1881–2, quoted in Lottman 1979: 617–18. It is perhaps worth noting here that after Camus was verbally harassed by the young Algerian, the Association des Algériens en Suède formally distanced themselves from this student's comments, adding in a letter to Camus that he was not a member of their organization or any other Algerian nationalist organization known to them (*E*: 1883).

57   Speech as reported in *Le Monde*, reprinted in *E*: 1881–2. See Eveno & Planchais 1990: 196–7; Winock 1997: 537. It is worth noting, finally, since the statement was only ever published in *Le Monde*, that Camus did write to the editor of the newspaper in order to clarify some issues in the report, but never disputed the accuracy of the comment regarding his mother and justice. Indeed, in the letter he states that he felt a great deal of sympathy for the Algerian student, who was motivated not by hatred, but by a sadness over the current situation in Algeria, a sadness that he (Camus) shares (*E*: 1882–3).

58   De Beauvoir 1968: 396, 362. Noting the uncertain origins of the term *pied-noir*, Philip Dine suggests that it may derive from the footwear of the first French settlers (army boots) or from the dirty bare feet of the impoverished European settlers who came after the soldiers (Dine 1994: 9).

59   In March 1956 to his friend Emmanuel Roblès, and again in the 1958 preface to *Chroniques algériennes*, where he also comments on the "strange" controversy it provoked (*E*: 1843; Roblès 1988: 48; *E*: 892; *RRD*: 113). See also Camus's letter to Jean Amrouche (*C3*: 238). Alec Hargreaves 1986: 80 mentions, without endorsing, the "Freudian slip" interpretation.

60   Nacer-Khodja 2004: 158. See *ibid*.: *passim* and Le Sueur 2001: 113–15, for details of Sénac's criticism of Camus. Camus's friend, Jules Roy, also a *pied-noir*, made a similar claim: "It is not a question of preferring one's mother to justice, but of loving justice as much as one's mother" (Roy 1960: 215).

61   In May 1957 the FLN massacred over 300 civilians in the MNA stronghold of Melouza. Whereas the editor of *Esprit*, J. M. Domenach, compared Melouza to Nazi massacres in Lidice and Oradour-sur-Glane (quoted in Obuchowski 1968: 93), Sartre believed that journalists were mistaken in even reporting the massacre, arguing that "Politics imposes a constraint to remain silent about certain things. Otherwise one is a 'beautiful soul' and is not acting politically" (Daniel 1973: 251–2). In an interview in 1973 he expressed the same view: "Can one conceive of Algerian independence without the elimination of the MNA by the FLN? And how can the FLN be reproached for violence when for years it confronted daily repression, torture, and massacres by the French army? Inevitably, the revolutionary army

ends up by striking at some of its own members at the same time. I believe this is an historical necessity which we can do nothing about" (Burnier 1988: 42).

62   "Lethal frivolity" in Daniel 1973: 257; "it seems to me revolting to beat one's *mea culpa*, as our judge-penitents do, on someone else's breast" (*RRD*: 120; *E*: 897). Already, in *L'Express* in 1955, Camus asked whether it was necessary that *pieds-noirs* "be offered up for slaughter to expiate the immense sins of French colonialism[?]" (*CAC6*: 73). Jean Daniel, himself a supporter of Algerian independence, was to note in 1956 that there was now an "orthodox anticolonialism", the "dogma" of which "is not the well-being of the colonised but the mortification of the colonisers" (quoted in Le Sueur 2001: 46).

63   *RRD*: 145*; *E*: 1012. In 1956, Camus told Jean Daniel that whereas there had been an Algerian state [*Etat*] and there was presently an Algerian homeland or country [*patrie*], "none of this has anything to do with the concept of nation. And in any case, Algeria is today a territory occupied by two peoples . . . each with an equal right to justice and to preserve their homeland [*patrie*]" (Daniel 1973: 258).

64   "Had I discovered the Algerian nation [*nation*] I would be a nationalist and I would not blush as though I had committed a crime . . . I will not die for the Algerian nation [*patrie*] because that nation does not exist. I have not found it. I have examined history, I questioned the living and the dead, I visited cemeteries: no one spoke to me about it" (Ferhat Abbas, "La France c'est moi", *L'Entente*, 23 February 1936, quoted in Julien 2002: 100). Abbas made this claim at a time when he supported assimilation, a policy he was later to reject.

65   According to their 1954 manifesto, the FLN sought "the restoration of the sovereign, democratic and social, Algerian state, within the framework of Islamic principles" (quoted in Thomas 2003: 5, 112). See Said 1990: 147 (where he misquotes Camus); Said 1993: 216–17; Dunn 1998: 353.

66   *CAC6*: 72. "At present the Arabs do not alone make up all of Algeria. . . . The Algerian French are likewise, and in the strongest meaning of the word, natives" (*RRD*: 145; *E*: 1012).

67   *El Moudjahid*, 1 December 1957, quoted in Meynier 2002: 254. See also Camus's letter to Jean Amrouche quoted in the conclusion.

68   *RRD*: 146–7; *E*: 1014. Although Nasser was to disappoint the FLN's hopes for substantial material aid for its cause, it was headquartered for a time in Cairo, from where it launched the insurrection in 1954 (Horne 1977: 79, 85, 94).

69   *RRD*: 147–8; *E*: 1014–15. According to Ronald Aronson, Camus declared "that colonialism was over while insisting that its essential political relations be retained" (2004: 219). In contrast, and I think more accurately, Susan Tarrow, writing about his journalism of the 1930s, suggests that "in a sense what Camus advocated was decolonisation, in that he called for the abolition of a power structure in which Muslims were always at the bottom of the hierarchy. To him, as a man who had never lived anywhere but Algeria, colonialism was a power structure, not a conflict between European and Muslim: the system could be changed without the eviction of inhabitants" (Tarrow 1985: 62).

70   *RRD*: 148; *E*: 1015. In a letter published in *Combat* in 1949, protesting against the death sentence handed down to two Algerian soldiers for desertion, Camus and his friend René Char note the extreme severity of the sentence compared to those handed down to many French collaborators, and observed that "it is extremely rare for Algerian subjects to enjoy the rights of French citizenship, even though they are subject, as we have seen, to the same duties". He concludes by noting the "singular lesson in morality that our courts have just administered to the people of France and Algeria" (*CC*: 309).

71   *RRD*: 150–51; *E*: 1016–17. Horne notes that before the outbreak of violence in 1954, the Lauriol Plan might have proved acceptable to moderate Muslims, but it would always have met with opposition from the *pieds-noirs* (Horne 1977: 235).

72   *RRD*: 149, 150, 153; *E*: 1016, 1018. This was indeed to be Camus's last public statement on Algeria. In private he seems to have been less optimistic: "I believe as you do that it is undoubtedly too late for Algeria. I did not say so in my book because . . . historical randomness must have its chance – and because one does not write to say that everything is screwed up. In that case, one remains silent. I am preparing myself for that" (Camus & Grenier 2003: 187).

73   Ronald Aronson, for example, calls the Lauriol Plan "a masterpiece of bad faith". By endorsing it, says Aronson, "Camus claimed to serve justice as well as his own people, while actually serving neither. It was, of course, impossible to end colonialism *and* leave existing French rights intact, a fact that Camus never faced" (Aronson 2004: 214). Although believing the Lauriol Plan was "doomed to failure by the furious pace of events" in Algeria, Jeffrey Isaac offers a more sympathetic reading of the plan and Camus's endorsement of it (Isaac 1992: 203–4).

74   *RRD*: 141–2; *E*: 999. This last striking image alludes to Camus's remarkable story "The Renegade" (written in 1955). See David Carroll's important reading of this story (Carroll 2007a: 121–9); see also *C3*: 56–7 and Tarrow 1985: 187.

75   Jean Sénac, an enthusiastic supporter of the FLN through the war, remained in Algeria after independence, where he lived in increasing obscurity, shunned by the new state because of his outspoken views and his homosexuality; in 1973 he was murdered in obscure circumstances. Another of Camus's *pied-noir* friends, Jules Roy, who was a fierce critic of the French war in Algeria, felt unwelcome in independent Algeria. As with more than a million other *pieds-noirs*, Roy left Algeria after independence, considering himself *un sans-patrie* (without a homeland).

76   Sartre's preface to Fanon 1967: 19–20. Sartre later notes "A fine sight they are too, the believers in non-violence, saying that they are neither victims nor executioners" (*ibid.*: 21; cf. Sartre 1974c: 252–3).

77   Fanon 1967: 31–2. *RRD*: 117; *E*: 894. According to Albert Memmi, "Like many other defenders of the colonized, [Fanon] had in him a certain dose of revolutionary romanticism. The Colonizer was the complete bastard; the colonized, the integrally good man . . . the day that oppression ceases, the new man has to immediately appear. But, and I say this without any pleasure, what decolonization precisely shows us is that this is not true" (Memmi, "Note on Frantz Fanon and the Notion of Inadequacy", in *Dominated Man: Notes toward a Portrait* (New York: Orion, 1968): 87, quoted in Carroll 2007a: 216n.14).

78   One of the most controversial aspects of the period of decolonization was the treatment of the *Harkis*, Muslim Algerians who had fought with the French against the FLN. Some escaped to France; others remained in Algeria with their families, where as many as 150,000 were massacred (Horne 1977: 533, 538).

79   Yacine 1994: 52. For fragments of correspondence between Camus and Yacine see Todd (1996: 519; 1998: 287) and the preface to Yacine's novel *Nedjma* (1996: 1).

80   See Taleb Ibrahimi 1966, 1973. For an account of Taleb Ibrahimi's criticism of Camus see Le Sueur 2001: 118–21.

81   James Le Sueur, for example, alleges that Camus "separated 'Arabs' loosely into the Kabyles and the 'Muslims' – an inconsistent distinction because the Kabyles are Berber by ethnicity and Muslim by religion. The interaction of these divisions can be found in almost all Camus' writings on Algeria" (Le Sueur 2001: 91). This is quite simply false: we have seen already that Camus notes that in Algeria "there are a million Frenchmen who have been here for a century, millions of Muslims, either Arabs or Berbers, who have been here for centuries, and several rigorous religious communities" (*RRD*: 136; *E*: 994–5). For another version of this post-colonial commonplace see Apter 1997: 506.

82   Taleb Ibrahimi 1973, quoted in Stora 2001: 181. See Benrabah 2004 for a sociolinguistic account of the extent and impact of this policy of Arabization and Islamization.

83   Stora 2001: 181, 174. In 1980 the Algerian government banned a conference in Tizi-Ouzou on the Berber language, prompting a general strike in Kabylie.

84   Zoubir 1994: 742. According to R. W. Johnson, "That blending of peoples and civilisations on the North African littoral was, despite the cruelties and deformations of colonialism, a precious thing and the victory of the FLN destroyed it utterly. The messianic promises of socialism, revolutionary democracy and all the rest were simply false. Women were forced back into the veil; there was corruption, authoritarianism, social regression and, for thirty years, no free elections were held. The present civil war – the aftermath – had already cost at least 60,000 lives" (Johnson 1997: 25).

Conclusion

1   *E*: 1710. For an alternative translation see *SCHC*: 213.

2   *MS*: 35; *E*: 122. He refers to the Marxist "deification of history" in *The Rebel* (*R*: 146; *E*: 554). If Camus perceives the same *démesure* in existentialism, Marxism and, indeed, the actions of the FLN, it is hardly surprising that he would disagree with both Sartre's effort to merge existentialism with Marxism and his enthusiastic support for the FLN.

3   Interview with *Servir*, December 1945 (*E*: 1427; see also *TRN*: 1743). "Reason does not preach, or if it does, it is no longer reason. That is why historical reason is an irrational and romantic form of reason, which sometimes recalls the false logic of the insane and at other times the mystic affirmation of the word" (*R*: 221; *E*: 625). Camus makes reference to "crimes of reason" or "rational crimes" in *The Rebel* (*R*: 103–4; *E*: 511). For a detailed account of Camus's "anti-rationalism" see Henry 1975.

4   Conor Cruise O'Brien, for example, suggests that Camus's novel *La Chute* (*The Fall*), first published in 1956, reveals a confession that "he who had talked so much of justice must now abjure such language, since there is something he prefers to justice . . . if France in Algeria was unjust, then it was justice that had to go, yielding place to irony". The political significance of this transformation is most apparent, for Cruise O'Brien, in "the only public statement of Camus on the subject of the Algerian war that has the ring of complete candour", i.e. his assertion "I believe in justice but I will defend my mother before justice". As we have seen, for Cruise O'Brien this meant only that "the defence of his mother required support for the French army's pacification of Algeria" (Cruise O'Brien 1970: 83, 85, 75).

5   Robin 1986: 186, 188. Taleb Ibrahimi, as Minister for Education in independent Algeria, spoke of "a new Algerian" and "a new Algeria", and the necessity that a new generation of Algerians "learn to think in Arabic" (Taleb Ibrahimi 1973: 98, quoted in Benrabah 2004: 67).

6   A similar view of the FLN was expressed by Isaiah Berlin, who, in November 1960, was asked to add his name to a manifesto supporting their struggle. Although Berlin accepted the right of Algerians to self-determination and had condemned the brutality of the French in dealing with the insurrection, he refused to endorse the FLN's use of terrorism against civilian targets, writing to Stephen Spender: "I do not see how one can sign a document supporting a pro-FLN manifesto, if, in fact, one thinks that the consequences of their success, if carried out by methods which they are employing, would be worse than even the horrible present situation. I could not have signed the manifesto for Lenin or Béla Kun or the Jewish terrorists either" (quoted in Ignatieff 1998: 234; 330n.43).

7   Camus noted in *Soir Républicain* (6 November 1939): "Nations . . . are like individuals. It is in the depths of suffering that they forge their will for power" (quoted in Parker 1965: 49).

8   *C3*: 237. In January 1958 Amrouche published a full-page article in *Le Monde*, in which he condemned colonial France as "racist, greedy, oppressive, inhuman, and destructive", and saw declaring independence as the only solution to the Algerian question (Todd 1998: 385; Todd 1996: 710–11). Camus's letter, dated only "19 November", was probably written in response to this and other articles.

9   *Révolution prolétarienne*, October 1957, reprinted in *Le Monde Libertaire*, No. 33, December 1957, reprinted in Camus 2002: 177–8; *R*: 22; *E*: 431.

10 David Ohana suggests that other "exemplars" of Mediterranean humanism are the Tunisian-French Jewish Albert Memmi, the French-Moroccan Tahar Ben-Jelloun, the Spanish Jorge Semprún, the Egyptian Najib Mahfouz and the Egyptian Jewish Edmond Jabès (Ohana 2003: 59).

BIBLIOGRAPHY

Frequently cited texts are identified using abbreviations (see p. xi).

Works by Camus

Works in French

1952. "Lettre au directeur des 'Temps Modernes'". *Les Temps modernes* **82** (August): 317–33.

1962. *Théâtre, Récits, Nouvelles*, J. Grenier (pref.); R. Quilliot (ed.). Paris: Gallimard.

1962. *Carnets I, mai 1935–février 1942*. Paris: Gallimard.

1964. *Carnets II, janvier 1942–mars 1951*. Paris: Gallimard.

1965. *Essais*, R. Quilliot (intro.); R. Quilliot & L. Faucon (eds). Paris: Gallimard.

1971. *Cahiers Albert Camus I: La Mort heureuse*. Paris: Gallimard.

1973. *Cahiers Albert Camus II: Le Premier Camus suivi d'Écrits de Jeunesse d'Albert Camus*. Paris: Gallimard.

1978. *Cahiers Albert Camus III: Fragments d'un Combat 1938–1940: Alger Républicain* [2 volumes]. Paris: Gallimard.

1978. *Journaux de voyage*. Paris: Gallimard.

1984. *Cahiers Albert Camus IV: Caligula – version de 1941 suivi de La Poétique du premier Caligula par A. James Arnold*. Paris: Gallimard.

1987. *Cahiers Albert Camus VI: Albert Camus – éditorialiste à* L'Express, *mai 1955–February 1956*. Paris: Gallimard.

1989. *Carnets III, mars 1951–décembre 1959*. Paris: Gallimard.

1994. *Cahiers Albert Camus VII: Le Premier homme*. Paris: Gallimard.

2002a. *Cahiers Albert Camus VIII: Camus à Combat: éditoriaux et articles d'Albert Camus 1944–1947*, J. Lévi-Valensi (ed.). Paris: Gallimard.

2002b. *Réflexions sur le terrorisme*, J. Lévi-Valensi *et al.* (eds). Paris: Nicholas Philippe.

2006. *Œuvres Complètes: Tome 1, 1931–1944*, J. Lévi-Valensi *et al.* (eds). Paris: Gallimard/Pléiade.
2006. *Œuvres Complètes: Tome 2, 1944–1948*, J. Lévi-Valensi *et al.* (eds). Paris: Gallimard/Pléiade.

Camus, A. & J. Grenier 1981. *Correspondance 1932–1960*, M. Dobrenn (ed.). Paris: Gallimard.
Camus, A. & P. Pia 2000. *Correspondance 1939–1947*. Y. M. Ajchenbaum (ed.). Paris: Fayard/ Gallimard.
Camus, A. & A. Koestler 2002. *Réflexions sur la peine capitale*. Paris: Gallimard/Folio [contains previously unpublished correspondence from Camus concerning capital punishment].
Camus, A. & R. Char 2007. *Correspondance 1946–1959*, F. Planeille (ed.). Paris: Gallimard.

Works in English

1948a. "We too Are Murderers", L. Abel (trans.). *Art and Action: Twice a Year 1938–1948*, 74–5.
1948b. "Chamfort", L. LeSage (trans.). *Sewanee Review* **56**(1): 12–23.
1949. "The Artist as a Witness of Freedom", B. Frechtman (trans.). *Commentary* **8**(6): 534–8.
1954. "The Artist in Prison", A. White (trans.). *Encounter* **2**(3): 26–9.
1956. *The Rebel: An Essay on Man in Revolt*, rev. edn, A. Bower (trans.); H. Read (fwd). New York: Knopf.
1957a. "Parties and Truth", *Encounter* **8**(4): 3–5.
1957b. "M. Camus Replies . . .", *Encounter* **8**(6): 68.
1958. *Caligula & Three Other Plays*, S. Gilbert (trans.). New York: Knopf.
1960. *Resistance, Rebellion, and Death*, J. O'Brien (trans.). New York: Knopf.
1960. *The Plague*, S. Gilbert (trans.). Harmondsworth: Penguin. [Original publication 1948]
1962. *Exile & the Kingdom*, J. O'Brien (trans.). Harmondsworth: Penguin.
1963. *The Fall*, J. O'Brien (trans.). Harmondsworth: Penguin.
1963. *Notebooks 1935–1942*, P. Thody (trans.). New York: Knopf.
1964. "Neither Victims nor Executioners", D. Macdonald (trans.). In *Seeds of Liberation*, P. Goodman (ed.), 24–43. New York: George Braziller.
1965. *Notebooks 1942–1951*, J. O'Brien (trans.). New York: Knopf.
1968. *Lyrical & Critical Essays*, E. C. Kennedy (trans.); P. Thody (ed.). New York: Knopf.
1973. *A Happy Death*, R. Howard (trans.). Harmondsworth: Penguin.
1975. *The Myth of Sisyphus*, J. O'Brien (trans.). Harmondsworth: Penguin.
1979. *Selected Essays & Notebooks*, P. Thody (trans., ed.). Harmondsworth: Penguin.
1980. *Youthful Writings*, E. C. Kennedy (trans.). Harmondsworth: Penguin.
1983. *The Outsider*, J. Laredo (trans.). Harmondsworth: Penguin.
1984. *Caligula & Other Plays*, S. Gilbert *et al.* (trans.). Harmondsworth: Penguin.
1992. "Métaphysique chrétienne et néoplatonisme." In J. McBride (ed.) *Albert Camus: Philosopher and Littérateur*, 93–171. New York: St Martin's Press. [An English translation of Camus's DES thesis, written in 1935–6.]
1996. *The First Man*, D. Hapgood (trans.). Harmondsworth: Penguin.
2001. "Democracy Is an Exercise in Modesty", A. van den Hoven (trans.). *Sartre Studies International*, **7**(2): 12–14.
2001. *The Plague*, R. Buss (trans.). London: Penguin Press.
2004. "A Letter to the Editor of *Les Temps modernes*". In *Sartre and Camus: A Historic Confrontation*, D. Sprintzen & A. van den Hoven (eds & trans.), 107–29. New York: Humanity.
2006. *Camus at 'Combat': Writing 1944–1947*, A. Goldhammer (trans.); J. Lévi-Valensi (ed.); D. Carroll (fwd). Princeton, NJ: Princeton University Press.

Camus, A. & J. Grenier 2003. *Correspondence 1932–1960*, J. Rigaud (trans.); M. Dobrenn (ed.). Lincoln, NE: Nebraska University Press.

Other works

Abbas, F. 1980. *Autopsie d'une guerre: l'aurore*. Paris: Garnier.

Achour, C. "Camus and Algerian Writers", A. King & F. Majdoub (trans.). In *Camus's* L'Etranger: *Fifty Years On*, A. King (ed.), 89–100. New York: St Martin's Press.

Albérès, R. M. *et al.* 1964. *Camus*. Paris: Hachette.

Albert, A. 1962. "Study in Brown (II): de la mentalié [*sic*] coloniale", *Les Temps modernes* (August): 332–46.

Alleg, H. 1958. *La Question*. Paris: Minuit.

Amiot, A.-M. & J.-F. Mattéi (eds) 1997. *Albert Camus et la philosophie*. Paris: PUF.

Anderson, K. 1995. *Lenin, Hegel and Western Marxism: A Critical Study*. Urbana, IL: University of Illinois Press.

Anderson, T. 1993. *Sartre's Two Ethics*. Chicago, IL: Open Court.

Apter, E. 1997. "Out of Character: Camus's French Algerian Subjects". *Modern Language Notes* **112**: 499–516.

Arban, D. 1945. "Entretien avec Albert Camus". *Opera* 17 November: 2.

Archambault, P. 1972. *Camus' Hellenic Sources*. Chapel Hill, NC: University of North Carolina Press.

Arendt, H. 2002 [1946]. "What Is Existenz Philosophy?" In *The Phenomenology Reader*, D. Moran & T. Mooney (eds), 345–61. London: Routledge.

Arendt, H. 1947. "La Philosophie de L'Existence" and "L'Existentialisme français vu de New-York". *Deucalion* **2**: 217–52.

Arendt, H. 1961. *Between Past and Future: Six Exercises in Political Thought*. New York: Viking.

Arendt, H. 1970. *On Violence*. New York: Harcourt, Brace & World.

Arendt, H. & K. Jaspers 1992. *Correspondence 1926–1969*, R. & R. Kimber (trans.); L. Kohler & H. Saner (eds). San Diego, CA: Harcourt, Brace.

Aron, R. 1955. *L'Opium des Intellectuels*. Paris: Calmann-Lévy.

Aron, R. 1975. *History and the Dialectic of Violence: An Analysis of Sartre's* Critique de la raison dialectique. Oxford: Blackwell.

Aron, R. 1983. *Mémoires*. Paris: Julliard.

Aron, R. 1994. *In Defense of Political Reason*, D. J. Mahoney (ed.). Lanham, MD: Rowman & Littlefield.

Aronson, R. 1980. *Jean-Paul Sartre – Philosophy in the World*. London: Verso.

Aronson, R. 1987. *Sartre's Second Critique*. Chicago, IL: University of Chicago Press.

Aronson, R. 2001. "Sartre, Camus and the *Caliban* articles". *Sartre Studies International* 7(2): 1–7.

Aronson, R. 2002. "Camus vs Sartre". *Times Literary Supplement* 27 September: 14–15.

Aronson, R. *et al.* 2003. "Sartre and Terror: The New Orleans Session – March 2002". *Sartre Studies International* **9**(2): 3–25.

Aronson, R. 2004. *Camus & Sartre: The Story of a Friendship and the Quarrel that Ended It*. Chicago, IL: University of Chicago Press.

Aronson, R. 2005. "Camus versus Sartre: The Unresolved Conflict". *Sartre Studies International* **11**(1/2): 302–10.

Aronson, R. 2006. "Camus and Sartre on Violence: The Unresolved Conflict". *Journal of Romance Studies* **6**(1/2): 67–77.

Aronson, R. & A. van den Hoven (eds) 1991. *Sartre Alive*. Detroit, MI: Wayne State University Press.

Aubery, D. 1968. "Albert Camus et la classe ouvrière". *French Review* **32**(1): 14–21.

Ayer, A. J. 1945. "Jean-Paul Sartre (Novelist-Philosophers V)". *Horizon* **12**: 12–26, 101–10.

Ayer, A. J. 1946. "Albert Camus (Novelist-Philosophers VIII)". *Horizon* **13**: 155–68.

Ayer, A. J. 1950. "Jean-Paul Sartre's Doctrine of Commitment". *Listener* 30 November: 633–4.

Ayer, A. J. 1955. "Philosophy at Absolute Zero: An Enquiry into the Meaning of Nihilism". *Encounter* **5**(4): 24–33.

Ayer, A. J. 1977. *Part of My Life*. London: Collins.

Bair, D. 1990. *Simone de Beauvoir: A Biography*. London: Cape.

Barnes, H. 1961. *The Literature of Possibility: A Study of Humanistic Existentialism*. London: Tavistock.

Barnes, H. 1997. *The Story I Tell Myself: A Venture in Existentialist Autobiography*. Chicago, IL: University of Chicago Press.

Baudelaire, C. 1976. *Œuvres complètes*, vol. II, C. Pichois (ed.). Paris: Gallimard/Pléiade.

Baudelaire, C. 2006. *The Flowers of Evil*, K. Waldrop (trans.). Middletown, CT: Wesleyan University Press.

Beckett, S. 1952. *En Attendant Godot*. Paris: Minuit.

Beckett, S. 1984 [1949]. "Three Dialogues". In *Disjecta – Miscellaneous Writings and Dramatic Fragments*, R. Cohen (ed.), 138–45. New York: Grove.

Belinsky, V. G. 1948. *Selected Philosophical Works*. Moscow: Foreign Languages Publishing House.

Bell, L. A. 1993. *Rethinking Ethics in the Midst of Violence: A Feminist Approach to Freedom*. Lanham, MD: Rowman & Littlefield.

Benrabah, M. 2004. "Language and Politics in Algeria". *Nationalism and Ethnic Politics* **10**: 59–78.

Berdyaev, N. 1948. *The Origins of Russian Communism*. London: Geoffrey Bles.

Berlin, I. 1998. *The Proper Study of Mankind: An Anthology of Essays*. London: Pimlico.

Berman, P. 2003. *Terror and Liberalism*. New York: Norton.

Berne, M. (ed.) 2005. *Sartre*. Paris: BNF/Gallimard.

Berns, W. 1979. *For Capital Punishment: Crime and the Morality of the Death Penalty*. New York: Basic Books.

Bernstein, R. J. 2003. "Rorty's Inspirational Liberalism". In *Richard Rorty*, C. Guignon & D. R. Hiley (eds), 124–38. Cambridge: Cambridge University Press.

Bieber, K. 1954. *L'Allemagne vue par les écrivains de la Résistance française*, A. Camus (pref.). Geneve: Droz.

Bieber, K. 1955. "The Translator – Friend or Foe?" *The French Review* **28**(6): 493–7.

Bieber, K. 1956. "*Engagement* as a Professional Risk". *Yale French Studies* **16**: 29–39.

Bieber, K. 2001. "Traduttore, Traditore: la réception problématique de *L'Homme révolté* aux Etats-unis". In *Albert Camus 19*, R. Gay-Crosier (ed.), 143–8. Paris: Lettres modernes.

Birchall, I. 1990. "The Labourism of Sisyphus: Albert Camus and Revolutionary Syndicalism". *Journal of European Studies* **20**: 135–65.

Birchall, I. 1994. "Camus contre Sartre: quarante ans plus tard". In *Albert Camus: Les Extrêmes et l'Equilibre: Actes du Colloque de Keele, 25–27 mars 1993*, D. H. Walker (ed.), 75–87. Amsterdam: Rodopi.

Birchall, I. 1999. "Neither Washington nor Moscow? The Rise and Fall of the Rassemblement Démocratique Révolutionnaire". *Journal of European Studies* **29**: 365–404.

Birchall, I. 2004. *Sartre against Stalinism*. New York: Berghahn.

Blanchot, M. *et al.* 1967. *Hommage à Albert Camus*. Paris: Gallimard.

Bocca, G. 1968. *The Secret Army*. Englewood Cliffs, NJ: Prentice-Hall.

Boudraa, N. 2006. "Was Edward Said Right in Depicting Albert Camus as an Imperialist Writer?" In *Paradoxical Citizenship: Edward Said*, Silvia Nagy-Zekmi (ed.), 187–200. Lanham, MD: Lexington.

Boulouque, S. 2001. "Anarchisme et syndicalisme révolutionnaire aux origines de la révolte camusienne". In *Albert Camus: la révolte: Actes du 3ème Colloque International de Poitiers [mai 1999]*, 219–50. Poitiers: Pont-Neuf.

Bowman, E. & R. Stone 1986. "Dialectical Ethics: A First Look at Sartre's Unpublished 1964 Rome Lecture Notes". *Social Text* **13/14**: 195–215.

Bowman, E. & R. Stone 1991. "Sartre's *Morality and History*: A First Look at the Notes for the Unpublished 1965 Cornell lectures". In *Sartre Alive*, R. Aronson & A. van den Hoven (eds), 53–82. Detroit, MI: Wayne State University Press.

Bowman, E. & R. Stone 2004. "The End as Present in the Means in Sartre's *Morality and History*: Birth and Reinventions of an Existential Moral Standard". *Sartre Studies International* **10**(2): 1–27.

Braun, L. 1974. *Witness of Decline: Albert Camus, Moralist of the Absurd.* Madison, NJ: Fairleigh Dickinson University Press.

Brée, G. 1951. "Albert Camus and *The Plague*". *Yale French Studies* **8**: 93–100.

Brée, G. 1961. *Camus*, rev. edn. Piscataway, NJ: Rutgers University Press.

Brée, G. (ed.) 1962. *Camus: A Collection of Critical Essays.* Englewood Cliffs, NJ: Prentice-Hall.

Brée, G. 1972. *Camus and Sartre: Crisis and Commitment.* New York: Delta.

Brisville, J. C. 1970. *Camus*, rev. edn. Paris: Gallimard.

Brochier, J.-J. 2001 [1970]. *Albert Camus, philosophe pour classes terminales.* Paris: La Différence.

Bronner, S. 1999. *Camus – Portrait of a Moralist.* Minneapolis, MN: University of Minnesota Press.

Broyelle, C. & J. Broyelle 1982. *Les illusions retrouvées: Sartre a toujours raison contre Camus.* Paris: Grasset.

Bruckberger, Père R. L. 1981. *Tu Finiras Sur L'Echafaud suivi de La Bachaga – Mémoires.* Paris: Flammarion.

Bruckberger, Père R. L. 1989. *A l'Heure où les Ombres s'Allongent – mémoires.* Paris: Albin Michel.

Buber, M. 1937. *I and Thou*, R. G. Smith (trans.). Edinburgh: T. & T. Clarke.

Buber, M. 1949. *Paths in Utopia*, R. F. C. Hull (trans.). London: Routledge & Kegan Paul.

Burnham, J. 1948. "The Extreme and the Plausible", *Partisan Review* **15**(9): 1020–24.

Burnier, M.-A. 1968. *Choice of Action: The French Existentialists on the Political Front Line*, B. Murchland (trans.). New York: Random House.

Burnier, M-A. 1988 [1973]. "On Maoism: An Interview with Jean-Paul Sartre". In *Critical Essays on Jean-Paul Sartre*, R. Wilcocks (ed.), 34–45. Boston, MA: G. K. Hall.

Busch, T. 1999. "Albert Camus: Absurdity, Solidarity, and Difference". In *Circulating Being: From Embodiment to Incorporation: Essays on Late Existentialism*, 1–27. New York: Fordham University Press.

Caracciolo, P. 1957. "M. Camus and Algeria". *Encounter* **8**(6): 68.

Carroll, D. 1997. "Camus's Algeria: Birthrights, Colonial Injustice, and the Fiction of a French-Algerian People". *Modern Language Notes* **112**: 517–49.

Carroll, D. 2001. "The Colonial City and the Question of Borders: Albert Camus' Allegory of Oran". *L'Esprit Créateur* **41**(3): 88–104.

Carroll, D. 2007a. *Albert Camus, the Algerian: Colonialism, Terrorism, Justice.* New York: Columbia University Press.

Carroll, D. 2007b. "Rethinking the Absurd: *Le Mythe de Sisyphe*". In *The Cambridge Companion to Camus*, E. Hughes (ed.), 53–66. Cambridge: Cambridge University Press.

Castoriadis, C. 1977a. "The Diversionists". *Telos* **33**: 102–6.

Castoriadis, C. 1977b. "Reply to André Gorz". *Telos* **33**: 108–9.

Castoriadis, C. 1988. "Sartre, Stalinism and the Workers". In *Political and Social Writings I*, 207–41. Minneapolis, MN: University of Minnesota Press.

Caute, D. 1964. *Communism and the French Intellectuals 1914–1960.* London: Deutsch.

Caute, D. 1970. *Fanon.* London: Fontana.

Caute, D. 1973. *The Fellow-Travellers – A Postscript to the Enlightenment.* London: Weidenfeld & Nicolson.

Caute, D. 2003. "Dirty Hands: The Political Theatre of Sartre and Camus". In *The Dancer Defects: The Struggle for Supremacy during the Cold War*, 306–36. Oxford: Oxford University Press.

Champigny, R. 1959. *Sur Un Héros Païen.* Paris: Gallimard.

Champigny, R. 1969. *A Pagan Hero – An Interpretation of Meursault in Camus' The Stranger*, R. Portis (trans.). Philadelphia, PA: University of Pennsylvania Press.

Champigny, R. 1972. *Humanism and Human Racism: A Critical Study of Essays by Sartre and Camus.* The Hague: Mouton.

Chaulet-Achour, C. 1999. *Albert Camus, Alger – L'Etranger et Autres Récits.* Paris: Séguier.

Chérifi, Y. 2007. " 'Misère de la Kabylie': les inoubliables reportages". *La Dépêche de Kabylie*, 27 January http://www.depechedekabylie.com/qsearch.php.

Chesson, J. P. 1990. "Colonialism and Violence: Camus and Sartre on the Algerian War". *The Maghreb Review* **15**(1/2): 16–30.

Chiaromonte, N. 1948. "Albert Camus and Moderation". *Partisan Review* **15**: 1142–5.

Chiaromonte, N. 1962. "Sartre versus Camus: A Political Quarrel". In *Camus: A Collection of Critical Essays*, G. Brée (ed.), 31–7. Englewood Cliffs, NJ: Prentice-Hall.

Christensen, P. G. 1993. "Camus and Savinkov: Examining the Problems of Terrorism". *Scottish Slavonic Review* **21**: 33–51.

Clayton, A. J. 1972. "Note sur Augustin et Camus". In *Albert Camus 5*, A. Abbou & J. Lévi-Valensi (eds), 267–70. Paris: Lettres modernes.

Coady, C. A. J. 1985. "The Morality of Terrorism". *Philosophy* **60**: 47–69.

Cohen, G. A. 1978. *Karl Marx's Theory of History: A Defence*. Oxford: Clarendon Press.

Cohen-Solal, A. 1986. "Camus, Sartre et la guerre d'Algérie". In *Camus et la Politique: Actes du Colloque de Nanterre 5–7 June 1985*, J. Guérin (ed.), 177–84. Paris: L'Harmattan.

Cohen-Solal, A. 1987. *Sartre: A Life*. New York: Pantheon.

Cohen-Solal, A. 1998. "Camus, Sartre and the Algerian War". *Journal of European Studies* **28**(1/2): 43–50.

Collot, C. & J.-R. Henry (eds) 1978. *Le movement national algérien: texts 1912–1954*. Paris: L'Harmattan.

Comte-Sponville, A. *et al.* 2001. *Albert Camus – de l'absurde à l'amour*. Paris: La Renaissance du Livre. [Contains previously unpublished letters from Camus to René Leynaud, his widow and his daughter.]

Connelly, M. 2002. *A Diplomatic Revolution: Algeria's Fight for Independence and the Origins of the Post-Cold War Era*. Oxford: Oxford University Press.

Cooper, B. 1979. *Merleau-Ponty and Marxism: From Terror to Reform*. Toronto: University of Toronto Press.

Cooper, D. E. 1990. *Existentialism: A Reconstruction*. Oxford: Blackwell.

Courrière, Y. 1969. *La Guerre d'Algérie II: le temps des léopards*. Paris: Fayard. [Originally published as "Camus devant la Guerre d'Algérie". *Le Figaro littéraire* 2–8 June 1969: 8–11; "Albert Camus devant la Guerre d'Algérie II. 1956: L'échec de la trêve civile". *Le Figaro littéraire* 9–15 June 1969: 10–13.]

Cranston, M. 1962. *Sartre*. Edinburgh: Oliver & Boyd.

Cranston, M. 1969. "Herbert Marcuse". *Encounter* **32**: 38–50.

Cranston, M. (ed.) 1971. *The New Left: Six Critical Essays on Che Guevara, Jean-Paul Sartre, Herbert Marcuse, Frantz Fanon, Black Power, R. D. Laing*. New York: Library Press.

Crenshaw Hutchinson, M. 1978. *Revolutionary Terrorism: The FLN in Algeria, 1954–1962*. Stanford, CA: Hoover Institution Press.

Crowley, M. 2007. "Camus and Social Justice". In *The Cambridge Companion to Camus*, E. Hughes (ed.), 93–105. Cambridge: Cambridge University Press.

Cruickshank, J. 1960 [1959]. *Albert Camus and the Literature of Revolt*. Oxford: Oxford University Press.

[Cruise O'Brien, C.] O'Donnell, D. 1946. "Dada Comes of Age". *Irish Times* 7 September.

Cruise O'Brien, C. 1955. "France as the Conscience of Europe", *Listener* 20 January, 105–6.

Cruise O'Brien, C. 1960. "Albert Camus: A Rejoinder". *Spectator* 26 February: 293–4.

Cruise O'Brien, C. 1970. *Camus*. Glasgow: Fontana.

Cruise O'Brien, C. 1971. "Violence in Ireland: Another Algeria?" *New York Review of Books* 23 September: 17–19.

Cruise O'Brien, C. 1976. "Monsieur Camus Changes His Climate". In *Writers and Politics: Essays and Criticism*, 96–103. Harmondsworth: Penguin.

Cruise O'Brien, C. 1982. "The Angel of the Absurd". *Times Literary Supplement* 7 May: 505.

Cruise O'Brien, C. 1988 [1986]. "A Neo-Conservative Ideologue: Norman Podhoretz". In *Passion and Cunning: Essays on Nationalism, Terrorism & Revolution*, 247–55. New York: Simon and Schuster.

Cruise O'Brien, C. 1994. "Foreword". In *The Deaths of Louis XVI Regicide and the French Political Imagination*, S. Dunn (ed.), ix–xi. Princeton, NJ: Princeton University Press.

Cruise O'Brien, C. 1995. "The Fall". *The New Republic* 16 October: 42–7.

Cruise O'Brien, C. *et al.* 1986. "The Intellectual in the Post-Colonial World – Response and Discussion". *Salmagundi* **70/71**: 65–81.

Daniel, J. 1960. "Une patrie algérienne, deux peuples . . .". *Études Méditerranéennes* **7**: 19–24.

Daniel, J. 1973. "Malraux, Sartre, Camus et la Violence (entretiens)". In *Le temps qui reste: essai d'autobiographie professionnelle*, 243–59. Paris: Stock.

Daniel, J. 1990. "La visite à Jean Paul Sartre". *Les Temps modernes* October/December: 1192–200.

Daniel, J. 2006. *Avec Camus: comment résister à l'air du temps*. Paris: Gallimard.

Davies, H. 1987. *Sartre and "Les Temps Modernes"*. Cambridge: Cambridge University Press.

Davis, C. 2007. "Violence and Ethics in Camus". In *The Cambridge Companion to Camus*, E. Hughes (ed.), 106–17. Cambridge: Cambridge University Press.

de Bazin, J. 1969. *Index du Vocabulaire de* L'Etranger *d'Albert Camus*. Paris: Nizet.

de Beauvoir, S. 1948a. *L'Existentialisme et la sagesse des nations*. Paris: Nagel.

de Beauvoir, S. 1948b. *The Ethics of Ambiguity*, B. Frechtman (trans.). New York: Citadel.

de Beauvoir, S. 1951. "Faut-it brûler Sade? [I] ", *Les Temps modernes* **74**: 1002–33.

de Beauvoir, S. 1952. "Faut-it brûler Sade? [II]". *Les Temps modernes* **75**: 1197–230.

de Beauvoir, S. 1954. *Les Mandarins*. Paris: Gallimard.

de Beauvoir, S. 1962. "Must We Burn Sade?" A. Michelson (trans.). In *The Marquis de Sade*, P. Dinage (ed.), 9–82. London: Calder.

de Beauvoir, S. 1965. *The Prime of Life*, P. Green (trans.). Harmondsworth: Penguin.

de Beauvoir, S. 1968. *Force of Circumstance*, R. Howard (trans.). Harmondsworth: Penguin.

de Beauvoir, S. 1984. *Adieux: A Farewell to Sartre*, P. O'Brien (trans.). London: Deutsch & Weidenfeld and Nicolson.

de Beauvoir, S. 2004. *Philosophical Writings*, M. A. Simons *et al.* (eds). Urbana, IL: University of Illinois Press.

de Boisdeffre, P. 1954. *Des Vivants et des morts . . .* Paris: Editions Universitaires.

de Chamfort, N. 1970. *Maximes et pensées/Caractères et anecdotes*, A. Camus (pref.); G. Renaux (ed.). Paris: Livre de Poche.

de Sade, M. 1991. *Justine, Philosophy in the Bedroom and Other Writings*. London: Arrow.

Debout, S. 1998. "Sartre et Camus face à Hiroshima". *Esprit* January: 151–8.

Deneen, P. J. 1999. "The Politics of Hope and Optimism: Rorty, Havel, and the Democratic Faith of John Dewey". *Social Research* Summer: 577–609.

Deneen, P. J. 2004. "Christopher Lasch and the Limits of Hope". *First Things* December: 26–30.

Derogy, J. 1990. *Resistance & Revenge – The Armenian Assassination of the Turkish Leaders Responsible for the 1915 Massacres and Deportations*, pref. G. Chaliand; A. M. Berrett (trans.). Piscataway, NJ: Transaction.

Devoyod, P. 1955. *Les Délinquants*. Reims: Editions Matot-Braine.

Dine, P. 1994. *Images of the Algerian War: French Fiction and Film 1954–1992*. Oxford: Clarendon Press.

Djebar, A. 2000. *Algerian White: A Narrative*, D. Kelley & M. de Jager (trans.). New York: Seven Stories Press.

Djemaï, A. 1995. *Camus à Oran: récit*. Paris: Michalon.

Dobson, A. 1993. *Jean-Paul Sartre and the Politics of Reason*. Cambridge: Cambridge University Press.

Domenach, J.-M. 1953. "Camus–Sartre Debate: Rebellion vs. Revolution". *The Nation* 7 March: 202–3.

Doubrovsky, S. 1962. "The Ethics of Albert Camus". In *Camus: A Collection of Critical Essays*, G. Brée (ed.), 71–84. Englewood Cliffs, NJ: Prentice-Hall.

Drake, D. 1999. "Sartre, Camus and the Algerian War". *Sartre Studies International* **5**(1): 16–32.

Drake, D. 2002. *Intellectuals and Politics in Post-war France*. Basingstoke: Palgrave Macmillan.

Druon, M. 1957. "Le respect qu'on doit à l'esprit". *La Nef* December: 94.

Duff, R. A. & S. E. Marshall 1982. "Camus and Rebellion: From Solipsism to Morality". *Philosophical Investigations* **5**: 116–34.

Dunn, S. 1989. "Revolution from Burke to Camus". *Salmagundi* **84**: 214–29.

Dunn, S. 1994. "Camus and Louis XVI: A Modern Elegy for the Martyred King". In *The Deaths of Louis XVI: Regicide and the French Political Imagination*, 140–64. Princeton, NJ: Princeton University Press.

Dunn, S. 1998. "Albert Camus and the Dubious Politics of Mercy". In *Ideas Matter: Essays in Honour of Conor Cruise O'Brien*, R. English *et al.* (eds), 345–56. Dublin: Poolbeg.

Dunn, S. 1999. "Review of *Albert Camus: A Life* by Olivier Todd". *America* 27 February.

Dunwoodie, P. 1993. "Albert Camus and the Anarchist Alternative". *Australian Journal of French Studies* 30(1): 84–104.

Dunwoodie, P. 1998. *Writing French Algeria*. Oxford: Clarendon Press.

Duvall, W. 2005. "Albert Camus against History". *The European Legacy* 10(2): 139–47.

Eckermann, J. 1883. *Conversations of Goethe with Eckermann and Soret*, rev. edn, J. Oxenford (trans.). London: George Bell.

Elshtain, J. B. 1999. "Limits and Hope: Christopher Lasch and Political Theory". *Social Research* Summer: 531–43.

Elshtain, J. B. 2003. "Don't Be Cruel: Reflections on Rortyian Liberalism". In *Richard Rorty*, C. Guignon & D. R. Hiley (eds), 139–57. Cambridge: Cambridge University Press.

Etiemble 1947. "Peste, ou Péché". *Les Temps modernes* 3(26): 1911–20.

Etiemble 1948. "Chronique littéraire: un travail de Sisyphe". *Les Temps modernes* 3(28): 1911–20.

Evans, M. 1997. *The Memory of Resistance: French Opposition to the Algerian War (1954–1962)*. Oxford: Berg.

Eveno, P. & J. Planchais (eds) 1990. *La Guerre d'Algérie: dossier et témoignages*. Paris: La Découverte/Le Monde.

Fanon, F. 1967. *The Wretched of the Earth*, J.-P. Sartre (intro.); C. Farrington (trans.). Harmondsworth: Penguin.

Fanon, F. 1970 [1965]. *A Dying Colonialism*, H. Chevalier (trans.). Harmondsworth: Penguin.

Fauré, C. 2000. "Albert Camus, Nicolas Lazarévitch et le populisme russe". *Communisme* 61: 111–18.

Femia, J. 1993. *Marxism and Democracy*. Oxford: Clarendon Press.

Feraoun, M. 2000. *Journal 1955–1962: Reflections on the French-Algerian War*, M. E. Wolf & C. Fouillade (trans.); J. D. le Sueur (ed.). Lincoln, NE: University of Nebraska Press.

Ferhi, Y. 2004. "Doulce France". *El Watan* 25 November: http://www.elwatan.com/spip.php?page=article&id_article=8551.

Feuillade, L. & N. Lazarévitch (eds) 1950. *Tu peux tuer cet homme . . . Scènes de la vie révolutionnaire russe*. Paris: Gallimard.

Foley, J. 2007. "A Postcolonial Fiction: Conor Cruise O'Brien's *Camus*". *Irish Review* 36/37: 1–13.

Forsdick, C. 2007. "Camus and Sartre: The Great Quarrel". In *The Cambridge Companion to Camus*, E. Hughes (ed.), 118–30. Cambridge: Cambridge University Press.

Fouchet, M-P. 1968. *Un jour, je m'en souviens . . . Mémoire parlée*. Paris: Mercure de France.

Foxlee, N. 2006. "Mediterranean Humanism or Colonialism with a Human Face? Contextualising Albert Camus' 'The New Mediterranean Culture'". *Mediterranean Historical Review* 21(1): 77–97.

Frank, B. 1957. "Une bonne oeuvre". *La Nef* November: 61–3.

Freeman, E. 1971. *The Theatre of Albert Camus: A Critical Study*. London: Methuen.

Friedman, M. 1967. *To Deny Our Nothingness*. New York: Delacorte.

Fukuyama, F. 1992. *The End of History and the Last Man*. Harmondsworth: Penguin.

Furet, F & M. Ozouf (eds) 1989. *A Critical Dictionary of the French Revolution*, A. Goldhammer (trans.). Cambridge, MA: Harvard University Press.

Gabhart, M. 1994. "Mitigated Scepticism and the Absurd". *Philosophical Investigations* 17(1): 67–83.

Gallimard, R. 1999. "Sartre versus Camus". *Newsweek* (Atlantic Edition) 19 July: 55.

Garaudy, R. 1948. *Literature of the Graveyard: Jean Paul Sartre, François Mauriac, André Malraux, Arthur Koestler*, J. M. Bernstein (trans.). New York: International Publishers.

Garfitt, J. T. S. 1983. *The Work and Thought of Jean Grenier (1898–1971)*. London: Modern Humanities Research Association.

Gaudeaux, J.-F. 2006. "Sartre: The Violence of History". *Sartre Studies International* 12(1): 50–58.

Gay-Crosier, R. (ed.) 1980. *Albert Camus 1980*. Gainesville, FL: University of Florida Press.

Gay-Crosier, R. 1985. "La Révolte en Question". In *Albert Camus 12*, R. Gay-Crosier (ed.), 3–4. Paris: Lettres modernes.

Gay-Crosier, R. & J. Lévi-Valensi (eds) 1985. *Cahiers Albert Camus V: Albert Camus: oeuvre fermée, oeuvre ouverte? Actes du colloque du Centre Culturel International de Cerisy-la-Salle*. Paris: Gallimard.

Gearty, C. (ed.) 1996. *Terrorism*. Aldershot: Dartmouth.

Geifman, A. 1993. *Thou Shalt Kill – Revolutionary Terrorism in Russia 1894–1917*. Princeton, NJ: Princeton University Press.

Gellner, E. 1993. "The Mightier Pen: Edward Said and the Double Standards of Inside-Out Colonialism". *Times Literary Supplement* 19 February: 3–4 [see also related correspondence: 26 February, 5 March, 19 March, 2 April, 9 April, 4 June, 11 June 1993].

Gerassi, J. 1971. "Sartre Accuses Intellectuals of Bad Faith". *New York Times Magazine* 17 October: 38–9, 116, 118–19.

Gerassi, J. (ed.) 1973. *Revolutionary Priest: The Complete Writings and Messages of Camilo Torres*. Harmondsworth: Penguin.

Gerassi, J. 1989. *Jean-Paul Sartre: Hated Conscience of his Century. Volume 1: Protestant or Protester?* Chicago, IL: University of Chicago Press.

Gide, A. 1937a. *Back From the USSR*. London: Secker & Warburg.

Gide, A. 1937b. *Afterthoughts on the USSR*. London: Secker & Warburg.

Ginestier, P. 1964. *Pour connaître la pensée de Camus*. Paris: Bordas.

Girard, R. 2001 [1964]. "Camus's Stranger Retried". In *Albert Camus's* The Stranger, H. Bloom (ed.), 57–82. Philadelphia, PA: Chelsea House.

Glicksburg, C. 1963. *The Tragic Vision in Twentieth Century Literature*. Carbondale, IL: Southern Illinois University Press.

Glover, J. 1999. *Humanity: A Moral History of the Twentieth Century*. London: Cape.

Golomb, J. 1994. "Camus's Ideal of Authentic Life". *Philosophy Today* **38**(3): 268–77.

Golomb, J. 1995. "Camus's return to authentic morality". In *In Search of Authenticity – from Kierkegaard to Camus*, 168–99. London: Routledge.

Gorz, A. 1977. "Sartre and the Deaf". *Telos* **33**: 108–9.

Gras, C. 1971. *Alfred Rosmer (1877–1964) et le mouvement révolutionnaire International*. Paris: Maspero.

Greacen, R. 1952. "Men Who Live Peace (2): Albert Camus". *Peace News* 11 July: 3.

Green, J. 1975. *Oeuvres complètes* vol. IV, J. Petit (ed.). Paris: Gallimard/Pléiade.

Grenier, J. 1949. "L'Histoire a-t-elle un sens?" *Empedocle* **1**: 35–42. [This issue of *Empedocle* also contains two pieces by Camus: "Le Meurtre et l'absurde" and "L'artiste et le témoin de la liberté".]

Grenier, J. 1953. "L'époque des sibylles". *La Nouvelle Revue Française* 1 February: 203–13.

Grenier, J. *et al.* 1958a. "A propos de Camus". *La Nef* January: 96.

Grenier, J. 1958b. "Orthodoxy Against the Intellect", B. A. Price (trans.). In *From The N.R.F. – An Image of the Twentieth Century from the Pages of the Nouvelle Revue Française*, J. O'Brien (ed.), 268–81. New York: Farrar, Straus & Cudahy.

Grenier, J. 1959. *Les Îles*, Albert Camus (pref.). Paris: Gallimard.

Grenier, J. 1967 [1938]. *Essai sur l'esprit d'orthodoxie*. Paris: Gallimard.

Grenier, J. 1968. *Albert Camus: souvenirs*. Paris: Gallimard.

Grenier, J. 1982 [1948]. *Entretiens sur le bon usage de la liberté*. Paris: Gallimard.

Grenier, R. 1953. *Les Monstres*. Paris: Gallimard.

Grenier, R. (ed.) 1962. *A Albert Camus, ses amis du livre*. Paris: Gallimard.

Grenier, R. (ed.) 1982. *Album Camus*. Paris: Gallimard.

Grenier, R. 1991 [1987]. *Albert Camus – soleil et ombre: une biographie intellectuelle*. Paris: Gallimard.

Grimaud, M. 1992. "Humanism and the 'White Man's Burden': Camus, Daru, Meursault and the Arabs". In *Camus's L'Etranger: Fifty Years On*, A. King (ed.), 170–82. New York: St Martin's Press.

Grupp, S. (ed.) 1971. *Theories of Punishment*. Bloomington, IN: Indiana University Press.

Guérin, J. & D. Wood 1980. "Albert Camus: The First of the New Philosophers". *World Literature Today* **54**(3): 363–7.

Guérin, J. 1984. "Noces de Sang: Albert Camus". *Esprit* **10/11**: 147–55.

Guérin, J. (ed.) 1986. *Camus et la Politique: Actes du Colloque de Nanterre 5–7 June 1985*. Paris: L'Harmattan.

Guérin, J. (ed.) 1990. *Camus et le Premier Combat 1944–1947: Colloque de Paris X-Nanterre*. Nanterre: Erasme.

Guérin, J. 1993a. *Camus: portrait de l'artiste en citoyen*. Paris: François Bourin.

Guérin, J. 1993b. "L'Urgence et la limite: essai sur la violence dans l'œuvre de Camus". *Hebrew University Studies in Literature & the Arts* **20**: 7–26.

Guérin, J. 1994. "Actualité de la politique camusienne". In *Albert Camus: Les Extrêmes et l'Equilibre: Actes du Colloque de Keele, 25–27 mars 1993*, D. H. Walker (ed.), 103–14. Amsterdam: Rodopi.

Guerney, B. G. (ed.) 1943. *A Treasury of Russian Literature*. New York: Vanguard.

Haddour, A. 2000. *Colonial Myths: History and Narrative*. Manchester: Manchester University Press.

Haddour, A. 2003. "The Camus–Sartre debate and the colonial question in Algeria". In *Francophone Postcolonial Studies: A Critical Introduction*, C. Forsdick & D. Murphy (eds), 66–76. London: Arnold.

Hallie, P. 1954. "Camus and the Literature of Revolt". *College English* **16**(1): 25–32, 83.

Hallie, P. 1979. *Lest Innocent Blood be Shed*. London: Michael Joseph.

Halpern, M. 1948. "The Algerian Uprising of 1945". *Middle East Journal* **2**: 191–202.

Harbi, M. (ed.) 1981. *Les Archives de la révolution algérienne*. Paris: Jeune Afrique.

Hare, R. M. 1972. "Nothing Matters". In *Applications of Moral Philosophy*, 32–47. London: Macmillan.

Hargreaves, A. G. 1986. "Caught in the Middle: The Liberal Dilemma in the Algerian War". *Nottingham French Studies* **25**(2): 73–82.

Hargreaves, A. G. 1987. "Camus and the Colonial Question in Algeria". *Muslim World* **77**(3/4): 167–74.

Hargreaves, A. G. 1992. "History and Ethnicity in the Reception of *L'Etranger*". In *Camus's L'Etranger: Fifty Years On*, A. King (ed.), 101–12. New York: St Martin's Press.

Harrow, K. 1971. "Albert Camus and the Algerian Dilemma", *Journal of Modern Literature* **2**(1): 143–7.

Havel, V. 1987a. "Doing without Utopias: An Interview with Václav Havel", by Erica Blair [pseud. John Keane]. *Times Literary Supplement* 23 January: 81–3.

Havel, V. 1987b. *Living in Truth*. London: Faber.

Havel, V. 1990. *Disturbing the Peace: A Conversation with Karel Hvizdala*. London: Faber.

Havel, V. 1991. *Open Letters: Selected Prose 1965–1990*. London: Faber.

Hayman, R. 1986. *Writing Against: A Biography of Sartre*. London: Weidenfeld & Nicolson.

Hegel, G. W. F. 1977. *Phenomenology of Spirit*, A. V. Miller (trans.); J. N. Findlay (ed.). Oxford: Oxford University Press.

Hegel, G. W. F. 2005. *Hegel's Preface to the Phenomenology of Spirit*, Y. Yovel (ed.). Princeton, NJ: Princeton University Press.

Heidegger, M. 1962. *Being and Time*, J. Macquarrie & E. Robinson (trans.). New York: Harper & Row.

Henry, P. 1975. *Voltaire and Camus: The Limits of Reason and the Awareness of Absurdity*. Banbury: Voltaire Foundation.

Herzen, A. 1982. *My Past and Thoughts: The Memoirs of Alexander Herzen*, C. Garnett (trans.); H. Higgens (rev. trans.); I. Berlin (intro.); D. Macdonald (ed.). Berkeley, CA: University of California Press.

Herzog, A. 2005. "Justice or Freedom: Camus's Aporia". *European Journal of Political Theory* **4**(2): 188–99.

Hirsh, A. 1982. *The French Left: A History and Overview*. Montreal: Black Rose.

Hitchens, C. 1990 [1979]. "Camus: un Copain". In *Prepared For the Worst – Selected Essays and Minority Reports*, 93–6. London: Hogarth Press.

Hitchens, C. 2002a. *Orwell's Victory*. London: Penguin Press.

Hitchens, C. 2002b. *Unacknowledged Legislation: Writers in the Public Sphere*. London: Verso.

Hobsbawm, E. J. 1999. "The Rules of Violence". In *Revolutionaries*, 248–55. London: Abacus [1969/1973].

Hochberg, H. 1972. "Albert Camus and the Ethic of Absurdity". In *Contemporary European Ethics – Selected Readings*, J. Kockelmans (ed.), 323–47. New York: Anchor.

Honderich, T. 1980. *Violence for Equality: Inquiries in Political Philosophy*. Harmondsworth: Penguin.

Honoré, T. 1988. "The Right to Rebel". *Oxford Journal of Legal Studies* **8**(1): 34–54.

Horne, A. 1977. *A Savage War of Peace: Algeria 1954–1962*. London: Macmillan.

Hudon, L. 1960. "*The Stranger* and the Critics". *Yale French Studies* Spring: 59–64.

Hudson, R. 1989. "Et Bourreaux, et Victimes! Eye-Witness Reactions to the First Phase of the French war of Decolonisation in Indochina, Les Temps Modernes 1946–1950". *Journal of European Studies* **19**: 191–204.

Hughes, E. 2001. "Camus and the Resistance to History". In *Writing Marginality in Modern French Literature*, 102–34. Cambridge: Cambridge University Press.

Hughes, E. (ed.) 2007. *The Cambridge Companion to Camus*. Cambridge: Cambridge University Press.

Humbaraci, A. 1966. *Algeria: A Revolution that Failed – A Political History since 1954*. London: Pall Mall Press.

Humpheries, T. (ed.) 1950. *Kravchenko versus Moscow: The Report of the Famous Paris Case*. London: Wingate.

Husserl, E. 2001. *Logical Investigations Vol. 1*, J. N. Findlay (trans.); D. Moran (rev. trans.). London: Routledge.

Ignatieff, M. 1998. *Isaiah Berlin: A Life*. London: Chatto & Windus.

Irwin, R. 2006. *The Lust for Knowing: The Orientalists and Their Enemies*. London: Penguin Press.

Isaac, J. 1992. *Arendt, Camus and Modern Rebellion*. New Haven, CT: Yale University Press.

Isaac, J. 2004. "The Camus Sartre Controversy Revisited". In *Sartre and Camus: A Historic Confrontation*, D. Sprintzen & A. van den Hoven (eds & trans.), 251–71. New York: Humanity.

Jakobiak, B. 1968. "Camus le colonisateur sublimé". *Souffles* **12**: http://oumma.com/spip.php?article2319 (accessed 25 February 2007).

Jay, M. 1984. *Marxism and Totality: The Adventure of a Concept from Lukács to Habermas*. Cambridge: Polity.

Jeanson, F. 1947a. *Le Problème moral et la pensée de Sartre*, lettre-préface de J.-P. Sartre. Paris: Myrte.

Jeanson, F. 1947b. "Albert Camus ou le mensonge de l'absurde". *Revue Dominicaine* **1**(53): 104–7.

Jeanson, F. 1947c. "Une évolution dans la pensée de Camus". *Erasme* **2**(22–4): 437–40.

Jeanson, F. 1948a. "Une évolution dans la pensée de Camus". *Revue Dominicaine* **2**(54): 223–6.

Jeanson, F. 1948b. "La Morale de l'histoire". *Esprit* **5/6**: 904–17.

Jeanson, F. 1950. "Pirandello et Camus à travers *Henri IV* et *Caligula*". *Les Temps modernes* **61** (November): 944–53.

Jeanson, F. 1952a. "Albert Camus, ou l'âme révoltée". *Les Temps modernes* **79** (May): 2070–90.

Jeanson, F. 1952b. "Pour tout vous dire . . .". *Les Temps modernes* **82** (August): 354–83.

Jeanson, F. 1955. *Sartre par lui-même*. Paris: Seuil.

Jeanson, F. 1997. "Une Exigence de sens: trois conversations avec Francis Jeanson". *Le Bord de l'Eau* **22**: 11–121.

Jeanson, F. 2002. "The Third Man in the Story: Ronald Aronson Discusses the Sartre–Camus Conflict with Francis Jeanson". *Sartre Studies International* **8**(2): 20–67.

Jeanson, F. 2004a. "Albert Camus, or the Soul in Revolt". In *Sartre and Camus: A Historic Confrontation*, D. Sprintzen & A. van den Hoven (eds & trans.), 79–105. New York: Humanity.

Jeanson, F. 2004b. "To Tell You Everything". In *Sartre and Camus: A Historic Confrontation*, D. Sprintzen & A. van den Hoven (eds & trans.), 163–203. New York: Humanity.

Jeanson, F. 2005 [1966; 1965; 1990]. *Sartre Devant Dieu* suivi de *Un quidam nommé Sartre [&] De l'alienation morale à l'exigence éthique*. Paris: Editions Cécile Defaut.

Jeanson, F. & C. Philip 2000. *Entre-Deux: Conversations Privée 1974–1999*. Latresne: Le Bord de l'Eau.

Johnson, R. W. 1997. "Mediterranean Man". *London Review of Books* 16 October: 24–5.

Judt, T. 1992. *Past Imperfect: French Intellectuals 1944–1956*. Berkeley, CA: University of California Press.

Judt, T. 1994. "The Lost World of Albert Camus". *New York Review of Books* 6 October: 3–5.

Judt, T. 1998. *The Burden of Responsibility: Blum, Camus, Aron and the French Twentieth Century*. Chicago, IL: University of Chicago Press.

Julien, C.-A. 2002. *L'Afrique du nord en marche: Algérie, Tunisie, Maroc 1880–1952*. Paris: Omnibus.

Kamber, R. 2002. *On Camus*. Belmont, CA: Wadsworth.

Kaplan, A. 2000. *The Collaborator: The Trial and Execution of Robert Brasillach*. Chicago, IL: University of Chicago Press.

Kateb, G. 1963. *Utopia and Its Enemies*. New York: Free Press.

Kaufmann, W. (ed.) 1975. *Existentialism from Dostoevsky to Sartre*, rev. edn. New York: Meridian.

Keane, J. 2000. *Václav Havel: A Political Tragedy in Six Acts*. New York: Basic Books.

Khilnani, S. 1993. *Arguing Revolution – The Intellectual Left in Postwar France*. New Haven, CT: Yale University Press.

Kierkegaard, S. 1938. *The Journals of Søren Kierkegaard*, A. Dru (trans. & ed.). London: Oxford University Press.

Kierkegaard, S. 1941. *Kierkegaard's Concluding Unscientific Postscript*, D. Swenson & W. Lowrie (trans.). Princeton, NJ: Princeton University Press for American-Scandinavian Foundation.

Kierkegaard, S. 1956. *Purity of Heart: Is to Will One Thing?* D. V. Steere (trans.). New York: Harper.

King, A. 1964. *Camus*. Edinburgh: Oliver & Boyd.

King, A. (ed.) 1992. *Camus's L'Etranger: Fifty Years On*. New York: St Martin's Press.

Koestler, A. 1941. *Darkness at Noon*, D. Hardy (trans.). New York: Modern Library.

Koestler, A. 1945. *The Yogi and the Commissar, and Other Essays*. London: Cape.

Koestler, A. 1956. *Reflections on Hanging*. London: Gollancz.

Koestler, A. *et al.* 1950. *The God that Failed: Six Studies in Communism*. London: Hamish Hamilton.

Kojève, A. 1980 [1969]. *Introduction to the Reading of Hegel: Lectures on* The Phenomenology of Spirit, assembled by R. Queneau; J. H. Nichols Jr (trans.); A. Bloom (ed.). Ithaca, NY: Cornell University Press.

Kolakowski, L. 1971 [1969]. *Marxism and Beyond: On Historical Understanding and Individual Responsibility*, J. Z. Peel (trans.). London: Paladin.

Kolakowski, L. 2001. *Metaphysical Horror*, rev. edn, A. Kolakowska (trans.). Chicago, IL: University of Chicago Press.

Kolakowski, L. 2005. *Main Currents in Marxism*, rev. edn, P. S. Falla (trans.). New York: Norton.

Konrád, G. 1984. *Antipolitics: An Essay*. London: Quartet.

Kravchenko, V. 1947. *I Chose Freedom*. London: Hale.

Kravchenko, V. 1951. *I Chose Justice*. New York: Scribners.

Kréa, H. 1961. "Le malentendu algérien". *France observateur* 5 January: 16.

Kritzman, L. 1997. "Camus's Curious Humanism or the Intellectual in Exile". *Modern Language Notes* **112**: 550–75.

Kuhn, T. 1996. *The Structure of Scientific Revolutions*, 3rd edn. Chicago, IL: University of Chicago Press.

Kushnir, S. 1972. "Albert Camus et la peine de mort". *Cahiers des amis de Robert Brasillach* **17**: 48–50.

Lamont, R. 1988. "Two Faces of Terrorism: *Caligula* and *The Just Assassins*". In *Critical Essays on Albert Camus*, B. Knapp (ed.), 128–40. Boston, MA: G. K. Hall.

Lampert, E. 1957. *Studies in Rebellion*. London: Routledge & Kegan Paul.

Lampert, E. 1965. *Sons against Fathers: Studies in Russian Radicalism and Revolution*. Oxford: Clarendon Press.

Lasch, C. 1969. "The Cultural Cold War: A Short History of the Congress for Cultural Freedom". In *The Agony of the American Left*, 69–114. New York: Knopf.

Lasch, C. 1991. *The True and Only Heaven: Progress and Its Critics*. New York: Norton.

Lavrov, P. 1967. *Historical Letters*, J. P. Scanlan (trans. & ed.). Berkeley, CA: University of California Press.

Lazere, D. 1973. *The Unique Creation of Albert Camus*. New Haven, CT: Yale University Press.

Lazere, D. 1981. "American Criticism of the Sartre–Camus Dispute: A Chapter in the Cultural Cold War". In *The Philosophy of Jean-Paul Sartre*, P. A. Schilpp (ed.), 408–21. La Salle, IL: Open Court.

Lazere, D. 1996. "Camus and His Critics on Capital Punishment". *Modern Age* Fall: 371–80.

Lebjaoui, M. 1970. *Vérités sur la révolution algérienne*. Paris: Gallimard.

Le Blanc, J. R. 2002. "Camus, Said, and the Dilemma of Home: Space, Identity, and the Limits of Postcolonial Political Theory". *Strategies* 15(2): 239–58.

Lenzini, J. 1987. *L'Algérie d'Albert Camus*. Aix-en-Provence: Édisud.

Lefort, C. 1948. "Kravchenko et le problème de l'URSS". *Les Temps modernes* 29 (February), 1490–516.

Le Sueur, J. D. 2001. *Uncivil War: Intellectuals and Identity Politics During the Decolonization of Algeria*, fwd P. Bourdieu. Philadelphia, PA: University of Pennsylvania Press.

Lévinas, E. 1969. *Totality and Infinity: An Essay on Exteriority*, A. Lingis (trans.). Pittsburgh, PA: Duquesne University Press.

Lévi-Valensi, J. (ed.) 1970. *Les critiques de notre temps et Camus*. Paris: Garnier.

Lévi-Valensi, J. *et al.* 1999. *Europe* 77(846) [Special Number on Camus].

Lévi-Valensi, J. 2002. "Albert Camus et la question du terrorisme". In *Réflexions sur le terrorisme*, J. Lévi-Valensi *et al.* (eds), 9–40. Paris: Nicholas Philippe.

Lévy, B.-H. 1995. *Adventures on the Freedom Road – The French Intellectuals in the Twentieth Century*, R. Veasey (trans.). London: Harvill.

Lévy, B.-H. 2003. *Sartre: The Philosopher of the Twentieth Century*, A. Brown (trans.). Cambridge: Polity Press.

Lottman, H. 1979. *Camus – A Biography*. London: Weidenfeld & Nicolson.

Lottman, H. 1982. *The Left Bank: Writers, Artists and Politics from the Popular Front to the Cold War*. London: Heinemann.

Lottman, H. 1986. *The Purge*. New York: Morrow.

Lowenstein, J. 1980. *Marx against Marxism*, H. Drost (trans.). London: Routledge & Kegan Paul.

Lowrie, W. 1938. *Kierkegaard*. London: Oxford University Press.

Lustic, I. S. 1993. *Unsettled States, Disputed Lands: Britain and Ireland, France and Algeria, Israel and the West Bank–Gaza*. Ithaca, NY: Cornell University Press.

McBride, J. [n.d. 1973?] "*L'Étranger* of Albert Camus". *Philosophical Studies* 22: 53–62.

McBride, J. 1992. *Albert Camus: Philosopher and Littérateur*. New York: St Martin's Press.

McBride, W. 1991. *Sartre's Political Theory*. Bloomington, IN: Indiana University Press.

McBride, W. 2004. "After a Lot More History Has Taken Place". In *Sartre and Camus: A Historic Confrontation*, D. Sprintzen & A. van den Hoven (eds & trans.), 225–49. New York: Humanity.

McCarney, J. 2000. *Hegel on History*. London: Routledge.

McCarthy, P. 1982. *Camus*. New York: Random House.

McCarthy, P. 1994. "The *pied-noir* story". *Times Literary Supplement* 24 June.

McCarthy, P. 2004. *Camus: The Stranger*, 2nd edn. Cambridge: Cambridge University Press.

Macdonald, D. 2001. *A Moral Temper: The Letters of Dwight Macdonald*, M. Wreszin (ed.). Chicago, IL: Dee.

Macquarrie, J. 1973. *Existentialism*. Harmondsworth: Penguin.

Mahon, J. 1997. *Existentialism, Feminism and Simone de Beauvoir*. Basingstoke: Palgrave Macmillan.

Majault, J. 1965. *Camus: révolte et liberté*. Paris: Centurion.

Mandouze, A. 1998. *Mémoires d'outre-siècle (Tome 1: d'une résistance à l'autre)*. Paris: Viviane Hamy.

Maquet, A. 1955. *Albert Camus ou l'invincible été*. Paris: Debresse.

Maquet, A. 1958. *Albert Camus: The Invincible Summer*, H. Briffault (trans.). New York: George Braziller.

Marcuse, H. 1968 [1966]. "Ethics and Revolution". In *Ethics and Society – Original Essays on Contemporary Moral Problems*, R. T. De George (ed.), 133–47. London: Macmillan.

Margalit, A. 2003. "The Suicide Bombers". *New York Review of Books* 16 January: 36–9.

Martinet, D. 1960. "Albert Camus aux *Groupes de liaison internationale*". *Témoins* May: 6–7.

Marx, K. 1935. *Selected Works – in Two Volumes*, vol. I, V. Adoratsky (ed.). Moscow: Co-operative Publishing Society of Foreign Workers in the USSR.

Marx, K. 1971. *Early Texts*, D. McLellan (ed.). Oxford: Blackwell.

Marx, K. & F. Engels 1969. *Marx and Engels: Basic Writings on Politics and Philosophy*, L. Feuer (ed.). London: Fontana.

Marx, K. & F. Engels 2002. *The Communist Manifesto*, G. Stedman Jones (ed.). Harmondsworth: Penguin.

Mathieu, A. 2004. "Jean-Paul Sartre et la guerre d'Algérie". *Le monde diplomatique* November: 30–31.

Mauriac, C. 1951 ."L'Homme révolté d'Albert Camus". *La Table Ronde* **48**: December: 98–109.

Mayne, R. 1971. "Camus' New Thriller". *The Listener* 30 September: 449–51.

Mayne, R. 1982. "Bogey Man". *London Review of Books* July/August.

Memmi, A. 1957. "Camus ou le Colonisateur de bonne Volonté". *La Nef* **12**: December: 95–6.

Memmi, A. 1969. "Albert Camus". In *Anthologie des écrivains français du Maghreb*, A. Memmi (ed.), 111–14. Paris: Présence Africaine.

Memmi, A. 1972 [1966]. *La Statue de Sel*, A. Camus (pref.). Paris: Gallimard.

Memmi, A. 1986. [Discussion of Camus and Algeria]. In *Camus et la Politique: Actes du Colloque de Nanterre 5–7 juin 1985*, J. Guérin (ed.) 194–5. Paris: L'Harmattan.

Memmi, A. 1991 [1965]. *The Colonizer and The Colonized*, H. Greenfeld (trans.); J.-P. Sartre (intro.); S. G. Miller (afwd). Boston, MA: Beacon.

Merleau-Ponty, M. 1947. *Humanisme et Terreur: Essai sur le problème communiste*. Paris: Gallimard.

Merleau-Ponty, M. 1964. "The USSR and the Camps". In *Signs*, R. C. McCleary (trans. & ed.), 263–73. Evanston, IL: Northwestern University Press.

Merleau-Ponty, M. 1969. *Humanism and Terror: An Essay on the Communist Problem*, J. O'Neill (trans.). Boston, MA: Beacon.

Merleau-Ponty, M. & J.-P. Sartre 1950a. "Les jours de notre vie". *Les Temps modernes* 5(51): 1153–68.

Merleau-Ponty, M. & J.-P. Sartre 1950b. "L'adversaire et le complice", *Les Temps modernes* 5(57): 1–11 [editorial signed only "T. M.", written in response to criticism of "Les jours de notre vie" above].

Merton, T. 1968. *Albert Camus' The Plague*. New York: Seabury Press.

Merton, T. 1981. "Seven Essays on Albert Camus". In *The Literary Essays of Thomas Merton*, P. Hart (ed.), 181–301. New York: New Directions.

Messali Hadj, 1982. *Les Mémoires de Messali Hadj 1898–1938*, R. de Rochebrune (ed.); A. Ben Bella (pref.); C.-A. Julien, C.-R. Ageron, M. Harbi (postf.). Paris: J. C. Lattés.

Meunier, J.-L. 2003. "La révolte et *La Rue*". In *En commune présence: Albert Camus et René Char*, 47–72. Bédée: Editions Folle Avoine.

Meynier, G. 2002. *Histoire intérieure du F.L.N. 1954–1962*, M. Harbi (pref.). Paris: Fayard.

Mijuskovic, B. 1977. "Camus and the Problem of Evil". *Sophia* **14/15**: 11–19.

Milosz, C. 1953. *The Captive Mind*, J. Zielonko (trans.). New York: Knopf.

Milosz, C. 1989 [1960]. "L'Interlocuteur fraternel". In *Preuves – Une revue Européenne à Paris*, P. Grémion (ed.), 385–9. Paris: Julliard.

Mimouni, R. 1994. "Camus et l'Algérie intégriste". *Nouvel Observateur* 9–15 June: 8.

Mitrany, D. 1951. *Marx against the Peasant: A Study in Social Dogmatism*. London: Weidenfeld & Nicolson.

Modler, K. 2000. *Soleil et mesure dans l'oeuvre d'Albert Camus*. Paris: L'Harmattan.

Molnar, T. 1958. "On Camus and Capital Punishment". *Modern Age* Summer: 298–306.

Molnar, T. 1996. "A Reply to 'Camus and his Critics on Capital Punishment'". *Modern Age* Fall: 380–82.

Monasterio, X. 1970. "Camus and Violence". *The New Scholasticism* 44(2): 199–222.

Morin, E. 1959. *Autocritique*. Paris: Julliard.

Mouralis, B. 2003. "Edward Said et Albert Camus: un malentendu?" In *Albert Camus et les écritures du XXe siècle*, S. Brodziak *et al.* (eds), 239–54. Arras: Artois Presses Université.

Murchland, B. 1968. "Sartre and Camus – The Anatomy of a Quarrel". In *Choice of Action: The French Existentialists on the Political Front Line*, M.-A. Burnier, 175–96. New York: Random House.

Nacer-Khodja, H. 2004. *Albert Camus, Jean Sénac ou le fils rebelle*. Paris: Paris-Méditerranée. [Contains previously unpublished correspondence between Camus and Sénac.]

Nagel, T. 1979. "The Absurd". In *Mortal Questions*, 11–23. Cambridge: Cambridge University Press.

Natanson, M. 1962. "Albert Camus: Death at the Meridian". In *Literature, Philosophy and the Social Sciences: Essays in Existentialism and Phenomenology*, 141–52. The Hague: Nijhoff.

Nietzsche, F. 1961. *Thus Spoke Zarathustra*, R. J. Hollingdale (trans.). Harmondsworth: Penguin.

Nietzsche, F. 1997. *Untimely Meditations*, R. J. Hollingdale (trans.); D. Breazeale (ed.). Cambridge: Cambridge University Press.

Nora, P. 1961. "Pour une autre explication de *L'Etranger*". *France observateur* 5 January: 16–17.

Norrie, A. 2004. "Law and the Beautiful Soul". *Kings College Law Journal* 15: 45–62.

North, H. 1947. "A Period of Opposition to *Sophrosyne* in Greek Thought". *Transactions and Proceedings of the American Philological Association* 78: 1–7.

North, H. 1966. *Sophrosyne: Self-Knowledge and Self-Restraint in Greek Literature*. Ithaca, NY: Cornell University Press.

North, H. 1979. *From Myth to Icon: Reflections of Greek Ethical Doctrine in Literature and Art*. Ithaca, NY: Cornell University Press.

Novello, S. 2004. "Du nihilisme aux théocraties totalitaires: *Les Sources et le Sens du communisme russe* de Berdiaev dans les *Carnets* de Camus". In *Albert Camus 20*, R. Gay-Crosier (ed.), 175–95. Paris: Lettres modernes.

Novick, P. 1968. *The Resistance versus Vichy – The Purge of Collaborators in Liberated France*. New York: Columbia University Press.

Obuchowski, C. 1968. "Algeria: The Tortured Conscience". *The French Review* 42(1): 90–103.

Odajnyk, W. 1965. *Marxism and Existentialism*. New York: Anchor.

Ohana, D. 2003. "Mediterranean Humanism". *Mediterranean Historical Review* 18(1): 59–75.

Ollivier, A. 1945. "*Caligula* d'Albert Camus". *Les Temps modernes* 1(3): 574–6.

Onimus, J. 1970. *Albert Camus and Christianity*, E. Parker (trans.). Dublin: Gill & Macmillan.

Orwell, G. 1938. *Homage to Catalonia*. London: Secker & Warburg.

Orwell, G. 1953. *Such, Such Were the Joys*. New York: Harcourt, Brace.

Ouzegane, A. 1962. *Le Meilleur combat*. Paris: Julliard.

Oxenhandler, N. 1996. *Looking for Heroes in Postwar France – Albert Camus, Max Jacob, Simone Weil*. Hanover, NH: Dartmouth College & University Press of New England.

Parker, E. 1965. *Albert Camus: The Artist in the Arena*. Madison, WI: University of Wisconsin Press.

Petersen, C. 1969. *Albert Camus*, A. Gode (trans.). New York: Ungar.

Petit, P. 1981. "Tuberculose et sensibilité chez Gide et Camus". *Bulletin des Amis d'André Gide* 51: 279–92.

Peyre, H. 1958. "Albert Camus: An Anti-Christian Moralist". *Proceedings of the American Philosophical Society* 102(5): 477–82.

Peyre, H. 1960. "Camus the Pagan". *Yale French Studies* Spring: 20–25.

Peyre, H. 1962. *Albert Camus Moraliste* (The First Kathleen Morris Scruggs Memorial Lecture). Randolph-Macon Women's College.

Pieper, J. 1966. *The Four Cardinal Virtues*. Bloomington, IN: Indiana University Press.

Pierce, R. 1966. *Contemporary French Political Thought*. London: Oxford University Press.

Pisarev, D. 1958. *Selected Philosophical, Social and Political Essays*. Moscow: Foreign Languages Publishing House.

Plato 2005. *Meno and Other Dialogues: Charmides, Laches, Lysis, Meno*, Robin Waterfield (trans.). Oxford: Oxford University Press.

Podhoretz, N. 1986. "Camus and His Critics". In *The Bloody Crossroads: Where Literature and Politics Meet*, 33–49. New York: Simon and Schuster.

Popper, K. 1960. *The Poverty of Historicism*. New York: Basic Books.

Popper, K. 1963. "Utopia and Violence". In *Conjectures and Refutations: The Growth of Scientific Knowledge*, 355–63. London: Routledge and Kegan Paul.

Popper, K. 1966. *The Open Society and its Enemies*, 5th edn. London: Routledge & Kegan Paul.

Poster, M. 1975. *Existential Marxism in Postwar France: From Sartre to Althusser*. Princeton, NJ: Princeton University Press.

Postgate, R. W. (ed.) 1962. *Revolution – from 1789 to 1906*. New York: Harper.

Pouillon, J. 1947. "L'Optimisme de Camus". *Les Temps modernes* 3(26): 921–9.

Principe, M. A. 2000. "Solidarity and Responsibility: Conceptual Connections". *Journal of Social Philosophy* 31(2): 139–45.

Quandt, W. 1969. *Revolution and Political Leadership: Algeria, 1954–68*. Cambridge, MA: MIT Press.

Quilliot, R. 1962. "Albert Camus's Algeria". In *Camus: A Collection of Critical Essays*, G. Brée (ed.), 38–47. Englewood Cliffs, NJ: Prentice-Hall.

Quilliot, R. 1970a. *La Mer et Les Prisons – essai sur Albert Camus*, rev. edn. Paris: Gallimard.

Quilliot, R. 1970b. *The Sea and Prisons: A Commentary on the Life and Thought of Albert Camus*, E. Parker (trans.). Tuscaloosa, AL: University of Alabama Press.

Quinn, R. 1967. "Albert Camus devant le problème algérien". *Revue des Sciences humaines* 32: 613–31.

Quinn, R. 1969. "Le thème racial dans *L'Etranger*". *Revue d'histoire littéraire de la France*, November/December, 1009–13.

Rader, M. 1979. *Marx's Interpretation of History*. Oxford: Oxford University Press.

Ramadan, T. 2001. *Islam, the West and the Challenges of Modernity*, S. Amghar (trans.). Markfield, Leicester: The Islamic Foundation.

Ransome, A. 1919. *Six Weeks in Russia in 1919*. Glasgow: The Socialist Labour Press.

Rauschning, H. 1939. *The Revolution of Nihilism: Warning to the West*, E. W. Dickes (trans.). New York: Alliance.

Rawls, J. 1999. *A Theory of Justice*, rev. edn. Oxford: Oxford University Press.

Reed, J. 1997. *Ten Days that Shook the World*. New York: St Martin's Press.

Ricoeur, P. 1999 [1956]. "L'Homme révolté". In *Lectures 2*, 121–36. Paris: Seuil.

Rigaud, J. "The Depiction of the Arabs in *L'Etranger*". In *Camus's* L'Etranger: *Fifty Years On*, A. King (ed.), 183–92. New York: St Martin's Press.

Rimbaud, A. 1972. *Œuvres completes*, A. Adam (ed.). Paris: Gallimard/Pléiade.

Rizzuto, A. 1981. *Camus' Imperial Vision*. Carbondale, IL: Southern Illinois University Press.

Robin, M. 1986. "Remarques sur l'attitude de Camus face à la guerre d'Algérie". In *Camus et la Politique: Actes du Colloque de Nanterre 5–7 juin 1985*, J. Guérin (ed.) 185–90. Paris: L'Harmattan.

Roblès, E. 1988. *Albert Camus et la trêve civile*. Philadelphia: Ceflan Edition Monographs.

Roblès, E. 1990. "Albert Camus et la trêve civile". In *Les Rives du fleuve bleu*, 209–50. Paris: Seuil.

Roblès, E. 1992. "Camus, Our Youthful Years", A. King (trans.). In *Camus's* L'Etranger: *Fifty Years On*, A. King (ed.), 18–23. New York: St Martin's Press.

Roblès, E. 1995. *Camus – Frère de Soleil*. Paris: Seuil.

Rorty, R. 1989. *Contingency, Irony, and Solidarity*. Cambridge: Cambridge University Press.

Rorty, R. 1998a. "The End of Leninism, Havel and Social Hope". In *Truth and Progress: Philosophical Papers Vol. 3*, 228–43. Cambridge: Cambridge University Press.

Rorty, R. 1998b. *Achieving Our Country: Leftist Thought in Twentieth Century America*. Cambridge, MA: Harvard University Press.

Rorty, R. 2002. *Against Bosses, Against Oligarchies: A Conversation with Richard Rorty*. Chicago, IL: Prickly Paradigm Press.

Rorty, R. 2003. "Humiliation or Solidarity?" *Dissent* Fall: 23–6.

Rorty, R. & G. Vattimo 2005. *The Future of Religion*, S. Zabala (ed.). New York: Columbia University Press.

Rosmer, A. 1953. *Moscou sous Lénine – les origines du Communisme*, A. Camus (pref.). Paris: Pierre Horay.

Rosmer, A. 1972. *Moscow under Lenin*, I. Birchall (trans.). New York: Monthly Review Press.

Rossfelder, A. 2000. "Poker avec Camus". In *Le onzième commandement*, 377–91. Paris: Gallimard.

Roth, L. 1955. "A Contemporary Moralist: Albert Camus". *Philosophy* **30**(115): 291–303.

Roth, M. 1988. *Knowing and History: Appropriations of Hegel in Twentieth Century France*. Ithaca, NY: Cornell University Press.

Rousseau, J.-J. 1968. *The Social Contract*, M. Cranston (trans.). Harmondsworth: Penguin.

Roy, J. 1960. *La Guerre d'Algérie*. Paris: Julliard.

Roy, J. 1968. "Depuis l'indépendence de l'Algérie, je suis un sans patrie". *Le Figaro Littéraire* 5–11 February: 20–21.

Roy, J. *et al.* 1970. "Pour et contre Camus". *Le Figaro Littéraire* 5–11 January: 10–13.

Roy, J. 1989. *Mémoires barbares*. Paris: Albin Michel.

Royle, P. 1982. *The Sartre–Camus Controversy: A Literary and Philosophical Critique*. Ottawa: University of Ottawa Press.

Sagi, A. 1994. "Is the Absurd the Problem of the Solution? *The Myth of Sisyphus* Reconsidered". *Philosophy Today* **38**(3): 178–284.

Sagi, A. 2002. *Albert Camus and the Philosophy of the Absurd*, B. Stein (trans.). Amsterdam: Rodopi.

Said, E. 1990. "US Intellectuals and Middle East Politics". In *Intellectuals: Aesthetics, Politics, Academics*, B. Robbins (ed.), 135–51. Minneapolis, MN: University of Minnesota Press.

Said, E. 1993. *Culture and Imperialism*. London: Chatto & Windus.

Said, E. 2000. "My Encounter with Sartre". *London Review of Books* 11 June.

Saint-Just, L.-A. 1946. *Le Gouvernement révolutionnaire jusqu'à la paix*, J. Gaucheron (ed.). Paris: Raisons d'être.

Saint-Just, L.-A. 1957. *Discours et rapports*, A. Soboul (ed.). Paris: Editions sociales.

Santoni, R. 1988. "Philosophers and the Nuclear Threat". *Philosophy Today* Spring: 75–8.

Santoni, R. 2003. *Sartre on Violence: Curiously Ambivalent*. University Park, PA: Penn State University Press.

Sarocchi, J. 1968. *Albert Camus*. Paris: PUF.

Sartre, J.-P. 1943. *L'être et le néant: Essai d'ontologie phénoménologique*. Paris: Gallimard.

Sartre, J.-P. 1946a. "Fragment d'un portrait de Baudelaire". *Les Temps modernes* **8** (May): 1345–77.

Sartre, J.-P. 1946b. "Et Bourreaux, et victimes . . .". *Les Temps modernes* **15** (December) [unsigned and unpaginated editorial, between p. 384 and p. 385].

Sartre, J.-P. 1946c. *L'Existentialisme est un humanisme*. Paris: Gallimard.

Sartre, J.-P. 1947a. "Qu'est-ce que la littérature?" *Les Temps modernes* **22** (July): 77–144.

Sartre, J.-P. 1947b. *Baudelaire*, M. Leiris (pref.). Paris: Gallimard.

Sartre, J.-P. 1948. *Situations, II*. Paris: Gallimard.

Sartre, J.-P. 1950. *Baudelaire*, M. Turnell (trans.). New York: New Directions.

Sartre, J.-P. 1952. "Mon Cher Camus . . .". *Les Temps modernes* **82** (August): 334–53.

Sartre, J.-P. 1955a. *Literary and Philosophical Essays*, A. Michelson (trans.). London: Rider.

Sartre, J.-P. 1955b. "L'Algérie n'est pas la France". *Les Temps modernes* **119** (November): 577–9 [signed T. M.].

Sartre, J.-P. 1956. *Being and Nothingness*, H. E. Barnes (trans.). New York: Philosophical Library.

Sartre, J.-P. 1962a. "An Explication of *The Stranger*". In *Camus: A Collection of Critical Essays*, G. Brée (ed.), 108–21. Englewood Cliffs, NJ: Prentice-Hall.

Sartre, J.-P. 1962b. "Tribute to Albert Camus". In *Camus: A Collection of Critical Essays*, G. Brée (ed.), 173–5. Englewood Cliffs, NJ: Prentice-Hall.

Sartre, J.-P. 1963. *Search for a Method*, H. E. Barnes (trans.). New York: Knopf.

Sartre, J.-P. 1964a. *Saint Genet: Actor and Martyr*, B. Frechtman (trans.). London: W. H. Allen.

Sartre, J.-P. 1964b. *The Words*, B. Frechtman (trans.). New York: George Braziller.

Sartre, J.-P. 1964c. *Situations, IV – portraits*. Paris: Gallimard.

Sartre, J.-P. 1964d. *Situations, V – colonialisme et néo-colonialisme*. Paris: Gallimard.

Sartre, J.-P. 1965. *Situations*, B. Eisler (trans.). New York: George Braziller.

Sartre, J.-P. 1967. *What is Literature?* B. Frechtman (trans.). London: Methuen.

Sartre, J.-P. 1968. *The Communists and Peace: with a Reply to Claude Lefort*, M. H. Fletcher, J. R. Kleinschmidt & P. R. Berk (trans.). New York: Braziller.

Sartre, J.-P. 1970. *Les écrits de Sartre: Chronologie, bibliographie commentée*, M. Contat & M. Rybalka (eds). Paris: Gallimard.

Sartre, J.-P. 1974a. *The Writings of Jean-Paul Sartre, Volume 1: A Bibliographical Life*, R. C. McCleary (trans.); M. Contat and M. Rybalka (eds); Evanston, IL: Northwestern University Press.

Sartre, J.-P. 1974b. *The Writings of Jean-Paul Sartre, Volume 2: Selected Prose*, R. C. McCleary (trans.); M. Contat and M. Rybalka (eds). Evanston, IL: Northwestern University Press.

Sartre, J.-P. 1974c. *Between Existentialism and Marxism*, J. Matthews (trans.). New York: Pantheon.

Sartre, J.-P. 1976a. *Situations, X – politique et autobiographique*. Paris: Gallimard.

Sartre, J.-P. 1976b. *Sartre on Theatre*, F. Jellinek (trans.); M. Contat & M. Rybalka (eds). London: Quartet.

Sartre, J.-P. 1977. *Life/Situations*, P. Auster & L. Davis (trans.). New York: Pantheon.

Sartre, J.-P. 1978a. *Sartre by Himself*, R. Seaver (trans.). New York: Urizen.

Sartre, J.-P. 1978b. *Existentialism & Humanism*, P. Mairet (trans.). London: Eyre Methuen.

Sartre, J.-P. 1981. *Œuvres Romanesque*, M. Contat & M. Rybalka (eds). Paris: Gallimard.

Sartre, J.-P. 1984. *War Diaries: Notebooks from a Phoney War November 1939–March 1940*, Q. Hoare (trans.). London: Verso.

Sartre, J.-P. 1988. *'What is Literature?' and Other Essays*, B. Frechtman *et al.* (trans.). Cambridge, MA: Harvard University Press.

Sartre, J.-P. 1989. *No Exit and Three Other Plays*, S. Gilbert & L. Abel (trans.). New York: Vintage.

Sartre, J.-P. 1991a. *Critique of Dialectical Reason Volume 1: Theory of Practical Ensembles*, A. Sheridan-Smith (trans.). London: Verso.

Sartre, J.-P. 1991b. *Critique of Dialectical Reason Volume II [Unfinished]*, Q. Hoare (trans.); A. Elkaïm-Sartre (ed.). London: Verso.

Sartre, J.-P. 1992. *Notebooks for an Ethics*, D. Pellauer (trans.). Chicago, IL: University of Chicago Press.

Sartre, J.-P. 1993 [1947]. *Critiques littéraires: Situations, I*. Paris: Gallimard/Folio.

Sartre, J.-P. 1996. *Hope Now: The 1980 Interviews*, A. van den Hoven (trans.). Chicago, IL: University of Chicago Press.

Sartre, J.-P. 2001. "To Be Hungry Already Means that You Want to Be Free", A. van den Hoven (trans.). *Sartre Studies International* 7(2): 8–11.

Sartre, J.-P. 2004. "Reply to Albert Camus". In *Sartre and Camus: A Historic Confrontation*, D. Sprintzen & A. van den Hoven (eds & trans.), 131–61. New York: Humanity.

Sartre, J.-P. 2006. *Colonialism and Neocolonialism*, A. Haddour *et al.* (trans.); R. C. Young (pref.); A. Haddour (rev. intro.). London: Routledge.

Sartre, J.-P. 2007. *Typhus: Scénario*, A. Elkaïm-Sartre (ed.). Paris: Gallimard.

[Saurel, R.] R. S. 1959. "Le Théâtre: *Les Possédés* d'Albert Camus, d'après Dostoïevski". *Les Temps modernes* 14(156/7): 1508–9.

Savinkov, B. 1931. *Memoirs of a Terrorist*, J. Shaplen (trans.). New York: Albert & Charles Boni.

Savinkov, B. 1982. *Souvenirs d'un terroriste*, R. Gayraud (trans.). Paris: Champ Libre.

Scarry, E. 1999. *On Beauty and Being Just*. Princeton, NJ: Princeton University Press.

Schalk, D. L. 2004. "Was Algeria Camus's Fall?" *Journal of Contemporary European Studies* 23(3): 339–54.

Schalk, D. L. 2005. *War and the Ivory Tower: Algeria and Vietnam*, 2nd edn. Lincoln, NE: University of Nebraska Press.

Schuessler, K. F. 1971. "The Deterrent Influence of the Death Penalty". In *Theories of Punishment*, S. E. Grupp (ed.), 181–95. Bloomington, IN: Indiana University Press.

Sénac, J. 1983 [1957] "Camus au secours de Lacoste?" In *Poésie au Sud: Jean Sénac et la nouvelle poésie maghrébine d'expression française*, 69–72. Marseille: Archive de la ville Marseille.

Senancour, E. P. de 1909. *Obermann*, A. E. Waite (ed.). London: William Rider.

Senancour, E. P. de 1984. *Obermann*, J.-M. Monnoyer (ed.). Paris: Gallimard/Folio.

Servan-Schreiber, J.J. 1957. *Lieutenant in Algeria*, R. Matthews (trans.). New York: Knopf.

Shaw, D. 1986. "Absurdity and Suicide: A Reexamination". *Philosophy Research Archives* 9: 209–23.

Shklar, J. N. 1982. "Putting Cruelty First". *Daedalus* 111(3): 17–27.

Siblot, P. & J.-L. Planche 1986. "Le 8 Mai 1945: éléments pour une analyse des positions de Camus face au nationalisme algérien". In *Camus et la Politique: Actes du Colloque de Nanterre 5–7 juin 1985*, J. Guérin (ed.) 153–71. Paris: L'Harmattan.

Simon, P. H. 1962. *Présence de Camus*. Paris: La Renaissance du Livre.

Sirinelli, J.-F. 1995. *Deux Intellectuels dans le Siècle: Sartre et Aron*. Paris: Fayard.

Smith, C. 1964. *Contemporary French Philosophy: A Study in Norms and Values*. London: Methuen.

Smith, E. T. 1978. "Original Innocence in a Passionate Universe: the Moral Anthropology of Camus". *Thomist* 42: 69–94.

Solzhenitsyn, A. 1980. *The Oak and the Calf – A Memoir*, H. Willetts (trans.). London: Collins.

Souvarine, B. 1938. *Stalin – A Critical Study of Bolshevism*, C. L. R. James (trans.). London: Secker & Warburg.

Souvarine, B. 1989 [1956]. "Les Archives entrouvertes". In *Preuves – Une revue Européenne à Paris*, P. Grémion (ed.), 251–63. Paris: Julliard.

Sperber, M. 1960. *The Achilles Heel*, C. FitzGibbon (trans.). New York: Doubleday.

Spets, P.-F. 1985. *Albert Camus dans le premier silence et au-delà* suivi de *Albert Camus, Chroniqueur judiciaire à "Alger Républicain" en 1939*. Bruxelles: Goemaere.

Sprintzen, D. 1988. *Camus: A Critical Examination*. Philadelphia, PA: Temple University Press.

Sprintzen, D. & A. van den Hoven (eds & trans.) 2004. *Sartre and Camus: A Historic Confrontation*. New York: Humanity.

Starling, C. 1977. *Camus et Sartre: histoire d'une rupture*. PhD thesis, Lettres modernes, Université de Nice.

Steinberg, I. N. 1935. *Spiridonova: Revolutionary Terrorist*, G. David & E. Mosbacher (trans.); H. W. Nevinson (intro.). London: Methuen.

Steinberg, I. N. 1955 [1953] *In the Workshop of the Revolution*. London: Gollancz.

Stewart, J. (ed.) 1998. *The Debate Between Sartre and Merleau-Ponty*. Evanston, IL: Northwestern University Press.

Stora, B. 2001. *Algeria 1830–2000: A Short History*, J. M. Todd (trans.). Ithaca, NY: Cornell University Press.

Suetonius 1998. *[Lives of the Caesars] Volume 1*, J. C. Rolfe (trans.); K.R. Bradley (intro.). Cambridge, MA: Harvard University Press.

Taleb Ibrahimi, A. 1966 [1959]. "Lettre ouverte à Albert Camus". In *Lettres de prison 1957–1961*, 67–83. Algiers: SNED.

Taleb Ibrahimi, A. 1973 [1967]. "Albert Camus vu par un Algérien". In *De la décolonisation à la revolution culturelle 1962–1972*, 161–84. Algiers: SNED.

Tarrow, S. 1985. *Exile from the Kingdom: A Political Rereading of Albert Camus*. Tuscaloosa, AL: University of Alabama Press.

Taubman, R. 1960. "Albert Camus: Moralist". *Spectator* 26 February: 293.

Thody, P. 1956. "Albert Camus and *La Remarque sur la révolte*". *French Studies* 10(4): 335–8.

Thody, P. 1961. *Albert Camus 1913–1960*. London: Macmillan.

Thody, P. 1969. "Camus et la Politique", B. T. Fitch (trans.). In *Albert Camus 2*, B. T. Fitch (ed.), 137–47. Paris: Lettres modernes.

Thomas, H. 2003. *The Battlefield: Algeria 1988–2002: Studies in a Broken Polity*. London: Verso.

Tillion, G. 1958a. *Algeria – The Realities*, R. Matthews (trans.). New York: Knopf.

Tillion, G. 1958b. "Albert Camus et l'Algérie". *Preuves* **91**, 69–72.

Tillion, G. 1958c. "Algeria in 1958". *Encounter* **11**(1): 81–3.

Tillion, G. 1958d. "The Terrorist". *Encounter* **11**(6): 18–23.

Tillion, G. 1960. "Devant le malheur algérien". *Preuves* **110**, 25–7.

Tillion, G. 1961. *France and Algeria – Complementary Enemies*, R. Howard (trans.). New York: Knopf.

Todd, O. 1992. "Camus and Sartre". In *Camus's L'Etranger: Fifty Years On*, A. King (ed.), 244–51. New York: St Martin's Press.

Todd, O. 1996. *Albert Camus – une vie*. Paris: Gallimard.

Todd, O. 1998 [1997]. *Albert Camus – A Life*, B. Ivry (trans.). London: Vintage.

Todorov, T. 1998. "Politics and Truth". *The New Republic* **219**(26): 42–6.

Todorov, T. 1999. *Facing the Extreme: Moral Life in the Concentration Camps*, A. Denner & A. Pollack (trans.). London: Weidenfeld & Nicolson.

Todorov, T. 2003. *Hope and Memory: Reflections on the Twentieth Century*, D. Bellos (trans.). London: Atlantic.

Toma, P.A. 1966. "Failures in Communist Revolutionary Strategy". In *Issues of World Communism*, A. Gyorgy (ed.), 222–43. Princeton, NJ: D. Van Nostrand.

Troisfontaines, R. 1946. *Le Choix de J. P. Sartre: exposé et critique de L'Etre et le néant*, rev. edn. Paris: Aubier.

Troisfontaines, R. 1948. *Existentialisme et pensée chrétienne*, rev. edn. Paris: Vrin.

Trottier, Y. & M. Imbeault 2006. *Limites de la violence: lecture d'Albert Camus*. Saint-Nicolas: Presses de l'Université Laval.

Uniacke, S. 1994. *Permissible Killing – The Self-Defence Justification of Homicide*. Cambridge: Cambridge University Press.

Vanney, P. 1994. "Quelques remarques sur l'idée de trêve dans l'oeuvre politique d'Albert Camus". In *Albert Camus: Les Extrêmes et l'Equilibre: Actes du Colloque de Keele, 25–27 mars 1993*, D. H. Walker (ed.), 115–28. Amsterdam: Rodopi.

Vattimo, G. 1988. *The End of Modernity: Nihilism and Hermeneutics in Post-Modern Culture*, J. R. Snyder (trans.). Cambridge: Polity Press.

Vattimo, G. 2004. *Nihilism and Emancipation: Ethics, Politics, & Law*, W. McCuaig (trans.); S. Zabala (ed.); R. Rorty (fwd). New York: Columbia University Press.

Venturi, F. 2001. *Roots of Revolution: A History of the Populist and Socialist Movements in 19th Century Russia*, rev. edn. London: Phoenix.

Viggiani, C. 1968. "Notes pour le futur biographie d'Albert Camus". In *Albert Camus 1*, B. T. Fitch (ed.), 200–18. Paris: Lettres modernes.

Viggiani, C. 1982. [Review of the French translation of *Albert Camus: A Biography* by H. Lottman]. In *Albert Camus 11*, R. Gay-Crosier (ed.), 137–43. Paris: Lettres modernes.

Vircondelet, A. 1998. *Albert Camus – Vérité et Légendes*. Milan: Éditions du Chêne.

Walker, D. H. (ed.) 1994. *Albert Camus: Les Extrêmes et l'Equilibre: Actes du Colloque de Keele, 25–27 mars 1993*. Amsterdam: Rodopi.

Walusinski, G. 1979. "Camus et les Groupes de liaison internationale". *Quinzaine littéraire* **297**: 22–4.

Walzer, M. 1977. *Just and Unjust Wars: A Moral Argument with Historical Illustrations*. New York: Basic Books.

Walzer, M. 1989. "Albert Camus' Algerian War". In *The Company of Critics: Social Criticism and Political Commitment in the Twentieth Century*, 136–52. London: Peter Halban.

Walzer, M. (ed.) 1992. *Regicide and Revolution: Speeches at the Trial of Louis XVI*, rev. edn, M. Rothstein (trans.). New York: Columbia University Press.

Wardman, H. W. 1992. *Jean-Paul Sartre: The Evolution of his Thought and Art*. Lewiston, NY: Edwin Mellen Press.

Warren, T. 1992. "On the Mistranslation of *La Mesure* in Camus's Political Thought". *Journal of the History of Philosophy* **30**(1): 123–30.

Weil, S. 1948. *La Pesanteur et la grâce*. Paris: Librairie Plon.

Weil, S. 1958. *Oppression and Liberty*, A. Wills & J. Petrie (trans.). London: Routledge & Kegan Paul.

Weil, S. 1959. *Waiting on God*, E. Craufurd (trans.). London: Collins.

Weil, S. 2002. *Gravity and Grace*, E. Crawford & M. von der Rhur (trans.); G. Thibon (ed.). London: Routledge.

Werner, E. 1972. *De la violence au totalitarisme – essai sur la pensée de Camus et de Sartre*. Paris: Calmann-Lévy.

Wetter, G. 1958. *Dialectical Materialism: A Historical and Systematic Survey of Philosophy in the Soviet Union*, P. Heath (trans.). New York: Praeger.

Weyembergh, M. 1998. *Albert Camus ou la mémoire des origines*. Paris/Brussels: De Boeck Université.

Willhoite, F. H. 1968. *Beyond Nihilism: Albert Camus's Contribution to Political Thought*. Baton Rouge, LA: Louisiana State University Press.

Wilson, A. 1960. "Albert Camus: Humanist". *Spectator* 26 February: 293.

Winock, M. 1997. *Le Siècle des intellectuels*. Paris: Seuil.

Wolf, J. B. 1979. *The Barbary Coast: Algeria under the Turks 1500–1830*. New York: Norton.

Wreszin, M. 1994. *A Rebel in Defence of Tradition: The Life and Politics of Dwight Macdonald*. New York: Basic Books.

Yacine, K. 1994. *Le poète comme un boxeur: entretiens 1958–1989*. Paris: Seuil.

Yacine, K. 1996 [1956]. *Nedjma*, avec une préface de G. Carpentier. Paris: Seuil.

Yarmolinski, A. 1962. *Road to Revolution – A Century of Russian Radicalism*. New York: Collier.

Zoubir, Y. 1994. "Algeria's Multi-Dimensional Crisis: The Story of a Failed State-Building Process". *Journal of Modern African Studies* **32**(4): 741–7.

INDEX